CONTENTS

CONTENTS

THE COMPLETE HISTORY OF WORLD WAR II

Abbeydale Press

ISBN: 978-1-86147-271-7

1 3 5 7 9 10 8 6 4 2

Published by Abbeydale Press,
an imprint of Bookmart Limited,
Registered Number 2372865
Trading as Bookmart Limited,
Blaby Road, Wigston,
Leicester, LE18 4SE,
England

Material from this book is taken from
Handbook of Great Aircraft of WWII,
published by Bookmart Limited
in 1997 and *Witness to World War II*,
published by Bookmart Limited in 1995

The publisher would like to thank the following
organisations for supplying photographs for use in this book:
straw-hat.co.uk/Alamy; Skyscan Photolibrary/Alamy;
Bettmann/Corbis; Hugo Jaeger/Timepix/Time Life Pictures/Getty
Images

Printed in Thailand

THE SOLDIER'S WAR

BLITZKRIEG!

With hindsight, it is easy to see how and why World War II erupted. Germany was enraged by the swingeing reparations imposed after its defeat in World War I, and suffered appalling economic disaster. Its people soon grew weary of being forcibly reduced to Europe's poor relation.

The time was ripe for a charismatic leader to sweep into power with the promise of returning Germany to its former glory. Unfortunately for the rest of Europe, those pledges for prosperity at home went hand in hand with an aggressive foreign policy. Nevertheless, Hitler offered the Germans an irresistible chance of stability, vitality and solidarity.

The only difficulty with which to wrestle is just how Britain and France missed the warning signs – catapulting them into a war in September 1939 for which they were ill-prepared and poorly armed.

Both countries were weary of war, still reeling from the enormous loss of manpower. At home they were too preoccupied with domestic problems to heed the warnings of the few who witnessed what was really happening in Hitler's Germany. Violent anti-semitism was put down to the work of a few extremists. Many in power had an admiration for Hitler who achieved so much by cutting unemployment and building prestigious new 'autobahns'. His admirers overlooked the fact that Germany had concentration camps, no free press and no free parliament. And few outside the Reich had any idea of the military strength and firepower that the Führer was amassing.

When Hitler marched into the demilitarised Rhineland in 1936, many considered he was only taking back what rightfully belonged to Germany. The annexation of Austria in 1938 was looked upon virtually as an internal matter. Only with Hitler's demands for land from Czechoslovakia later that same year did Britain and France begin to sense the threat.

Hitler relished the chance to 'free' fellow Germans from 'Polish barbarism'

A negotiated agreement with Hitler was designed to end his expansionism, but when Hitler marched into Prague in the face of that agreement, Britain and France finally realised the folly of their actions.

All thoughts turned to Danzig, the free city in a Polish-held corridor which split Germany from East Prussia, and which Hitler believed was part of Germany. He relished the chance to 'free' fellow Germans who he claimed were being subjected to Polish barbarism.

CARDBOARD TANKS

Much of Germany's rearmament had gone on covertly. Even when war broke out many British people were convinced that their former enemy had tanks made of cardboard. Indeed, the Germans did carry out military manoeuvres with

Left: Nazi book-burning ceremony. Only works regarded as acceptable to the fascist dictatorship were tolerated.
Far left: Hitler addresses a Nazi party rally at Nuremberg in 1938.

cardboard tanks in the early 1920s before secretly importing and building their own real ones. Meanwhile, France had the largest army and the most impressive air force in the world. Most of its citizens prided themselves on the fact that Germany was unlikely to begin hostilities against such a superior force. As England viewed the Channel as an impregnable wall

Hitler unleashed a new and frightening brand of warfare called 'Blitzkrieg'

of defence, so France had the much-vaunted Maginot line. It took nine years to construct the frontier defences, the brainchild of French minister André Maginot. The network of towers and tunnels was remarkable enough in itself. Had the Germans attacked the line directly, it might have served its purpose

BRITAIN'S FASCIST LEADER

Oswald Mosley became the creator of the British Union of Fascists in the early 1930s after having been a member of both Conservative and Labour parties and having been linked for a while with the Liberals.

He had a lively, sharp mind and a clarity of vision. He was even branded the best political thinker of the age. But his frustration at the confines of the accepted political doctrines cast him to the margins where he hit upon the fascism sweeping Europe.

The British, however, were not entranced with uniforms and salutes in the same way as the Germans, Italians or Spanish, among whom fascism flourished. He became a figure of fun, never taken seriously even after the outbreak of war. He was nevertheless jailed in 1940 for four years. Following his release, he was vilified in Britain and finally moved with his wife Diana Mitford and two small sons to France. He continued to exercise his mind around political problems but failed to find a platform for his views. He died in 1980.

well, albeit that it stretched only as far as the Belgian border, and not beyond it.

Static trench warfare, which had claimed so many lives, was now an outdated concept – yet France and Britain didn't realise it. When Hitler invaded Poland in September 1939, he unleashed a new and frightening brand of warfare into the world called 'Blitzkrieg'.

First to feel the heat of this 'lightning war', Poland lurched back in helpless horror when the German army crossed its borders at dawn on 1 September 1939. It took only a few hours for the invading force to quell Polish defences. As the German troops and tanks rolled through the Polish countryside, the country's major cities were being bombed by the Luftwaffe and its ports were being shelled by German ships.

Key to the success of Blitzkrieg was the use of tanks in large numbers and innovative style – they were still thought by Britain and France to be valid only as infantry support. The Panzer forces charged ahead independent of the troops, and wreaked havoc among defenders. Bursting through defensive lines, they harried the Poles from the rear, creating confusion and smashing supply lines.

The German air force had learned much by aiding Franco during the Spanish Civil War, which ended in May 1939. Now pilots were putting this knowledge to good use and after a month Poland capitulated.

Left: German soldiers survey the results of their fast-moving campaign in Poland.
Top: Britain was braced for attack months before it actually came.

Above: Germany used its tanks to thrust ahead during the Blitzkrieg. They were unleashed with great success against Poland, France and the Low Countries.

Poland's capital Warsaw held out for a few weeks longer than the rest of the country against the Third Reich. Heavy bombardment turned this once grand city to rubble. As it surrendered, the Germans were triumphant. The hated Treaty of Versailles, which had condemned them to international servitude since 1919, was at last eradicated.

This time Britain and France refused to sit back and watch their ally being dismembered by Hitler. Both declared war on Germany almost immediately – although failed to do anything which would materially assist Poland – and braced themselves for the onslaught. Thankfully, it never came.

Despite the success of the Polish campaign, many German officers were concerned about taking on the might of the French army backed by Britain. Hitler was persuaded to abandon thoughts of an immediate push through the Low Countries into France, in favour of launching a spring campaign.

REALITY OF WAR

The reality of war was slow to strike home in Britain. When the feared air raids and gas attacks failed to materialise, there was an almost euphoric mood as people busied them- selves sandbagging homes and putting up blackout screens in windows. The casualties in road traffic accidents caused by the rigorously enforced blackout far exceeded those caused in the war. Phrases full of mock indignation like 'put that light out' and 'don't you know there's a war on' typified the bureau- cracy pervading the country. Unemployment stayed high,

Above: *A French cottage is destroyed by advancing German troops, who put French and British defenders to flight.*

war production lamentably low. Reservists were being signed up for army duty surely but slowly, performing drills with bayonets and gas masks and sometimes wooden 'rifles'.

Nearly 200,000 soldiers in the British Expeditionary Force were sent to France where they dug in on the Belgian border. By this time, Germany had mobilised six million men.

Hitler was concerned at the ease with which the British navy had managed to raid a German ship in Norwegian waters. On 9 April 1940 Hitler's troops moved into Denmark and Norway for another short, sharp campaign. Denmark was without an army and acquiesced the following day.

Norway, deeply anti-militarist by tradition, nevertheless put up a fight despite the evident popularity with which the Germans were greeted in some quarters. Churchill himself was looking at the possibility of occupying Norway to reap the rewards of its strategic position. The government would do no more than lay mines in Norwegian waters to disrupt a vital German supply line. In fact, the Royal Navy was doing just that when some of the invasion force from Germany sailed up. There was a skirmish in which some damage was inflicted on German ships. That was the only glimmer of optimism in what turned into an otherwise disastrous escapade.

Churchill himself was looking at the possibility of occupying Norway

Britain sent landing parties to key points, but the small-scale campaign was ill-planned and improvised. The poorly equipped troops had no artillery and no air cover, whereas the Luftwaffe was in control of many Norwegian airstrips and was making full use of them. It wasn't long before the British, and the French forces with them, were forced to withdraw in disarray.

The debacle outraged many people and MPs in Britain, who feared the country was only making a half-hearted attempt at war. On 7 May there was a debate in the House of Commons in which Prime Minister Chamberlain made a statement on the Norwegian affair. The government won a vote of confidence by only 81 votes, too few for Chamberlain to continue.

BLITZKRIEG IN THE WEST

From 14 May 1940, German Panzer forces bridged the River Meuse and poured into Belgium and northern France, driving all before them. The XIX Panzer Corps under Guderian crossed at Sedan, the XLI Panzer Corps (Reinhardt) at Monthermé, the XV Panzer Corps (Hoth) at Dinant, while Höpner's XVI Panzer Corps swept down from the north east. Within days, the German tanks were at the English Channel, but then paused. The British attempted a counter-attack at Arras, while the French planned a similar move from the south. These efforts came to little, however, and by the end of May, with the German forces once again on the move, the British Expeditionary Force had its back to the sea at Dunkirk, awaiting rescue.

He resigned on 10 May, the same day that German troops made their first forays into Holland and Belgium. The

The spring campaign got underway with a vengeance in western Europe

spring campaign got underway with a vengeance as the horrors of Hitler's Blitzkrieg came to western Europe.

Airborne troops took the Belgian fortress of Eben Emael, chasing out the petrified defenders. At the same time in Rotterdam, 12 floatplanes landed on the River Maas. Out of each of them came an inflatable dinghy and a clutch of German troops ready to swarm over essential vantage points throughout the city.

HOLLAND FALLS

There were also more orthodox methods of invasion, by Panzer forces over the borders. The French army and the British Expeditionary Force prepared themselves for a surge of German troops coming through northern Belgium. To their surprise, Panzer divisions had crossed the Ardennes, condemned as impassable by Allied commanders. Amid confusion, a division led by Rommel began a headlong rush westwards.

Holland capitulated on 14 May. It was another hammer-blow to the morale of the French. Without a dynamic leader – their Commander-in-Chief Gamelin was inaudible, indecisive and thought to be suffering acutely from the

EYE WITNESS

Alf Turner joined a Territorial Army battalion in his home town of Barnstaple, North Devon, when he was 19.

❝In September 1940 we were stationed at Battle. Following Dunkirk it wasn't a case of "if the Germans invade", it was "when the Germans invade". So we had to put a minefield along the beach at Battle.

Not many people knew much about laying minefields. I was with a captain on the beach. We laid about four minefields and were starting on the fifth one. Our driver asked if he could help. The captain allowed him to lay a couple. The driver must have trodden on one and the explosion set lots of the mines off.

The captain and I were lucky to escape. A few days later our brigadier told us it was a vital area and asked us to go back to re-lay the minefield. I told the captain the chances of us coming out alive were only five percent. Still, we had a job to do.

We re-laid about four and I was leading the way when the captain said he should go first. Soon after he took over he pointed to his right. In the middle of a crater lay the head of the dead driver. The shock must have unbalanced him.

Then the ground seemed to open up and I felt I was going into a great big pit. Yet actually I was being blown upwards. Our new driver was waiting on a shelf some 40 feet above the beach. He saw me go into the air above him and go back down again.

I was cross-eyed, had a perforated ear-drum and an injured arm. Still, I managed to get out of there. I was put under sedation for 24 hours, during which time I jumped out of bed three times. They even asked me to go down to the minefield again. I went – but this time they decided it was too dangerous to tackle again.

I was given a week's leave. The medical officer said if I had had any more, I wouldn't have come back. Going home in the blackout was hard. I had to race across pools of darkness, imagining all the time that parts of a body were coming out at me.

A fellow lance corporal blamed himself for the captain's death. He was a religious man and prayed very hard for me, knowing it was a dangerous job. But he didn't pray for the captain and he felt guilty about that.❞

the operation to save British servicemen, was lifted and scores of small boats set sail for France to give aid to the Royal Navy. Experienced mariners set off alongside weekend sailors to pluck as many men as they could from the beach. It was a tough voyage on small craft but each skipper was imbued with a grim determination.

Before the surrender of the remaining defenders of Dunkirk on 4 June, 338,226 men – from Britain, France and Belgium – had been carried to safety. It was no mean feat, given that the official estimates for the evacuation were 45,000. Disastrously, most of Britain's armoury was left behind. There were too few guns remaining in Britain to arm the country's soldiers.

ravages of venereal disease – the French army fell away, their lack of commitment a world away from the fighting spirit they showed so often during World War I.

The British forces found themselves racing back to the French coast, barely keeping a step ahead of the German advance. Despite an attempt to counter-attack at Arras in northern France, it soon became clear the situation was hopeless. Their commander, General Lord Gort, ordered his men to Dunkirk where they would await evacuation.

DUNKIRK

Hitler ordered his most advanced Panzer divisions to halt, conserving his troops for the invasion of Paris. It gave the British time to install a defensive shell around Dunkirk, behind which they could stage a daring, dangerous and vital evacuation.

Courageous rearguard campaigners held off the German advance while the Royal Navy sent in ship after ship to remove the stricken forces. By 31 May the news blackout on 'Operation Dynamo', the code name for

PARIS OCCUPIED

French soldiers, supported in the west by some British fighters, continued to retreat. Two weeks following Dunkirk, Paris was occupied and region after region continued to fall. When French Prime Minister Reynaud resigned on 16 June, his successor Marshal Pétain immediately sued for peace.

The final humiliation for France came on 21 June when Hitler had its leaders sign an armistice in the same railway coach where the German surrender was authorised following World War I. Britain stood alone against the might of the Third Reich with only 21 miles of English Channel to save it from invasion.

Left: Bewildered soldiers and frightened civilians roam the streets of Dunkirk as the Germans close in.

BARBAROSSA– TARGET RUSSIA

Hitler has become infamous in history for his hatred of Jews. Yet he also singled out the Russians as a worthless, reviled race: he called them 'sub-humans'. It became his avowed aim to see the people in chains and Communism eradicated once and for all.

Before the war between Hitler's Germany and Stalin's USSR began, the German Führer laid down the ground rules to his generals. In essence, there were none:

'The war against Russia will be such that it cannot be conducted in a knightly fashion. The struggle is one of ideologies and racial differences and will have to be conducted with unprecedented, unmerciful and unrelenting harshness. The commissars are the bearers of ideologies directly opposed to National Socialism. Therefore the commissars will be liquidated. German soldiers guilty of breaking international law . . . will be excused. Russia has not participated in the Hague Convention and therefore has no rights under it.'

These words set the tone for a brutal and bloody conflict, far exceeding the ruthlessness shown so far by invading Nazi forces in western Europe.

Hitler's first problem, however, was how to bring the Russian Bear to battle at all. For months during 1939 the USSR's tyrant leader Stalin had been courted by Britain and France, both anxious to get Soviet support for the forthcoming hostilities with Germany. Hitler's disparaging views of Russia were very well documented, not least among the Soviet people themselves. In the

circumstances, it seemed Stalin was a natural ally of Britain and France.

FRAGILE PACT

Suddenly, however, the carefully wrought diplomacy collapsed like a house of cards. Out of the blue came the Berlin-Moscow Non-Aggression Pact, signed at the Kremlin by Ribbentrop, for Hitler, and Molotov, for Stalin, in August 1939. Hitler found himself the closest ally of his hated adversary. Stalin guessed it would at least buy him time before his country became involved in a war it neither wanted nor could afford.

Left: Joseph Stalin. Hitler feared and detested Communism and all other left wing ideologies. Stalin's regime in the USSR embodied all that Nazism opposed.

Above right: 'Barbarossa' unleashed the fury of Germany's erstwhile ally. Below: Hitler and Soviet Foreign Minister Molotov (left) reach an uneasy peace, 1939.

'The war against Russia... cannot be conducted in a knightly fashion'

And the reason behind the gleam in Stalin's eyes at the signing of the pact was revealed just a month later. Two weeks after German forces marched into Poland, Russian forces invaded from the east. The two countries proceeded to partition the helpless Poland as they pleased. If Stalin was concerned that he was dancing with the Devil, he comforted himself that

fight, using superior tactics and winning some impressive victories. It wasn't until March 1940 that the war was finally over with the surrender of little Finland, time enough for the Finns to have inflicted humiliation on their giant neighbour, which lost an estimated one million fighting men. Hitler noted the failings and flailings of the Red Army with more than a passing interest.

uprising against him. Whether the threat was imagined or real, no one can say. What is certain is that Stalin wrecked a terrible revenge to defend his lordly position.

By the end of 1938 three out of every five of the Red Army's

Below: General Heinz Guderian, architect of Blitzkreig in the west, keeping up morale in Russia in 1941.

Britain and France would tie up sufficient numbers of German troops on the Western front to make the opening of a second front an act of idiocy by Hitler.

In November, encouraged by his easy success, Stalin engineered a war with Finland. When the Finns flatly refused to hand over disputed territory, the Red Army marched in, anticipating another quick victory.

Six weeks later their hopes had been dashed. The vastly out-numbered Finns put up a fierce

Stalin was livid with the poor performance of his army. But there was no one to blame but himself for the debacle – as he

Stalin wreaked a terrible revenge to defend his lordly position

himself had ordered the deaths of many of his leading commanders during a devastating purge of the army in 1937. It happened after whispers of a military

marshals were dead as well as 13 out of 15 army commanders. More than a quarter of the army's brigadiers and more than half of the divisional comman-ders had been executed, too. There was also bloodletting among the politicos involved with defence. Those that remained were untalented and uninspiring. They hampered the progress of the fighting force with outdated ideas, which included the abandonment of automatic weapons and the halting of the comprehensive tank programme in favour of horsedrawn artillery. So the army was left woefully lacking in experience, for which it paid a terrible penalty.

Nevertheless it was still the largest army in the world, although Hitler had other considerations than this in preparing his battle plan.

GREEK DIVERSION

By 1941 he was convinced he could overwhelm the Soviet Union and kill off Communism there for good. But he was compelled to delay the invasion due to the German involvement in Greece, an unexpected diversion which cost the Reich valuable men and time.

It was a late spring that year, too, leaving roads clogged with mud and rivers swollen by the slow thaw. Germany needed the best possible weather to make a clean, quick strike into the heart of its foe.

By the beginning of June, all the indications were that Hitler was ready to pounce. As many as 76 different warnings came

to Stalin to that effect. Churchill gleaned top secret information from his Ultra decodes, telling of the proposed invasion. Spies stationed around the Axis world delivered similar warnings. One German soldier, a secret Communist, escaped across the border to warn Stalin of the impending attack.

Still the inscrutable leader refused to believe Hitler would wage war on him. He remained primarily concerned about his frontier with Japan, the growing menace in the east. Even the rapid and unexpected fall of France failed to persuade him that Russia would be next on the German Führer's hit list.

Stubbornly, Stalin dismissed the international warnings sent to Moscow as scandalous rumour-mongering and barred his top army commanders from mounting defences along the border, for fear of provoking Hitler. He even had the runaway German soldier shot.

His policy of appeasement designed to keep Russia out of the war stretched as far as sending train loads of oil, grain and metals to the Third Reich even while its troops were congregating

Left: The summer offensive against Russia progressed rapidly at first, until the German invaders ran out of good weather.

Below: A Red Army observer on the lookout for enemy aircraft in Moscow, 1941. The Soviets were ill-prepared for a German attack.

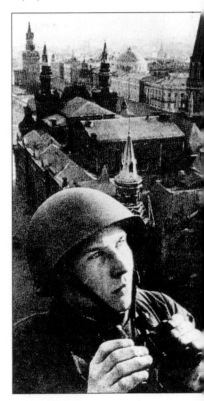

THE GREAT DEBATE

By 1940, America was caught up in 'The Great Debate', about whether or not it should enter the war.

The largest body of isolationists campaigning to keep America out of the conflict was the America First Committee, centred in the Mid-West where anti-British and pro-German sentiments were strongest. Fascists united with Communists and radical Irish Americans in wanting to keep America neutral. In opposition was the Committee to Defend America by Aiding the Allies, founded in May 1940.

Among those contributing to the debate was Colonel Charles A. Lindbergh, who in 1927 became the first aviator to cross the Atlantic non-stop, and whose two-year-old son was kidnapped and murdered in 1932. He had visited Nazi Germany, inspected the Luftwaffe and declared the force was invincible.

on the borders.

On 22 June 'Operation Barbarossa' got underway with 165 divisions trundling into Russia in a three-pronged attack. The 2,500,000 Germans in the invasion force were not alone. Lining up with them were divisions of Italians, Romanians, Hungarians, and Finns and one Spanish unit. Before the attack was launched there was no formal declaration of war.

Initially it was the familiar story of Blitzkrieg. The Panzer divisions ploughed through the Russian countryside heading for Kiev, Leningrad and Moscow. Occasionally the dirt track roads

Above: Farm workers and factory hands were called on to defend their country alongside Russia's soldiers, as the German onslaught swept in from the west.

were difficult to pass. Yet nothing could stop the motorised units for very long. In their wake the infantry marched at a pelt, straining to keep up with the successful advance and mopping up resistance along the way

They picked up thousands of prisoners, many caught by the rear sweep of the advance unit which snared them in a bag. Stalin engineered some of the major military disasters of the entire conflict when he refused

to allow his men to retreat.

Hundreds of planes in the sizeable Red Air Force were immediately knocked out. All was going according to plan for Germany. It seemed like the army would be at the gates of Moscow in six weeks as forecast.

Yet within a month the Soviets began fighting back. Their resolve began stiffening, their exploits became harder to contain. In fact, the Russian soldier was a formidable enemy in combat because he was prepared to fight to the death. Their readiness to make the ultimate sacrifice became particularly apparent as the war progressed. The Germans treated their Soviet prisoners with callous contempt. They were given fewer rations than other Allied prisoners of war and there was a catalogue of cruelty and atrocities. During the war, a staggering 3,300,000 Soviet prisoners of war died in German custody.

DEATH SQUADS

When the Russians got to hear of the treatment being meted out to their comrades they fought harder than ever. There was also increased incentive to fight to the last, as they knew that imprisonment would be worse than death. Equally, anything construed as cowardice by the soldiers and failure by their commanding officers led to execution by death squads of their fellow countrymen.

At the end of July Hitler made a controversial decision which perhaps cost him the war in Russia. Concerned at the rapid pace of the Panzers compared with the slow-moving infantry, he ordered a change in tack which had the advance units of his campaign veering off in another direction. The effect of this was to give the big cities valuable time to defend themselves.

His leaders in the field were mystified and outraged. In particular, General Heinz Guderian, who stood only 220 miles from Moscow, sought to disentangle himself from the order.

But despite some initial hesitation, Hitler was convinced

When the surge forward began the first winter chill crept into the air

he was right. It caused a flurry of resignations from his senior commanders, who knew instinctively that the time was right to press forward for Moscow. With the shelter the city offered to an army, the icy arctic winter might just be tolerable. Without it, the German hierarchy – who could only guess at the ravages such a winter would hold – gave an involuntary shiver.

When the surge forward began again, the first winter chill began to creep into the air. By September, Riga, Minsk, Smolensk and Kiev had fallen. A record 665,000 soldiers were taken prisoner when Kiev collapsed, the most ever taken during a single wartime operation. Leningrad, like Sevastopol

Left: German soldiers quickly realised the perils of fighting in a Russian winter when thick snow disabled much of their machinery.

in the Crimea, was under siege. Western Russia was pock-marked with destruction. Stalin had ordered a 'scorched earth' policy among his men which meant retreating armies torched everything in their wake to both hinder the enemy and deprive them of possible supplies.

The residents of Moscow and Leningrad had not wasted their unexpected breathing space that summer. An army of women, old men and children spent their every waking hour digging in. Between them they provided the key spots with miles of earthworks, anti-tank ditches, barbed-wire walls and pill-boxes.

TRENCHFOOT

During their labours, their spirits must have lifted with the first deluge of autumn. The Germans, now wearying, depleted in numbers and burdened by casualties, looked up to same endless grey skies in despair. The rains brought about cases of 'trenchfoot' – the vile affliction the Americans call 'immersion-foot'. The condition occurred when wet

An army of women, old men and children spent their every waking hour digging in

feet were not dried out for days or weeks on end. Numbed and uncomfortable, the infected feet frequently turned purple and, in severe cases, the nerve endings died and gangrene set in.

The Russian roads now turned into mires of mud. The German Panzers were literally bogged down and progressed at a painfully slow pace. Mechanical failures began to haunt each division as its desperate soldiers fought to keep the wheels turning.

The frosts of October came

HITLER'S LONELY LOVER

Eva Braun spent 12 years as mistress to the hypnotic German Führer and no more than a few hours as his wife.

Braun probably began her bizarre relationship with Hitler as early as 1931. Yet he refused to accord her the public recognition she desired despite his apparent regard for her.

Much of their relationship was spent apart, with the sporty, attractive Braun, born in 1910, waiting for Hitler to finish his state commitments before squeezing in some time with her. Hitler's chauffeur described her afterwards as 'the unhappiest woman in Germany. She spent most of her life waiting for Hitler.'

Even after her sister married General Fegelein, a member of

Himmler's staff, she was unable to persuade Hitler to formalise their relationship. She attempted suicide twice, in 1932 and 1935, on account of Hitler's involvement with other women.

On 15 April 1945 Eva Braun arrived in Berlin to join Hitler for what were clearly his final days. In the early hours of 29 April they were wed. The following afternoon they were dead, Hitler having shot himself and Braun having taken poison. Her body, clad in a dark dress, was placed in a shell hole at the rear of the Berlin bunker and set ablaze alongside that of her husband.

as a relief to the Germans. At least the ground was hard enough to support the tank tracks.

Haunted by the fate of the French Emperor Napoleon who had made mighty advances into Russia only to be crippled by the winter freeze, Hitler declared that Moscow was to be taken.

OPERATION TYPHOON

The final thrust of 'Operation Typhoon' brought German troops tantalisingly close to their goal. Some reports insist the leading units penetrated a suburb of the capital and saw sunlight glinting on the roof of the Kremlin itself. Even now they were able to take 660,000 more Russian prisoners. But their progress slowed and finally halted.

By now 200,000 members of the Germany army had been killed. The surviving German

Below: It wasn't just the weather that was bitter. Fighting between Russia and Germany on the Eastern front was some of the bloodiest of the entire conflict.

soldiers were no longer energetic. Five months of fighting had taken its toll. The resistance they found among the defenders of Moscow was fierce, the military machinery they relied on for spearheading their attack was failing. And now the relentless winter had set in, bringing with it snow storms and temperatures of minus 20 degrees Celsius.

German soldiers were inadequately clothed for the biting cold. The greatcoats they wore were scarcely thick enough to protect them from the bitter winds. In a feeble attempt to insulate themselves, they tore up paper and stuffed it inside their clothes. For snow camouflage they used bed sheets which again offered precious little warmth. Now frostbite was the worst enemy, claiming many more victims among the demoralised Germans than the fighting itself.

Vehicle oil froze unless it was kept warm, so the Germans were unable to move at all. The fine German horses used to pull artillery and supplies perished

by the thousand. Hitler had ordered 'no retreat', perhaps realising that any movement forward or backwards posed a danger to his troops. It would be three years before the supplies of winter clothing to German troops from the Reich were adequate.

The Soviet army was well used to the harsh weather. Sheepskins and furs were standard issue. Greatest among their assets were heavy-duty felt

---

Now frostbite was the worst enemy, claiming many more victims than the fighting

---

boots soon supplied in bulk by America where they were made to Russian specification. The Russians knew how to care for their animals throughout the coldest weather. A squad of crack Siberian troops was being called in, experts at winter warfare and at home on a pair of skis. The fate of Moscow hung in the balance.

JAPAN'S LIGHTNING WAR

With the success of Pearl Harbor under their belts, the Japanese were eager to capitalise on the supreme advantage of surprise. Defending British, Australian and American forces were caught off-guard throughout South East Asia and the Pacific as Japan began a 'Blitzkrieg' of its own.

Key targets were Hong Kong, the Philippines, Malaya, Singapore, Burma, Thailand, the Dutch East Indies and the stepping stone islands of Wake and Guam. Each offered the new Japanese empire mineral or agricultural wealth that was badly needed, or was a necessary land-base to protect precious cargoes.

Hong Kong was the first of the British domains to fall. Only 400 miles from Japanese air bases in Formosa (now Taiwan), it was vulnerable from the outset. The defence of Hong Kong and other British outposts had suffered thanks to the war effort in other parts of the world. During 1939 and 1940, troops, ships and aircraft were sent to trouble-spots like North Africa and the Mediterranean at the expense of the far-flung colonies, which appeared to be in no imminent danger.

By August 1940, Churchill accepted the view held by service chiefs that Hong Kong was practically indefensible and that the garrison on the island could be better used elsewhere. Japanese intentions were far from clear at this point. However, with growing indications that Japan was possibly hostile, no one acted further on the recommendation. The following year the Hong Kong garrison was strengthened by the addition of two Canadian battalions.

An initial strike made by the Japanese on 8 December proved to be devastating. The Allied troops were driven back to Hong Kong city within a matter of days. For a week, the Japanese were held at bay across the water barrier. Under the cover of darkness on 18 December, the inevitable Japanese landings on Hong Kong island began. Following Churchill's declared policy, resistance was slight. On Christmas Day one arm surrendered. Their comrades gave up the fight a day later. For the loss of 3,000 dead and wounded the Japanese had captured Hong Kong, together with its force of nearly 12,000 men.

The Philippines were to have suffered their first Japanese air bombardment on 8 December Although not an American possession, they were reliant on US support before becoming independent. In fact, morning fog grounded the aircraft based in Formosa, delaying take-off.

The Americans, meanwhile, were debating whether or not to carry out a bombing mission in Formosa. This indecision was to prove fatal. In the early afternoon, when the US B-17s were finally being prepared for a sortie, the overdue Japanese aircraft finally arrived. With the American planes presented on an airfield, the Japanese pilots did their destructive worst. A number of the planes intended to protect the Philippines were wrecked.

> ### For the loss of 3,000 dead and wounded the Japanese had captured Hong Kong

Left: *Victorious Japanese troops enter Rangoon after quickly annihilating opposition troops in Burma. The Burmese people gave them an indifferent welcome.*

Above: *Dejected British soldiers file through the streets of Singapore after the disastrous fall of the colony to the Emperor's forces.*

RATIONS

Rations were boosted – and cut – for Britons on the home front throughout the war. Here is a typical weekly allowance per person.

8oz sugar, 3oz cheese, 3oz cooking fat, 4oz bacon or ham, 2oz jam, 2oz sweets, 2oz tea or coffee 1 egg, 3 pints milk, 1lb meat
   Bread, fish and sausages, although not rationed, were scarce. Although there was no restriction on fruit and vegetables, many were impossible to get. Lemons, bananas, onions and even pepper were rarely, if ever, seen during the war years in Britain. Inventive housewives made chocolate truffle cake from potatoes, and banana pudding from parsnips.

Right: General-Marshal Homma makes an assisted landing on Luzon in the Philippines on 24 December 1941, ousting defending American troops.

The Japanese 14th Army quickly captured off-islands and made landings on Luzon, the largest Philippine island, as early as 10 December. There were continuing probes until the main landings, which took place on 22 December.

Coastal defences, comprising poorly trained and fearful Filipinos soon crumbled. A core of American troops was kept in the capital, Manila, by commander General MacArthur until it became clear that the defence of the island was an impossibility. He then ordered a withdrawal into the Bataan Peninsula in the hope the 31,000 troops could mount an adequate defence.

The Americans did manage to repel a number of raids. Then both sides became severely weakened through rampant malaria. Morale sank further in the American ranks when it became clear that little effort was being made to evacuate them. When the Japanese offensive began again on 3 April it took only six days to force a surrender.

Coastal defences, with poorly trained and fearful Filipinos, soon crumbled

There remained almost 15,000 Americans on the nearby island of Corregidor. The fight for this scrap of an island was to be fierce. The Japanese carried out daily artillery bombardments across the straits from Luzon as well as waves of air attacks. When much of the American artillery had been knocked out, the Japanese mounted an invasion with 2,000 troops. More than half were lost in the battle that ensued during the night of 5 May. But despite their losses, the Japanese managed to land some tanks, enough to crush the remaining resistance.

A surrender bid by American General Wainwright was hampered by guerrilla action adopted by the Americans. By 9 June all resistance was crushed.

The loss to the Americans had been considerable; likewise to the native forces. A combined total of 95,000 were taken captive by the Japanese. Yet the defenders had held out for six months with no outside assistance, a significant achievement given the domino fall of islands in the rest of the area.

On paper, it appeared the

British defenders of Malaya and neighbouring Singapore were more than a match for the invaders. There were about 100,000 Allied troops taking on just 30,000 incoming Japanese. In Britain there was confidence that Singapore particularly was a fortress with stout defences. It was unthinkable that the stronghold would be overrun. As so often happens during wars the unthinkable happened – at speed.

The defeat of the British and Allied forces at the hands of the Japanese was a shocking one for which few at home were prepared. Yet there were shortcomings in the defences of the countries invaded which allowed the enthusiastic Japanese to run rampant.

Despite the signs of militarism evident in Japan, the British government remained convinced this small country would not take on the combined might of America, Britain and Russia. After the war, Churchill admitted he among others had underestimated the threat posed by Japan, particularly in its air power.

The Allies had no tanks with which to blast the enemy while the Japanese rolled over the inhospitable terrain with something in the order of 300. And while the Allies possessed more than twice the amount of artillery, much of it was in Singapore facing seawards to repel a southerly invasion. The Japanese flooded in from the opposite direction.

OPPRESSIVE HEAT

As for aircraft, the Allies had only a sixth of the number of aircraft that the Japanese had at their disposal. In a war which proved air might was imperative, the British were left seriously under-equipped.

Japanese troops were trained for jungle warfare. The British and Australians were quickly wearied by the oppressive heat.

In command of the Japanese troops was General Tomoyuki Yamashita, a devoted servant of Emperor Hirohito and a military marvel. Among his troops, he was known as 'the tiger'. The Allies, meanwhile, were under General Arthur Percival, held with such low regard by his men that he was called 'the rabbit'.

On the day that the prize British capital ships *Prince of Wales* and *Repulse* were sent to the bottom of the sea, Japanese forces marched into Malaya. With waves of air cover, they were quickly able to force the British down the Malay Peninsula in a rolling retreat. The highly organised invaders cut quickly through any defences they encountered. About 4,000 British troops and their equipment were stranded in central Malaya when Japanese tanks broke through their lines and seized a road bridge, curtailing

Below: *Seasoned jungle warriors, the Japanese troops found far less difficulty operating in the tropics than their beleaguered enemies did.*

WAVELL VICTORIOUS

When British and Commonwealth troops under the command of General Sir Archibald Wavell drove Italian troops into a spectacular retreat early in 1941, there was rejoicing at home at the first glimpse of meaningful victory. The News Chronicle wrote:

'It is still too early for any complete estimate of General Wavell's happy and glorious achievement; but from what we already know two factors stand out and demand the most generous praise: the perfect co-ordination of land, sea and air forces and the superb Staff work that preceded the attack and made the co-ordination possible.'

Somewhat prematurely, it ended:

'Rapidly the Axis is becoming a meaningless phrase: an axis requires two ends, and, if it is to function, each end must perform an equal task. Otherwise the whole thing crumbles away. One day that will happen, and General Wavell, by his care and genius, has brought that day nearer than two months ago we dared hope.'

their withdrawal. The capital, Kuala Lumpur, was abandoned by the Allies on 11 January and still the retreat continued to gather pace.

MALAYA FALLS

It took the Japanese just 54 days to overcome the resistance in Malaya. Their casualties amounted to around 4,600, compared with the loss of 25,000 Allied troops, many of whom were now prisoners of war. Thousands of Indians recruited to fight for the Empire already had doubts about the wisdom of risking their lives for the country which oppressed their own. Now many took the opportunity to join brigades organised by the Japanese and were fighting against former comrades.

Fleeing British and Australian forces made a dash for Singapore and blew up the bridge connecting the island

Right: A Japanese artillery detachment making its way through the jungle in late 1941 during the Singapore campaign. They met little resistance.

with Malaya as they went. Japanese forces mustered threateningly on the other side. Singapore was bombed on the day the war with Japan began. The casualties were mostly among the civilian population. Perhaps for the first time, Churchill realised the folly of leaving the island of Singapore so woefully lacking in defences.

In January 1942, he declared: 'Not only must the defence of Singapore Island be maintained by every means but the whole island must be fought for until

every single unit and every single strongpoint has been separately destroyed. Finally, the city of Singapore must be converted into a citadel and defended to the death. No surrender can be contemplated.' On 8 February the Japanese troops put his words to the test by swarming across the Johore Strait which had so far barred them from the island. Some used small boats and dinghies. Others simply swam across. The Australian defenders in the region might have been expected to use the spotlights especially installed to light up their targets and blast the invaders out of the water.

The soldiers were left firing at darkened objects in the night

Yet the order to switch on the lights never came. The soldiers were left firing at darkened objects in the night. Not only that, the troops were soon ordered to fall back rather than to counter-attack. It was a symptom of the faulty lines of communication

EYE WITNESS

Bill Jenkins, from New South Wales, served in the Australian infantry from the outbreak of World War II to its close.

❝My battalion and another one from Victoria were probably the only Allied units to have fought all its enemies. We were up against the Italians in the desert, the Germans in Greece, the Vichy French in Syria and the Japanese in New Guinea.

The Japanese were the worst. They were a different culture – you didn't know what to expect next from them. No prisoners were taken on either side and they were very vicious. Yet the Japanese were good soldiers. I have got much respect for them but not for their culture which allows them to do such terrible things.❞

Above: US soldiers surrender to Japanese troops. Ahead of them is a gruelling march to a harsh prison camp.

that dogged the short campaign by the Allies to keep Singapore. The standard of leadership among the Allies was also continually poor, with tactical blunders being made time and again. Ill-thought-out orders to withdraw from strongly held positions around the coast gave the Japanese an open door.

SINGAPORE SHAME

Nor did the sight of thick black smoke rising over Singapore city do much to improve their state of mind. It plumed from oil tanks set alight by the British themselves in the harbour area to keep them from falling into Japanese hands. From it came a pungent black rain which fell across a wide area. A flurry of activity by Japan's supporters in Singapore added to the chaos and confusion in the city.

Food stocks were running low and the water supply was under threat by the time street battles commenced. Percival

realised that to proceed with the fight was futile. A package air-dropped to his headquarters in a cascade of red and white ribbons invited him to surrender. It bore the following sinister sentence from Yamashita: 'If you continue resistance, it will be difficult to bear with patience, from a humanitarian point of view.'

He chose to ignore Churchill's orders to fight to the bitter end. Percival marched to meet the triumphant Yamashita with a Union Jack and a white flag, held aloft side-by-side. This did little to endear him to the establishment at home. His signature ended the British domination of Singapore at a conference held in the Ford factory on Bukit Timah hill. Some 80,000 British, Indian and Australian troops were forced to face four years of captivity under the harsh Japanese regime

With the loss of Singapore came the realisation that Britain's proud boast of being able to defend its colonies no matter where they were in the world was now a sham.

It was later described as 'the greatest military disaster in [British] history'. For years Percival was an outcast and was held personally responsible. While his leadership was certainly flawed, he was only one of many Allied commanders who found themselves bowled over by the Japanese steamroller.

The extent of the Singapore debacle was only revealed fully after the war. Yamashita had considered himself on the brink of losing the vital campaign : 'My attack on Singapore was a bluff. I

Right: Japanese soldiers soon adapted in the jungle, making use of local elephants to forge a path through dense vegetation. The Allied defenders could not match the invaders proficiency in jungle warfare.

Below: General Tomoyuki Yamashita, one of Japan's most successful military leaders, pulled off a dramatic coup when he captured Singapore.

had 30,000 men and was outnumbered more than three to one. I knew that if I had been made to fight longer for Singapore I would have been beaten. That was why the surrender had to be immediate. I was frightened that the British would discover our numerical weakness and lack of supplies and force me into disastrous street fighting. But they never did. My bluff worked.'

December 1941 also saw the invasion of Burma. It was inadequately protected, with Malaya and Singapore seen as having greater requirement for military resources.

Once again, Japan had by far the most effective air force. It would become another story of inglorious retreat, this time over 1,000 miles into India.

The Burmese capital Rangoon was being bombed by Christmas. The British forces were once again forced back under the onslaught of the 35,000 invading Japanese troops, who proved themselves faster and more adept in jungle warfare. On 6 March 1942 the order came to evacuate Rangoon.

MONSOON SEASON

After both sides had reinforced, the British, assisted now by Chinese forces, defended a 150-mile line south of Mandalay. The Japanese sidestepped the line and enveloped the troops manning it. By April, the British troops not only had to consider the advance of the enemy but also the onset of the monsoon season, due in May, which would turn the roads vital for retreat into mires.

Burmese soldiers were deserting in droves to join the new national army that was fighting with the Japanese invaders.

Burmese soldiers, always unhappy about the colonial control of their country, were deserting in droves to join the new national army

British rearguard forces held up the Japanese advance before making the final dash for safety themselves. The tanks of the 7th Armoured Brigade made repeated counter-attacks to delay the enemy campaign.

A week before the monsoon season began, the majority of the British forces fell back behind the Indian frontier. They had lost much of their equipment and had suffered three times the number of casualties that the Japanese had incurred. It was a miracle that any succeeded in escaping at all.

The Dutch East Indies came

EYE WITNESS

Hugh Trebble, a local newspaper journalist, joined the Civil Air Guard before the war when it offered the chance to learn to fly for one penny per minute. In 1940 he was recruited into the Royal Air Force, in which he was a clerk.

I was posted overseas in June 1941 and got to Singapore by August. From there I went to RAF Butterworth, overlooking Penang Island in north west Malaya.

There was a lot of personnel in Malaya and Singapore but no equipment. At Butterworth we were still flying Bristol Blenheims. I never saw any combat aircraft the entire time I was there.

After the Japanese invaded down the east coast we were pulled back to Kuala Lumpur to a base called Sungeibesi. A few weeks later General Wavell flew in to assess the situation. As soon as his Hudson took off we blew it [the base] up. We retreated via a rubber plantation down to Singapore.

There, we were put in a camp at RAF Seletar. The last flight of so-called bombers that set off from there was made up of obsolete Vickers Wildebeest, twin-engined bi-planes. They took off but they never landed. They were destroyed before they could put down.

There was a desperate atmosphere in Singapore, even more so after the battleships *Prince of Wales* and *Repulse* were sunk. When they left port it was with a total absence of air cover and destroyer cover. They should never have been sent out in the first place.

In Singapore there were fixed guns facing over the sea – when the Japanese came overland. They Japanese soldiers easily overpowered anything we had. Some Allied soldiers got off troop ships and were taken prisoner virtually straightaway. They never fired a shot in anger. They had nothing to fight with anyway.

On 13 January 1942 I was among many who were evacuated from Kepple Harbour on the *Empire Star*, a Blue Funnel ship, heading for Java. Clearly, we were sent to Singapore for propaganda purposes – nothing else.

under attack in December 1941. These islands were rich in oil and thus an important target for the oil-starved Japanese. In a bid to halt the Japanese, the defending Dutch, Australian, British and American forces were put under a single command, known as ABDA, led by Britain's General Archibald Wavell.

Although the Dutch resistance was soon annihilated, the Australians proved a more formidable foe. Yet there was little they could do to protect the scores of tiny islands from Japanese occupation.

After the disastrous Battle of the Java Sea, which the Allies lost in February 1942, the Japanese could count the Dutch East Indies as their own.

EYES ON CEYLON

Other casualties in the Japanese war were Guam, Wake Island and the Gilbert Islands, which fell before the end of 1941. In the spring of 1942, the Bismarck Archipelago, the Solomon Islands and north eastern New Guinea all succumbed to Japanese forces.

Britain now feared attack from the Japanese navy in the Indian Ocean, where Ceylon was a prime target

Britain feared an attack from the Japanese navy in the Indian Ocean where Ceylon was a prime target. On 5 April 1942 the British braced themselves for attack following an air strike by more than 1,000 planes at Colombo the capital of Ceylon. Two British cruisers were sunk and the port was badly damaged. The distances were too great for an invasion to be sustainable, and the Japanese knew it. They withdrew behind the lines of their expanded empire and concentrated on defence.

THE EASTERN FRONT

Winter weather had brought the German advance in Russia to a complete standstill. Yet Stalin knew that freezing temperatures and snow flurries alone would not be enough to defeat the might of the Third Reich's army.

He was neither a gifted tactician nor a seasoned campaigner, unlike his enemy Hitler. In personal command of his army, Stalin was isolated at the top. The blunders he made as the campaign against his country got underway cost millions of lives. He would soon learn by bitter experience about how to run a war.

He enjoyed a certain degree of good luck and, in time, he used it well. To his advantage, he had a seemingly inexhaustible supply of men.

After Pearl Harbor, Stalin realised Japan was too embroiled with its actions against America to threaten Russia now. So the men tied up with defending its eastern rear were at last free to man the German front. In addition, there were countless thousands of reservists, recruited from all over the Soviet Union, to replace fallen comrades.

It was this perpetual sacrifice of men above all other factors that changed the course of the war. If Stalin had found his people with less resolve and more ready to capitulate, Hitler might have won on the Eastern front.

D-Day could not have gone ahead without the Russian front diverting German resources

A victory there would have ensured him triumph in the west. D-Day, the most decisive action of the entire war, could not have gone ahead without the Russian front diverting so

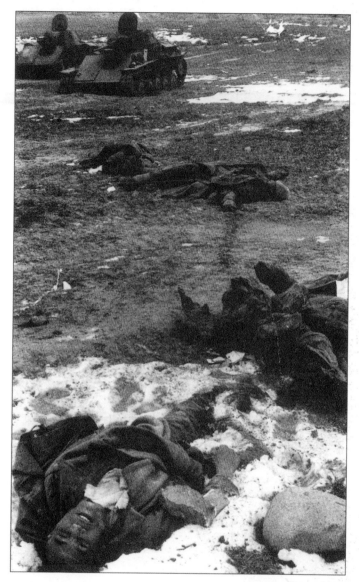

many German resources.

Somehow this massive country survived its appalling casualty rate. It prompted the frustrated German chief of staff Halder to comment: 'We estimated that we should contend with 180 Russian divisions; we have already counted 360.'

Above: *The half-frozen mud is littered with the bodies of dead Russian soldiers. Total Soviet losses, military and civilian, in the war may have exceeded 20 million.*

Left: *Resignation is etched on the face of a German soldier on the Eastern front, more than two years after 'Barbarossa'.*

Left: A smouldering tank is stopped in its tracks during the campaign.

World War I, aged 18, winning two medals before the Bolshevik revolution. By 1919 he was in the Red Army and a Communist Party member. Personal rapport with Stalin saved him during the military purge of 1937. He remained one of the few generals who was able to speak his mind to the Soviet dictator, although on at least one occasion he was demoted as a result of doing so.

RETREAT AND DIG

Not all the other Russian generals were so lucky. After war broke out, Stalin habitually telephoned commanders who had been compelled to pull back their armies and summoned them to Moscow. When they arrived they would face a quick court martial before being shot for dereliction of duty. Stalin was the only leader of World War II who continued with the outdated notion of shooting generals for failure in the field.

Russian generals were forced on the offensive by Stalin no matter what the odds, as it was the only

Wherever possible, the Soviet Union's heavy industry was moved nut by nut and bolt by bolt to the east of the country to prevent it being swallowed up in the German advance – from here productivity was now stepped up. While the Germans suffered from privation, with inadequate supplies being ferried along overstretched lines beginning in occupied Poland and beyond, the Russian forces had their needs seen to swiftly and without hindrance along railway tracks still running into Moscow despite the conflict.

Key among the Russian supplies was the new T-34 tank, heavily armoured, fast and tough. It was equal if not superior to the tanks being driven by the Germans. By 1943 Russian industry was able to produce twice as many tanks as its German counterpart.

MARSHAL ZHUKOV

Russia also received fresh stocks from the Allies. Perhaps the most significant of these was a mammoth consignment of trucks from America. It enabled Stalin to move men around his huge country at increased speed. He had a fine commander in the field in Georgi Zhukov, whose military genius shone out from the floundering incompetents left at the top of what remained of the Red Army.

Zhukov joined the Tsar's army as a conscript at the outbreak of

> ## When they arrived they would face a quick court martial before being shot

Below: Marshal Zhukov (left) pores over a battle plan as high-ranking Russians grapple with modern warfare techniques.

RICKY

In the treacherous task of clearing minefields, the British invasion force used specially trained dogs. When the dog sat down it was clear to his handler that a mine had been sniffed out.

Welsh sheepdog Ricky was clearing a canal bank in Holland when a mine blew up just three feet away from him. Ricky was wounded in the face while the blast killed the section commander. Regardless of his injuries, Ricky returned to his duties and found several more mines before retiring for treatment.

His courage won him the Dickin Medal, created by the People's Dispensary for Sick Animals, to recognise the courage of animals in the front line. Inscribed on it are the words 'For gallantry, we also serve'. Ribbons attached to the disc are green, brown and blue to represent sea, land and sky.

way he knew of achieving victory. Devoid of any inspiration until the arrival of Zhukov and his protégés, they would send waves of men 'over the top' to hurl themselves at the Germans, much as soldiers did during the trench warfare of 1914-18.

It took Stalin at least a year to realise that his strategies were fatally flawed. When he began lending an ear to the new breed of generals he finally realised that technique was everything in modern warfare. It was then that Russia began to turn the tables on its foe.

MOSCOW REPRIEVED

After an inconclusive Russian counter-offensive out of Moscow in December 1941, both sides suspended operations until May 1942 to give themselves time to recoup men and hardware. Moscow was saved from occupation but its people still suffered the deprivations of war.

While Stalin was convinced Moscow remained the Third Reich's prime target Hitler had other ideas. The need for more resources for his spiralling war effort became more pressing. He eyed the Soviet oilfields in

Below: Prepared for invasion. Moscow was lined with anti-tank devices to halt Hitler's progress.

the Caucasus greedily, knowing that success in capturing such prized assets would deprive Stalin of precious fuel resources as well.

Code-named 'Operation Blue', Hitler's drive east began at the beginning of May. In characteristic style the thrust was dynamic and 170,000 Russians were taken prisoner in the first week. Two Russian counter-attacks ended in disarray. The first German objective to take the tank-making town of Kharkov was achieved by the end of June.

But frustration followed victory as the Germans lost the initiative when they became involved in a battle for the city of Voronezh. Russian fighters, released from the order to stay their ground by Stalin, could finally strike and then melt away, causing maximum damage and nuisance to the Germans.

It delayed the German stab towards Stalingrad, the gateway to the Caucasus, which Hitler had earmarked as his own.

In October the German 6th Army reached Stalingrad and launched a bloody offensive with the aid of endless strikes by the Luftwaffe. Russian defenders of the city adopted the tactics of guerrilla warfare, going underground to snipe at the oncoming Germans.

OPERATION URANUS

Even as the winter set in, German commander Paulus braced himself and his men for a final effort, during November 1942. Although the killing went on, he achieved little.

The Russians were to use some of the devastating tactics they had learned the hard way, at the hands of the invading Germans. Paulus found his flanks surrounded by a mighty Russian force ready to put a

noose around the weakened 6th Army. This was Stalin's 'Operation Uranus', devised between himself, Zhukov and Chief of Staff General Vasilevsky.

When he heard about the

disaster, Hitler was furious. He pledged supplies would be dropped by the Luftwaffe to the beleaguered Paulus and organised a relief column. But he refused to give Paulus the lifeline he needed for himself and his men – the order to break out of the encirclement or retreat.

GERMANS BESIEGED

At Stalingrad, only a fraction of the food and medical supplies needed were arriving. Injury or sickness accounted for as much as one fifth of the 100,000-strong force.

Left: German pilots notched up some stunning successes on the Eastern front despite facing grim flying conditions.

EYE WITNESS

Dennis Goading, of Gosport near Portsmouth, England, was a British rifleman with the King's Royal Rifle Corps. As a light infantryman he was engaged in hand-to-hand combat with German troops throughout the 1944 advance across western Europe.

‘There are still so many myths about the war. If one of our men was wounded in an attack we didn't all stop and gather around him like you see in the movies. We didn't have time to think about it. We just carried on and completed our assignment.

Of course, you would help if you could. But it took four men to deal with one man wounded and you could end up going nowhere.

Then again I saw soldiers who didn't even realise they had been hit. It was only when one of their mates pointed out blood seeping through their uniform that they felt the pain.

Cracking up under fire is another aspect surrounded in mythology. Everybody thinks of these guys running away. I saw one lance corporal who just got up and wandered, babbling straight into enemy fire. He was what we called bomb happy, or shell-shocked. We never found his body.

I came across the same symptoms affecting Germans who surrendered to us after we took the Falaise Gap. Almost an entire German division was wiped out there and there were thousands of bodies and animal carcasses just heaped up in the streets. That was a sight no man should ever have to see.

The German troops had been shelled and bombed for days without end. By the time the Canadians and ourselves got to them, they had no fight left. You could tap them on the shoulder and they would follow you; they didn't know or care where you were taking them.

We always had to be alert. Once when we were clearing a forest a German infantryman popped out of his fox-hole a few yards away and levelled his gun at me. I heard one of my mates shout 'Look out Den' and then that man opened up on the German and killed him.

I'll never forget staring at his body and watching this very pale white cloud emerging from his chest, so faint you could hardly see it. Some soldiers later told me I'd seen the man's soul departing.’

Above: *Stalingrad proved a vital turning point for Germany in the war. Flouting Hitler's wishes, Third Reich troops surrendered to the Russians following a gruelling and costly winter battle.*

The Russian commanders were confident enough to offer Paulus an opportunity to surrender as early as 8 January 1943. Paulus knew the Führer would be maddened so he stood fast.

Another heavy bombardment rained down on Stalingrad a few days later, leaving the depleted fighting force even more demoralised and desperate. In a last-minute frantic gesture, Hitler promoted Paulus to the rank of Field-Marshal. Paulus knew well enough the politics behind the honour. No German Field-Marshal had ever surrendered. The message was clear, fight to the death.

In the misery of snow and ice, Paulus must have glanced at some of the bodies of the German soldiers who died in those weeks and wondered why.

Now Paulus found the courage to be the first Field-Marshal to wave a white flag. At the close of January his head-quarters was overrun and he surrendered to the elated Russians. He went on to join a turncoat regiment of Germans who, following capture, fought for the Russians. For the victors there was the prize of 110,000 prisoners. For the defeated, it was unmitigated disaster.

Germans were on the run elsewhere in Russia as well, chased by an increasingly confident Red Army who were at their best in winter. It was far from the end of the war at the Eastern front. But it was the beginning of the end for Germany even though Hitler remained blind to the fact for months to come.

Now Paulus found the courage to be the first Field-Marshal to wave a white flag

---

The subsequent drive by the Russian army between January and March was fruitless. Crack German Commander Field-Marshal Erich von Manstein staged a determined recovery. Hitler's morale was broken by the Stalingrad debacle, losing his self-confidence and intuition.

Fighting continued in explosive spats until the scene was set for a major confrontation at Kursk. Hitler allowed the planned offensive, 'Operation Citadel', to be delayed time and again while his commanders struggled to get sufficient numbers of tanks in position.

It was 5 July before the battle commenced. By 12 July there were some 2,700 German tanks and 1,800 German aircraft ranged against almost 4,000 Soviet tanks. It was the largest head-on tank battle in history, an epic test of firepower which would leave both sides battered and worn. Tank after tank went up in flames, its crew having little chance of escaping the inferno. At the end of the day there were 300 German tanks smouldering. The German advance had been halted. It spelled defeat once more for the Reich. The dramatic loss of so many tanks would take Germany many more weeks to recover than it would Russia, leaving their armoured divisions sorely lacking in firepower and mobility.

Now it was for Hitler to contemplate withdrawal. It was alien to his nature to pull out of territory fought over and won two years before. But the Red Army was flexing its muscles and was already chasing the German army out of the Crimea and the Baltic lands. The plan favoured

Below: The tank battle at Kursk was an epic trial of strength. In the end it was the Russians who triumphed.

DIEPPE

Twenty-one years after the disastrous raid at Dieppe which cost the lives of hundreds of Canadian servicemen an investigation was launched to probe whether an advertisement for soap flakes gave the enemy vital advance information.

The commando raid at Dieppe in August 1942 involved 5,000 Canadians, 1,000 British, 50 American Rangers and some Free French fighters. Only half returned. The rest were killed or captured after being pinned down on the beach by the Germans. A week before it took place English newspapers carried an advertisement for Sylvan soap flakes under the title 'Beach Coat from Dieppe'. The copy afterwards read: 'How could you have known when you bought it that sunny day before the war that such a flippant little coat would be so useful about the house in war-time?'

There was speculation that in the advertisement was hidden the message 'Beach Combined Operations at Dieppe'. The woman pictured carried secateurs. Were they in fact wire cutters? Scotland Yard and MI5 swooped on the advertising agency Graham and Gillies and on the manufacturers of the soap flakes. They were persuaded it was a horrible coincidence. But no one knows whether the Germans had read the advertisement and seen secret codes where none in fact existed.

by commanders like Manstein, to pull back to a single defensive line, soon became the only option. With sufficient supplies and men to build defences, Hitler may have held on to the gains he had made for longer. The Germans were unable to dig in along the 2,000-mile front and provide an effective defence. Hitler's dream to take Russia had turned into the same nightmare that afflicted Napoleon 150 years before.

By January 1944 the Red Army was at last able to lift the siege of Leningrad. The city had been encircled since November 1941, suffering months of artillery bombardment. When liberation came after 900 days, only one third of the original population of three million were left alive.

Just as the winter of 1941-42 caused devastation among the invaders, so it brought misery to the hemmed-in people of Leningrad.

Rationing was down to just nine ounces of bread per day for working people and half that amount for those too young or too old to be employed. Cats, dogs, even rats, were eaten in a bid to stave off starvation. In front of the desperate people lay the no-man's land of defences against the Germans. Behind them lay frozen Lake Ladoga, over which there was a narrow trail into free Russia.

When liberation came after 900 days, only one third of the original population of three million were left alive

Minimal supplies found their way across the trail at first and even the smallest relief attempts were harried by German air-craft. By the spring, residents

Above: The sight of Russian tanks lying uselessly by the roadside provides a grim spectacle for passing troops.
Right: Many German soldiers died as they vainly struggled to repair vehicles frozen in the snow.

had learned a harsh lesson.

Every available inch of land was cultivated and there were fresh vegetables available throughout the rest of their imprisonment. Electricity was also rationed, the sewers were brim full and clean water was in short supply.

When the saviour army lifted the blockade, they were greeted with a weary relief by the Leningraders.

Between March and April the Red Army reclaimed 165 miles of territory. Their greatest push was yet to come, however, in the form of 'Operation Bagration', which began in June, just as Hitler came under acute pressure from the D-Day landings in Normandy. Before it began, the partisans working for the Russians behind German lines set to work by

setting off a series of disabling explosions.

The operation was characterised by now-familiar tactics employed by the Red Army. A burst of artillery fire to 'soften up' the enemy followed by the rapid advance of the infantry. Thousands of German soldiers were taken prisoner as Minsk fell once again to the Russians. Their humiliation was to walk down the silent streets of Moscow on their way to prison camps, watched by the eyes of the city residents. Now the German forces in the east were

stretched to breaking point. Hitler refused to let his troops pull back even when they had been overrun. The Führer's behaviour only offered more to the Russians by way of enemy casualties and prisoners.

By August, the Russian troops were on the Polish border. They had been forced to contend with more than three times the number of troops facing the Allies in Normandy and had proved themselves equal to the task. For the first time, the war was to be carried into Reich territory.

A FORGOTTEN ARMY

Just like the British fighters in Burma and the American soldiers assisting the Chinese, the troops who fought to regain Italy believed they were 'a forgotten army'.

Theirs was a protracted campaign remembered mostly for its mud, miscalculation and unexpectedly high casualty rate. Churchill had described the Italian peninsula as 'the soft underbelly' of the Third Reich. Fierce German resistance proved his judgement to be wildly awry.

After nearly a year of strenuous fighting, the Allies took Rome on 4 June 1944. The trumpeted D-Day operations which began the following night swallowed the limelight. Forces who felt they had lost the recognition they deserved joked wryly thereafter about themselves being 'D-Day dodgers in sunny Italy'.

The opportunity to open a second front in Europe occurred when the fighting in North Africa was brought to a close in 1943. For months, the Americans had been pushing for a campaign in northern France. But Churchill and his commanders felt it was premature, preferring instead to squeeze the Germans from the south.

By July 1943, the invasion of Sicily, code-named 'Operation Husky', was in readiness. Montgomery was to lead his weary but able 8th Army in one assault while General Patton, heading the US 7th Army, came via a different route. The aim was to trap the defending German forces in a pincer movement.

Little did they know that the resolve of the Germans was harder than ever

During the course of the invasion, Italy swapped sides in the war, having overthrown the dictator Mussolini. A staggering 40,000 were able to slip through the British and American trap and escape to the mainland.

Sicily was in Allied possession by 17 August. An armistice was signed on 3 September as the 8th Army crossed the Straits of Messina to land in Calabria, in 'Operation Baytown'. The effect of the revelation of the Italian *volte face* on the troops poised to continue with the invasion of the mainland was disastrous. There were cheers and celebrations before the operation had even begun. The

Far left: The sky is decorated by a fireball, following a German dive-bomber attack on an American cargo ship during the invasion of Sicily.
Left, inset: Allied DUKW amphibious vehicles, nicknamed 'ducks', are loaded aboard a landing ship at Salerno harbour in preparation for the next phase of the invasion of Italy.

Above: Weary from a foot-slog in Sicily, US soldiers prop themselves up at the foot of an Italian memorial to the soldiers of World War I.

men believed southern Italy was theirs for the taking and they were mentally ill-prepared for the brutal fighting which awaited them.

SALERNO LANDINGS

On 9 September, 165,000 British and American servicemen from 500 ships were engaged in a large-scale amphibious landing. The landings at Salerno, code-named 'Operation Avalanche', were scheduled by US commander General Mark Clark to last three days. He had confidence in the ability of the troops to secure a quick victory. Within just 72 hours he expected Naples to have fallen, giving the Allies a crucial harbour facility.

In fact, it took 21 days of gruelling battle. An attack staged at Taranto designed to divert the Germans failed. Crack German troops held the British and Americans at Salerno until reinforcements had been brought forward.

Montgomery expressed doubts about the planning of the campaign from the outset, and encountered tough resistance as he and his men tried to rendezvous with the rest of the invasion force. He was horrified to find the German positions had been reinforced. Clark's and Montgomery's troops finally made the planned link up on 16 September. In those weeks 25,000 soldiers and civilians died.

Although a first vital foothold in Italy had been carved out, the fighting didn't get any easier. The terrain of rocky peaks and steep escarpments favoured defensive positions, all of which were held by the Germans. Time and again, the

Allied soldiers found themselves fatally exposed.

By 15 November the campaign was halted by winter weather. Relations between the British and American commanders were equally chilly.

The next tactic to bring

Above: *Allied artillery in action against Italian targets. The gunners, from 97 Heavy AA Regiment, Royal Artillery, feel the heat.*

about a breakthrough took the form of the Allied landings at Anzio in January 1944. In 'Operation Shingle', the beachheads were quickly secured, yet the Allies had difficulty spearheading an advance. Indeed, they only narrowly missed being driven back into the sea by a determined German counter-offensive. Soon Anzio was under seige. Conflicts there were bitter. The Allies were desperately seeking routes to push forward.

By now the Allied reinforcements consisted of British, American, French, Canadian,

New Zealand, South African, Greek and Brazilian troops. Even the Japanese were playing their part. The Nisei-Americans, Japanese settlers in America who had been reviled at home after Pearl Harbor, made several vital strikes on behalf of the Allies.

MONTE CASSINO

The road to Rome was marked by the architectural treasure of Monte Cassino, a sacred Christian site founded in 529 by Saint Benedict. It was filled with cultural riches gathered through the centuries, kept lovingly in archives by the monks who lived and worked at the abbey.

Perched high on a mountainous ridge, Monte Cassino looked down into the town of Cassino. Monastery and town were connected by a funicular railway which climbed the sheer rocky face of the peak with ease.

Cassino was in the hands of the Germans in January 1944, a major strength in its defences known as 'the Gustav line'. It was the target of Allied plane attacks but even a heavy pounding failed to eradicate the defenders. Soon, it became clear the Germans were using the abbey as a defensive stronghold, unassailable at the mountain top.

The Americans then took one of the most controversial decisions of the conflict – to bomb the delightful monastery which was consequently smashed to smithereens.

Little was achieved. Allied forces were left clinging to the mountainside, scrambling forward a few yards whenever they

Right: The German forces in Italy finally surrendered to the Allies on 2 May 1945.

A Million Of The Enemy Lay Down Arms

FULL SURRENDER OF NAZIS IN ITALY

FALL OF BERLIN

could. It wasn't until May that the Allies by-passed the hazard, leaving the ruins of the abbey to fall to the Polish army in the rear. With heavy casualties, the Polish, assisted by a British contingent, took 1,500 prisoners – men of the German 4th Parachute Regiment.

To capture Monte Cassino, the Allies used 27 divisions with 1,900 tanks, together with 4,000 aircraft. Casualties on both sides were appalling, with some 105,000 Allied soldiers killed or wounded alongside 80,000 Germans.

FALL OF ROME

Although Rome fell soon afterwards and the incoming troops received a tumultuous welcome from its citizens, it was not the end of fighting in Italy. Still Germany threw men and ammunition at the advancing Allies. Pockets of resistance around Rimini and Bologna held the advance until the winter months, when by necessity it all but ground to a halt. Allied troops were forced to dig in during the inclement weather, experiencing the same dreadful conditions that faced their forebears in the trenches of World War I.

Right: The fierce battle at Monte Cassino left the monastery a shattered wreck.

As late as 9 April 1945, the Allies were compelled to begin another offensive. It wasn't until 2 May that a surrender was negotiated with the weary and disillusioned Germans.

OVERLORD!

It was the day that Europe had been waiting for, when Allied soldiers would tread again on French soil. In the event, many had to step over the bodies of fallen comrades lying lifeless in the Normandy surf before their feet touched Nazi-occupied France.

The Americans had been pressing for an assault on occupied Europe virtually since their entry into the war. Cautious British commanders, stung by heavy losses during the foray at Dieppe two years previously, at last thought the time was right to begin the liberation of the continent. A defeat could have been a death-blow to Britain's war effort, leaving her without an army. The commanders were finally convinced that victory was likely to be theirs.

The Germans, too, had been waiting with trepidation for the day that their enemies would try to get a foothold once more in Europe and had fortified the French coastline accordingly. Construction on the lines of tunnels, guns and bunkers to protect Hitler's Europe stretching 3,000 miles from Holland to the south of France began in September 1941 and got underway in earnest when Rommel took charge of the huge task in 1943.

German intelligence was good yet they still had no idea when and how the invasion would come. Norway, the Balkans and Calais were all strong possibilities. The imminence of the invasion, however, was beyond doubt in anyone's mind.

Hitler hoped it would be Disaster-Day for the Allies, with the German defenders casting the invaders back into the sea. He guessed rightly that the outcome of the attack would

Left: When Utah beach was secured, troops and supplies flooded ashore from the scores of ships in the Channel.

Right: *Dwight Eisenhower sent a 'good luck' message to all those who took part in 'Operation Overlord', the Allied invasion of occupied France.*

decide the war. Fulfiling everybody's expectations, the invasion came in early June. 'Operation Overlord' was the culmination of more than a year's work. It was an elaborate plan involving thousands of soldiers, sailors and airmen. The troops who would be scrambling up the shores and overwhelming the German opposition could only guess at what fate held in store for them when they set sail across the Channel for France. The shortest route from Britain would have been from Dover to Calais, where German and British troops could already spy each other on clear days. German defences were tight on that section of the French coast in readiness for an Allied invasion.

Despite the advantage of the brief crossing, the beaches around Calais posed too great a threat to the troops. Allied commanders had to look elsewhere. Further west, they found the answer to their conundrum – the long, golden beaches of Normandy. Here the German defences were comparatively thin.

Before 'Operation Overlord' got underway, there were key factors to consider which would help the Allies triumph in the war. First was the training of the men involved. Although amphibious landings had been

tried and tested during the war, nothing of the same magnitude had ever been attempted. British, American and Canadian soldiers were posted around Britain for rehearsals.

Coastal resorts such as Woolacombe, Gosport, Westward Ho!, Salcombe, Studland Bay and Slapton Sands played host to hundreds of soldiers sent to practise beach landings in an environment similar to that which they would encounter in France.

Slapton became a scene of disaster when live ammunition killed some of the soldiers taking part. Then, On 28 April 1944, mass devastation was wrecked when German E-boats slunk into a convoy in training off the coast, sinking two landing craft and killing 749 soldiers and sailors.

'OPERATION OVERLORD'

During the night of 5/6 June 1944, the armada carrying 21st Army Group – the 'Operation Overlord' strike force – approached the coast of Normandy. The assault was to be concentrated on five beaches: the two in the west (code-named 'Utah' and 'Omaha') were the responsibility of the Americans under Bradley; the three in the east ('Gold', 'Juno' and 'Sword') were the target of the British under Dempsey. The army group was under the overall command of Montgomery. Early in the morning of the 6th, the reconquest of continental Europe began as the first Allied forces hit the beaches and struggled to establish beachheads. German resistance was tough, but the liberation was underway.

Support for the soldiers and sailors promised to be greater than anything known before. Construction firms all over the United Kingdom set to work on a top secret engineering project, each company manufacturing a different component for a giant concrete jigsaw. Few of the workers involved could guess that they were building massive harbours called 'Mulberries', to be towed across to France for docking purposes by 150 tugs. Now the invading forces didn't have to capture a ready-built harbour, always a costly exercise in terms of human lives. Tanks, trucks, big guns and supplies would roll along the Mulberries with ease.

PLUTO

A pipeline under the ocean (codenamed 'Pluto'), made from steel or sometimes steel and lead, was installed to bring essential fuel quickly from Britain to France; it was laid on the sea bed by slow-moving tugs. After the war, it was salvaged to provide plumbing for 50,000 houses.

Reconnaissance was meticulously detailed. Air force pilots flying Spitfires stripped of ammunition to make them as speedy as possible photographed as much of the coastline as they could. In addition, an appeal for holiday photographs and postcards of the region reaped thousands of pictures of the area. Further aided by maps provided by the French Resistance, cartographers began to build up a three-dimensional impression of the targeted Normandy beaches.

Midget submarines went on dangerous nightly missions to the Normandy coast. Their occupants braved the water and the German patrols to bring back soil and sand samples and up-to-date information on the position of German defences.

The British authorities began a highly detailed decoy campaign to fool the Germans, who were equally involved in reconnaissance.

Along the Kent coast, some 150 miles from the British heart of 'Overlord', there was an impressive collection of armour and shipping being prepared. Only on close inspection was it revealed that the tanks were rubber and the ships were made from plywood. Lines of tents were empty apart from army cookers puffing smoke through the chimneys to make them appear authentic. The oil depots, planes and jetties that

> ## Only on close inspection was it revealed that the tanks were rubber

mushroomed in the area were also shams, designed to convince the Germans that the Allied thrust would be launched against Calais.

'Operation Fortitude' was vital to the success of the invasion. The Allied forces could still be driven back if the Third Reich descended on them within the first few days of the assault. With a variety of bogus intelligence messages, the commanders behind 'Fortitude' managed to convince the Germans that the invasion in Normandy was only a diversion and that the real attack was coming at Calais. Given that information, the Germans refused to move their forces from Calais, thereby saving the Allies from an onslaught.

EYE WITNESS

William Ryan, of the US 16th Infantry Regiment, was in the first wave to land at Omaha beach. At 18, it was his first action. He went on to serve 30 years in the army and is a veteran of the Korean and Vietnam wars.

❢We loaded up the transports at Portland, Weymouth, about 2 June. We were supposed to attack on 5 June. They cancelled it due to weather. We were on the ship all those days.

Everyone was sea-sick. At about 2am on 6 June we loaded on to small 36ft LCVPs, we were 12 miles out. They wanted to surprise the enemy. The seas were six or eight feet high. By now most of the men were so sick they didn't care whether they lived or died. They were too sick to be scared. Even coxswain was sick. I ran the boat for five miles until he started to feel better.

My company was assigned six boats. We lost two boats almost immediately – they were swamped with heavy waves. Heading for the beach the coxswain lost his bearings. When he realised we were off course he had to try again. The guys from the next sector blew over into our beach – their boats filled the beach so we couldn't get in. We had to circle around like sitting ducks. When we finally started into the beach we lost all four boats with the fire from the German 88s.

I was blown over the side and knocked unconscious. I was told later that two of the men in the boat with me dragged me through the water and propped me up against an embankment. Otherwise I would have drowned. At first there were five or six wounded with me. Then there were hundreds. I laid on the beach in that same position from about 8am until 10pm when they evacuated us. I had concussion in addition to shell fragments in my head, shoulder and leg. All this time I was going in and out of consciousness, looking down on Omaha beach. It was just a madhouse.

Troops were pinned down by the gun emplacements. Eventually a US Navy destroyer came in as close to the beach as possible without running aground and started firing at all the German emplacements. In a little while two or three other destroyers started shelling as well. In my opinion, that is what saved Omaha beach from defeat.

I heard afterwards the skipper on the ship was ordered to go back to a safe position. Apparently he said he wasn't leaving while US soldiers were pinned down on the beach. He could have been court martialled for what he did. But he should have got a medal.

I didn't have anything to eat all day. In the afternoon a US soldier came over the hill with a couple of bottles of French red wine which he gave to us. You are never going to beat Americans in war. They are crazy.❢

A double stood in for Monty and made a public departure for Algiers – when the real Monty was safely ensconced in 'Overlord' headquarters, which was based at Southwick House, Portsmouth.

The initial landings were to be made by 156,000 men, mostly Britons, Americans and Canadians. The line-up included an armoured division from France, one Belgian brigade, one Dutch brigade, one Polish division, as well as multi-national seaborne forces. In the skies, the main air forces were joined by squadrons from Norway, Czechoslovakia, France, Poland, Australia and New Zealand.

More men and equipment were held in reserve for future operations in Europe. It took an armada to ferry the men for the first action across the Channel. By late May, 359 warships, 1,000 minesweepers and associated vessels, 4,000 landing craft, 805 merchantmen, 59 blockships and 300 other small craft were at the ready.

> ### Local people became used to the sight of tanks and trucks lining the streets, as major military traffic jams built up

Overhead, more than 11,000 aircraft were assembled. Some would be towing gliders to be released over France. Each of these carried some 30 troops, tasked with tackling inland enemy positions, including vital landmarks which would halt a German advance, like Pegasus Bridge. The seas and the skies both belonged to the Allies. Montgomery had promised his men that the invasion would not go ahead until that umbrella of protection was firmly in place.

Anyone living on the south coast of England could have had no doubt that an invasion was poised to go ahead. Local people became used to the sight of tanks and trucks lining the streets, as major military traffic jams built up on the main roads to Portsmouth. Now there were 1,500,000 American troops alone massed on British shores. Then, one morning, they were gone.

Beginning on 2 June, the hordes of men and machinery bound for Normandy boarded their ships. The weather had been unseasonably poor, putting the entire operation at risk. It had to be postponed once from 5 June. General Dwight Eisenhower, supreme Allied commander, considered a further postponement in the face of the driving winds and rains which could wreak havoc with a seaborne landing force. The next date in June when the tides and the light were compatible was not for almost another two weeks. Some commanders favoured waiting. Others, like Montgomery, believed the strike should go ahead. It would, after all, be impossible to keep aboard ship those men already embarked. Each soldier and marine had already been interned in a camp for at least three weeks and was primed and ready for action. Any postponement could only

Above: A US ship returns to a British port loaded with 'Overlord' casualties, while in France the action continues.

have led to a deterioration in their mental and physical fitness.

Eisenhower smoked and read Westerns while he pondered the dilemma. Finally he made his decision. Heartened by predictions of a break in the weather, he signalled the go-ahead for 6 June, with the words 'OK, let's go'.

IKE SPEAKS

Eisenhower, fondly known as 'Ike', gave this message to the departing men of the Allied Expeditionary Force: 'You are about to embark upon the Great Crusade, toward which we have striven these many months. The eyes of the world are upon you. The hopes and prayers of liberty-loving people everywhere march with you. In company with our brave Allies and brothers-in-arms on other Fronts, you will bring about the destruction of the German war machine, the elimination of Nazi tyranny over the oppressed peoples of Europe and security for ourselves in a free world.

'Your task will not be an easy one. Your enemy is well equipped, well trained and battle-hardened. He will fight savagely.

'But this is the year 1944! Much has happened since the Nazi triumphs of 1940-41. The United Nations have inflicted upon the Germans great defeats, in open battle, man-to-man... The tide has turned! The free men of the world are marching together to Victory.'

The only message to reach the expectant public that day was a short, sharp statement, reading: 'Under the command of General Eisenhower, Allied naval forces, supported by strong air forces, began landing Allied armies this morning on the northern coast of France.'

As the soldiers and sailors bobbed in darkness on a choppy sea, they were nervous, tense, euphoric and excitable. Some were sea-sick, some prayed, many fought an overwhelming feeling of doom. Still more found enough spirit to tell jokes.

The huge size of the armada involved in 'Operation Neptune', which got them across the Channels only served to inflate their confidence.

The troops heard the drone of aircraft overhead – a big boost to their morale. Not only were the planes going to bombard enemy positions along the coast in preparation for the landings. Some were carrying paratroopers who, in the first leg of 'Overlord', were being

EYE WITNESS

Henry 'Marty' Martin, from Chicopee, Massachusetts, USA, witnessed the tragedy of 'Operation Tiger' at Slapton Sands while training for D-Day.

❛When the German E-boats attacked we just thought it was just part of the exercise. I was right in that exercise and I didn't find out for another 43 years that 749 men had drowned. These guys were wearing their life jackets around their waists when they should have been up around their armpits. With 30-35lb packs on their backs they were just tipped upside down in the water and couldn't right themselves.

I can understand why the government kept it secret at the time because the news would have been a terrible blow to morale. I only question why it took so long for the facts to come out.❜

dropped at 2am into east and west flanks of the landings.

When they approached the beach, they saw what appeared to be men walking on water. These were crew members of the midget submarines used to guide in the flotillas of landing craft. Men lashed themselves to the masts of their tiny submarines, which floated low in the water to signal to the captains of much larger vessels.

H-HOUR, D-DAY

Just a few hours later, naval guns were joining the aircraft in the pounding of enemy positions. Before 6am, the first men were ashore, putting months of rigorous training to the test.

British and Canadian troops were destined for the easterly beaches between Arromanches and Ouistreham. The three beaches earmarked for landings were code-named Gold, Juno and Sword.

In the west, the Americans tackled beaches Utah and Omaha, stretching between Les Dunes de Varreville and Colleville. On each beach there were barbed-wire hazards, anti-tank stumps entrenched in the sand and other menaces. First to come off the boats were the commandos who were to knock out the pill-boxes, and the sappers, charged with clearing a safe path up the beach.

The operation surprised the Germans, who at first believed the landings were a diversionary

tactic. Rommel was unprepared for the Allied arrival and was in Germany celebrating his wife's 50th birthday when the landings occurred. After Rommel heard of the invasion at 10.15am, he began a frantic drive back from Germany to his post.

After the war, Rommel's son Manfred recalled how his father had told Hitler many times that the invasion battle could not be won. Hitler refused to listen. 'All my father could do was to pull the front further and further back and, until he was wounded, carry out his duty.'

When he was told of the early morning events of 6 June, Hitler ordered his troops to clean

---

The Führer refused to release two Panzer divisions from the east of France

---

up the beachheads before nightfall. He knew the only way to save his extended empire was to throw the Allies back into the sea. But convinced it was a false alarm, the Führer refused to release two Panzer divisions from the east of France to counter the Allied attack until 3.40pm.

Troops on Sword, Juno and

Gold made solid progress in spite of casualties, although many soldiers landed without their guns and ammunition, which were lost in the water. They had to wait in huddles until the beach was taken before resuming their war. On Utah beach, the German defences found it impossible to keep the swarms of Americans at bay. It was speedily taken with fewer than 200 lives lost.

HELL OF OMAHA

On Omaha beach, bad weather, combined with strong currents and fierce resistance, made the landings a nightmare.

More than 2,000 men lost their lives. They were drowned when they were swept away by a changing tide with heavy equipment strapped to their backs. Some died when they trod on mines. Others perished from artillery, machine-gun, mortar and rifle fire from beach pill-boxes and from positions on cliffs above the beach. Wounded men strewn on the beach were in danger of being run over by tanks. There was little shelter and no escape.

Lieutenant-General Omar Bradley considered a withdrawal. It would have been disastrous

EYE WITNESS

George Ross, from Glasgow, was called up in 1939 when he was 19 years old. He recalls how as Sergeant Major of 101 Company, 5th Beach Group, he landed on Sword beach in the early hours of D-Day.

❝We didn't know what we were going to come up against. The crossing was rough. Our craft was led by a chief petty officer. He had been at sea 25 years and never been sea-sick. But he was sick as a dog that morning.

Coming ashore, the first thing we noticed was a camouflaged pill-box. We got underneath the slits and launched a grenade attack. Our job was to establish a route where our tanks could come through. I honestly cannot say I was nervous. I was anxious but I had been warned about what to expect during six months of lectures beforehand.

There were bodies in the water of both British and Germans. One of the officers told us afterwards how, when he was walking up the beach, he felt he was walking on cushions. It was bodies of dead soldiers he was walking on.❞

for the invasion, offering an opening for the Germans to attack both British and American flanks. Yet hardy US Rangers finally scaled the coastal heights to tackle the guns and alleviate the problems on the beach.

LONGEST DAY

Some of the men on the beaches were battle-hardened veterans. There was, however, a large contingent of raw soldiers, particularly among the Americans. They were pitched into the most intense, violent battleground, and forced to pick their way among the dead and dying amid the roar of big guns overhead and the sensation of small-

arms fire whizzing past their ears. The air was filled with the pungent smell of flesh, blood and cordite.

Particularly on Omaha but also true of the other beaches, the first wave of men forced to fight their way ashore were cut down. Preparing to take to the beaches, the second wave witnessed the carnage then ran past the bodies of their comrades.

Each flash of cowardice displayed by frightened, confused men was matched ten times by instances of heroism and stoicism. Each man was focused only on surviving for the next minute, the next hour and into the following day.

Ahead of them lay the task of capturing German-held towns, some of which fell more quickly than others. Russians who had been forced into German uniforms after being captured on the Eastern front were eager to lay down their arms. The French people rushed out to greet the

Below: *A Sherman tank, nicknamed 'Bessie', goes ashore to fight the battle of Normandy.*

liberating Allies, offering drinks, flowers and greetings. Residents near the beaches braved the conflict to aid the wounded.

Tales of outstanding courage filled the newspapers for months and years afterwards. One commando corporal led his men up the beach past enemy pillboxes, bellowing encouragement. He fell only when he had passed the pill-boxes – he had received more than 50 wounds.

The defending Germans were mostly in chaos. One senior commander reported that American gliders were landing Volkswagen cars in Normandy which were driven by American troops in German uniforms. The confusion and indecision that paralysed many Germans was countered by the heroic efforts of the Allied troops.

By the end of the longest day, 10,000 Allied soldiers had fallen. The figure was a third of that estimated by Allied command. But there was no turning back. The Allies had achieved the Normandy landings. Nothing and nobody was going to force them out of France again.

TANKS COME OF AGE

The tank came of age during World War II and proved to be a battle winner – or loser. The first tanks had been designed by Sir Ernest Swinton and saw action in the Somme offensive of World War I in 1916. Caterpillar tracks enabled them to cross treacherous terrain where no other vehicle could go. They were equipped with one or more guns, the crew sitting behind armour plating and firing off salvos at the enemy.

Now German General Heinz Guderian used the outbreak of World War II to put his own theories about the use of tanks to the test. Tanks should not be pinned down to flanking foot soldiers, he argued. Their purpose was to break out against the enemy, putting a speed into land-based warfare which it had never known before.

With that in mind, he formed his highly efficient Panzer divisions. The tanks were fast but lacked adequate protective armour. Nevertheless, they were an integral part of 'Blitzkrieg', the lightning war, a tactic with which Hitler easily won Poland, France, Holland and Belgium.

The technique took Britain and France by surprise. Although France had 2,475 tanks at its disposal their effectiveness was muted because of the way in which they were deployed. Instead of combining the fire-power as Guderian did, each tank was evenly spaced down a long defensive line. In time Allied commanders mimicked Guderian to get the best out of their tanks. Used individually, they were easy targets.

When a tank 'brewed up', the escape hatches were wholly inadequate, or blocked

If tankmen in World War I were better protected than their colleagues in the infantry, the same could not be said of their counterparts 20 years on. In fact, there were few infantrymen who would willingly change places with tankmen. For while

Above: *Tank crews during World War I were rightly delighted with the new hardware, which provided them with ample protection. But in World War II, a variety of anti-armour weapons existed to make life hell for the tankman.*
Far left: *The men of an armoured division running through the smoke-filled streets of the German town of Wernberg.*

tanks stole a march on the enemy in the the killing fields of Flanders, technology had now caught up. Now there was a wide range of anti-armour artillery designed to knock tanks out. Men inside a stricken tank had little or no chance of escape.

And for the first three years of the war, German tanks and anti-tank weapons were better than their British counterparts. For example, the Mark II Matilda was known for its weak steering clutches, the Valentine offered only limited vision to its commander, the Crusader was mechanically unreliable. It took only an armour-piercing shell from one of the new breed of anti-tank guns used by the Germans to finish them.

That's when infantrymen remained glad they had the job they did. For when a tank caught fire, or 'brewed up', the tiny escape hatches on the tanks were wholly inadequate and were often blocked. Sometimes there was a matter of seconds

before fire took a hold and the tank's ammunition began to explode. Sometimes there was not. Nicknames for tanks during the war included 'steel coffins', 'tommy cookers' and 'Ronson burners', because, like the products of the same name, they would always 'light first time'.

BLACKENED DOLLS

One witness gruesomely detailed the effects on the men trapped inside: 'Little blackened dolls about two feet high have been found in tanks. Once these were men.'

As the war progressed, the Germans learned about the short-comings of their tanks, which

Left: Matilda tanks were favoured by the British military but they failed to match the firepower of German Tigers, pictured below.

some – but not all – of the difficulties. Yet no design, no matter how superior, could compensate for the problems thrown up by the terrain the tanks were working in. Every theatre of war offered its pitfalls to tanks. In Europe

were lacking in firepower and suffered from flimsy armour. Their most painful lesson came on the Eastern front when their troops encountered the fearsome T-34 tanks of the Russian armoured divisions.

They introduced the Panther, in July 1943, and the Tiger, in September 1942, which were battle winners thanks to the enormous range of their guns, quite outstripping the British models, which were unable to get close enough to counterattack effectively.

THE DEADLY 88

By the time the British developed the six-pounder gun, the Germans had in their armoury the heavier 75 mm weapon. As the Americans caught up, with their own 75 mm gun, the Germans leaped ahead again, fitting the deadly 88 mm guns, which were originally designed as anti-aircraft guns but wreaked havoc when mounted on the Tiger tank.

As an illustration of the immense advantage kept in hand by the Germans in terms of tank technology, a single Tiger tank operating in

Normandy knocked out 25 British tanks, 28 armoured vehicles and killed an additional 80 infantrymen.

It seemed as if the British had learned nothing from their experiences in the desert a full two years earlier. The poor state of British and American tank

---

The poor state of Allied tank technology was little short of a scandal

---

technology was little short of a scandal and left Allied tank crews disheartened.

A later generation of Allied tanks, including Shermans and Churchills, began to overcome

the rain made the earth unacceptably boggy; in North Africa the desert dust clogged engines and sharp stones tore the tracks; in Asia, where there were few tanks, the humidity affected the engineering. In nine days of fighting in Germany in 1945 the 9th Royal Tank Regiment and the 147th Regiment suffered 85 tank casualties. 17 were due to enemy action, 36 succumbed to mechanical problems, while 32 got stuck in the mud. This time the innovators were the British. A series of modified tanks were used to breach the beaches at Normandy. Witnesses reported that some German soldiers threw down their guns and ran at the sight of this bizarre new breed.

Behind them was Major-General Sir Percival Hobart. Like

A series of modified tanks were used to breach the beaches at Normandy

his brother-in-law Montgomery, Hobart was outspoken and did not suffer fools gladly. His forthright manner won him few friends at the War Office and by 1940 he was retired. It was the personal intervention of Winston Churchill which installed Hobart back in the fight against Hitler.

HOBART'S FUNNIES

Mindful that Allied troops would encounter all manner of defences during the landings, his priority was to install tough armour to protect the troops. Then he looked at ways of tackling an amphibious landing, crossing a minefield, blasting a well-fortified pill-box and travelling with heavy vehicles across boggy ground.

To get hefty tanks ashore from landing craft, he came up with the Duplex Drive, an amphibious tank with propellers and a canvas skirt to protect it from the water. When the tank made it to the shore, the canvas was lowered.

An adaptation of the Churchill tank helped to combat the threat of minefields. On the front a large rotating drum hung with heavyweight chains, was turned by power from the engines. This 'Crab' would explode the hidden mines without causing damage. The 'Ark', a tank with four long

ROMMEL – DESERT FOX

Erwin Rommel, courageous soldier and gifted leader of men, became known as the Desert Fox thanks to his cunning in North Africa.

The son of a teacher, Rommel joined the army from his home town of Württemberg as an officer cadet and proved his early promise during World War I. Between the wars he taught at Germany's military academies and authored a book about infantry strategies which was published in 1937.

When war broke out, Colonel Rommel was put in charge of the troops guarding Hitler. Frustrated with his behind-the-lines role, he seized the opportunity early in 1940 to command the 7th Panzer Division which he took into action in France before it was occupied, striking as far north as the Channel coast.

A year later he was put in charge of the German troops sent by Hitler to bail out the beleaguered Italians in North Africa. He shone in his new role, despite his misgivings about his wavering Italian allies. His impressive early victories won him the rank of Field-Marshal.

He was held in high esteem by his men for his initiative and bravery. In an example of his charismatic leadership, he once leapt from a car to address a division of men: 'There is an English Armoured Brigade getting ready to attack you from the north and in the south there is an English mixed force which is advancing. Take care that you are finished with the first before the second arrives!' Yet he was all but ready to pull out his exhausted men when Hitler ordered a strike on Cairo in Egypt. Once again, he found remarkable success until his supply lines became hopelessly overstretched as he ventured further into British-held territory. Weakened by lack of essentials and wearied by months of fighting, he was finally defeated and pursued out of Africa.

In 1944 Rommel was ordered by Hitler to secure the French coastline against Allied invasion. Even though he was already convinced the war was unwinnable, he tackled the unenviable task with a deep professional pride. Yet he received little practical support from the Führer despite his warnings that all would be lost if the enemy penetrated the insubstantial coastal defences.

Although at heart he was non-political, Rommel was recruited by plotters who wanted Hitler replaced. The popular and realistic Rommel was their chosen leader. It is unlikely, however, that he knew about plans to assassinate the Führer for he was deeply opposed to killing for political ends.

In any event, an attack by British bombers put Rommel in hospital with serious injuries when the abortive coup took place. Hitler himself was reluctant to expose Rommel as part of the plot against him. He knew only too well that he was vulnerable to the grass-roots affection won by Rommel. So he dispatched two generals to see his reluctant adversary to offer a deal. Rommel and his family would escape the shame of public exposure if he would take poison and eliminate himself as a threat to Hitler. On 14 October 1944 Rommel did as his leader asked and was buried with full military honours.

Right: Rommel (left) confers with a subordinate during the desert campaign.

beams at each corner, became a bridge to span small ravines and enable troops and armoured cars to cross.

Providing a roadway for troops and vehicles through soft ground became the job of the 'Bobbin' tank. It had a large, rolled, heavy-duty canvas roadway attached to its front. As the tank trundled along, it unfurled the roadway for following traffic. But perhaps the most fearsome of his designs was the 'Crocodile' another modified Churchill tank, designed to throw a scorching flame for 120 yards. Attached behind was its own fuel depot on wheels. So feared was this flame-thrower that when SS troops captured the crew of a Crocodile, they would shoot them straightaway.

RIFLES AND GUNS

In just four years, the advances in gun capabilities had been enormous. When the war started, the Allied stock of rifles dated mostly from the previous world war or before.

Rifles were smaller and lighter than ever before and fired faster too. Rates of fire were up in the machine guns as well. The

> ## When SS troops captured the crew of a Crocodile, they would shoot them

British Bren could now dispense around 500 rounds a minute, the same as the US Browning. New mortars were light enough for infantrymen to carry with them into battle.

The pack of equipment loaded onto the back of the infantryman was very heavy. Soldiers had to rely on mules in some cases to transport the guns to the top of high, hostile escarpments in rugged terrain.

Even then the pre-prepared defences installed by the enemy were strong enough to resist the firepower of such weapons. Only bombs would have a sufficiently devastating effect and that required air support.

Given the firepower, the men used it, expending thousands of rounds of ammunition daily. The prospect of any shortages of fuel or ammunition, was a daunting one. World War II showed that a fighting force was only as good as its supply line.

Left: Jeeps were put through their paces in Normandy during the autumn of 1944. These rugged, four-wheel-drive vehicles were used to transport the wounded.

the thousand in America to reach the battle fronts and replenish the men.

WILLYS JEEP

Transport had to be reliable and tough to be of any use. In 1940, the Jeep made its debut, its name derives from the full name first given it general purpose (i.e. 'GP') vehicle. First constructed by the Willys Overland Company, this legendary creation had speed and agility and was an instant hit with the army. It could tackle even the roughest terrain and was useful for transporting troops, small arms and other light loads. It further helped to make horses redundant on the battlefield.

In Burma the Chindits had an advantage over their Japanese enemy through the regular supplies dropped in by aircraft. In Europe and Africa improving methods of amphibian landings allowed the trucks which were being turned out by

---

EYE WITNESS

Sydney Hartley suffered a badly injured leg when he was in the third of three tanks sent forward to pinpoint the whereabouts of the enemy during a battle in the Tunisian campaign. It was later amputated just above the knee. He was 28 years old.

❝I knew the dangers of crossing open ground on enemy territory but I clearly remember thinking that, with a bit of luck, we might again just get out of this unscathed with us being the last tank in a line of three.'

After about 150 yards I heard the voice of the squadron leader come through my headphones. "Third troop, halt. Turn right and engage the enemy tanks." As we turned we realised we had run into a trap. Just coming into their final positions were two German tanks or self-propelled guns. We were all taken by surprise.

I knew this was the moment of truth, life or death. I quickly estimated the range, our big 75 mm gun was loaded, I put the sights on the target and fired. It was impossible to follow the tracer bullet because the sun was lying just behind the target. Then it didn't matter as I saw the German tank's gun flash and a split second afterwards our world exploded. Everything suddenly went black and I felt what seemed like a red-hot poker against my right leg.

Flames were rising and I knew I had to get out quickly. I tried to pull myself out of the turret but at waist high I realised something was holding me back, because I was still wearing my headphones. Then I made a superhuman effort and flung myself the eight-foot drop to the ground. I knew something was terribly wrong with me. I heard this soul-destroying scream – it could have been any one of us. I dragged myself away. Looking at my right leg, the shock was more mental than physical. The armour-piercing shot had taken away half of my calf and broken up the calf bone. The foot was dangling from what flesh remained.

I took out a large field-dressing from my pocket and made a tourniquet. It looked like the driver and co-driver hadn't made it out of the tank. The next tank in line was burning although the crew got out safely. Mortar bombs were dropping all around. The troop corporal carried me to the rest of the men which was excruciatingly painful. I had morphine tablets but felt faint from blood loss. I didn't know which was most painful, my leg or the burns on my hands and face. The top skin of my hands peeled back like roller blinds. I had a very bumpy ride on a Bren-gun carrier back to the echelon alongside an injured German soldier and his friend.

I was laid out on a stretcher, looking up at the sky, when I saw a Messerschmitt 109 come into view. It appeared to be heading straight for me. He started machine-gunning us. It was the first of three aircraft attacks before I was put in the ambulance and driven away.❞

THE PACIFIC

Sweeping Japanese gains left the Allies with their work cut out, yet there was a grim resolve among them to push the invaders back. The rocky road to triumph over the extended empire of the Rising Sun began in New Guinea.

Japanese plans to take the unoccupied sector of New Guinea with a seaborne invasion were dashed following the Battle of the Coral Sea in May 1942. But they had not given up hope of seizing the island. Another offensive was planned, this time overland.

On 21 July 1942 an advance party of 2,000 Japanese soldiers landed at Buna, Papua, without a shot being fired. Their aim was to take Port Moresby, still in Allied hands. Ahead of them was a choice of two jungle tracks across the 1,200 ft Owen Stanley mountains – hostile and steamy terrain. They chose the most accessible or least impassable.

Defensive forces on New Guinea at the time comprised some scattered Australian brigades backed up by a limited number of indigenous New Guinea riflemen.

The Japanese forces seized the interior in little more than a week, scaling the rocky heights of the mountain range. Racing against time, the Australians rushed through reinforcements. By 12 August Lieutenant-General F. Rowell, in command at Port Moresby, decided he had enough troops at his disposal to send an expedition into the mountains.

PORT MORESBY

Another Japanese force, numbering about 11,500, was landed, enabling a significant thrust to take place against the Australians. The prospects looked bleak for the Allies as the Australians fell back and back. The Australian commandos were swallowed up in the Japanese advances.

But by now the Japanese were encountering some difficulties of their own. Allied aircraft were making a fine job of disrupting the already treacherous lines of supply. It meant soldiers fighting in the most torrid conditions were left without adequate food and medical supplies.

In addition, the spectre of dysentery and other debilitating diseases loomed. Troops were

Troops were weakened by highly infectious wasting diseases in jungle conditions

weakened by highly infectious wasting diseases which medics were unable to counter in jungle conditions. By September their advance had run out of steam. They were brought to a halt just 32 miles from Port Moresby.

The Australians had little time to even draw breath. More Japanese troops had landed at Milne Bay, to the east, with orders to occupy the all-important airfield there. Approximately 2,000 Japanese soldiers fought fiercely to reach the edge of

Above: Japanese marines begin their march on New Guinea, confident of yet another victory.
Left: One of the Emperor's vessels lies wrecked off Guadalcanal, which became a graveyard for ships.

the airstrip. Then the tide of battle turned against them. The Japanese had thought the Australian presence there was depleted. In fact there were nearly two brigades of men, two fighter squadrons and plenty of established artillery.

In a counter-attack at the end of August by the 18th Australian Brigade, the Japanese were chased back to the sea. Finally, on 6 September, the remnants of the landing force were withdrawn.

Now the focus was back on the Japanese holed up in the mountain range. Australian troops reinforced by Americans forged up the Kokoda trail, the same route the invading Japanese had followed but in the opposite direction. A parallel force hoping to outflank the enemy embarked up the Kapa Kapa trail, even more remote and difficult.

Ahead of them lay the Japanese, securely dug into three defensive positions at the peak of the Kokoda trail. On 16 October the first Japanese post was taken by an Australian brigade. Yet the supreme effort in the face of determined opposition sapped what little strength the Australian soldiers had left.

Without the help of their trusted Melanesian porters,

The Australians were equally vulnerable to disease. The main cause of dysentery in New Guinea was polluted water. Springs were fouled by natives and the fighting men themselves, who were often too far away from their latrines to use them.

JAPANESE ROUT

It took fresh troops, who finally relieved the exhausted

astray, the Allies were better off than their Japanese counterparts, who were still dependant on supplies coming in by sea and being passed up country. Australian troops found the bodies of their foe were emaciated and diseased. There were signs of cannibalism as no doubt starving soldiers had resorted to eating human flesh to stay alive.

Below: US marines heading for Japanese front lines at Guadalcanal. **Right:** *US soldiers resting after action on New Guinea.*

EYE WITNESS

Bob Cartwright, from Wimbledon, south west London, was a lance corporal in the Royal Army Medical Corps who saw action in North Africa before being posted to the Far East. He served as a Chindit in the 44th Recce Regiment on the force's second foray.

❬There were 400 men in every column. The men from the medical corps like me travelled either at the front or the back. Conditions were ruddy awful. The recce men had to tackle unmapped mountains with gradients of one in one. They were so steep that men had to crawl on their hands and knees. Even the mules fell by the wayside. They plunged down ravines and couldn't get out.

On my back was a 60 lb first aid bag. For six weeks we were living on bully beef and biscuits and on any rice we could scrounge from local Burmese people, which wasn't much. Then US 'K' rations were airdropped to us. In one of the daily meals there was usually a bar of chocolate. We used to melt it on to the rice to make a pudding. We were on our way to Kohima to relieve the siege there when we were ambushed in a teak forest. The leaves of teak trees are very big and crisp. We had to wait until it rained before we could get out without the Japanese hearing our every footstep.

We had to take malaria and salt tablets. If you weren't wet from perspiration you were wet with the rain. Men suffered from malaria, tick bites and ulcers. I don't know anyone who didn't lose weight. Everyone thought the world of Orde Wingate, the man behind the Chindits, even though he wasn't liked by the big shots in India. All they did was criticise him.

He had eyes that looked right through you and a really magnetic personality. I met him on two occasions. He inspired the troops. We marched 600 miles through the jungle. I was out there about six months before they flew us out. The men were in excellent spirits. I don't think I heard anybody moan about what we were doing. It was only the weather that bothered us.

There must be many unmarked and unknown graves in Burma. ❭

---

who carried their equipment and sometimes the men themselves, they would not have got so far. Try as they might, they could not budge the invaders from the other two dug-outs. Casualties mounted from sniper fire, with the Japanese apparently secure in their fox-holes.

Australians, to add impetus to the assault. After intense fighting in swampy insect-ridden undergrowth the Japanese were finally routed. All the while, the Australian and American troops were benefiting from supplies dropped by air in the jungle. While some consignments went

Every mile of the jungle was bitterly contested by the two sides. The stop-start campaign was at its most deadly when the Japanese were cornered in wellbuilt defences, with their backs to the sea. Both prongs of the Allied forces joined up but there was stalemate as the Japanese sat tight in their well-dug positions.

Even the arrival of new Allied troops to wage the battle brought piecemeal results. For every fighting soldier, the conditions were nothing short of appalling. Allied troops were forced to pick off Japanese men and guns one by one as the doomed and diminishing force refused to capitulate. It wasn't until 3 January 1943 that the last of the Japanese resistance was ended. It had taken six months and cost an estimated 5,700 Australian, 2,800 American and 12,000 Japanese casualties.

As Australians and Americans fought to free Papua New Guinea, so US Marines were battling to liberate Guadalcanal, an island in the Solomons crucial in importance because of its airfield, Henderson Field. Frequent rain squalls in the sauna heat made it a perfect breeding ground for mosquitoes. Malaria was rife among soldiers already weakened by the humidity. Documents from Japan's high command captured later revealed the immense importance they attached to the island. 'Success or failure in recapturing Guadalcanal is the fork in the road which leads to victory for them or us.'

GUADALCANAL

On 7 August 1942 11,000 US Marines landed on Guadalcanal, surprisingly, without opposition. It would take a long time before Japan's soldiers on the island were eradicated, however. Japanese forces on neighbouring islands gave a more rousing reception to landing parties. On Tulagi, there was a hectic battle. At the end of it, the Marines were victorious. Tulagi was theirs. In total 108 US Marines had died while the Japanese force of an estimated 1,500 was wiped out.

> ## *Frequent rain squalls in the sauna heat made it a perfect breeding ground for mosquitoes*

Like the Australians and the British, the American forces fighting the Japanese in the Pacific discovered that jungle warfare was a battle of nerves. The vegetation was host to scores of unusual animals making terrifying noises. Sounds of birds, lizards and insects echoed through the night, each one sounding like an approaching sniper. And sometimes it was indeed the enemy, creeping in the dark before moving in for a kill. It was vital for guns to remain quiet unless there was an attack, since a burst of fire pinpointed a soldier's position for the enemy.

The Japanese, throughout the Pacific and South east Asia, displayed a mastery of cunning jungle warfare tactics. They knew a grenade thrown from somewhere in the night would result in havoc in an Allied camp. Startled and confused, the Allied soldiers would fire wildly and draw their knives, often injuring their comrades in the subsequent chaos. Meanwhile, the Japanese melted back into the darkness.

There were reports of Japanese soldiers leaping

Below: A tense moment as US soldiers, with guns at the ready, probe a jungle hideout in search of Japanese snipers.

suddenly into Allied foxholes brandishing knives – then quickly jumping out again.

The Allied soldiers were left tussling among themselves in panic with weapons drawn. In the darkness, a voice might sound: 'Please, Johnny, help me.' It was tempting for the soldiers to rise up and respond to a

---

The Japanese displayed a mastery of cunning jungle warfare tactics

---

call for help. If they did so, it would spell their doom. Here was yet another technique used by the Japanese to get the enemy to reveal itself. The US occupation of Guadalcanal sparked some vital sea battles. But the first land-based reprisals from the Japanese came on 18 August when 1,000 Japanese troops were landed on

Guadalcanal. All were killed and their commander Colonel Ichiki committed suicide.

Aircraft from the US carriers patrolling in the region deterred further large-scale landings although there were numerous small-scale attacks mounted by Japanese units, all successfully repulsed. Japanese commanders had grossly underestimated the number of American troops stationed on Guadalcanal. The American garrison, now numbering 19,000, was able to prevent wholesale Japanese landings with naval and air support even though the empire gathered 20,000 men from around the region for an October offensive.

The Americans were, however, handicapped by the frequent attacks on Henderson Field made by battleships and aircraft, as well as by the nuisance raids led by the Japanese who had made successful landings on

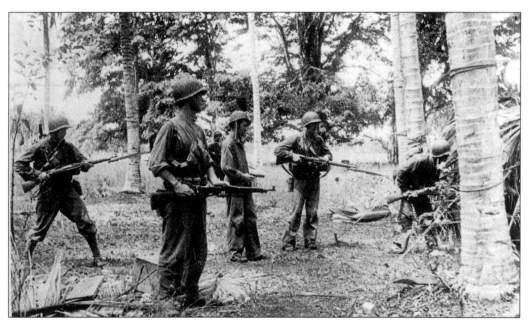

Guadalcanal. It wasn't until the three-day Battle of Guadalcanal at sea that the hard-pressed American defenders enjoyed some respite.

It was then that the Japanese navy decided to pull back from Guadalcanal and defend a different line. Senior navy commanders recognised the increasing strength of the Americans reduced the chances of taking Guadalcanal to virtually nil.

CHINDITS

The army was keen to continue the campaign, confident that the 30,000 troops based on the island would eventually triumph. But without naval co-operation, transporting reinforcements or supplies to the island, would be impossible.

Here was a chance at last for the Marines to withdraw for some recuperation after four months of jungle warfare. Their replacements finally totalled about 50,000 men, who were fit enough to drive the remaining Japanese forces from the island with relative ease. By February 1943, all had been evacuated by sea.

Above: B-25 Mitchell medium bombers of the US 5th Air Force deliver destruction to a Japanese airstrip on New Guinea in March 1944.

In Burma, the Japanese were still holding their own. The British had one card left, which may not have been a winner but certainly kept them in the game. This was the first ever deployment of Long Range Penetration Groups, later known as the Chindits.

Behind the Chindits was Orde Wingate, an unorthodox soldier with broad experience of organising guerrilla operations. His men from the 77th Indian Brigade derived their name from the mythical Burmese temple guardian, the chinthe, half lion and half eagle.

Earlier in the war, Wingate had attempted suicide by stabbing himself in the neck while suffering from malaria and depression. He was saved and a year later brought his charismatic brand of leadership to an enthusiastic bunch of men.

INTO BURMA

Their aim was to operate behind enemy lines, causing disruption and damage. They had to be skilled jungle fighters, able to fade away quickly into the forested landscape. Those in demand for the first Chindit expedition in February 1943 were men who were masters of demolition skills and also able radio operators. The radio operators were vital to the success of the mission as they were responsible for contacting base and requesting supplies. These were dropped by air, giving the Chindits an essential advantage of endurance.

EYE WITNESS

Bill Jenkins joined the Australian armed forces in 1939 when he was 18 years old and served until 1945, seeing action on the infamous Kokoda trail in New Guinea.

❝We had just come back from the Middle East. I had three days' leave after two and a half years at war when I was recalled and put on a boat headed for New Guinea. Things were getting pretty desperate. The Japanese were in rowing distance of Australia itself. The pitifully small forces there to meet them were militiamen or home guard members who were decimated. We joined them and gradually drove the Japanese back over the Owen Stanley range of mountains. Sickness was terrible, with scrub typhoid, malaria and malnutrition claiming many lives. It was difficult for the planes to spot us and drop supplies. My brigade began with about 2,500 men. Less than 200 were evacuated at the close of the campaign. I returned weighing less than seven stones instead of 12 stones.❞

Together with elephants, mules and buffaloes, two groups comprising 3,200 men set off into occupied Burma, each ready to sub-divide into columns to achieve its aim. They set off with the poetic words of Orde Wingate ringing in their ears:

WINGATE'S WORDS

'It is always a minority that occupies the front line. It is a still smaller minority that accepts with a good heart tasks like this that we have chosen to carry out. We need not, as we go forward into conflict, suspect ourselves of selfish or interested motives. We have all had the opportunity of withdrawing and we are here because we have chosen to be here; that is, we have chosen to bear the burden and heat of the day. Men who make this choice are above the average in courage. We need therefore have no fear for the staunchness and guts of our comrades.

Our motive may be taken to be the desire to serve our day and generation in the way that seems nearest to our hand. The

---

EYE WITNESS

Alf Turner was a member of the 6th Battalion, The Devonshire Regiment, when he was posted to the Far East in 1943.

❜Our sergeant major told us it was the best draft of all and that we wouldn't do anything for six months. That was a load of tripe. After arriving at a reinforcement camp we were sent up to Bhopal to do a month's jungle training. Then we set off for Burma.

All you can see around you in the jungle are trees. If somebody fires, you don't know which way it is coming from. Being a country boy, I found it a bit easier than the Londoners out there who weren't used to night-time noises and wildlife.

The Japanese soldiers would shout out in the night: "Tommy, where are you?" And they would beat bamboo sticks to unnerve us. They tried to get us to give away our positions. After one attack an apparently wounded Japanese soldier was calling: "Tommy, help me, help me". One of our officers who couldn't stick it any more went out to him. We told him not to go. When he got near, the soldier jumped up and threw a grenade at him. The officer lost his leg.

The Japanese put grenades under dead bodies in the hope you would turn them over. Near the Irrawaddy river we came across a village where all the men had been beheaded by the Japanese and all the women were hung up by their hands and disembowelled. They were cruel fighters.

We took very few prisoners. Those who were wounded would rip their bandages off after being treated. They wanted to die in battle.

We belonged to the 20th Indian Division and I was a technical sergeant in charge of transport. I had to use sticky tape to repair tyres. We came across some Japanese supplies and used those to keep the trucks going.

There were giant ant hills. In the monsoon season they would collapse and you could find yourself knee deep in earth with ants crawling all over your legs. Then there were the leeches. The only way to get them off was with a lighted cigarette butt. We also had snakes slithering over our legs, jungle sores and prickly heat.

In France and Germany the troops had fleets of invasion craft. When they liberated towns, the people came out to cheer them. In Burma we had a few 'ducks' but mostly we had to make our own rafts to see us across the rivers. And we were never welcomed by the people. They didn't seem to care if it was us or the Japanese.❜

Left: British troops of the 14th Army advance cautiously on the mud huts in the newly taken prize of Meiktila in Burma, March 1945.

battle is not always to the strong nor the race to the swift. Victory in war cannot be counted upon but what can be counted upon is that we shall go forward determined to do what we can to bring this war to the end which we believe best for our friends and comrades in arms, without boastfulness or forgetting our duty, resolved to do the right so far as we can see the right.'

Wingate's bold and unexpected plan took the Japanese by surprise. When forces crossing the main Irrawaddy and Chindwin rivers were spotted, commanders believed these were small groups on reconnaissance who would be easily dispatched. Only when major railway bridges were blown

That the Japanese were now aware of their presence made life increasingly difficult

up did the Japanese suspect an orchestrated attack against them. At that stage, two divisions were sent to flush the British out of the jungle.

By now, the Chindits were dispersed into smaller, isolated groups, some faring better than others. That the Japanese were now aware of their presence made life increasingly difficult for the jungle warriors, who became trapped in the dense vegetation while their enemies had the rule of the roads and tracks. Inevitably, the tightly planned operation began to fall apart. When food ran short, they ate their mules. But then they had no transport.

BAREFOOT TO INDIA

Four months later, some 2,200 men returned to India, hungry, physically frail and many with hare feet, veterans of a remarkable physical trial and fully conversant with both jungle and guerrilla

Above: Gurkha troops march past giant statues of chinthe — after which the Chindits were named – having liberated a key Burmese city.

tactics. The important principles of warfare had been tried and tested by them, including that of air-dropping supplies. The soldiers rarely visited local villages for food and drink, where they might have been captured.

The Chindits were a difficult enemy for the Japanese to pin down, moving as they did under cover of darkness. So concerned were the Japanese army by the exploits of the Chindits that they revised their defensive policies in upper Burma, which not only tied up forces but ultimately laid them open to defeat.

REICH IN RUINS

By the end of 1943, the Germans were on the run from Stalin's forces. The Battle of the Atlantic had ended in their defeat and U-boats were being systematically blown out of the water. Germany itself was suffering a barrage of bombing campaigns, Italy had changed sides and, to many in the Nazi hierarchy, it seemed the war was already lost.

The following year brought little by way of relief. The long-awaited landings of thousands of Allied soldiers finally occurred in Normandy in June. When German soldiers were unable to defend the beaches, it was clear the destination for the Allies was nothing short of the German Fatherland itself.

During their first few weeks on French soil, the Allied armies encountered some strong resistance, particularly centred at Caen. Here was a professional SS division and a green German unit culled from the Hitler youth. Some fighters were as young as 16, they proved to be formidable opponents.

The British forces failed to capitalise on their surprise attack to gain their D-Day objectives and paid the penalty for their short delay while regrouping, as the Germans dug in with a vengeance. It took two major pushes, code-named 'Epsom' and 'Goodwood' to oust the few hundred Germans,

costing hundreds of Allied lives.

Countless numbers of French civilians died, mostly in the enormous air raids launched by the Allies which reduced the historic town of Caen to rubble. Fires raged in Caen for 11 days after the main bombing attack. Estimates put the number of French dead as high as 10,000. Still the German resistance held fast. The net effect of the air raids was simply to provide new hazards, like blocked roads, for the Allied ground forces.

TANK BATTLES

There were bitter tank battles between the British and Canadian forces and the Panzer units which rushed to the area from eastern France and Poland. Supplies began to falter when a gale blew up in the Channel on 19 June, wrecking the Mulberry harbours, onto which the Allies were unloading.

There was talk of sacking Montgomery for his failure to move forward. While German reserves were embroiled in the battle,

other Allied divisions were given a free hand elsewhere on the coast.

The American troops, having captured the Cherbourg peninsula, broke out to make a sweep through central Normandy and discovered too the horrors of fighting in the Normandy bocages. This was the ancient hedgerow and field system which covered the countryside providing havens for German snipers and hazards for Allied tanks and infantrymen.

Churchill and the American leaders were filled with angry frustration

The German reinforcements, which had at last made their way to Normandy, created more firmly held pockets of resistance, which were tough to shift. Falaise, Metz and a number of other towns formed serious blockages in the arteries of the Allied invasion.

Soldiers who on D-Day had never fired a shot in anger or seen a dead body were within a matter of weeks brutalised by the harshness of conflict. If they were fearful, they hid their feelings. Many were overwhelmed with elation when they killed an enemy soldier. As one US Ranger explained: 'It was not joy that I had killed him but that he hadn't killed me.'

Far left: French inhabitants and US soldiers rejoice after Cherbourg is won from the Germans.
Left: German soldiers surrender to the US military near Toulon, in southern France, following the invasion of the south of the country in August 1944

By 15 August 1944 the Germans found southern France was also at risk. 'Operation Dragoon' got underway 10 weeks after D-Day, with the forces of the US 7th Army making landings between Toulon and Cannes and meeting only mild opposition. One of the soldiers to land south of St Tropez was Audie Murphy, later to be a Hollywood hearthrob, who single-handedly wiped out an enemy machine-gun nest.

The advance through France was known as the 'Champagne Campaign'

The US forces drove up France, to link up with their comrades swinging down from the north. Such was the joy of their reception by the French, it soon became known as the 'Champagne Campaign'. Paris was liberated by Free French forces on 25 August.

ARNHEM

By September, Montgomery and American General Omar Bradley had thrust through Belgium and Luxembourg. The fighting remained gruelling with British paratroops experiencing horrific losses when they tried to take Arnhem, Holland, at the end of September.

The successes of the Allies began to take their toll. The front line forces were running out of ammunition and supplies while enemy soldiers were making

Right: *Although General de Gaulle was never popular among Allied war leaders, he won the undying adoration of his people for his uncompromising views.*

EYE WITNESS

Rudolf Valentin was among the German soldiers who fought at Monte Cassino, and revealed some of his experiences to New Zealand author Alex Borrie. He saw some tough fighting as the Germans tried to recapture Hangman's Hill.

❝Our situation was not an enviable one. Whoever came out of cover during the day became a sure victim for the Indian sharp-shooter. The Gurkhas on Hangman's Hill were in a similar position. They also had to make themselves scarce during the day otherwise they drew German fire.

The set of circumstances meant that almost all attacks were switched to night-time. Just after the onset of darkness, we had to repel the first attack and two others followed. With the beginning of the new day, we had to creep into holes again which we enlarged with the spikes of our jack knives. We had to survive the armed attacks in these holes.

In the evening the murderous close-combat began again. During this one often had to let the enemy advance until only metres away before one was able to recognise him by the shape of his helmet. In addition to this, hunger and especially thirst were also becoming factors.

At dawn on 19 March the 1st/FJR 4 [a German paratroop unit] came out to us with about 120 men from the monastery with the order to capture Rocca Janula again. After approximately 10 minutes of machine-gun fire and shelling our comrades overwhelmed the Rajputanis at the lower hairpin curve and stormed the walls.

A terrible hand-to-hand combat flared up there. The Germans were attempting to scale the walls. They succeeded in blasting a hole in the wall. But the enemy from the Essex Battalion fought with the same determination and beat off the attack causing heavy casualties. Courage and the willingness to make sacrifices did not help at all. The castle could no longer be captured. This attack cost the lives of half the comrades, the rest had to retreat.

But the English and the Indians also suffered such heavy casualties that they had to abandon their intentions to capture the monastery in this way. On this day a ceasefire lasting several hours was agreed upon in order to recover the dead and wounded. It was at this point that we exchanged cigarettes with the enemy and helped each other out with bandages. The English even lent us stretchers to transport our wounded to the monastery. At the same time the Gurkhas took their wounded through our positions. A short time later the men who helped each other out in such a comradely fashion were once again the bitterest of enemies. What madness!❞

stronger stands than before. The Allied initiative ground to a halt in December 1944 before going on to make headway in Germany.

The infantrymen were heartily relieved. It had been a long, arduous haul which cost many lives. Combat exhaustion as well as other maladies were striking the servicemen who had survived the fighting. Seemingly ceaseless rain and acres of mud weighed their spirits down.

SLOW ADVANCE

Many soldiers were weary of the inch-by-inch advance they had experienced on the Western front, which resembled the trench warfare known by their fathers two decades earlier. A rash of self-inflicted wounds began bringing waves of soldiers to the sick bays. Anyone suspected of having deliberately injured himself was instantly court martialled.

Their commanders were frustrated in their desire to push relentlessly onwards. Hitler seized the opportunity to strike back.

The fury of the American and British air forces was brought to bear on the Germans

Choosing the same route which had served him so well some four years earlier, he proposed a surprise attack through the Ardennes with the intention of driving a wedge between the Allied forces and capturing

Antwerp, the Belgian port through which vital Allied supplies were being brought.

Luck was with the Germans as the offensive got underway on 16 December. Low cloud kept the Anglo-American reconnaissance aircraft on the ground. The Allied commanders had no idea of what was coming until it arrived.

Field-Marshal von Rundstedt commanded the German forces, comprising ten armoured divisions and 14 other divisions. However, only the 6th SS Panzer Army was up to full strength and adequately equipped. When the weather cleared, the fighting raged on over Christmas and into the New Year, with the Allies gradually gaining the upper hand. The Battle of the Bulge, as it was called, was over by 23 January when the Allies took St Vith, the last remaining German stronghold. Another, less substantial German thrust into northern Alsace which began on 1 January 1945 was also quickly suppressed.

The cost of the two German

assaults was high. Both had weakened the German defences elsewhere, a fact that didn't go unnoticed by Allied commander General Patton. At last the fortified Siegfried line, built to protect Germany, was in danger.

February saw a further big offensive in north west Europe from the Allies. In a series of pushes the Allied armies managed to link up to form a formidable front line.

REMAGEN

They were bucked when a sharp-eyed US sergeant spotted a railway bridge left intact by the retreating Germans, spanning the Rhine at Remagen. The Germans had viewed the Rhine in much the same way as the English saw the Channel, a vital line of defence which would be hard to penetrate. Now troops forged along the bridge while further up- and downstream their comrades made less comfortable crossings on swiftly assembled pontoons. The defences of the Fatherland had been breached.

EYE WITNESS

LeRoy Stein, from Michigan, USA, was 24 when he joined up and was a member of the 87th Division in Patton's 3rd Army in the battle for Normandy.

❝It was very frightening. I was in a mine platoon which was shaky work. We laid mines and booby traps and would take them up if they had no more use. Each one was supposed to be removed. A permanent record was supposed to be kept on the whereabouts of these explosives. But they were not properly taken up. There are still people being killed by them today.❞

Airborne troops helped capture stalwart German towns. By early May, key regions including the Ruhr, Hamburg, Bavaria and Austria were in the hands of the Allies. The German defences were cleverly conceived and included mines and booby traps.

Frequently, the morale of troops was low. In addition to seeing bloody action and burying their friends, the infantry had to endure apparently endless hours of foot-slogging. Their rations were pitiful, consisting mostly of tinned spam, corned beef and soya sausages. Despite the strong camaraderie of men forced to suffer unspeakable hardships, there were numerous instances of insubordination and desertion in the field.

Meanwhile, Russian troops had been pouring into Germany from the east, their target Berlin. Even the most hopeful of German commanders must

Right: US army engineers attempt to put rails across the bridge at Remagen. Four hours after the picture was taken, the bridge collapsed into the Rhine.

have realised the end was near when a tidal wave of Russian troops overran the Silesian industrial basin in January. Albert Speer, head of war production, wrote a memo to Hitler, beginning with the words: 'The war is lost.' Speer realised that Germany could not sustain its industry or defence when the region which produced 60 per cent of its coal had been snatched from it. But Hitler refused to listen.

RED FLAG RISES

Russian generals Zhukov and Konev encircled Berlin by 25 April and began another relentless advance towards the very heart of the Reich. Fierce street fighting raged as loyal Nazis battled to stop the Russians closing in on their beloved Führer. Despite their efforts, a Red Flag was raised over the Reichstag on 2 May 1945.

Hitler finally summoned his long-time mistress Eva Braun to be at his side in the middle of April, realising that his days were numbered.

His 56th birthday on 20 April was marked by more catastrophes in the field. Nazis including Goebbels, Göring, Himmler, Ribbentrop and Bormann joined him for the celebrations. They urged him to flee south but Hitler refused to leave Berlin. In fact, he rarely left the 18-room bunker beneath Berlin's Chancellery that had become his home. With him were the commanders who had remained close to him, and his most valued aides.

He slept for no more than three hours at a time, partly as a result of the pounding of the incessant air raids. Incredibly, Hitler still talked of inflicting

Albert Speer, head of war production, wrote a memo to Hitler beginning with the words: 'The war is lost'

defeat on the Allies. The next day he ordered a last-ditch stand against the Russians, bellowing that every last man should be thrown in. When Hitler finally realised there was no hope, he erupted in a volcanic fury, accusing all his closest commanders of cowardice and treachery. For the first time he

Above: Soldiers of the US 9th Army flush out German soldiers in a battle-scarred town over Germany's western border. Meanwhile Russian troops bore down on Berlin from the east.

spoke of killing himself. Still, he refused to abandon the war effort, a stand which cost the lives of countless German soldiers.

Inside the bunker the tension among its occupants reached new heights. Hitler exploded in rage when he heard that his hitherto faithful lieutenants Göring and Himmler were both making advances to the Allies for peace.

On 27 April, Hitler carried out a macabre rehearsal of his suicide and the deaths of the faithful still at his side. However, it wasn't until 29 April that he dictated his will to his secretary. There was no expression of remorse for the misery and death he had caused worldwide, only the same tired tirade against those he held responsible for his misfortunes: 'More than thirty years have now passed since in 1914 I made my modest contribution as a volunteer in the First World War which was forced upon the Reich. In these three decades I have been actuated solely by love and loyalty to my people...

'It is untrue that I, or anyone else in Germany, wanted the war in 1939. It was desired and instigated solely by those international statesmen who were either of Jewish descent or who worked for Jewish interests.'

The last paragraph in Hitler's will read: 'Above all I charge the leaders of the nation and those under them to scrupulous observance of the laws of race and to merciless opposition to the universal poisoner of all peoples, international Jewry.'

HITLER'S END

In the early hours of the same day, Hitler married Eva Braun and had a champagne celebration with Bormann, Goebbels, his secretaries and his cook. Within hours he heard of the death of Mussolini shot with his mistress Clara Petacci and then hung by the ankles in a square in the centre of Milan.

On the afternoon of 30 April, with the Russians just a street away, Hitler said his final farewells, retired to a sitting room with his wife and shot himself. Eva chose to end her life by taking poison.

The instructions he left for the disposal of his body were carried

out, with his remains being burned by petrol fire in the yard of the bunker. His successor as Führer, Grand Admiral Karl Dönitz, Commander in Chief of the German navy, tried negotiating a peace settlement but the Allies wanted unconditional surrender. German resistance capitulated and the surrender was finally signed on 7 May 1945.

BLACK SANDS OF IWO JIMA

America's mighty war machine was now in top gear. In the field the US had the latest and the best military equipment. At home its colossal industrial muscle provided seemingly endless supplies of hardware. There were ranks of young men drawn from all over the States queuing up for action, full of grit and determination.

In opposition, an over-extended Japan was war-weary. The country's battle losses in ships and planes far outstripped the number of replacements being produced on the home islands. Japan itself was being starved of the materials it desperately needed by the naval blockade imposed by America. Its industry was targeted for devastating air raids. Long-term jungle fighting had taken its toll among the surviving troops, despite their rigorous training.

Against all odds, the Japanese soldiers were determined to hold back the American advance. In-bred in the Emperor's men was an oriental code of honour which dictated that they must fight to the death. In most cases, this is just what they did, costing many Allied lives. The hallmark of the Pacific campaign was prolonged savage fighting and huge loss of life.

The hallmark of the Pacific campaign was savage fighting and huge loss of life

With a victory established in New Guinea by the start of 1943, Allied Commander of the South West Pacific General Douglas MacArthur was already pondering his route to the Philippines, a campaign dear to his heart. Before he could take it, there

Left: General MacArthur remained determined to push the Japanese out of the Pacific.
Right: An island beach devastated by gunfire becomes a depot for US troops.

Right: Admiral William Halsey, Commander of the 3rd Fleet, sits deep in thought on the bridge of the USS New Jersey *en route for the Philippines.*

was a selection of Japanese strongholds on New Guinea still to be beaten.

Meanwhile, Admiral Halsey, of the South Pacific sector, already had the Russell Islands, Vella Lavella and Bougainville in the Solomon Islands under his belt.

Both MacArthur and Halsey recognised the value of leap-frogging many Japanese-held islands and outposts, picking for attack mainly those that were inadequately defended. The rest were left to 'wither on the vine', increasingly isolated from Japanese lines of communication.

TARAWA

Now nine crucial atolls under Japanese control, collectively known as the Marshall Islands, had to be taken. One of them,

Tarawa, was defended by 5,000 Japanese. When a similar number of US Marines landed on the island on 21 November 1943 they found themselves pinned down on the open beach. Before night had fallen, 500 of the Americans were dead and a further 1,000 wounded. Japanese gun positions were only silenced when their entire crew was killed. Only an additional landing of troops won victory for the Americans. In all 1,000 Marines died along with virtually all the Japanese.

The Americans learned a valuable lesson. When it came to taking another atoll in the group, Kwajalein, there were no landings until a heavy bombardment neutralised much of the defence.

Fleas, flies, lice and mosquitoes were liable to be carrying appalling disease

---

Although the American campaign was fast, there was immense hardship for the troops brought about by the conditions. Fleas, flies, lice and mosquitoes plagued them. More than just pests, they were liable to be carrying appalling disease. It wasn't until 1944 that DDT sprays were introduced to combat the insect swarms.

Once an island was taken, it became a top priority to bury the dead on both sides. For the corpses attracted not only flies but also rats, which came in droves.

MARIANAS

Truk, a key naval outpost for the Japanese navy, came under fire on 18 February 1944 in a raid orchestrated by Vice-Admiral Marc Mitscher. There were 30 separate strikes at the base which destroyed 275 aircraft and 39 ships.

Next stop was Saipan in the Mariana Islands, a fearsome task given that 32,000 Japanese soldiers were garrisoned there. Nevertheless, it was a dual disaster for the Japanese. For soon after the American landings on 15 June

EYE WITNESS

Ito Masashi spent 16 years in hiding in the jungle of Guam after it was overrun. He describes his reason for not surrendering in his book _The Emperor's Last Soldiers._

❝By the start of October the only sound we heard was the shell fire so far off that it sounded like distant thunder. But the fighting continued. The enemy no doubt considered it simply mopping up but for us it was a full-scale and bloody battle.

We had eaten what little there was of our portable battle rations of dried bread and now we lived on what berries and fruits we could find. We kept up a vain defiance with nothing left to help us but our grenades. But now the vital will to fight was absent. Our commanders sent messages advising us to end the senseless resistance, to give up our arms and pack it in. But somehow we didn't. We were afraid to.

Afraid that our useless rifles and guns – marked with the noble crest of the Imperial Chrysanthemum – might fall into enemy hands, we buried them deep in the ground. And we prepared, quite resignedly, for death as the only possible outcome. For us soldiers of Japan, the only thing left to our way of thinking was to deck out our last moment as nobly and bravely as we could.

By now there was no supply base for us to go back to and we didn't know whether there still existed any company or battalion headquarters where we could have got orders. So we formed sad and sorry little squads, hardly alive, now hiding ourselves away in the jungle, now moving aimlessly along the paths and lanes. We had been reduced to the status of a ragged band of stragglers. Even during this period however there were a number of incidents when we tangled with Australian troops backed by tanks or fell foul of a line of pickets. Fortunately, we always managed to get in our grenades and escape. But on every occasion the number of our already small band would dwindle by the odd one or two.❞

came the Battle of the Philippine Sea, in which their Fleet Naval Air Arm was decimated. By July the defenders of Saipan were running short of ammunition. They chose to kill themselves by the score, along

with the 22,000 civilians who had been living on the island since before the war, when it was a Japanese dominion. American troops looked on helplessly as women and children joined their menfolk in plunging from high cliffs to be dashed on the rocks below rather than face the ultimate shame of surrender. Saipan was under US control by 9 July.

The islands of Tinian and Guam were the next to go. Then the Palau group of islands. It didn't take nearly as long to achieve victory here as it had done on Saipan. It frequently included suicidal rushes at secure American positions by shrieking Japanese soldiers, who were duly mowed down in their masses. With fighters refusing to surrender in even the most hopeless of battles, the Americans were forced to use armoured flame-throwers to clear well-protected pockets of resistance.

By October 1944 the Americans were ready to redeem the Philippines. The island of Leyte was their chosen point for invasion, poorly defended by just 16,000 men. While a memorable victory was quickly carved out for the Americans at sea, the land-

based struggle for supremacy lasted longer, with the Japanese counter-attacking in December. The losses on both sides were heavy. The Americans mourned 15,500 fighters, while the Japanese suffered the bodyblow of 70,000 deaths. Yet once Leyte was won for the Americans, the rest of the Philippines fell to them with gratifying ease.

At Iwo Jima the US Marines were cut down in droves by the defenders

Now it was time to approach the Japanese home islands. Choosing to by-pass several strongholds, including Formosa, the Americans decided to take the Ryuku Islands, less than 400 miles from Japan itself. A stepping-stone island between the Philippines and the Ryukus was necessary as a rendezvous for American planes. Iwo Jima

Above: US Marines hold their weapons aloft as they wade ashore on the stepping-stone island of Tinian, unsure about what awaits them beyond the beach.

in the Bonin Islands was selected for invasion in February, while an operation to capture Okinawa, the largest of the Ryuku Islands, was time-tabled for April.

At Iwo Jima the US Marines were cut down in droves as they tried to penetrate the complex defensive system constructed by the defenders. Bombardment by battleship prior to the landings had not obliterated the defences as hoped. In fact, the Japanese were so deeply entrenched it had made little noticeable difference.

Amphibious landing transports were beached and blown up and the Marines found themselves without an iota of cover on their route up the beach. There was also little

'FRIENDLY FIRE'

'Friendly fire' took its toll during World War II, particularly during the Normandy campaign.

Bombers had failed to dislodge German gun emplacements before D-Day. This should have acted as a warning against so-called precision bombing. Yet American heavy bombers were called on in July 1944 to target the German lines. Instead, the bombs fell on US troops, killing 25 and wounding 131. The next day, the same mistake was made again, only this time 111 American servicemen were killed and 490 were wounded. Among the dead was US Lieutenant-General Lesley McNair, the highest-ranking Allied officer to be killed in the Normandy campaign.

Three weeks later 'friendly fire' claimed more Allied victims from above. This time 77 Canadians and 72 Polish soldiers died. 'Friendly fire' incidents occurred through poor weather conditions, imprecise briefings, lack of training and sometimes through nervous fingers being on the trigger.

opportunity to remove the wounded from the firing line.

The Japanese commander Lieutenant-General Kurihayashi's order to his men was acidly clear: 'No man must die until he has killed ten of the enemy.' He added that each of his men must think of his defence position as his grave-yard. It was widely considered to be the worst landing the Marines experienced in the war. Iwo Jima finally fell into American hands on 16 March after they had used bulldozers to bury defenders in their bunkers. The tally of dead

Below: *Pinned down by mortar fire, marines of the 5th Division inch their way up the slopes of Mount Suribachi, determined to seize Iwo Jima.*

among the Americans amounted to 6,821 but yet again there was a far more devastating number for Japan as virtually all the 21,000 troops were killed.

On 1 April the landings by the Marines on Okinawa, as part of 'Operation Iceberg', were in stark contrast to the blood-bathed beaches of Iwo Jima. An estimated 50,000 Americans got ashore barely hearing a shot and for the following five days there was hardly a skirmish. It was a deliberate lull engineered by the Japanese before they unleashed a storm of incredible violence.

The Japanese had drawn up a defence plan code-named 'Ten-Ichigo', which involved

thousands of 'kamikaze' missions. The Japanese commanders were even prepared to sacrifice their prized battleship *Yamato* in a suicidal attack. On 6 April the ship left its base with sufficient fuel for a one-way journey to Okinawa. Its aim was to wreak havoc there among the landing forces.

KAMIKAZE

However, soon picked up on radar, the great warship came under fire from 280 US aircraft until she was finally crippled and sunk on 7 April with her 2,300 crew still aboard.

Meanwhile, swarms of kamikazes were setting about the US Navy as it cruised off Okinawa. On the first day, three destroyers, two ammunition ships and an LST (Landing Ship Tank) were destroyed. It temporarily halted the drive forward, through lack of ammunition. On the next day a battleship, a carrier and two destroyers were hit. Of the 16 destroyers sent forward to give early warning of kamikaze raid, 14 were

Right: On Okinawa, advancing Americans were forced to use fire power to oust tough Japanese resistance.

of minimal strategic value. The story goes that one destroyer's crew erected a poster complete with arrow bearing the words: 'To Jap Suiciders. Carriers are that way.' And still kamikaze fliers descended on the fleet.

During the battle to secure Okinawa, which raged between April and August, there were an estimated 2,000 kamikaze raids carried out by both army and navy aircraft as well as about 5,000 conventional sorties. In total 20 ships were sunk by kamikazes, against six sunk by other aircraft manoeuvres. Kamikaze planes notched up a further 217 strikes against ships.

Japanese resources were feeling the strain. After two months of sustained kamikaze raids, there were few aircraft left for such missions.

On land the fighting was equally horrific. In one of the early battles, to win the off-island of Ie Shima and its landing strip, more than 4,700 of the 5,000 Japanese defenders died in battle. Towards the end of the eight-day confrontations local women, some with babies strapped to their backs, draped demolition charges around their necks and rushed at American positions.

It took until the last days of June to eradicate the last of the Japanese land-based resistance on Okinawa. American losses amounted to almost 7,000 men as well as numerous ships and 763 planes. The Americans found themselves taking prisoners, some 7,400 in all. 110,000 Japanese died in battle with all the senior officers committing ritual suicide in their offices, and there was carnage among the population. The Japanese stood the loss of 7,800 aircraft.

After two months of sustained kamikaze raids, there were few aircraft left

Hostilites in South East Asia were just as gruesome for the troops involved. Following the Chindit Offensive into Burma the Japanese commander in Burma, General Renya Mutaguchi, decided that attacking the British in India was probably the best form of defence.

On 6 March 1944 the 'U-Go' offensive opened, with three Japanese divisions setting off for Kohima and Imphal, high in the

Left: Billowing smoke marks the path of a kamikaze plane which caused devastation on the USS Bunker Hill, *hit off Okinawa on 11 May 1945.*

Assam hills. For the first time in the conflict, British troops stood firm against Japanese aggression in defence of India.

KOHIMA

Both Kohima and Imphal were under siege by the first week in April. There followed some of the harshest fighting of the war.

Japanese soldiers were in the majority but the Commonwealth troops were in no mood to be routed this time. The bitterest of the fighting was at Kohima. Japanese soldiers had killed everything in their path until they reached the tennis court of what was once the Deputy Commissioner's bungalow. They dug in on one side while the defenders were holed up just 20 yards away.

Grenades and mortar bombs rained down on Commonwealth forces taking a toll on the troops. However they repelled the frequent Japanese charges with surprising ease. Each one was accompanied by

the traditional 'banzai' cry and screaming. The Allies were able to open fire and cut them down. There was little opportunity for the Allies to collect their dead. Bodies lay rotting on the ground, emitting a terrible stench. Sometimes they were buried where they had fallen, in shallow, inadequate graves with arms or knees left exposed. A cloud heavy with the pungent smell of burning flesh hung over the Allied position as the Japanese cremated fallen comrades.

Both sides were exhausted and riddled with disease

Both sides were exhausted and riddled with disease. After 16 days of gruelling fighting the defending regiments were relieved by the 1st Royal Berkshire Regiment.

They left behind 1,419 dead among them 19-year-old Lance

Above: *After a siege by the Japanese, the British 14th Army was finally able to open the Imphal-Kohima road.*

Corporal John Harman who ran up to a Japanese machine gun, shot the crew and hoisted it up on to his shoulders to bring it back behind his own lines.

Further he stormed a bakery held by the Japanese, set it on fire and came back to his dug-out with a wounded Japanese soldier under each arm. It was as he was returning from one of these astonishing feats that he was fatally wounded. He was awarded the Victoria Cross posthumously for his incredible efforts.

Airlifts by the American Air Force and RAF continued to aid the defenders of Kohima and Imphal. The Japanese soldiers had pitiful rations by comparison. It was a staggering 80 days before the Japanese were compelled to withdraw with just a quarter of the original force left on their feet. Over half the casualities were claimed by sickness.

WAR AT SEA

WEAPONS AT SEA

For years naval warfare had remained largely unchanged. It was a case of tactics combining with firepower to achieve the victories sought after by the seafaring nations.

Britain excelled at the art of the sea battle and was proud of her navy traditions. By 1939, however, the rules of the game had changed and, unfortunately, nobody informed the major players.

No longer was it enough to have impressively large ships capable of blasting the enemy vessels out of the water. In fact capital ships were a positive disadvantage as they were large targets which could only move slowly to evade enemy fire. It meant Germany's *Bismarck* and *Tirpitz* ships and Japan's *Yamato* were obsolete when they originally rolled down the slipway in time to see action during World War II. The great hopes that they carried with them were badly misplaced.

The power lay with aircraft and a navy was only as good as its fleet air arm. Britain didn't have a fleet air arm at all as it had been incorporated into the Royal Air Force. Many British naval chiefs refused to believe the age of the big ships had drawn to a close. It took the death of the battleship *Prince of Wales* and battle cruiser *Repulse* off the coast of Malaya in December 1941 at the hands of Japan's skilful fliers to convince them of the fact.

The power lay with aircraft and a navy was only as good as its fleet air arm

Now ships would stay out of reach of enemy guns and send in versatile and effective planes to wreak havoc with opposition navies. As the range of the aircraft increased through the war, the big ships could stay hundreds of miles away from the hub of the fighting.

Britain was, however, better placed regarding the advent of navy planes than Germany. At least the British could call on seven aircraft carriers including the *Ark Royal* and *Illustrious* during the conflict. Hitler, in contrast had only one aircraft carrier in his navy *Graf Zeppelin* which was never completed.

ARMOUR PLATING

The importance of air battles at sea in turn made the bodily defences of each ship key to its survival. Each navy discovered to its cost that only the thickest armour plating was impervious to bombs dropped by planes. Those ships which crumpled easily under fire from above were the first casualties of the conflict.

Left: Mangled wreckage after the surprise Japanese strike at Pearl Harbor, revealing the scale of damage inflicted.
Below: Illustrious was one of Britain's few aircraft carriers at the outbreak of war.

At the start of the war Britain had the largest navy in the world – 12 battleships, 3 battle cruisers, 15 heavy and 45 light cruisers, 184 destroyers, 58 submarines and 27 motor torpedo boats. The navy was probably in better shape than the army or the air force but still unprepared for war. At least there was a construction programme that would considerably improve the size of the navy. The largest British ship was *Hood* sunk by *Bismarck* in 1941.

EYE WITNESS

George Miles enlisted in the Australian Army in 1940 when he was 17 years old. He was injured at El Duda in North Africa, and was being ferried to hospital in December 1941 when his ship was blown up in the Mediterranean.

There were about 600 people on the Chaktina, mostly wounded although there were some prisoners of war. Only 200 survived, including a German general. Out of 17 members of my battalion, I was among three who lived. We were headed for the 62nd General Hospital in Alexandria. It was night-time when the Italian dive-bombers struck. The sky lit up as if it was day. The ship was blown apart. In the melée you didn't get a chance to worry about anything.

I had a life jacket on. I spent time in a life raft or clinging to the side – it was so crowded that you had to take your turn.

We pushed dying men over the side to let the rest live. It was the following night when we were picked up by a Norwegian corvette.

Left: Human torpedoes, nick-named 'pigs', were launched from this tiny hatch on the Italian tanker Olterra.

The largest of the British ships was Hood, sunk by Bismarck in 1941

which consisted of six modern battleships, 19 cruisers, 132 destroyers and torpedo boats and 107 submarines.

In Japan's navy when it entered the war in 1941 the number of aircraft carriers outnumbered the number of battleships by 11 to ten. This accounts for Japan's success on the high seas in the opening months of the war. Also lining up under the emblem of the rising sun were 23 cruisers, 129 destroyers, 67 submarines and 13 gunboats.

Much of the American strength in the area was decimated by the attack on Pearl Harbor. US shipyards laboured to repair the damage wrought by the Japanese planes and refloated many of the sunken vessels. America only had three

On the other hand the German navy was the least favoured branch of Hitler's armed forces. He promised his Admiral Erich Raeder plenty of time to prepare for war in Europe. The conflict arrived about five years too early as far as Raeder was concerned.

He had two battleships *Scharnhorst* and *Gneisenau* in readiness as well as three pocket battleships. In addition there were seven cruisers, 21 destroyers and 12 torpedo boats in the fleet. His strengths lay in U-boats, of which he had 159 and planned many more. He also made good use of auxiliary cruisers or armed raiders as they were better known. Merchant ships in their appearance and war ships in their weaponry, they launched bandit attacks on shipping throughout the world.

Italy had a sizeable navy

operational aircraft carriers in the Pacific, 24 cruisers, nine battleships, 80 destroyers and 56 submarines. The hidden weapon that America possessed was its ability to produce sufficient replacements and reinforcements for its navy throughout the war.

Submarines also came of age during World War II although only Germany and America fully grasped the potential offered by this sleek sinister vessel.

The German U-boats could very well have changed the entire course of World War II if only there had been enough of

The Allies possessed radar which helped them considerably in their war at sea. Pioneering scientist Sir Robert Watson-Watt developed the system and oversaw its use for the benefit of all the British military.

Astonishing advances made in code-breaking offered plenty of new chances to the fleet

Radar detects distant objects by sending out a microwave pulse beam. The reflection of the beam indicates the position of the object.

one-man crew. The bows of the boat were packed with explosives which would fire on impact. It wasn't a suicide vehicle. The courageous pilot escaped by throwing himself backwards with a float before the EMB made contact with its target.

Also among their gadgets was a torpedo submarine measuring about 22ft which was driven by a two-man crew sitting astride the strange weapon. Cast into the water by full-sized submarines the men wearing diving suits guided this timed missile towards its target and attached it to the underside of a

them during the crucial early years. Hitler saw too late the massive opportunity he had passed up by reining in resources due to his navy.

American submarines executed a brilliant strategic move against Japan destroying the vast majority of its merchant shipping and isolating the four home islands from outside trade effectively starving the people and industry of vital goods. Any other country which did not have the shame and dishonour of surrender woven deeply into its culture would have surrendered on the strength of the submarine stranglehold alone.

Its advantage to the Allies was that they would get warning of approaching enemy ships and planes. Bad weather was no longer the cloak to vision it once had been. Action under cover of darkness would now achieve more accurate results.

CODE-BREAKINGS

Also at sea the astonishing advances made in code-breaking offered many new chances to the fleet who were forewarned about enemy movements.

The Italians came up with some ingenious waterborne methods of attack. The first was an Explosive Motor Boat with a

Above: *It took courage and endurance to man the Italian torpedoes which wreaked havoc in the Mediterranean.*

ships hull before making an escape.

The British had their midget submarines, based on an early design, it was 51ft long, eight and a half feet wide and ten feet high. Inside there was enough space for four crew members. a commander, a lieutenant to operate the engine, a navigator and an engineer. The capabilities of the midget submarines were most impressive. They could dive to a depth of 300ft and boasted a speed of four knots.

THE GRAF SPEE AND DUNKIRK

When war was declared, the British people expected an instant torrent of bombs to fall from a sky blackened by enemy aircraft. The wail of the air raid siren sent people scurrying for the bomb shelters clutching their gas masks, fearful of being enveloped in a cloud of poisonous chemicals.

It didn't happen and soon the opening stages of the war were labelled 'the Phoney war' or even 'the Bore War'. The sceptics at home who believed the war would be over once Hitler had his way in Poland had to wait nearly a year to see action over Britain. But at sea it was an entirely different story.

A lone U-boat set the tenor of the sea-farers conflict when the liner *Athenia* sailing out of Glasgow was sunk off Ireland the day after hostilities were officially opened. U-boat captain Fritz-Julius Lemp believed he had an auxiliary cruiser or troopship in his sights. In all, 112 lives were lost including 28 Americans. There was shock at such an atrocity, and it prompted orders to the U-boat commanders, to target only freighters and Navy ships. It was only a matter of months before the tighter rules which governed the U-boats were disregarded once more.

More than 800 sailors died when a U-boat slid into Scapa Flow and destroyed a battleship

The brutal attack on *Athenia* sparked an Allied blockade of Germany in which ships were stopped and searched at the rate of 100 a week. Although the Royal Navy did capture some German ships this way, it caused acrimony between Britain and other neutral countries who resented the intrusive action.

By the end of September 1939, 20 Allied ships had been floored by U-boats, including HMS *Courageous*, lost in the Atlantic with 515 men. Even neutral boats heading to Britain bearing vital supplies were not safe from the prowling German submarines.

MAGNETIC MINES

Britain's mariners fared little better in October. More than 800 sailors died when a U-boat slid into Scapa Flow, the anchorage of the British Fleet 10 miles off the north coast of Scotland, which was thought to be a safe haven, and destroyed a large British battleship. Under the command of Captain Gunther Prien, the submarine manoeuvred through a narrow, unguarded channel leading into the harbour area and dealt a deadly blow to the *Royal Oak*. Claims that the battleship's armour could withstand a torpedo

attack proved to be nothing more than a pipe dream. Just 396 members of the 1200-strong crew survived.

Germany was laying hundreds of mines, with devastating effect.

The Reich had pioneered a deadly magnetic mine which could be dropped by air on to the sea bed, to later rise and attach itself to any passing ship, with deadly consequences. It was far superior to the mines being laid by Britain, designed to defend its shipping.

Fortunately, one of the mystery mines was jettisoned in error on land. Thanks to one courageous naval officer who tackled the explosive, its secret of success became known. The antidote was 'de-gaussing', with an electric cable fitted to ships which neutralised magnetism. The plague of the magnetic mine at least to British ships was quickly overcome.

Above the waves were the determined ships of the Reich's navy equally adept at picking off

Above: *After the Battle of the River Plate the* Graf Spee *limped into Montevideo for repairs. However, it could not escape its predators.*
Left: *U-boat Captain Gunther Prien was hailed a hero in his homeland for penetrating Scapa Flow.*

British vessels. Among them was the pocket battleship *Admiral Graf Spee*. By agreement before the war, the Germans were only to build ships up to a certain size. These were tagged pocket battleships, larger than cruisers but smaller and less effective than battleships.

The *Graf Spee* slipped out of port just before war was declared, sidestepped the Royal Navy blockade and headed for the South Atlantic. It was then the pride of the German navy with its high speed and thick protective plating. In the first three months of the war, it had notched up nine British ships, including the liner *Doric Star*.

British commander Commodore H. Harwood guessed that it was only a matter of time before the *Graf Spee* was lured to the River Plate, Uruguay, attracted

Exeter, and two light cruisers, *Ajax* and *Achilles*, one from Britain and one from New Zealand.

CRUISERS DAMAGE

Graf Spee's Captain Hans Langsdorff, believing the heavy cruiser was accompanied only by destroyers, opened fire inflicting serious damage on the *Exeter* and the *Ajax*. The reply from the British ships crippled his own. With smoke pouring from the German ship, the *Graf Spee* headed for the safety of Montevideo in Uruguay.

Although Uruguay was a neutral country, it supported the Allies. In international law, the *Graf Spee* was only entitled to stay in its capital, Montevideo, for 72 hours and the Uruguayans refused to extend its deadline.

Uruguayan territorial waters, British ships waited for a kill. He believed the mighty *Renown* and *Ark Royal* had joined the pursuit when they were, in fact, hundreds of miles away.

Langsdorff deemed the situation hopeless and asked Berlin for permission to scuttle his ship, rather than have it fall into enemy hands. Consent duly came.

Crowds had gathered on the waterfront eager to witness the great sea battle

On 17 December the *Graf Spee* set off slowly for the middle of the harbour. Crowds had gathered on the waterfront eager to witness the great sea battle that would surely follow. When the majority of the crew had safely disembarked, a huge explosion wrecked her and she sank to the estuary floor.

Langsdorff considered the incident a grave disgrace. Three days afterwards he wrapped himself in the flag of his beloved fatherland and put a bullet through his head.

NEUTRAL NORWAY

Churchill, First Lord of the Admiralty, instantly trumpeted the achievement of his navy even though it was gained by luck and misunderstanding on behalf of the enemy. Yet while Britain celebrated the triumph, it was far from the end of its troubles at sea.

Within a week in January three submarines, HMS *Grenville* and destroyer HMS *Exmouth* were sunk. There was little more by way of encouraging news for

---

EYE WITNESS

Bill Gamble, from Derbyshire, joined up in 1939 when he was 22. The following year, he became one of the thousands of men of the British Expeditionary Force evacuated from Dunkirk.

❛The Germans kept the beach under fire. I had never been under shell fire before. The Luftwaffe planes were strafing the beaches There were rows and rows of fellows waiting to get on a boat. There was no panic because officers were there. They would have shot you if you had panicked.

I have got a vivid memory of the Welsh guards who formed the rear guard action which helped us escape. They were courageous men. I don't think I had properly fired a rifle until then. We didn't have half the equipment we should have had and there had been no training. We were just like civilians in uniform.

I was dead scared. Finally, I got on to a little barge and then on to a destroyer. When the waves came up we had to jump from one to the other. I landed in England on June 2. A few days later that destroyer got blown up. All those brave lads on the ship died.

At least when it came to D-Day, I wasn't bothered about it. By then I was properly trained. I had a job to do and I did it.❜

---

by the British shipping there.

At dawn on 13 December the *Graf Spee* was spotted at the river estuary. Lined up before it were the ships in Harwood's force; the heavy cruiser HMS

It gave Langsdorff time to transfer his injured seamen to a German merchant ship. The most pressing repairs were carried out. But Langsdorff knew that outside the protection of

Above: *With Hitler's consent the pocket battleship* Admiral Graf Spee *was spectacularly scuttled off Montevideo.*

the British until February when HMS *Cossack* carried out a top secret raid on a German supply ship sheltering in the waters of neutral Norway. Aboard the *Altmark*, concealed in filthy conditions in a hold, were 300 British POW's taken by the *Graf Spee*. Regardless of international regulations which banned such action, the *Altmark* was boarded and the prisoners released. Norway protested about the violation of its neutrality, but the Norwegian authorities had already searched the ship and apparently not found the captives. This persuaded Hitler that Norwegian waters should be under German control if his navy was to get the protection it deserved.

The Royal Navy continued its efforts to contain the U-boat threat and the activities of the German fleet until May 1940 when a task of much greater

importance beckoned.

At the start of May, German forces had moved into Belgium. With characteristic speed, the Reich's forces overran Belgium, Holland and northern France. The lightning pace of the attack left everyone gasping for breath, not least the British Expeditionary Force, numbering some 200,000 men, which was sent to France at the outbreak of war to bolster French defences. The British soldiers

---

The Reich's forces overran Belgium, Holland and northern France

---

were driven relentlessly back amid some bloody fighting. With them was a section of the French forces, weary and disenchanted with apparently no hope of escape.

Commander of the BEF, General Lord Gort, had quickly realised there was no option but to withdraw his men by sea. The

best and shortest route would have been from Calais to Kent, but the French port was almost in the hands of the Germans already. Dunkirk seemed to be the single remaining point from which any kind of meaningful evacuation could take place.

British and French soldiers staggered on to the beach at Dunkirk. All semblance of order was gone after the hasty retreat in which bands of men lost sight of their units. Communication between commanders and their men was cut inland. The soldiers, now acting on initiative, got to Dunkirk as best they could.

The French forces' Commander in Chief, General Gamelin, had been bemused by the German advance. His tanks, evenly spaced down the frontier, were unable to provide a striking action against the rear of the Germans. So while the Panzer armies were tiring and running short of supplies, there was no one to exploit their vulnerability.

Ironically, it was Hitler himself who called a halt to the German march. Concerned that vital tank divisions were at risk if they went into action against the by-now concentrated strength of the Allies on treacherous marshlands and would be unable to complete the invasion of France, Hitler stopped the key Panzer advance. He was made even more anxious by the counter-offensive of sorts that the Allies had managed to stage at Arras.

DUNKIRK

The strategy was perhaps sound. Hitler's decision came on 24 May when a comprehensive rout of the enemy seemed assured. Its unavoidable side effect was to give Allied troops two days' grace without which an evacuation from Dunkirk would surely have been impossible. Historians have subsequently speculated that, had the BEF been lost in northern France, Britain would have sought peace at any price as there would have been no army left to fight with.

As early as 20 May, Admiral Bertram Ramsay, the Flag Officer at Dover, had been gathering a small fleet capable of crossing the English Channel to rescue soldiers. At this stage it was believed just 35,000 men would be saved.

Still more men were straggling on to the beach until the ragged throng numbered 38,000. Many were by now unarmed. There were still rations of sorts, but many soldiers had been without sleep for days. Between periods of calm and order there was panic.

Each hour the shelling grew ever closer. Dunkirk itself was being blown to bits, offering little by way of protection for the British and French forces. There were attacks by the Luftwaffe, too. The low whine of oncoming aircraft followed by the clatter of its guns sent men diving to the ground for cover

'Operation Dynamo', the evacuation at Dunkirk, was officially begun on 26 May 1940

There was a feeling of resentment among many that the Royal Air Force was not doing its bit to aid the plight of the soldiers. In fact, its pilots were going up time and again, helping the rear guard defenders of Dunkirk or hampering the Luftwaffe high above the clouds. But the pilots' role was invisible to the eyes of the stranded soldiers – who were looking for someone to blame for their appalling predicament.

In peacetime Dunkirk had ample harbour facilities from which a major evacuation could have been carried out with ease. Now the town was rubble and the harbour installations in tatters. The only useful jetty left was wooden planking extending a mile into the sea. Yet it was valueless to the big ships for embarkation. Even the mildest wind would have blown the vessel into its concrete foundations causing damage below the waterline. As time went by it became clear that men would have to be taken off the beaches, no matter how cumbersome the task.

Operation Dynamo, the evacuation at Dunkirk, was officially begun shortly before 7pm on 26 May although in fact some support units had already been brought back to Britain. Before midnight fewer than 8,000 men had been brought home.

When the depth of the dilemma facing the bulk of Britain's army became clear, a flotilla of small boats was called upon to assist. Such boats already had to be registered with the government. Now they were recruited for the still-secret operation, with many civilian captains being allowed to stay with their ships.

The British public finally got to hear about 'Operation Dynamo' on 31 May, when about 194,000 British troops had been brought back under the guidance of the Royal Navy. When news about the crisis was broadcast, many more owners of small boats set sail immediately. This was the brave face of Dunkirk that haunts history.

CIVILIAN COURAGE

Their task was no easier than that faced by the Royal Navy. Bombardments by the Luftwaffe continued claiming the lives of servicemen and civilians alike. On 1 June the courage of the civilian boat owners reaped dividends when 64,429 soldiers were rescued. Having ferried their battle-worn cargo to safety, boat owners turned back to face the risks all over again in a bid to haul yet more soldiers to safety. Not least of their worries were the minefields that lay between them and their destination .

By any standards, the rout of the British Army in France by

The courage of the civilian boat owners reaped dividends

Hitler's forces was nothing short of outright defeat. Yet the way in which the cream of the British army slipped through the Führer's grasp and the courage of the evacuation gave an element of heroism to the event, and has ensured it a special place in British military history.

The soldiers who made it back were full of criticism for the army that had sent them to France inadequately armed and supplied. Yet within a few days or weeks, most were posted again, often back to France where remnants of the British contingent were still fighting with the French to keep Hitler out of Paris.

The last Allied boat pulled away from the beaches of Dunkirk on 4 June with the remnants of the 338,000 rescued British and French soldiers aboard. Each man was precious and represented the future fighting force of Britain. Yet behind the retreating force lay its equipment without which no army could fight. Before leaving, the BEF had sabotaged 63,900 vehicles, 289 tanks and 2,472 guns.

EYE WITNESS

Miner Wilf Cowie was 25 when he joined the army and was part of the British Expeditionary Force in France which evacuated from Dunkirk.

❛We were in France on the Belgian border for about six months with very little happening, just a bit of bombing and shelling.

When the retreat started, we had to make our way over fields because the Germans were patrolling the roads. The worst thing I ever saw were the refugees streaming out of Belgium pushing prams and carrying beds just machined gunned by German planes. Hundreds of them were killed.

I was one of the last to get out of Dunkirk. It was horrible on the beach. We were lying in bomb craters on the beach, expecting every day to get away. Every day seemed to take forever. Luftwaffe planes were firing at us and then there was the shelling. That was the worst thing of all. The shells screamed as they were going over the top of you and you never knew where they were going to land.

Once I took shelter in a bomb hole with three other lads. I was the only one who came out alive. The others were killed by a machine gun blast from an aeroplane.

There were hundreds of lads killed. We had to go and get the identity discs from the bodies and give them to our superiors. It was a bit upsetting but it was just a job that had to be done. We saw so many young men dead that in the end we didn't worry about it.

I came back in a trawler. It took 36 hours to reach the east coast after the skipper diverted to avoid mines. Several men on the boat died when they were hit by machine gun fire from Luftwaffe planes passing overhead.❜

Above: Devastation of the beaches of Dunkirk following the evacuation.

U-BOAT MENACE

If Britannia ruled the waves in 1939, the kingdom beneath the sea was in the hands of the Germans. Lurking in the murky depths were the U-boats, relatively few in number, but none the less terrifying for that.

Just a mention of the name could strike fear into the stout hearts of the English sailors. Winston Churchill confessed later that the U-boat threat in the Battle of the Atlantic was 'the only thing that ever really frightened me during the war'.

For U-boats (Unterseeboot in German) had a habit of creeping up on British shipping and sinking it without warning. At first merchant ships seemed very much like sitting ducks if U-boats were in the area. There appeared to be little opportunity to dilute the threat.

Britain, Canada and America lost thousands of tons of cargo and scores of seamen, to the U-boats. Bitter experience finally taught the Allies effective defences and, later, vital offensive tactics which would ultimately neutralise the stealthy foe.

U-boats soon began to hunt in 'wolf packs', an idea thought

Above: German U-boats came close to their goal of strangling Britain.

up in Germany in the mid-1930s in which a group of submarines orchestrated their attacks on convoys. At first, the concept was thwarted by a lack of boats. Sometimes, in the early stages of the war, there were only a handful of submarines to put to sea, the others being in dock for repairs or in use for training. The lack of air support

By the summer of 1940 there were two 'wolf packs' operating in the Atlantic

from the Luftwaffe to the U-boat service also slightly lessened their menace, since they were compelled to search, sometimes for days, for convoys.

However Raeder, Commander in Chief of the Kriegsmarine was conscious of the golden opportunity that was open to him. While finding it almost impossible to keep more than six U-boats in the sea at a time before February 1941, he devoted much time and energy to rectifying the short-coming. Before the year was out the number of

U-boats in his fleet had been increased tenfold.

By the summer of 1940 there were two wolf packs operating in the Atlantic, preying on the convoys as they supplied troops to Britain from America. Submarine commanders could now pinpoint convoy positions thanks to the German Radio Monitoring Service (B-Dienst). Slung across the Atlantic, the U-boats formed a deadly chain from which the convoys could not escape. The aim was for the boat which first spotted the convoy to shadow it until other submarines could gather for a mass attack. In October, three convoys lost 38 ships to U-boats in the space of just three nights.

U-BOAT TECHNIQUE

The technique used by the U-boats continued to improve. At first, commanders attacked from positions both above and below the waves. Their firepower was far more accurate, however, when the U-boats were on the surface. It became accepted

Above: Admiral Karl Dönitz knew the potential of his U-boat fleet.
Left: The Allies also had submarines.

procedure for the boats to sneak into the centre of a convoy, surface after dark and wreak havoc, disappearing before daybreak when the first of the Allied flight escorts arrived. On the surface, the sleek machines, powered by diesel engines, could outrun larger convoy escort vessels with relative ease.

> ## On the surface, the sleek machines could outrun larger convoy escort vessels

There followed a 'happy time', as it was known among German submariners, in which dozens of merchant ships were sent to the bottom. They were picking off targets with ease and convoy escorts were floundering with exasperation, not knowing how to halt the rising casualty toll. In 1940, U-boats accounted for more than 1,000 ships while just 16 U-boats were knocked out. The following year

Right: Sailors keeping watch from a surfaced submarine got a drenching.

followed a similar pattern with 24 U-boats being sunk.

AMPLE WARNING

Had there been a greater number of U-boats operating at that time, Britain would have been in grave danger of being throttled. Hitler was delighted with the success of the U-boats. Always sceptical of the power of his naval fleet, he became a convert and lavished his favours on the U-boat arm. If he had devoted more resources to them in 1939 instead of waiting until 1941, the outcome of the war might have been very different. By the

Above: One U-boat torpedo was enough to break a ship's back.

time his confidence was raised in the potential of the U-boats, it was just one of many services forced to get in line for the available resources.

As it was, technology came to the rescue for the Allies. Britain finally cracked the German radio code signals. Now operators could give ample warning to the convoys as to the whereabouts of the U-boats. Ships began to successfully bypass the waiting packs which were now forced to stretch out over huge distances, diminishing their effect.

Although the sinking of the liner *Athenia* at the beginning of the war did serve to tighten up the rules of engagement which governed U-boats, these were soon relaxed, in part because it was difficult for submariners to

---

Operators could give ample warning as to the whereabouts of the U-boats

---

abide by such rules without putting themselves into considerable danger. Stipulations like the one laid down in the 1935 London Submarine Agreement that submarines must stop intended victims and order the crew into lifeboats before opening fire were soon forgotten. The hunter quickly became the hunted if he lingered too long trying to establish the identity and purpose of a ship. In the Atlantic neutral, shipping was also at risk from German U-boats. Some vessels flying the flags of unaligned

Below: *In 1942 the remains of a convoy approach beseiged Malta.*

EYE WITNESS

The following personal account of life aboard a patrolling British submarine in the Mediterranean appeared in the *Daily Express* in June 1942.

The captain is wearing shorts with a sweater handy in case it is chilly. His favourite dress while submerged in action is a towel wrapped around his loins.

The crew are wearing overalls, shorts, shirts, vests – anything they fancy. There are no badges of rank and it is impossible to tell the captain from the cook.

Life goes on quietly, almost dully, for some days while the submarine continues towards her patrol station. There are only seven gramophone records, some of them scratched and indistinct through constant wear. The captain tells the first lieutenant he will brain the first rating to play *Frankie and Johnnie were lovers* – he swears he has heard it 3,000 times.

At midday the next day the captain is resting in his cabin. The first lieutenant is at the periscope. He swings it, sees smoke on the horizon. Without ceasing to look he says: "Captain, in the control room". The murmur is taken up and goes around the boat. Within a matter of seconds the captain is at the periscope clothed in his towel. He looks and says: "There is smoke on the horizon – a couple of masts."

Then the orders come fast. "Diving stations, full speed ahead together, starboard 25, steer 320." The hum of the motors can be heard through the otherwise silent submarine.

There are three merchant ships escorted by six Italian destroyers. The captain grabs his slipping towel as he snaps the range – 8,000 yards.

Excitement in the submarine is terrific and suppressed. Nobody speaks except the captain. At times the silence is so intense that a movement by a rating sounds like thunder.

As the torpedoes jump from the tubes the submarine shudders a bit. The captain's towel falls off. Nearby ratings chuckle at naked authority.

Stop watches have already started to mark the time the torpedoes take to reach the target. The captain's: "I'll have a cup of tea, please," is hardly necessary. The electric stove was switched on some minutes before. It is a ritual. Everybody in the service knows that you must have a cup of tea before the depth charging begins.

In 55 seconds the explosion which means the target has been hit rocks the submarine. The captain sits on the engine-room artificer's tool box, sipping his tea. Then the first depth charge arrives.

The captain's cup leaps off the tool chest. The submarine vibrates with the clangour of charges exploding nearby.

For two hours the racket of the depth charges goes on. The men behave as if they were on tiptoe. Barely a word is spoken. As the noise of the depth charges dies away the submarine creeps to periscope depth. The captain sees three destroyers picking up survivors from the sunken merchantmen.

One of the ratings off duty has already got hold of the "Jolly Roger" skull and cross bones flag of the submarine service and is preparing to stitch another chevron to the other battle honours. They will fly it when they get back from patrol.

countries were hit by accident. Others, suspected of aiding the British, were rammed or torpedoed on purpose.

In November 1939 neutral countries were warned by Germany that their ships could not be guaranteed a safe passage in waters around the British Isles. Meanwhile, secret instructions to U-boat commanders gave them the go-ahead to sink tankers and other key commercial ships approaching Britain unless they were identified as Russian, Japanese, Italian, Spanish, Greek or American. To cover their tracks, the U-boat commanders were told to use only electric torpedoes which did not leave a tell-tale wake in the water. This meant the explosion could be blamed on an engine fault or a mine.

It wasn't only in the Atlantic that the U-boats plied their deadly trade. Six were broken into pieces and transported by road to Linz in Austria where

the water was deep enough for re-assembly and were then launched into the Black Sea. The first to go into action there took to the water on 28 October 1940.

It wasn't only in the Atlantic that the U-boats plied their deadly trade

Operation in the Mediterranean was difficult for the U-boats – which were known by numbers rather than names – as their dark forms could be quickly spotted in the shallow, clear water by aircraft above or nearby ships. Also, the fast flowing eastern currents assisted the U-boats as they sailed into the warm seas but thwarted their exit.

Nevertheless, it was there that the U81 sank HMS *Ark Royal* on 13 November 1941, one of the prestige ships of the Royal Navy.

Above: Relief as a German U-boat and its crew return safely to port after a long spell on patrol.

Far easier was the task of the U-boats in the waters off America and Canada. Until Japan's attack on Pearl Harbor and Germany's subsequent declaration of war on America, Hitler had ordered that any ship bearing the stars and stripes standard be allowed freedom of the waters. There had been sinkings of US vessels before December 1941, but presumably these were in error.

When America and Germany were eventually pitted against each other, the U-boats seized the opportunity for yet another 'happy time'. U-boat commander in chief Karl Dönitz, the man who was later to take over from Hitler as Führer of Germany, knew his forces had to pounce before America became wise to the threat.

Five of the largest submarines, called Type IX boats,

EYE WITNESS

Stoker Fernand 'Pedro' Guinard, 69, from Halifax, Nova Scotia, served on several Canadian warships including HMCS *St. Laurent*.

❝My first contact with the enemy came early in the war when we picked up 27 survivors from the German submarine U31. We were four days out of Newfoundland.

A lot of these guys were Czechs and Poles. They told me they'd been offered the chance to fight in the navy or go work in a slave camp. You couldn't really blame them for joining up. I got quite close to them because I had to detail them to hand pump the bilges.

Even that got me into trouble. When we docked and disembarked the POWs, two of the Germans came over to shake hands and say goodbye. That didn't go down well with the officers. I got warned in no uncertain terms not to fraternise with the prisoners.

We only killed one submarine in my first three years of service. But we saw plenty of attacks on our convoys. I remember one time when a wolf pack began torpedoing our boats at sunset. It was so sad to see these ships going down. There were people in the water everywhere but to be honest we didn't give a bag about them. There were guys in a life raft obviously looking for help and we just rode straight through them throwing out depth charges. All we cared about was getting the submarine.

Was I scared? I didn't have much time to be scared. I was part of a team and you just got on with your job.❞

were dispatched from the Mediterranean to commence operations in North American coastal waters in 'Operation Paukenschlag'.

EASY TARGETS

Americans living along the eastern seaboard had so far been virtually untouched by the war. There were no blackouts, built-in defences, or restrictions on radio use. Even navigation lights remained helpfully in place. Not only did the U-boats have easy targets but, after the 'kill', the pursuing submarine hunters were inexperienced and ill-prepared. There was little to stop the U-boats getting clean away. In 'Operation Paukenschlag', each boat averaged almost six 'kills' before returning to home waters. Some of the boats sunk were those who had traversed the Atlantic in a convoy to pick up a cargo only to be sunk, as the British saw it, through a reckless lack of defence on behalf of the Americans.

A further wave of 12 smaller boats did their utmost to match the grand total but, thankfully for the Americans, fell short of the target. Within a few months, America began using convoy systems in its home waters and mimicked the successful British methods of hunting U-boats.

The tentacles of the U-boat campaign also spread into the southern oceans. There were plenty of ships carrying essential goods which were poorly equipped to deal with U-boat attack. In addition, it further stretched the Royal Navy ships

> ## Within a few months, America began using convoy systems in its home waters

Below: *Living conditions on a U-boat were cramped and uncomfortable, with restricted fresh food and air.*

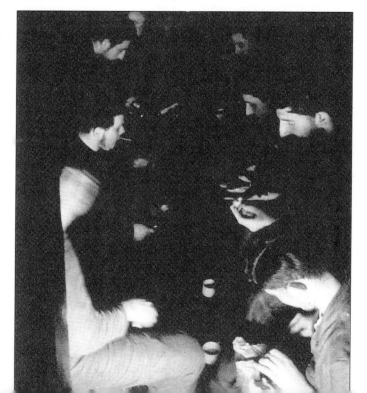

charged with hunting for submarines.

Not all of the 1,300 U-boats put to sea by Germany during World War II saw action. Some U-boats were used for training, others for supplying the roving hunters. Still more U-boats

were employed carrying goods from the Far East to the Fatherland.

Men who served in the U-boat arm of the Kriegsmarine (German Navy) were considered the elite by their countrymen – although they were loathed and detested by the British. There can be little doubt that they had strong nerves and plenty of courage. Some were volunteers, attracted by the excitement the service

appeared to offer. This was perpetuated by the public accolades which were awarded to U-boat aces like Gunther Prien and Joachim Schepke. U-boat men also got about double the rates of pay awarded to other sailors. Other men who found themselves serving on the U-boats were naval recruits who had been drafted.

Above: A U-boat in harbour is loaded with supplies before embarking on another lengthy ship-bagging voyage.

The day-to-day life for those who had to live on board a U-boat was far from glamorous. Conditions were cramped. There was a curtained-off cabin for the captain but there were not enough beds for every member of the crew. Some men slept in hammocks, while others slept on the floor.

LIFE EXPECTANCY

Until hostilities started with America, the U-boat commanders had little idea of the distances their crafts were able to travel. They were pleasantly surprised to find they could cruise far further than they ever thought possible if they conserved fuel by keeping to reasonable speeds and travelled on the surface.

More supplies were needed on a long voyage. However, they took up valuable living accommodation, leaving the crew of about 50 even fewer comforts.

MASCOTS

Animals featured as mascots to the branches of army, navy and air force throughout the war. On HMS *Duke of York*, the ship's tabby cat was Whiskey who became famous for sleeping soundly through the battle which sunk the *Scharnhorst*. A cat called Susan made herself at home on a Royal Navy tank landing craft and even attended the D-Day invasion. A St Bernard by the name of Bamse was the mascot of the Norwegian fighting ship *Thorod*. He assured himself a place in the heart of his crew by rounding them up from shore leave by visiting their favourite bars and clubs – even boarding a bus to patrol the more far-reaching destinations.

One of the more unusual mascots of the war was a Syrian bear by the name of Voytek, adopted as a cub by the Second Polish Transport Company in Persia. He was thought of as human by his soldier pals who watched distressed as he cried like a child when his carer, Lance Corporal Peter Prendys, disappeared from sight. His love of water led to the shower room having to be locked to prevent him from exhausting the water supply. When he discovered an Arab spy, he was acclaimed a hero and allowed a morning's free play in the bath.

It was as a hero he was greeted in Scotland at the end of the war where he served the army until 1947 when his owner was demobbed. It was then he was handed over to Edinburgh Zoo where he had to get used to a new life behind bars.

Water was rationed and the opportunities for washing were very few. The atmosphere was squalid, sweaty and unpleasant.

Early models were very spartan. There was inadequate heating aboard. So men soaked from taking their turn on the watch when the boat was on the surface found themselves unable to dry their sodden clothes. Men wore layers of jumpers and still felt chilled.

Above: A U-boat is armed with a giant torpedo before a trip.
Left: Sailors stood little chance when a U-boat was blown up.

When the most primitive U-boats were forced to submerge, the men had to wear breathing masks to prevent poisoning by carbon dioxide. Later, more sophisticated air purifiers were built into the wall of the ships, so masks became obsolete.

Voyages lasted for months at a time and there was little chance

The greatest shadow over a U-boat crewman was his brief life expectancy

to breath fresh air. U-boat men operating in the darkened Arctic region during the winter months were known to queue up patiently for a glimpse of sunlight.

Perhaps the greatest shadow over the life of a U-boat crewman, though, was his brief life expectancy.

During the first two years of war, their existence was perilous

Left: Depth charges were one antidote to roaming U-boats.

became more impotent which prompted the desperate Dönitz, by now Admiral of the entire Kriegsmarine, to order a kamikaze-style attack by them following D-Day.

RECKLESS ATTACK

On 11 June 1944 he issued an order which read: 'The Invasion Fleet is to be attacked with complete recklessness. Every enemy vessel that aids the landing, even if it puts no more than half a hundred men or a tank ashore, is a target calling for all-out effort from the U-boat.

'It is to be attacked even at the risk of losing one's boat. When it is necessary to get to grips with the enemy landing fleet, there is no question of any regard to danger through shallow water or possible minefields.'

Even with the benefit of hindsight it is difficult to discern whether the U-boat captains, carried out assaults and were

due entirely to the shortcomings in their torpedo systems. Then, when they bore the brunt of Allied air and sea power, U-boats became an endangered species. Apart from torpedoes and mines, the only weapon the

---

German sailors grew into the habit of calling their craft 'iron coffins'

U-boats could use against their enemies was an undersized machine gun. German sailors grew into the habit of calling their craft 'iron coffins'.

After attacking, there are examples of U-boat captains displaying concern for their victims, passing on food and water and radioing their position so help could be sent. Survivors were never allowed on board, however.

Equally, there were stories of men from sunken ships being machine-gunned to death by callous U-boat captains as they lay helpless in the water. While that may have occurred, there is the strong possibility such stories were used for propaganda

purposes by a Ministry of Information which depicted U-boat captains as callous, dedicated Nazis.

The most successful U-boat was U48, which came into service in April 1939 and sank a record 59 ships before being sunk itself in October 1943. Many of the submarines sunk five or fewer ships, many making no hits at all before they were sent to the ocean bed.

The U-boat force gradually

ORAN DILEMMA

In one of the most controversial moves of the war, Churchill turned British guns against former ally France a little more than a week after the French armistice with Germany was signed.

A British squadron led by Vice Admiral James Somerville encircled the pride of the French fleet harboured in the Algerian port of Oran on 3 July 1940 as part of 'Operation Catapult' and issued an ultimatum to the ships sheltering there to sail for Britain or America. When the order was refused, the mighty force of British ships including the ill-fated battle cruiser *Hood* opened fire.

Prestige ships, among them the *Provence*, *Bretagne* and *Dunkerque* were sunk or badly damaged and 1,300 French sailors were killed. The aim was to prevent the ships falling into German hands but it caused a major outcry in France and among French-speaking nations around the world.

Churchill said he regretted the loss of life but insisted the action was necessary. 'I leave the judgement of our actions with confidence to Parliament. I leave it to the nation and I leave it to the United States. I leave it to the world and to history.'

The French ships in British ports were confiscated with barely one shot being fired.

Above: U-boat construction sites became priority targets for Allied air forces.

defeated or if indeed the U-boat force was already so depleted and poorly supplied that they were unable to take any meaningful action. Certainly, there is little evidence of U-boat activity in the Channel following D-Day.

Despite the Allied successes in combatting the U-boat menace, the Nazi hierarchy continued to pin great hopes on the success of a renewed campaign. Hitler, keeping faith with the U-boat service, was convinced the newest model designed by Germany was a war-winner. In his diaries, dated 6 March 1945, his aide Goebbels reflected those optimistic opinions. With the Allies crossing the borders of Germany into the Fatherland, he wrote: 'There is considerable hope for us here. Our U-boats must get to work hard; above all it may be anticipated that as the new type gets into action, far greater results should be achieved than with our old U-boats...' Later, on 28 March, barely a month before the collapse of Hitler's Germany, he noted the Allied bombing campaign against the new submarines in dock at Bremen and penned with satisfaction: 'Clearly the revival of our U-boat war has made a great impression on the war.'

Below: Another convoy ship falls victim to U-boats, Hitler's underused war weapon.

BATTLE OF THE ATLANTIC

During World War II, German U-boats almost succeeded in severing the supply routes from America and Canada to Britain. Without shiploads of goods, including fuel, from overseas the prospects for Britain were dim.

Unable to support herself, Britain had for years relied on trade to keep her people fed, clothed and employed. If those vital links were cut during conflict, Britain would have been forced to capitulate or see her population starve. Now in World War II the grim scenario was being played out once more. U-boats, in tandem with the German Navy or Kriegsmarine, were set to exploit the Achilles heel of the British Empire. They nearly succeeded.

Both Britain and Germany's navies had been unprepared for war. Navy chief Erich Raeder had far fewer U-boats at his disposal than he would have liked. In addition, the submarine construction programme was almost at a halt. Hitler had little faith in his navy and earmarked only limited resources for it.

Meanwhile, Britain had a mighty fleet of Royal Navy vessels and numerous merchant ships. But the Admiralty appeared to have devoted little time or effort in the years between the wars in looking at ways to counter the U-boat threat. It still believed in the outdated notion that wars could be won with offensive action by battleships.

Putting their lives on the line alongside sailors in the Royal Navy were volunteer merchant seamen. It was their job to ferry the all-important supplies to Britain, mostly from America and Canada across the Atlantic. Instantly, they became targets for the roaming U-boats. Their pay was £9 a month with an additional two shillings and sixpence in danger money.

The major threat in the Atlantic was always from U-boats

Immediately, the convoy system when merchant ships banded together and travelled under armed escort was in use once again, as it had been with marked success in World War I. There were some drawbacks, however, which made shortages more acute on the homefront. For example, it took valuable time for a convoy to be assembled and some ships were compelled to travel by a longer route than they otherwise would have done. Speedier ships were impeded by

Left: *Freezing weather in the Atlantic had the crew thawing out anchor chains.*
Below: *U-boats on far-flung missions were dependent on supply ships.*

the pace of slower vessels. Also, dockyards became hopelessly congested when a glut of ships arrived all at once.

ESCORT SHIPS

Nevertheless, the accompanying Royal Navy ships at least offered some protection to the merchant fleet. At first, however, the short range of the accompanying ships meant that escorts could only be offered for some 200 miles out of Britain. The convoy was then on its own until it met with a reciprocal Canadian escort a few hundred miles from the other side. It offered a mid-Atlantic gap which was ideal for hunter U-boats.

Even the proximity of the armed destroyers at the outset and close of the voyages proved little deterrent to the U-boats in the opening years of World War II. The major threat in the Atlantic was always from U-boats and sometimes from merchant ships fitted out with weaponry, known as armed raiders.

Hitler was unwilling to risk his capital ships in the open sea after the *Bismarck* disaster. Lacking any aircraft carriers, the Germans were unable to launch air bombardments out of range of their airfields.

By the close of 1940, more than 4,700,000 tons of British shipping was lost

---

If they operated at night, the U-boats often went unnoticed by the escort ships even on the surface. Low in the water and much smaller than a surface ship, the most vigilant watch could be forgiven for letting the streamlined craft slip by.

The only technology available to counter the threat from U-boats was Asdic, a sonar device which sent out underwater impulses that could, by the sound of the echoes, indicate the presence of solid objects. Not only was it almost useless at speed or against surface objects, but early models were also unable to produce an accurate range and operators were very inexperienced.

In a bid to flush out U-boats during the early months of the war, Royal Navy warships attempted sweeps of convoy routes. The U-boats would simply dive and wait for the danger to pass. Even if their presence was detected, there was every chance the depth charge dropped by a pursuing vessel would fall short of its intended mark.

As the war progressed, Germany eased the way for its U-boat captains in their task of sinking trans-Atlantic shipping by providing new ports from which they could operate. The fall of Norway and France offered plenty of fresh and friendly harbours for repairs and restocking. In port, the U-boats were housed in specially built bunkers with two metre thick walls. That meant that although the docks came under heavy fire during Allied bombing raids the U-boats remained safe. It wasn't until 1944 that the Allies found sufficient fire power to shatter these solid defences.

By the close of 1940, more than 4,700,000 tons of British shipping had been lost in the form of 1,281 vessels, about one fifth of the pre-war merchant fleet.

EYE WITNESS

Dennis Bell, 67, of Waterlooville, Hampshire, was one of the youngest seamen to sail with the D-Day invasion fleet. At 16 he was a galley boy in the merchant navy, serving aboard the converted troop ship *Liberation of Europe*. His pay was £2 per week, including £1 3s 4d 'war risk money'.

❝ I spent the early months of 1944 chugging along the south coast to drop off soldiers for secret beach-storming exercises. Looking back, I was incredibly naïve about the whole business of war. I was only a kid and I knew nothing. I used to think I'd be all right because I was wearing my lifejacket.

By D-Day I'd already had a taste of the Atlantic War. At 15 I was galley boy aboard a crude carrier called the *Robert F. Hind*, bringing oil from the States to Britain and North Africa. Nobody would ever tell me what was going on – they would just shout at me to get back to the galley and work.

I soon cottoned on to the fact that none of the escort ships wanted to come too close to us. Obviously a tanker was a nice juicy target for the U-boats and if we'd gone up in flames we'd have lit up the sky. ❞

Left: Crewmen on board an escort warship observe the progress of a southbound convoy.

Above: Always alert, seamen knew the threat of attack was never far away. **Right:** Germany housed her precious U-boats in sturdy concrete bunkers.

In May 1941, the first convoy to receive protection for the entirety of its voyage set sail. It was an important first step towards victory in the Battle of the Atlantic.

Soon after came the introduction of radar, still far from foolproof but a huge boon to the navy ships charged with

Now, at last, aircraft could be brought to bear against the undersea menace

spotting predators. Radar also aided Coastal Command aircraft as to the whereabouts of U-boats. Now, at last, aircraft could be brought to bear against the undersea menace and the planes posted to coastal duties appeared to be reaping a reward. Britain's Admiralty, without a fleet air arm, was

constantly battling to keep those few planes in place when many in the RAF and the war office thought they would be better employed bombing land-based targets in Europe. It took several years for the Germans in command to become fully aware of the danger posed by radar to its U-boats.

Also, the British cashed in on a fatal flaw of the wolf pack system used by U-boats, in which a handful of craft operated

together during a convoy attack. To alert nearby boats to the presence of a convoy, the German commanders had to use their radios. The prospect of the British being able to track the signals was dismissed out of hand by the Germans for months. But that is just what did happen when the High Frequency Direction Finder was pioneered, affectionately known as 'Huff-duff'. When the U-boat position was fixed by the radio operators, it gave Royal Navy vessels far greater scope in their attack.

Convoy defences were reorganised so that extra escort boats could loiter over submerged submarines for up to two days, waiting for the craft to surface for air. Then it was an

1941 proved to be a key year for the Allies in their fight against the U-boats

easy target. Other vessels manoeuvred themselves around the precious convoy ships to fill the gap left by the lingering vessel for fear that another U-boat would make merry in the unexpected opening.

In the British armoury, too, was the increasing ability of the decoders to pinpoint the position of U-boats. At the start of the war, the translation of the messages sent between the German admiralty and its ships was slow and provided only retrospective information. With practice, the 'tapping' system speeded up, providing accurate and detailed assistance for convoys and British ships on the whereabouts of the enemy. While the German commanders suspected a breach in security, they never identified where the leak was.

So 1941 proved to be a key year for the Allies in their fight against the U-boats. Although 432 ships were sunk, the total was less than in the previous year. The

Above: A US destroyer pulls alongside HMS Norfolk to refuel mid-voyage.

U-boat arm lost 35 of its craft.

When the U-boats turned their attentions to the pickings off America in early 1942, the pressure on the Atlantic convoys eased. But when the U-boats returned to Atlantic waters, it was with a vengeance.

AIRCRAFT ATTACKS

At last U-boat manufacture was approaching the levels hoped for by Dönitz. Every month, 20 new U-boats left the ship yards. The boost for the Kriegsmarine was bad news for British sailors in the Atlantic who found themselves once more at the heart of a fierce battle for survival.

EYE WITNESS

Forbes Brown, from Victoria, British Columbia, joined the Royal Canadian Navy in 1941, training as an Asdic operator.

❮Being a Canadian ship, we didn't drink much tea. When we were docked in Londonderry, my pal Bob took me to see 'Black Dan'. He sold 'Black Dan' an enormous box of tea for £1. Bob took the money and later that night tied the box of tea to a rope and lowered it down the side of the ship to the dockside where Dan was waiting.

When I next went ashore, Bob asked me to find 'Black Dan' and offer him a bag of sugar for £1. When Dan came to collect the sugar he tasted it before handing over the money to Bob and making off.

Two nights later I was on gang plank duty when Bob was brought back with a great gash in his head. He had concussion and was severely bruised up. I went to see him later on.

He confessed there was only a fraction of sugar in the bag he had sold 'Black Dan'. The rest was salt, dirt cheap even then. I never went back to see 'Black Dan' again after that and neither did Bob.❯

Although the extended air patrols aided the safety of the ships and significantly improved the rate at which U-boats were knocked out, it was still a fearful fight to the death. U-boats began to attack once more during daylight hours, a sign of their boosted confidence.

During the two months of August and September

U-boats – helped by the German advances in cracking British codes – found 21 convoys and sank 43 ships. By the end of 1942, Allied tonnage totalling 7,500,000 had been sunk, more than the combined totals for the three previous years of war.

Allied aircraft stepped up the number of attacks against

Above: When a convoy put to sea, the Atlantic throbbed with activity.

Below: A cargo ship is lost amid smoke following an air attack.

U-boats during 1943 after the long-awaited allocation of more long-range aircraft. Between March 1943 and the end of the

> **Between March 1943 and the end of the war, air attack accounted for 290 U-boats**

war, air attack accounted for 290 U-boats alone. A surface U-boat could offer little by way of defence to an aircraft as its guns were so small as to be useless.

Suddenly, the campaign against U-boats was accelerating. That spring eight U-boats were lost in the battle to protect one convoy. During May alone 41 U-boats were sent to the bottom of the ocean, causing a concerned Dönitz to pull the ranks of remaining U-boats out of

The importance of the Battle of the Atlantic suddenly loomed large for Hitler

the Atlantic for a few months. Still, he failed to question the security of his cipher system.

The importance of the Battle of the Atlantic suddenly loomed large for Hitler, who had previously been wholly absorbed in his bid to conquer Russia.

In January 1943 Admiral Raeder was replaced as the Commander in Chief of the

Kriegsmarine by Dönitz. Hitler saw Dönitz with new eyes after the impressive successes of the U-boat war. Now Dönitz found it impossible to achieve similar standards.

U-boat production was still

relatively healthy, despite an increasing shortage of manpower in the dockyards. However, the lack of crews was becoming a dilemma for Dönitz who was compelled to send barely trained men into action despite the fact he believed the success of the U-boats lay at least in part with a rigorous training for the men aboard.

LIBERTY SHIPS

The Allies, meanwhile, had the bonus of Liberty ships – US built craft which went to replace the mercantile fleet decimated by U-boat action. By July 1943,

Left: Young, fit men were always needed for the fight against the U-boats.

"SUB SPOTTED – LET 'EM HAVE IT!

LEND A HAND – Enlist in your Navy today

the number of new ships coming out of the American yards was greater in total than the amount being lost.

With losses being so severe, the pack formation was abandoned in the autumn of 1943 and U-boats returned to the Atlantic hunting alone, cutting their effectiveness

In looking at the Battle of the Atlantic, it is vital to remember the contribution made by Britain's own submarines. During the war they sank 15 U-boats. Only three British submarines were sent to the bottom by U-boats. Submarines were never sighted by their own kind until they were at very close range. For a successful attack to be pressed home, the two could be no more than half a mile apart. The first U-boat fell victim to HMS *Salmon* as early as December 1939.

COST OF CONFLICT

In the last four months of 1943, the U-boats succeeded in sinking 67 ships at a cost of 64 U-boats.

Clearly, the Battle of the Atlantic was lost by the Germans although it would be months before shipping in the

Above: A convoy reaches port, thanks this time to the Royal Canadian Navy.

Atlantic was completely safe from U-boat attack.

At the end of the war, it became clear that the conflicts at sea – chiefly the Battle of the Atlantic – had been costly for both sides. During the war, the Allies lost 5,150 merchant ships, 2,828 of them to U-boats. The number of merchant seamen whose lives were lost amounted to 50,000. The U-boat tally also included 148 Allied warships.

As for the U-boat arm, 785 of its 1,131 strong fleet were lost, costing the lives of at least 27,491 crew and officers. Approximately 5,000 were taken prisoner of war.

EYE WITNESS

J. H. Blonk, from Eindhoven, Holland, was blinded in one eye in 1941 when he was serving as an engineer on the cargo ship *de Friesland* which was hit off the English coast.

*We knew that if we were hit, we were on our own – the other ships would not and were not allowed to turn back otherwise they would be easy targets. The ship sank so fast that we didn't even manage to get a float from the deck.

I can still remember how the wireless operator who I shared a cabin with was standing beside me. Then the water came and I never saw him again, I just felt his hand on my leg.

I was in the water for four hours. I held on to a panel from the deck that had gone overboard. An English communications officer was holding on to the other side. After an hour or so he said to me: "I think I'm going to let myself go, I'm so tired, I can't hang on any more."

I begged him to keep going. After he went, I lost all conception of time and that is the greatest danger for a drowning man – he thinks he is bobbing around for hours when in reality it is a much shorter time.

After four hours a trawler returned from the convoy to see if there were any survivors. Thirteen members of a 27-man crew were saved.*

MATAPAN

Jostling for position in the Mediterranean, the tussle between the Italian and British navies was set to be of epic proportions. In the event, the British navy pulled off a tactical master-stroke which decided the debate before Italy celebrated its first anniversary at war.

Britain had its own Mediterranean fleet. Key bases for Britain were Gibraltar, at the teeth of the Mediterranean, the hard-pressed island of Malta and Alexandria, the Egyptian port operating under Admiral Sir Andrew Cunningham, from which supplies were being shipped to Greece.

Italy had well-established ports of its home territory opening into the Mediterranean and the Aegean as well as control of Albania and Libya, on the northern coast of Africa.

When war broke out, the British had a grasp of Italian naval codes and gathered enough information to sink nine Italian submarines before the end of June 1940. But a fortuitous switch in cipher systems by the Italians in July prevented the British from cracking the codes again.

The Italian air force wasted no time in bombing the British big ships when they were at sea. Italian intelligence about British

---

The Italian air force wasted no time in bombing the British big ships

---

sea traffic was good. It enabled her captains to circumnavigate all convoys to Libya around the British forces.

Against this background, Cunningham was determined to punish his Italian enemies and put to sea 16 times between June and October 1940. Yet he only managed to track Mussolini's ships three times.

So it was a priceless morale

booster for the British when, on 11 November 1940, the Fleet Air Arm attacked Taranto, an Italian port. In port were six Italian battleships. A dozen Swordfish aircraft from the aircraft carrier *Illustrious* took off at dusk and flew 170 miles to attack the Italian navy vessels, struggling to gain height with their heavy load of explosives.

They notched up two strikes against the battleships *Cavour* and *Littorio*. A second wave of Swordfish arrived less than an hour afterwards, directed to their target by the blaze now roaring at the base. Together, they damaged the battleship *Duilio*. At a cost of two aircraft, the Italian fleet was deprived of three valuable battleships – *Cavour* permanently; *Littorio* and *Duilio* until the late spring of 1941.

At the turn of the year, Fliegerkorps X, the Luftwaffe's anti-shipping force, transferred 200 of its aircraft to Sicily. By 10 January 1941 bombers from the precision corps bombed *Illustrious* and also struck

Warspite, although neither ship was terminally damaged.

It demonstrated, however, the need for air superiority if the Allies were to control the Mediterranean. Unfortunately, there was a shortage of Allied aircraft in the area, worsened when the *Illustrious* was hit again while in dock at Malta. Air attacks against Malta were so heavy and so frequent that it proved impossible to carry out adequate repairs to the much-needed aircraft carrier there. Consequently she had to be withdrawn from the Mediterranean.

ITALIAN THREAT

The British resolve to eradicate the Italian naval threat hardened and its objective was carried out in spectacular fashion, off Cape Matapan, in Greece. On 27 March 1941, a British plane

Below: *Italian cruisers* Flume, Gorizia *and* Pola *undergoing manoeuvres.*
Left: *HMS* Revenge *sets sail from Malta in 1939, before the siege.*

spotted a large gathering of Italian ships. The squadron comprised eight cruisers, the prestige battleship *Vittorio Veneto* and a host of destroyers. *Vittorio Veneto* was the pride of the Italian fleet. Her sister ship *Littorio* had been holed by the British at Taranto. Now she was poised with her support vessels to blow convoys destined for Greece out of the water.

Cunningham was instantly informed at his base in Alexandria. To back the aircraft

Below: The big guns of the Vittorio Veneto *unleash their fire power.*

DAKAR DEBACLE

Among the military calamities faced by Britain in the first half of the war was the debacle of Dakar. British ships sailed to the colony of French West Africa with the aim of landing Free French Forces who would take control from the Vichy regime.

❝As they anchored off the main port of Dakar on 23 September 1940, General de Gaulle broadcast a series of messages to the colony's governor stating his intention to land troops. All of the messages were ignored. Five messengers sent ashore with similar news were likewise rebuffed.

De Gaulle began threatening to use force. In reply, the coastal guns and ships at anchor in the port let off a barrage at the British ships, preventing the planned landing. The next day the exchange of fire continued with the British battleship *Barham* being struck. Twenty four hours later the battleship *Resolution* was hit, this time sustaining more serious damage.

At this the British commanders and de Gaulle realised that their carefully laid plans to steal a march on Vichy France was quite literally being shot to pieces. Consequently, the ships pulled out of the engagement and returned humiliated to Freetown, the capital of Sierra Leone. Apart from the damage to its ships, the British also had to endure a reprisal air raid by the leaders of Vichy France directed against Gibraltar.❞

sighting there were messages passed through the Italian secret service cipher which had been broken by the Allies. He grouped together three battleships, the aircraft carrier *Formidable*, four cruisers and as many destroyers as he could muster. If trouble was coming, the Royal Navy together with its Australian contingent were prepared.

Admiral Cunningham then made a move to protect the secrecy of the British activities which has since gone down as wartime folklore. A very keen golfer, he played regularly in the same club in Alexandria as the Japanese consul who reported every move made by the British Mediterranean Fleet to its enemies. Not only did Cunningham take his clubs to play golf that afternoon but

ostentatiously carried a suitcase, clearly bound for a night ashore. Having duped the tell-tale consul, he abandoned the case and slipped back aboard the battleship *Warspite* in time for an evening departure. Fortunately, the British ships did not pull out until after the Italians had carried out aerial reconnaissance of Alexandria harbour which revealed all were still at anchor. Italian Admiral Iachino believed the British posed no danger.

The British launched waves of aircraft to pester the Italians

The two forces first clashed in the morning of 28 March. After 40 minutes of exchanging shells, neither side had scored a hit and the action was broken off. The British launched waves of aircraft to pester the Italians who were themselves left virtually unprotected by their own air forces – which were stationed within easy range.

Above: Vittorio Veneto *was the jewel in the Italian navy crown.*

Vittorio Veneto was hit by one torpedo but still managed to escape the ravages of the air bombardment. However the cruiser *Pola* was stopped in her tracks by British firepower. Iachino, who was without the benefit of radar and apparently oblivious to the presence of British big ships, ordered two other cruisers to assist her. That night all three were attacked at short range. Two were quickly sunk without firing a shot. *Pola* and two other vessels were also sent to the bottom.

TIMED EXPLOSIVES

The British ships in the vicinity picked up 900 survivors before being scared off by the arrival of Luftwaffe planes. A further 270 men were plucked from the sea in the subsequent days but still the Italian casualties amounted to a devastating 2,400. The Battle of Matapan had been the biggest naval

engagement of the war so far and dealt a serious blow to the Italian navy.

Vittorio Veneto was not to escape for long. A British submarine torpedoed her again in December 1941.

Despite the inferiority of Allied air cover, the Royal Navy continued to carry out admirable harrassing manoeuvres against the Italians and the Germans in the Mediterranean. Most notable were the contributions made by the cruisers *Aurora* and *Penelope* operating out of Malta who targeted convoys destined for Libya with immense success. Hitler and Mussolini were counting the cost of the contribution to the North African campaign made by the small island.

But the British didn't have it all their own way. When U-boats arrived in the Mediterranean, the fleet was deprived of the aircraft carrier *Ark Royal* which was sunk in November 1941, as well as the battleship *Barham* and two cruisers.

In the naval armoury were minute submarines, nick-named 'pigs' by their crew who were clad in frogmen's suits and sat astride the 22ft long craft. The 'pigs' were carried close to their position by regular submarines. Then it was the job of the crew to go in close to the target and attach timed explosives.

The Italians had made two abortive attempts using 'pigs' against the British during August and September 1940. This time there were to be no mistakes.

The Battle of Matapan dealt a serious blow to the Italian navy

After dark on 18 December an Italian submarine picked its way quietly and cautiously through mined seas to the approach of Alexandria harbour. There it off-loaded three 'pigs' and six crew, with a noiseless ripple on the water.

Beneath the waterline of the Royal Navy battleship *Queen*

Elizabeth, one team placed an explosive charge. Unseen, the two divers went ashore and posed as French sailors until they were seized by Egyptian police some time afterwards.

The second Italian team struggled to affix explosives to the side of a tanker. They were cold and stricken with sickness after spending too long under-water. But they didn't emerge from the water until their task had been completed. Egyptians arrested them as they attempted

Below: Vittorio Veneto *smokes after attack by British Albacore planes.*

to pass the first control post of the harbour.

The men were still there when an explosion sent the ship lurching to portside

One member of the third team passed out but bobbed back to the surface and clutched a buoy until his partner finished the job in hand. The latter was having problems of his own, meanwhile, with a torn diving suit exposing him to lethal cold. Then the 'pig' plunged to the sea bed. Despite the growing

Above: *Probably the last photo taken of the Italian big ships before Matapan.*

effects of exposure, he dived to retrieve it, manhandled it 60 feet back to the base of his target, the *Valiant,* and set the detonator.

He and his partner, now recovered, were picked up out of the water by a British motor-boat and interrogated aboard *Valiant.* When they refused to speak about their operation, they were sent into the bowels of the ship close to where the charge was planted. The men were still there when an explosion sent the ship lurching to portside. They

MALTESE CROSS

Malta was awarded the George Cross in April 1942 after four months of continuous bombardment by the Axis air forces. As the Royal Navy battled to get convoys containing vital supplies through to the island, they were hampered by U-boats and airborne attacks which wrecked merchant shipping. It wasn't until August 1942 that a convoy arrived intact. With the volley of bombs coming from the sky the people of Malta and the beleaguered defending forces were subject to the most appalling privations. Yet Malta was a key point in the Allied defences. Had it fallen into the hands of Germany, Rommel would probably have won the battle for North Africa and the outcome of the war might have been different.

witnesed the effects of the blasts on the *Queen Elizabeth* and the tanker.

The Italian navy with Luftwaffe assistance continued to blockade Malta, the island which held the key to victory in North Africa. In December 1941 the Germans flew 169 bombing raids over Malta. In January 1942 the number rose to 262. The devastation took effect and Axis convoys began seeping through again as Allied ships were put out of action, deprived

themselves of fresh supplies. Nevertheless, Churchill was determined to keep Malta in Allied hands at all costs.

DAILY BOMBINGS

It wasn't until March 1942 that a British convoy managed to slip through the Italian net bringing in vital supplies. Attempts to get supplies to the island in June failed. Yet still the vicious air bombardment continued. Much of the island was laid waste by the daily

bombings as Hitler and Mussolini plotted an invasion.

The Allies planned a convoy of unprecedented size and strength in 'Operation Pedestal'. Setting off from Gibraltar were three aircraft carriers, two battleships, seven cruisers, 34 destroyers and eight submarines. The US carrier *Wasp* was also in evidence to bring new air forces to the island. The convoy departed on 10 August 1942 and came under repeated air attack. Both the Luftwaffe and Italy's Regia Aeronautica launched endless attacks with dive bombers, torpedo

---

Churchill was determined to keep Malta in Allied hands at all costs

---

bombers and fighter aircraft.

In the four day battle which pursued the convoy, the carrier *Eagle* was lost when it was sunk by U73, the cruisers *Cairo* and *Manchester* and the destroyer *Foresight*. Many of the surviving escort ships were damaged. The Italian navy, denied air cover by its own airforce. refused to join the offensive and fell victim to a British submarine as it made its way back to port.

CRITICAL LOSSES

Although the losses were critical, Malta was saved. Supplies that did filter through, amounting to some 30,000 tons, allowed the islanders and its battered forces to rebuild. It continued as a vital Allied base and deprived the Axis powers of a toehold which would have given them access to North Africa and the Middle East.

Woollen skull cap covered with a fine mesh camouflage net

Mouthpiece and airtube

Rubber tunic, water tight at the wrists, neck and waist

Underwater breathing equipment and oxygen bottle

Rubber trousers

Frogmen feet

SINKING THE BISMARCK

Majestic and mighty, the brand new battleship which sailed under the swastika for the first time in May 1941 drew gasps of admiration from friend and foe alike.

The *Bismarck* cut an awesome sight as it sped through the waves. More than 800 feet long and almost 120 feet wide, it was heavy with armour plating and bristled with giant guns yet was still sleek and fast. Who could blame the proud Germans for believing it was unsinkable?

It was down to the Royal Navy to send the great ship to the ocean floor and it was an urgent task which they were eager to undertake. A powerful battleship like the *Bismarck* posed an enormous threat to the convoys bringing essential food and materials from across the Atlantic. Without this lifeline from America and Canada, Britain would have quickly been strangled.

Left: *Deck of the mighty* Bismarck.
Below: *The battleship* Bismarck *undergoing sea trials.*

On *Bismarck*'s maiden voyage it confronted HMS *Hood*, elegant queen of the Royal Navy and sank it with the loss of almost all the crew. It was a devastating blow to navy pride and one which had to be avenged. The humblest sailor and the most powerful admiral in the British fleet felt to a man that *Bismarck*'s maiden voyage must also be its last.

Bismarck was built in Hamburg long before the opening salvoes of World War II were fired. The vessel was launched amid great pomp and ceremony on 14 February 1939. Nazi top brass, including navy chief Raeder, Göring, Goebbels and Hess, joined Hitler on a lofty podium when the great hull rumbled down the slipway. There to christen the ship was Dorothea von Loewenfeld, granddaughter of the celebrated German Chancellor Bismarck

after whom the ship was named.

After World War I, the German navy had been stripped of virtually all its assets and the Treaty of Versailles had strictly forbidden the creation of military muscle like the *Bismarck*. Hitler had been rebuilding the fleet and *Bismarck* was the largest addition to date. It was officially listed at 35,000 tons, some 7,000 tons lighter than it actually was.

A powerful battleship like the Bismarck posed an enormous threat to the convoys

When war came, *Bismarck* stayed in dock while having chunky plating affixed to its sides and decks, the 22 sealed chambers beneath its waterline made watertight and the latest technology installed on the bridge. It was being fitted out for conflict to become, as Germany's Admiral Tirpitz put it, 'an unsinkable gun platform'.

Its first taste of sea salt came when it left Hamburg on 15 September 1940 for trials in the shelter of Kiel Bay. There were teething troubles and *Bismarck* had to slink back to Hamburg for modifications. It wasn't until the following May that the ship was ready to set forth.

AIRCRAFT COVER

Hitler arrived at Gotenhafen (now Gdynia) for an inspection of his seaborne gem on 5 May, where *Bismarck* was patiently waiting to embark on its first trip. He was, it appears, kept unaware that its sailing date was imminent. The Führer was wary of losing his prize vessel and admiralty chiefs feared he would scupper their chances of getting underway at last.

Grand Admiral Erich Raeder believed it was vital to get *Bismarck* to sea. Germany now had the advantage of Atlantic

EYE WITNESS

Frank Hewlett joined the Royal Marines in 1939 when he was 20 years old.

❛I was on HMS *Aurora*, an escort to the *Hood*. We followed her a day after she left Scapa Flow. When *Hood* was sunk we were 40 miles away. We saw a big flash on the horizon. When we heard the news, nobody believed it.

Then the *Prince of Wales* came within our sights. She was damaged and we escorted her back to Iceland. There was an unexploded shell inside her bows. If it had gone off it would have destroyed the ship. When the shell was removed, it was full of sand. It must have been sabotaged in Germany.

Afterwards, we went to Newfoundland and sank the supply ship *Max Albrecht*, sister ship to the *Altmark*. She went down with a U-boat still attached to her.❜

In one sense, the Bismarck *was out of date even before setting sail*

ports in occupied France to provide bolt holes for its ships. There was now extended aircraft cover from the Luftwaffe operating out of France and the lighter nights would significantly reduce the cover which was needed to spirit the ship into the Atlantic through the British sea blockade. There was also the increasing threat of America joining the war on the side of the Allies. The United States' naval power would dwarf that of Nazi Germany.

Fleet commander Gunther Lutjens was as confident in the strength of his new ship as the rest of Germany. But he had one nagging doubt that was shared by many senior officers in the Germany navy. It was the wisdom of going to sea without round-the-clock aircraft cover. In one sense, the Bismarck was out of date even before setting sail. The sun was rising on the

Below: HMS Hood, *like the* Bismarck, *was thought by admirals to be invincible.*

between Iceland and Greenland. As they dashed for cover in the icy fog, the *Bismarck* registered their presence and fired off a warning shot.

DEADLY BLOW

The mood was tense among officers and men on the *Hood* and the *Prince of Wales* as the hunt for their fearsome quarry continued. All th crew were poised to strike but lost their chance when their ships slipped past the giant battleship in the darkness as it skirted the Greenland ice pack.

Bismarck continued altering it course, not greatly but enough to put the ships commanded by Vice Admiral Lancelot Holland in a quandary. The initial plan had been to creep up on the *Bismarck* under cover of darkness in a short range strike. Now the *Hood* was forced to make a broad sweep at the

fleet air arms which could offer much more by way of flexibility and accuracy. While both Japan and America were gearing up their navies for the new age, Germany and Britain were lagging behind, both caught unawares by the outbreak of war.

Lutjens was a veteran of the sea assaults in World War I, he had already earned the distinction of a Knight's Cross during World War II through his courage in the Norwegian campaign of 1940.

It was only a matter of time before sighting of this monster was confirmed to London

---

Loyal to his country, 51-year-old Lutjens was not a Nazi and refused to offer the party salute. Instead he preferred the time honoured navy salute and wore the old fashioned insignia of the Kaiser's navy instead of a swastika.

On 19 May the *Bismarck* sailed under cover of darkness to begin 'Operation Rheinubung'. In the company of the 17,000-ton heavy cruiser *Prinz Eugen*, itself a formidable ship, the

Bismarck purred off into the Baltic to be joined by other German vessels for its historic voyage. Its aim was to sink the battleships protecting convoys while the smaller *Prinz Eugen* picked off the merchantmen.

VULNERABILITY

Slipping down the Danish waterways and shadowing the Swedish coastline, it was only a matter of time before the sighting was confirmed to London. Sir John Tovey, Commander in Chief of the Home Fleet, went into action. At the pinnacle of his plan would be HMS *Hood*, 20 years old but still an inspiring sight. It was a match for the *Bismarck* in size and gunnery but its weakness lay in the thin armour plating which covered its body and decks. It was this vulnerability that *Bismarck* exploited to the full.

On 22 May, just a day after news of the *Bismarck* arrived in London, *Hood*, the *Prince of Wales* and six other vessels set off from Scapa Flow. The following day, two of the fleet, the *Norfolk* and the *Suffolk*, encountered the *Bismarck* in the Denmark Strait,

Above: *Following his encounter with* Hood, *Admiral Lutjens bolted for France.*

HUNTING THE BISMARCK

On 19 May the *Bismarck* sailed under cover of darkness to begin Operation Rheinubung. In the company of the heavy cruiser *Prinz Eugen*, *Bismarck* headed through the Skagerrak to the Norwegian coast. Passing so close to the Danish and Swedish coasts, it was only a matter of time before the two warships were sighted by British agents, and the news transmitted to London. Sir John Tovey was ordered to get the *Bismarck*.

On 22 May, just a day after news of the *Bismarck* arrived in London, the largest ship in the Royal Navy, HMS *Hood*, and the brand-new battleship HMS *Prince of Wales* set off from Scapa Flow in the Orkneys, accompanied by six other vessels.

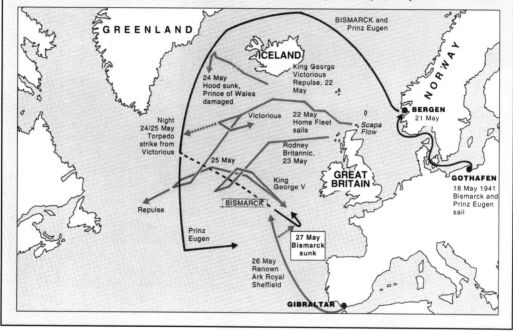

enemy and would be exposed to the brunt of its firepower.

When they sighted *Bismarck*, the *Hood* and *Prince of Wales*, travelling in close formation, were about 17 miles distant. At Admiral Holland's command, both ships began a charge at the enemy.

Lutjens was under orders to engage only the escorts of convoys. He wasn't looking for a duel and had hoped to avoid one. But now he had no choice. When the *Hood* and *Prince of Wales* closed the gap to 13 miles, they fired. Seconds later, the *Bismarck* and the *Prinz Eugen*

replied in kind. And while the British ships failed to find their targets, the Germans had them well and truly in range.

The initial plan had been to creep up on the Bismarck under cover of darkness

The second salvo from *Prinz Eugen*'s guns struck the *Hood*, igniting anti-aircraft ammunition. Another hit and then a third slaughtered many of the gun crews taking shelter. Still the guns from both sides continued firing.

It was during a manouevre by the *Hood* trying for a better angle that the deadly blow was delivered by the *Bismarck*. A shell plunged down into the heart of the ship, penetrating the deck with apparent ease. Somewhere in the bowels, it silently sparked an ammunition store, maybe two. The effect was catastrophic. Observers from both sides were astonished to see a massive plume of fire and smoke burst from the middle of the ship when there had been no explosion. The *Hood*, the most prestigious ship in old England, folded in two and

Above: Prinz Eugen was released from escape duty to escape the Royal Navy.

plunged to the bottom of the sea.

With it went the vast majority of the 1,400 crew, trapped in the wreckage. It was several hours before a British cruiser

The Hood folded in two and plunged to the bottom of the sea

came hunting for survivors. It found only three, cold and near death, clinging to small rafts in the middle of an oil slick.

The *Prince of Wales* was soon reeling from the effect of shells. It had been hit seven times, lost two officers and 11 men and was plagued with difficulties in its gunnery, making its own attack ineffective. Moments after its stunned crew saw the *Hood* ditching into the sea, it was decided to withdraw. The showdown had lasted just 21 minutes.

Britain was devastated by the loss of the *Hood* and its men. After the shock, the public were baying for revenge – or feared the *Bismarck* really was indestructible. There was no time for sentimentality among the naval officers now in hot

pursuit of the *Bismarck*.

The battleship *Prince of Wales*, plus the cruisers *Norfolk* and *Suffolk* shadowed the *Bismarck* as it moved south. Admiral Tovey, aboard *King George V*, was in command of *Victorious, Repulse,* four cruisers and nine destroyers hoping to intercept *Bismarck* from the south.

Visibility was poor, however, and the radar used by *Suffolk* to track its movements was patchy. *Bismarck* had, in fact, not escaped unscathed. It was holed twice by British shells which forced it to reduce speed and lost the vessel valuable fuel.

BISMARCK HURT

Lutjens felt he had no choice but to head for France for repairs. He released the *Prinz Eugen* to make a clean getaway, firing lazily at the *Prince of Wales* by way of distraction. Then he set a course which he hoped would take him to friendly France or within the torpedo range of a protective U-boat.

It was with some degree of surprise that he and his crew looked up to the skies some hours later and saw a group of circus-style planes buzzing

towards them. These were the Swordfish planes which had set off from the *Victorious* in order to wreak havoc on the *Bismarck*. With their single propellers and stacked wings they look like something from a different age. Nevertheless, the torpedo they carried beneath their fuselage was powerful enough to reckon with. The pilots of the Swordfish planes flew in low despite the barrage of anti-aircraft fire.

Below: Hitler failed to share the nation's pride in the navy.

KRIEGSMARINE

EYE WITNESS

Able Seaman Robert Kilburn was one of the three who survived the sinking of the *Hood*.

❛ I was a member of the anti-aircraft gun crew but, of course, we weren't needed. There were only two other people with me at the time. The others were in a shelter deck – a shell had gone in there and killed all of them, about 200 men – but I didn't know that at the time.

One of the shells hit one of the ready-fuse lockers for the four inch guns and there was a fire on board the upper deck and the ammunition was exploding. We were laid on the deck and then there was this terrific explosion. It was most peculiar, the dead silence that followed it – I don't know if we were deaf.

One of the other men was dead and the other one had his sides cut open and all his innards were tumbling out. I went to the ship's side to be sick. I noticed that the ship was rolling over and the bows were coming out of the water so I started taking off my tin hat, gas mask, anti-flash gear, overcoat, oilskin, so that I would have a chance to swim. With the ship rolling over, I just went into the water and the water came up to me.

I was terrified. I had a small rubber life belt on which you blew up – it was partially blown up. I started swimming away from the ship. The ship rolled over and the yard arms which had been broken during the action hit me across the legs and the wireless aerials tangled around my legs, pulling me down with the ship. I cut my seaboots off with the knife and shot up, like a cork out of a bottle. I must have been about 10ft down by then. The ship was around 10 yards away from me with her bows straight up in the air – and she just sank. ❜

In 1989 a team led by Dr Robert Ballard located the crusted hulk of the *Bismarck* (above) nestling on the ocean floor. Dr Ballard, the man who found and photographed the wreck of the *Titanic*, was aboard the *Star Hercules* when he discovered the *Bismarck* three miles beneath the ocean during a 10-day expedition. Among the photographs he took with a remote controlled underwater camera were those of discarded boots, the teak deck which was still intact and a 14-inch gun with a sea anenome bursting from its barrel.

Just one torpedo hit the mark. Yet all the eight attacking Swordfish planes survived the hair-raising attack and landed safely back on *Victorious* in the dark with next to no fuel.

The damage sustained by *Bismarck* was enough to make Lutjens review his course. With masterly intuition he turned suddenly westwards and, in doing so, shook off the Royal Navy shadow. It took 31 hours for the British to locate the *Bismarck* again.

By now most of the British ships in reach had been called in to help. Yet due to a series of mishaps and misunderstandings, they were unable to find the roaming battleship, having

On 26 May intrepid Swordfish planes found Bismarck again and attacked

turned in the wrong direction. In addition, many were running short of fuel and had to splinter from the body of the fleet to find more. Navy top brass was becoming increasingly nervous. Unaware that the *Bismarck* had been wounded, they knew its path must be taking it towards the 11 Allied convoys presently crossing the Atlantic.

On 26 May intrepid Swordfish, this time from the *Ark Royal*, found *Bismarck* again and attacked. Two torpedoes struck the big ship, wrecking the steering gear and ruining a propeller. It meant that *Bismarck* not only had to slow down further but also became locked on to a course which brought it directly into the path of the opposition, thanks to the jammed rudder.

The following day *Bismarck* came within range of the battleships *Rodney* and *King George V*. They weren't alone and soon the *Bismarck* was surrounded by British ships firing when they could. *Bismarck* took punch

Above: The Prince of Wales *was one of many ships to hunt the* Bismarck.

after punch, losing men and guns with the merciless onslaught. Fires raged fore and aft while ammunition exploded all around. Yet still it stayed afloat.

Afterwards, British sailors admitted they felt little joy seeing the enemy ship battered so badly. However, they had no option but to continue the barrage while the *Bismarck* still fired back.

HITLER'S OUTRAGE

When streams of German sailors plunged into the sea, the shelling stopped. Admiral Tovey was mindful of their safety as well as that of his own men. Fuel and ammunition were running desperately low in his fleet. It would not be long before the lurking U-boats would turn up looking for easy pickings.

Satisfied the *Bismarck* would no longer menace the shipping lanes of the Atlantic, he gave orders for the British ships to withdraw. The only ship left with torpedoes, the *Dorsetshire*, remained to finish off the job.

Controversy raged afterwards whether it was a British torpedo or a German sailor who sank the *Bismarck* by opening the sea-cocks.

At first the *Dorsetshire* and the destroyer *Maori* hauled up survivors. But their goodwill came to an abrupt end following the reported sighting of a U-boat. The ships pulled away from the bobbing survivors, leaving them to suffer a lingering death in the waves. Two other vessels rescued a handful of survivors between them.

Only 115 of the crew escaped with their lives out of a total of 2,206.

When news of the sinking reached Hitler he was outraged. Never mind that a fleet of five battleships, three battle cruisers, two aircraft carriers, 13 cruisers, 33 destroyers and eight submarines had been involved in the execution. He bitterly regretted ever putting his classic ship to sea.

Below: How the incredible story of pursuit was told to the British public.

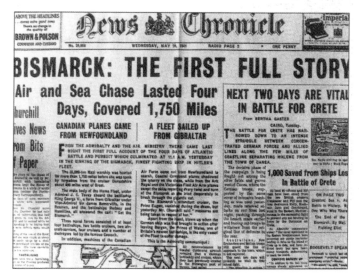

ARCTIC CONVOYS

Manning a ship on one of the treacherous Arctic convoys was perhaps the bleakest role in the whole war. For on these storm-lashed northern routes the weather collaborated with the enemy to make each day more miserable than the last.

Arctic convoys began after Soviet Russia was invaded by Germany and became an eminent ally of Great Britain. It wasn't a matter of survival to Britain as in the case of the Atlantic convoys.

Here was an exercise designed to appease Russia's leader Stalin. To exploit the opportunities for trade between the two countries, ships had to travel in the vicinity of the north pole where, for winter weeks on end, the sun never rose.

Hidden dangers under the waves included icebergs as well as U-boats. In the air the threat lay in frostbite alongside the dive-bombing planes of the Luftwaffe. The iron-grey steel hulls belonging to the powerful surface ships of the German navy were often masked by soupy fogs or dense blizzards.

REGULAR LOSSES

The sailors aboard knew they were being hunted. The buzz of a German reconnaissance plane overhead was a sure indication that an attack was being

Above: A U-boat crew operating in northern waters survey their iced-up weapons.

prepared. Sometimes, not often enough, the convoy skirted the edge of the polar ice and slid through the ocean without being noticed. Sole reward for the hapless mariners was the chance of arriving in one piece at their destination.

Ships carrying the precious cargoes travelled under protection of British and American warships in convoys, usually between Scotland or Iceland and Murmansk, Russia. These northern waters were particularly risky. After Germany invaded

Norway, it meant there were ports and airfields accessible to German forces within easy range. Hitler was also dedicated to victory over Russia. The

Hidden underwater dangers included icebergs and U-boats

sea battles to stop the convoys getting through to Stalin assumed greater importance given the personal interest of the Führer.

In reply the Allies did have the benefit of technology. Their grasp of the German naval secret codes was now accomplished. Yet despite re-routing to evade the attentions of the Arctic U-boats, convoys were still suffering regular losses. Virtually every convoy which

Far left: A British convoy leaves the warmth of British waters for Russia.
Left: Two Valentine tanks included in the aid sent to Russia.

set sail between March and June 1942 was attacked, either by U-boat or by the Luftwaffe. In all, 21 ships were lost in addition to the cruisers *Edinburgh* and *Trinidad*. Those losses were balanced against the safe arrival of 124 ships.

Now it seemed Germany was ready to pitch its prestige big ships into the fray. Britain's Admiralty was nervous.

> ## Virtually every convoy which set sail between March and June 1944 was attacked

Knowing that ships like the *Admiral Hipper* and *Admiral Scheer* were in northern waters, made the prospects for any future convoys seem gloomy. Also there was *Lutzow* formerly known as *Deutschland*. (Hitler changed the name because the sinking of a ship called 'Germany' would cause depression at home and would be the butt

EYE WITNESS

Forbes Brown, from Victoria, British Columbia, joined the Royal Canadian Navy in 1941 and trained as an Asdic operator.

❝My first trip was in a corvette, HMCS *Algoma*, across the North Atlantic as a convoy escort. With Asdic we transmitted a sound beam and it reflected back if there was a submarine under the water. I could hardly believe it when I picked up a contact. Action stations were sounded. It was about 600 yards ahead. About 40 depth charges were dropped.

Following the last one there was a tremendous explosion underwater. It blew out all the safety valves on the engine and there were blue flames shooting off the deck. We suspected the last charge hit a torpedo head. Still there were plenty of other U-boats about. We started off with 62 ships in the convoy and ended up with 41. It was hairy. After that trip we were supplied with sheepskins so we suspected we were going north. As usual, it was a foul up. We were off to the Mediterranean.❞

of jokes among his enemies.) Worst of all was the presence of the huge battleship *Tirpitz*, sister ship of the *Bismarck* and the pride of the German fleet, with awesome firepower and astonishing capabilities.

Code-crackers revealed the large boats were preparing to depart and do battle. Convoy PQ17, sailing out of Iceland's capital, Reykjavik, on 27 June, comprised 33 ships and a tanker with an escort of six destroyers, four corvettes, two submarines and two anti-aircraft ships.

Left: Some of the British and US ships involved in safeguarding the Arctic convoy routes.

In London, it was clear that the enemy could pounce at any time. At sea, the convoy captains were equally expectant, wondering where and when the ferocious strike would come. Each bank of fog came as a welcome relief as the convoy made its way steadily northwards.

Information now coming out of the cipher service indicated the big ships were setting out from their base. It was enough for Sir Dudley Pound, First Lord of the Admiralty, to order the convoy ships to scatter for their

the convoy. The information from the secret message service had been misconstrued – with devastating results. As ordered, the convoy scattered. Armed ships pulled away from the merchant ships to search for the

Watch officers scanned the horizon, expecting to see the massive vessel looming

Below: Scharnhorst *was the scourge of convoys in northern waters.*

The *Tirpitz* did sail on 5 July but was recalled following the success the attack had already achieved. Neither did the big ships take part in action against the subsequent convoy, PQ18. Hitler once again erred on the side of caution rather than risk another humiliating loss at sea to parallel the *Bismarck*. Before reaching safety, PQ18 lost ten ships to aircraft and three to U-boats. The escort ships which this time stayed close to their charges, claimed a number of planes with anti-aircraft fire and

best protection. Little did he know that Hitler himself had intervened in the operation. He barred the use of valuable, prestige ships like the *Tirpitz* unless complete safety could be guaranteed. That meant British and American aircraft carriers were safely out of range.

Tirpitz was not heading for

Tirpitz and its team. The watch officers scanned the horizon, expecting to see the massive vessel looming. Nothing appeared. Now their nagging anxieties lay with the fate of the ships they had left behind. Twenty of Convoy PQ17's vessels were lost when the U-boats and the Luftwaffe seized the golden opportunity.

Allied fighter aircraft while one U-boat was sunk.

When the might of the German navy next put to sea it was at the end of the year following some intensive exercises. Their target was a 14-ship convoy, JW51B, which set out from Scotland destined for Kola on 22 December. It was the second leg of a convoy, the first of which had crossed the sea without being spotted. A flotilla of destroyers joined up with the convoy on Christmas Day. Sailing to meet them were

The weather was poor, hampering visibility and identification of ships

the cruisers which had accompanied the first part of the convoy.

This time, the code-breakers let down the protection ships by failing to translate a vital enemy message in good time. *Admiral Hipper* and the pocket battleship *Lützow*, in the company of six destroyers, put to sea on 30 December. The British had no idea of the threat in the absence of deciphered enemy messages.

The weather was poor, hampering visibility and therefore the identification of ships whose shadows suddenly appeared in the mist. The first the Allied destroyers knew of the imminent danger was when the destroyer *Obdurate* was

fired on by one of the German destroyers.

While the convoy pulled back under the cover of a smoke screen, the destroyers set about repelling the advance. Four times the *Hipper* tried to break through to fire on the convoy and on each occasion the destroyers pushed it back. The only damage *Admiral Hipper* did was on the last attack when an eight inch shell ploughed into the *Onslow*. One other destroyer, *Achates*, was sunk along with the minesweeper *Bramble* before the Battle of the Barents Sea was over.

GERMAN DEFEAT

Hipper was forced to retire into a snow storm when it was hit three times. *Lützow*, although in a prime position to attack the convoy, kept its guns silent. A German destroyer which suddenly emerged from a snowstorm close to the *Sheffield*, by now pursuing *Hipper*, was soon sunk. The convoy continued on its way.

A squally, inconclusive battle, it was nevertheless a humiliating defeat for the German navy. One of its prestige ships was forced to pull away with substantial damage while the aim of the attack, the sinking of the convoy, was frustrated.

Hitler was furious at the debacle. On New Year's Day 1943 he threatened to decommission the German fleet completely and break up the big ships for scrap. Grand Admiral Raeder, he claimed, lacked the pioneering spirit of adventure that was necessary to win wars. Raeder responded immediately, by asking to be relieved of his command.

DARING PLAN

In his place came Admiral Karl Dönitz, hitherto commander of the U-boat service. Hitler much preferred Dönitz to his predecessor and, in turn, Dönitz was able to convince the Führer of the need to maintain the surface

Below: An X-craft, like those used against Tirpitz, *with its commander on deck.*

fleet. Nevertheless, he too was unable to find further successes, despite his efforts.

The British Admiralty chiefs appeared to have a greater faith in the destructive power of the German fleet than Hitler himself. In northern waters, they remained wary of the threat posed by *Tirpitz, Lützow* and *Scharnhorst.* Indeed, Arctic convoys were even cancelled on the basis that the big three might sail.

By September 1943 a daring plan was drawn up to rid the convoys of the naval menace once and for all. The aim was for that four-man midget submarines each armed with two one-ton charges to creep into the Norwegian anchorage at Altenfjord and place crippling explosives on the undersides of *Scharnhorst, Lützow* and *Tirpitz.* In utmost secrecy, the mission began with full-sized submarines towing the midgets to the mouth of the fiord.

Unluckily, *Scharnhorst* was at

sea for trials when the six midget submarines went into action. The tiny undersea craft assigned to blow up *Lützow* was lost as it made its way there. Another lost its tow and was forced to jettison the charges. A third caught fire and had to turn back. The success of submarines X5, X6 and X7 more than made up for the disappointing performances of the other three.

Hitler threatened to decommission the German fleet completely

---

When one of the midgets was spotted the alarm was raised. One was forced to surrender. The other sank with the loss of two lives and the third was sunk, although it is not known when and how. But all this unfolded after at least three of the charges had been laid. Although held captive on the ship itself, the seamen who surrendered refused to reveal the whereabouts of the explosives. Finally, the Germans got their answer when the mighty *Tirpitz* was lifted five feet out of the water. It would take seven months to fully complete the repairs. The two surviving submarine commanders, Lieutenants Donald Cameron and Godfrey Place, were rewarded after the war with the VC.

POOR WEATHER

Lützow abandoned the hunt for the Arctic convoys soon afterwards, returning to occupied Poland for operations in the Baltic. That left the last remaining danger – *Scharnhorst* – in Norwegian waters, fully equipped and ready for action. It was only a matter of time before she would venture forth to take on a convoy and this troubled the British commanders whose job it was to protect the merchant ships.

> ## Scharnhorst *had no idea It was heading towards the Royal Navy's big cruisers*

On Christmas Day 1943 the order to sail finally came through for the expectant *Scharnhorst* crew, eager as they were to salvage the good name of the German navy. The ship emerged from its protective fjord in the company of five destroyers that evening in search of convoy JW55B.

Poor weather once again played its part, this time to the advantage of the Allies.

Scharnhorst hived away from its destroyer escorts. Lacking the superior intelligence assistance open to the Allies, it had no idea it was heading towards some of the Royal Navy's big cruisers in the region.

First to fire on the German was HMS *Belfast* who picked up the enemy by radar. *Norfolk* then joined the battle by opening fire and scoring a hit. The British ships broke off their action, not wanting to scare *Scharnhorst* back into port.

Next to spy it was *Sheffield* some two hours later. In the spat that followed it was *Norfolk*'s turn to sustain damage. Yet the British cruisers did a brilliant job. They drove the unsuspecting *Scharnhorst* into the arms of Admiral Fraser on the *Duke of York*. At a range of 1,200 yards, the *Duke of York* opened fire with its devastating 14-inch guns. This time *Scharnhorst* fled to the east, making good ground against its pursuers. But critical damage forced the German ship to steady its speed. It gave British destroyers ample opportunity to unleash some torpedoes finally sinking the *Scharnhorst* at 7.45pm. Just 36 survivors were saved from a crew of 2,000.

Although *Tirpitz* rarely saw action, its presence alone was sufficient cause to divert air and naval craft from other duties. It would be aircraft that finally delivered the death-blows to this massive battlewagon.

TIRPITZ SUNK

The first sortie against Tirpitz began from Scapa Flow on 30 March 1944 with the *Duke of York*, *Belfast*, *Anson* and the aircraft carrier *Victorious* in 'Operation Tungsten'. On 3 April, 42 Barracuda aircraft loaded with powerful, armour-piercing bombs set off after their quarry, which was in Norway's Altenfjord, preparing to go to sea.

LEND-LEASE

Still hoping to keep his country out of war, President Roosevelt steered the Lend-Lease Act through Congress in March 1941. It gave the President powers to send military and material aid to countries at war with Germany and Italy with the sole provision being that they repay the loans at the end of the war. Although it was opposed fiercely by some factions, the Act had the beneficial effect of boosting the American defence industry even before the country went to war with Japan.

Above: *Wintry seas kept British sailors perpetually wet.*
Left: *Proud gunners on HMS* Duke of York *posed for the camera in front of their guns after sinking the German battlecruiser* Scharnhorst.

The action devastated the upper decks of *Tirpitz* and killed 122 men. Yet the super-ship stayed afloat, to the dismay of the Allies.

Several other bids to sink the ship by Fleet Air Arm aircraft were thwarted by poor weather. Aircraft were being lost in these vain attempts, forcing the Admiralty to think again. They called in the assistance of Bomber Command which had vast 'Tallboy' bombs.

Taking off from a Russian base on 15 September 1944, a cloud of Lancaster bombers rained 16 such bombs on the *Tirpitz*, causing extensive damage.

This time it would take nine months to make the repairs.

If the crippled *Tirpitz* had not moved to Tromsö that October, the Allies might have been satisfied. Germany wanted it as a floating gun platform to defend an expected invasion in the region by the Allies. Yet the Admiralty was disturbed by the ship's sudden activity and feared new attacks at sea.

On 29 October, 32 Lancaster bombers in 'Operation Obviate' caused considerable devastation. However, it wasn't until 'Operation Catechism' got underway involving the men and Lancaster aircraft of 617 Squadron – 'the Dambusters' – on 12 November 1944 that *Tirpitz* finally rolled over and died. About 1,000 crewmen were lost, trapped inside the great ship as it turned turtle.

CORAL SEA AND MIDWAY

Pearl Harbor may have been the most spectacular action that was undertaken by the Japanese navy but it certainly wasn't the last.

Here was the world's third most powerful navy staffed by efficient, skilled commanders and loyal sailors. It was their brief to roam the seas around Japan's newly acquired territories, protecting land-based flanks by fending off attacks from air and sea.

The Japanese navy played a major role in the domino fall of Asian and Pacific lands and islands, including that of Thailand, Hong Kong, the Philippines and Burma. Indeed, the noose put around Singapore by the Japanese navy during February 1942 ensured that none of the defending British or Australian troops could escape by sea and all those who survived the fighting were consequently taken prisoner.

When the Japanese cast their eyes in the direction of Java, the jewel they wanted in their crown, an allied naval force squared up to the challenge. Under Dutch officer Admiral Karel Doorman, a fleet of heavy and light cruisers and destroyers gathered from the British, American, Australian and Dutch navies determined to keep the Japanese out of the oil-rich colony.

BATTLE OF JAVA

The Battle of the Java Sea began on 27 February and was one of the largest naval confrontations the world had seen since World War I. Both sides seemed equally matched when they began a mutual bombardment with guns. But the Japanese wreaked havoc when they edged closer to the Allied fleet and opened up with torpedoes.

Hostilities ceased while the Allied ships refuelled only to resume within hours beneath the moonlight. Doorman was delighted when he once again encountered the Japanese and sought to end their plans to invade Java once and for all. Little did he realise that he was being snapped up in a tactical pincer. When more torpedoes blasted his force in a surprise

The Japanese wreaked havoc when they edged closer to the Allied fleet

Left: *Crews from USS* Lexington *go into action in the Coral Sea in May 1942.*
Below: *Carrying the wounded off USS* Marblehead *in Netherlands East docks after the* Battle of Java *in February 1942.*

from the carriers *Yorktown* and *Lexington* to attack two ports on Papua New Guinea which had just been overrun by the Japanese. Again, the results were negligible.

America determinedly began to gather its strength. US troops were sent to Darwin in Australia

The US felt confident enough only to take pot shots at the Japanese

and were by February under the command of General Douglas MacArthur. In fact, almost four times as many troops were sent from America to the Pacific at the time than took the shorter hop across the Atlantic to reinforce the Allied armies aiming to defeat Hitler.

Australian divisions, too, were recalled from the Middle East to help defend their homeland.

The tide of the Japanese successes was set to ebb as early as May 1942 with two historic seaborne clashes between Japan and America, one in the Coral Sea and the other around the island of Midway.

attack from a second angle there was chaos. In just seven hours, five Allied warships were sunk, while only one Japanese destroyer sustained damage. Doorman himself was lost when his cruiser *De Ruyter* went down.

BATTLE OF MIDWAY

So far the Emperor's fleet remained virtually unscathed by the ravages of war. During all its activities in the sea-borne invasions of Pacific and South East Asian islands only a total of four destroyers had been put out of action. Meanwhile, only four US destroyers had escaped to Australia from the treacherous waters around the Dutch East Indies. It seemed as if the

Japanese navy was invincible.

At the time the US felt confident enough only to take pot shots at the Japanese. The first skirmish took place in January when two US task forces bombed Japanese bases on the Marshalls and Gilberts. It was a tame event but nevertheless proved a small boost for American morale, being the first strike back at the enemy.

In March US planes took off

Above, right, far right: The triumphant Doolittle raid on Tokyo. A B-25 comes under starter's orders on its way to Japan. Doolittle is pictured later by his crashed aircraft in China.

BATTLE OF MIDWAY

Japan wanted a base within striking range of Hawaii. It also wanted the US fleet destroyed. Yamamoto hatched a plan to secure the base and lure the US Navy to its downfall in the process. He launched a diversionary attack on the Aleutians while he struck at Midway Island. Unfortunately for him the Americans knew he was coming and had put to sea. The first

wave of Japanese bombers caught many US aircraft on the ground at Midway. Nevertheless, enough got airborne to make a second Japanese strike necessary. It was while the Japanese were rearming that US *Admiral Spruance* struck. Aircraft from *Yorktown* and *Enterprise* destroyed four Japanese carriers; on the US side, *Yorktown* was sunk.

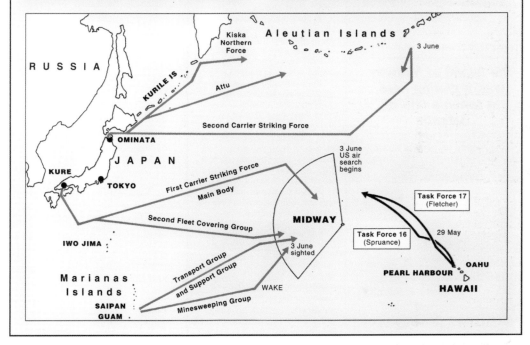

The Battle of the Coral Sea was not notable for its end result as the outcome was so murky it was difficult to distinguish a winner. Japan certainly wasn't defeated but its navy was for the first time halted. However, it was the first ever confrontation at sea to take place with the enemy ships placed hundreds of miles apart.

The firepower was carried to the opposition entirely by the planes stationed on the mighty carriers ranged against each other, capable of causing whole-sale devastation.

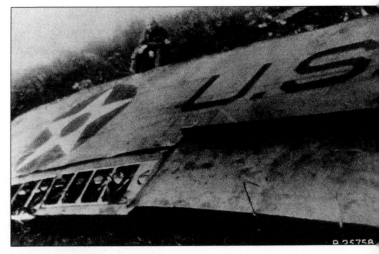

Meanwhile, the Battle of Midway proved to be a turning point in the fortunes of war and gave America the opportunity once more to assert naval superiority.

By May, Japan had control of New Britain, parts of Papua New Guinea and the majority of the Solomon Islands. It formed the outer edge of a

The island of Midway was a glaring hole in Japan's line of defence

Pacific empire which was fanning out towards Australia. The country's remaining aim was to secure the line of defence by conquering the remainder of Papua New Guinea.

Japanese priorities changed, however, with the most effective nuisance raid mounted by the Americans to date. It came with Lieutenant Colonel J. Doolittle's bombing raid over Tokyo in April mounted through an open

EYE WITNESS

Normand N. Silver, from Montreal, was a stoker first class. A member of the Royal Canadian Navy Volunteer Reserve, he served aboard aircraft carriers HMS *Thames* and HMCS *Punchuard* and also the minesweeper HMCS *Quatisino*.

❛I volunteered principally because I thought it was my duty. We all guessed that if Hitler wasn't stopped, then in 1945 or 1950 he might send his armies across to Canada.

The main action I saw was around the coast of Alaska in Quatisino. The Americans had a lot of their ships berthed up there and they didn't want another Pearl Harbor on their hands. Our job was to seek and destroy any Japanese subs that wanted to try their luck. This meant we were on round the clock patrol.

We were credited with killing one sub, but you could never be certain. In the engine room you didn't get to see much anyway.

It's hard to explain the pressure when you're fighting submarines. If you are a nervous person then you are in real trouble. You have to expect an attack every minute of every hour of every day. You don't know where the attack will come from and you don't know how long it will be before the next. You don't sleep much and you don't relax. I think that is the story of most men's war.❜

door from Midway. The island of Midway was held by a small garrison of American marines and was a glaring hole in Japan's line of defence. Although the damage caused during the 16-plane raid was light, it gave the Japanese hierarchy a shake up and compelled them to look again at domestic security.

FIRST BLOOD

Admiral Yamamoto confident in the continuing might of his navy, was appalled at the Tokyo air raid. He felt sure the best way ahead was to knock the heart out of the American navy once again. To do it he wanted to put Midway Island under threat.

Yamamoto knew America valued the island because of its proximity to Pearl Harbor and would defend it in force with its navy, so he planned to lure the remaining big ships into action and then destroy them.

Below: The last gasp of the Japanese carrier Shoho.

Meanwhile, the Japanese navy would also support a new thrust into Papua New Guinea where vital new forward bases could be installed.

Intelligence experts quickly grasped details of the preparations which would lead to the attack on Port Moresby, Papua New Guinea, after successfully decoding Japanese communications. Tempted by the presence of some of Japan's finest ships, America's Admiral Chester Nimitz hastily drew together as many ships as he could for a surprise rendezvous with the Japanese in the Coral Sea.

Australian cruisers which had gone ahead to secure a vital seaway for the heavier ships came under attack from Japanese planes but miracu-

lously escaped damage. So first blood in the four day battle went to the Americans when a wave of planes located the light carrier *Shoho* and blasted it out of the water. It left the Japanese in a quandary as they had no idea where the attacking aircraft had come from.

The US tally included three direct hits on the aircraft carrier Shokaku

---

As night fell, Japanese planes were launched to locate their hidden enemy but, hampered by low cloud, were forced to ditch their bombs and head back to base. En route, they happened across the USS *Yorktown* which sent up aircraft

Above: USS Lexington *sustains critical damage at the Battle of the Coral Sea.*

for a confrontation. In total 17 Japanese planes were lost that night against only three American casualties. In fact, for a while both sides suffered from the main disadvantage that this new, long-distance warfare offered. Neither could locate the enemy ships.

TACTICAL VICTORY

The next day both sides sent waves of aircraft in pursuit of the other. The US tally included three direct hits on the aircraft carrier *Shokaku* which was forced to limp back to its home port for major repairs.

Meanwhile, the Japanese struck the carriers *Yorktown*

and *Lexington*. The *Yorktown* escaped with comparatively minor damage while the *Lexington* was crippled by three bombs and two torpedoes. It was to sink days later following an internal explosion. Both admirals decided against continuing the battle and pulled away from their respective battle lines.

The Lexington *was to sink days later following an internal explosion*

Japan appeared to have inflicted the most damage on the opposition. In reality, the tactical victory belonged to the Americans. The Japanese had been contained and were forced to call off their strike at Port Moresby due to the large losses of essential aircraft.

EYE WITNESS

Mitsuo Fuchida, who led the air strike against Pearl Harbor, was aboard the aircraft carrier *Akagi* during the Battle of Midway.

❝For Japan, the Battle of Midway was indeed a tragic defeat. The Japanese Combined Fleet, placing its faith in "quality rather than quantity" had long trained and prepared to defeat a numerically superior enemy. Yet at Midway a stronger Japanese force went down to defeat before a weaker enemy.

Not only were our participating surface forces far superior in number to those of the enemy but the initiative was in our hands. Nor were we inferior qualitatively in the crucial element of air strength which played a major role throughout the Pacific War. In spite of this we suffered a decisive defeat such as the modern Japanese navy had never before experienced.

With Midway as the turning point, the fortunes of war appeared definitely to shift from our own to the Allied side. The defeat taught us many lessons and impelled our navy, for the first time since the outbreak of war, to indulge in critical self examination.

The Japanese public, of course, was not told the truth about the battle. Instead, Imperial General Headquarters announcements tried to make it appear that both sides had suffered equal losses. The United States, however, promptly announced to the whole world the damage inflicted on the Japanese accurately naming the ships damaged and sunk. Thus it was clear that our efforts to conceal the truth were aimed at maintaining morale at home rather than keeping valuable knowledge from the enemy.

I myself had a rather painful taste of the extreme measures taken to preserve secrecy. During the battle I had been wounded on board *Akagi* and then transferred to hospital ship *Hikawa Maru* which brought me to Yokosuka Naval Base. I was not moved ashore until after dark when the streets of the base were deserted. Then I was taken to the hospital on a covered stretcher and carried in through the rear entrance. My room was placed in complete isolation. No nurses or corpsmen were allowed entry and I could not communicate with the outside.

In such a manner were those wounded at Midway cut off from the rest of the world. It was really confinement in the guise of medical treatment and I sometimes had the feeling of being a prisoner of war.❞

Above: Shokaku, *pulled back to Japan following the Coral Sea battle.*

The Japanese High Command decided to abandon that first objective in favour of the capture of Midway, a far more ambitious undertaking. While the commanders had sought outright victory in the Coral Sea, they were convinced by their own glowing track record that the US navy could still be annihilated.

Once again intelligence reports gave the United States fair warning of the Japanese plans which they had tagged Operation MI. And again Admiral Nimitz called in as much support as he could from ships and submarines in the region. Aircraft carriers *Enterprise* and *Hornet* were

Japanese commanders were convinced that the US Navy could be annihilated

summoned along with the damaged *Yorktown* which had been hurriedly repaired so it could rejoin the action. They sailed with six cruisers, 14 destroyers

and 19 submarines to the north of Midway to await the attackers. On the island itself the garrison had been strengthened and increased numbers of aircraft brought in.

The Japanese strike force, including half the navy's aircraft carriers, came from several directions, one arm to land troops, another to tackle the American naval presence.

SUNRISE RAID

At dawn on 4 June, bombers took off from Japanese aircraft carriers and blasted the land-based defenders of Midway. Aircraft from the island attempting to deflect the invaders suffered huge losses and made little impact. It seemed the Japanese navy was to escape once more intact.

But before a second wave of bombers could be launched, Japan's Vice-Admiral Chuichi Nagumo was told of the presence of enemy ships signalled from the first attack by their planes. Instead of continuing bombardment of the already shattered small island, he decided to swing north and pursue the US Navy prey.

By now torpedo bombers from all the aircraft carriers had been launched and began a comprehensive strike lasting 55 minutes on three of Japan's aircraft carriers. Japanese pilots supported by anti-aircraft fire defended the ships fiercely. Of the 41 US planes which set out

Of the 41 US planes which set out on that mission, only six returned

on that mission, only six returned. It seemed victory was in the grasp of the Japanese. Yet they barely had time to congratulate themselves on their luck and judgement when the subsequent wave of dive-bombers sent by the Americans arrived on the scene.

As the Japanese sailors and airmen struggled to rearm in the disarray, bombs rained down on

Above: Akagi, *another Japanese navy gem, weaves its way out of fire at Midway.*

them and exploded on the decks which were crowded with aircraft. Afterwards, Japanese sailors told how the raid took them by surprise – which is why the prized planes were on deck. It took a matter of minutes to

It took a matter of minutes to reduce the carriers to smoking crates

reduce the carriers to smoking crates. Two of the Japanese carriers, the *Kaga* and *Soryu*, sank within hours. The *Akagi* drifted on hopelessly and helplessly until a Japanese submarine punctured it for the last time the following day.

Half an hour afterwards, bombers from an unscarred Japanese carrier, the *Hiryu*, went

Below: *The giant USS* Yorktown *lists helplessly following Midway.*

looking for revenge. Their target was the *Yorktown* on which the battle commander Rear Admiral Frank Fletcher was based. A volley of hits during two onslaughts finally put paid to the veteran carrier which was abandoned by its crew later the same day. A Japanese submarine sent its skeleton to the bottom two days later.

It was not the end of the bloody battle, however. At 5pm, less than 12 hours after the conflict began, USS *Enterprise* – nicknamed the 'Big E' – launched bombers in pursuit of the *Hiryu*. They caught up with their target and sparked a catastrophic blaze on board. The *Hiryu*, Japan's fourth and final aircraft carrier in the offensive, was finally laid to rest by a Japanese cruiser.

Admiral Yamamoto continued his assault on Midway from the heavy cruisers that remained.

But when two of them collided trying to evade an American submarine, he was finally convinced of its folly.

HUGE VICTORY

The American navy's Rear-Admiral Raymond Spruance risked one final foray against the Japanese, holing one of the already damaged cruisers and sinking the other. Even then Admiral Yamamoto was ready to spring a trap on the American fleet by luring them into combat with a light force and then pounce with much bigger guns.

Admiral Spruance was not to be drawn. Content with his enormous victory, he headed for home, leaving *Yamamoto* helpless in his wake. A Japanese submarine managed to claim one destroyer before Spruance pulled out of the region.

The decisive result was

Left: Admiral Raymond Spruance.

personnel, in which the Army, Navy and Marine Corps are all represented. They have added another shining page to their record of achievements.'

From a position of seemingly indomitable strength, the Japanese navy had within a few short days been for the first time mauled and gored. The defeat was so terrible that it was cloaked in secrecy in Japan for the duration of the war. While scores of heroic US pilots lost their lives in the battle, they inflicted devastation on their hitherto unbroken enemy and it was their courage alone that turned the tables. Four aircraft carriers, together with more than 300 aircraft and the cream of the Japanese naval pilots were

The steamroller successes of the Japanese forces had been stopped

at the bottom of the ocean. The steamroller successes of the Japanese forces had been stopped, Midway was saved and further plans by the Japanese to occupy other Pacific islands were shelved.

trumpeted around the Allied world. From Pearl Harbor Admiral Nimitz announced: '. . . the enemy's damage is very heavy indeed, involving several ships in each of the carrier, battleship, cruiser and transport classes. This damage is far out of proportion to that which we have received.

'The brunt of the defence to date has fallen upon our aviation

Below: Admiral Nimitz considers his next move from the bridge of a destroyer.

THE SOLOMONS

The Battle of Midway sent Admiral Yamamoto and his mariners home with a bloody nose. Yet the Japanese still fostered aggressive ambitions. Among them was a plan to sink the US Navy and once again win dominance over the islands and waters of the Pacific Ocean.

By May 1942 Japanese forces occupied Tulagi, one of the Solomon Islands. The Americans were keen to keep this Pacific route open as it represented a vital line of communication with Australia. So American military planners devised a plan, 'Operation Watchtower', to rout the Japanese from the region.

Initially, US and Australian troops were to liberate Tulagi and a few other selected islands. Then their aim was to free the rest of the occupied Solomon Islands and Papua in New Guinea. The final phase of the operation would be the capture of the Bismarck Archipelago; New Britain and New Ireland.

The Americans busied themselves gathering their forces, including three aircraft carriers,

a battleship, 14 cruisers and plenty of destroyers. After setting off from Wellington, New Zealand, on 22 July, there were four days of practice runs on a remote Pacific Island before the operation got underway.

Meanwhile, the Japanese were also making plans. They had high hopes of capturing Port Moresby in Papua, their target before the Battle of the Coral Sea. Instead of using a waterborne force this time,

they would go overland. A fleet comprising five heavy and three light cruisers, five submarines and a number of destroyers was based at Rabaul on New Britain and the Japanese further tried to strengthen their position by

Above: A Marine's eye-view of a Pacific landing operation, this one at Tulagi. *Left:* A Grumann Hellcat fighter returns to USS in the Pacific. *Below:* US Marines practise for their invasion of the Solomon Islands.

building new airfields right across the occupied territories.

The islands they were fighting over offered little more than strategic value to either side. The Solomon Islands had been a British Protectorate although two of the major islands fell

---

On 7 August, 11,000 US Marines landed on the Solomons without meeting opposition

---

under the domain of Australia. They stretch for some 600 miles encircling a waterway called The Slot.

It was a fighting man's nightmare. The climate was damp and humid encouraging thick jungle and forest to cling to the sides of the mountains throughout the centre of the isles alongside smokey volcanoes. On the coastal plains there were, apart from coconut plantations, acres of dense, spikey grass, sharp as a knife.

On the morning of 7 August, 11,000 US Marines landed on Guadalcanal in the Solomons without meeting any opposition. Within 24 hours they had taken the airstrip as their own.

The three battalions that landed on Tulagi were not so fortunate. The Marines encountered fierce resistance from the 1,500 Japanese defenders of the island. It cost the Marines 108 of their men before the island was theirs, in addition to many more wounded.

JAPAN ENRAGED

It was the work of a few days to win the islands. Ahead lay a bloody six months as they battled to keep them out of the hands of the Japanese.

The Japanese were surprised and enraged when they found out that one of their new prizes had been overrun. First response by Imperial General Headquarters was to send a convoy of 500 troops to reinforce

EYE WITNESS

Despite being sunk while a soldier in North Africa, Australian George Miles went on to join the US Army Small Ships Section.

❛I received a medical discharge from the Australian Army in 1943 but at the time nothing much appealed in civilian life in Sydney. Within six months I joined the US Army Water Transport Division and served in a couple of invasions in Indonesia, New Guinea and the Philippines.

With the amount of casualties suffered by the US merchant navy, they were prepared to make you a seaman in a matter of weeks. The first ship I signed on was all American. These men had never met an Australian before. They called me 'Limey' and reckoned I came from London. But there were a few Aussies in the force.

For the invasion at Leyte I was on a tug patrol. The amount of sea power the Americans had was incredible. There was no way they were going to lose.❜

Below: The first wave of Marines find their feet on the Solomons.

the islands. However, a US submarine put paid to the plan with a single torpedo. Those troops that survived were forced to turn back to New Britain.

However, their next strike was markedly more successful. Armed with reconnaissance information about the size and strength of the enemy forces, Admiral Mikawa and a rogue squadron slipped in to The Slot unnoticed by the watching Allied ships on 8 August, their silhouettes blotted out by bad weather.

SAVO ISLAND

Aided by flares dropped from his carrier planes, Admiral Mikawa gleefully caught sight of the Royal Australian Navy cruiser *Canberra* and the US Navy cruiser *Chicago*, patrolling The Slot. Both Allied ships were unaware their lines had been penetrated by enemy vessels. It meant the Japanese squadron was able to open up at point-blank range with shells and torpedoes.

Canberra came off worse.

Right: Japanese air power prior to the 'Marianas Turkey Shoot'.

The damage that the ship sustained was so bad it had to be abandoned. *Chicago* escaped with just one hit from a torpedo. But before its gunners could fire back, the Japanese squadron was heading north, straight towards another Allied patrol. Three more American cruisers were set alight and sank. The Japanese squadron pulled out at speed, completely unscathed. Even though they had left the transports delivering to Guadalcanal untouched, victory

in the Battle of Savo Island was theirs for the cost of 38 men, while more than 1,000 American and Australian sailors perished.

Eleven days later a sizeable force of Japanese soldiers charged with winning back Guadalcanal set off from Rabaul under the protection of two aircraft carriers, a light carrier, two battleships, five cruisers and 17 destroyers.

Allied ships were unaware their lines had been penetrated by enemy vessels

Ready to meet them this time was an Allied task force of three aircraft carriers and a battleship. Japan's Admiral Kondo sent his light aircraft carrier ahead as a decoy. It drew the fire of the American fleet air arm and sank on the afternoon of 24 August.

When the wave of Japanese aircraft arrived, there was a reception committee of US fighters to meet them. Although the Japanese lost a number of planes, the Battle of the Eastern Solomons was inconclusive. Both navies withdrew that night. It was the land-based bombers who later attacked the Japanese transports that forced them away from their destination.

The sorties were nicknamed the 'Tokyo Express' by the watching Marines

The Japanese navy ships sped down The Slot regularly, both to fire on the American positions and to land troops and supplies. The sorties were nicknamed the 'Tokyo Express' by the watching Marines.

At the end of August the US aircraft carrier *Saratoga* was torpedoed by a submarine and was forced back to Pearl Harbor for repairs. The US naval strength in the area, already inferior to Japan's, continued to take a battering from both submarines and aircraft attacks.

America had to wait six weeks before replying in kind. A squadron escorting some American transporters happened on a Japanese naval force which was preparing to fire on a US-controlled airstrip. In the confrontation that followed one Japanese cruiser and two destroyers were sunk for the cost of one American destroyer.

A major Japanese effort to recapture Guadalcanal was knocked back to the end of October but still the Japanese would not give up. At the ensuing Battle of Santa Cruz, the outnumbered Americans lost seventy aircraft compared to an estimated 100 downed from the Japanese ranks. All Japan's ships stayed afloat although five sustained damage.

SAVAGE ACTION

It wasn't until the three-day naval battle of Guadalcanal that the American Navy found the outright victory which had eluded it so far. It began with a savage encounter between a small American escort force against a powerful Japanese squadron. Although the US contingent was cut through during the battle, which lasted just 24 minutes, it saved the Guadalcanal airstrip from bombardment and it bought valuable time for the pursuing US task force.

Two days afterwards, the Americans unleashed their fire-power at the Japanese with another close range bloody battle at sea. A Japanese battleship was so badly damaged she had to be scuttled. One Japanese and three American destroyers were sunk. The key to the American success was the attack the following day on the transports bringing an attacking Japanese force to Guadalcanal. Three-fifths of the landing troops were annihilated. The rest were rendered an ineffective fighting force, trapped as they were without supplies.

The final conflict in seas surrounding the Solomons was the Battle of Tassaronga, which turned out to be equally damaging to both Japan and America. The losses suffered by the Japanese navy were sufficient to persuade its leaders not to venture again into such fateful waters.

Japanese destroyers went to the Solomons just once more, to help in the evacuation of

tally of damage to the Japanese was a destroyer which sank and damage to seven cruisers and three more destroyers. In later air battles an estimated two-thirds of the Japanese carrier aircraft were gunned down, the cream of its pilots lost forever. It finally squeezed the Japanese navy out of Rabaul once and for all.

US SUPERIORITY

At home Japan tried to nurture a new generation of navy pilots to

by Admiral Spruance. At last the Americans had found an antidote to Japan's Zero fighter. The new US Hellcat was faster and more powerful.

It was known among Americans as 'The Great Marianas Turkey Shoot' after waves of Japanese planes were bagged and brought down. In total the Japanese lost 223 aircraft. Only 17 aircraft returned from an attacking force of 69 in the first wave of aircraft.

EYE WITNESS

Swedish-born Nels Olson, 72, from Chicago, USA, was a gunner in the US Navy Armed Guard, who later served in the Pacific at the time of the Japanese surrender.

❮My war ended in the Pacific. I arrived on the island of Okinawa two or three weeks after the Japanese surrender. All the guys wore guns when they went ashore but there were no problems. The Japanese bowed to us whenever they saw us. It was like they went out of their way to show they did not want to fight.

For a country that caused us such problems I was amazed at how primitive some of the people were. I once had to supervise the unloading of coal from a cargo ship. They did it by sending men on board with two buckets strapped to their shoulders. It was amazing to watch.❯

troops from Guadalcanal in January 1943.

With every month that passed the Americans managed to reinforce their navy and its vital fleet air arm. There was little the Japanese could do to replace its lost ships, planes or pilots.

The Japanese Navy took its next severe pounding in port at Rabaul in October 1943. Aircraft from the growing number of American carriers in the region launched two raids. The

replace those it had lost in the Solomons and soon afterwards. Their destination was the Marianas, a series of islands being heavily reinforced by the Japanese to fend off US invasion.

But the students were ill-equipped to deal with intense warfare and they were lost in their droves. In the two-day Battle of the Philippine Sea in June 1944 the Japanese navy received yet another drubbing from Task Force 58 commanded

In the next wave the Japanese lost 98 out of its force of 130 planes and in the disastrous fourth wave, just nine survived out of 82. The Americans were down by just 29 aircraft. In addition, three Japanese aircraft carriers were sunk.

The Americans outnumbered the Japanese in all classes of ship. None of the four Japanese aircraft carriers had planes aboard and all were listing from battle damage.

AMPHIBIOUS WARFARE

When British, Australian and New Zealand troops tried to land at Gallipoli during World War I, the sea ran with their blood.

Bullets from defending Turkish guns rained down on unfortunate troops as soon as they emerged from boats just short of the shore line. It remains one of the most appalling military disasters in history in which there were more than a quarter of a million casualties on the Allied side alone.

Winston Churchill, then First Lord of the Admiralty and a keen exponent of the plan, resigned over the Gallipoli debacle and it blighted his career for years afterwards.

The adventure achieved little, but served to illustrate the gap in military manoeuvres which reduced soldiers, trying to take a fortified coast, to cannon fodder.

The lesson was not lost on Major Earl Ellis in the United

Left: *The Americans led the field in the development of amphibious techniques.*
Below: *LVTs and LCWs approach the island of Aguni Shima in the Pacific.*

States. He realised the importance of safe transport of troops from ship to shore during invasion. His aim was to give American Marines the best chance of survival. As early as 1921 he had written a 50,000-word plan which was intended as a blueprint for a Marine advance in the Pacific. He argued that men should be specifically trained to overcome the hazards of amphibious warfare and that the Marines were the best task force to undergo that instruction.

LANDING VEHICLES

Ellis wrote: 'It is not enough that the troops be skilled infantry men and jungle men or artillery men of high morale. They must be skilled water men and jungle men who know it can be done – marines with marine training.'

By 1933 the Fleet Marine Force came into being to oversee the challenge of amphibious landings. There followed a series

of experiments with tracked landing vehicles which could travel in the sea, offering protection to soldiers on leaving landing boats. It wasn't until the war years, however, that an effective ship-to-shore craft was constructed, the LVT or Landing Vehicle, Tracked. Even then, due to its mechanical

'It wasn't until the war that an effective ship-to-shore craft was constructed

shortcomings, the 'amtrac' was mainly used to travel up beaches rather than on to them.

Boatbuilder Andrew Higgins, from New Orleans, then came to the notice of the US Marines after he built a shallow craft vessel for crossing the Mississippi River. It beached with ease and could be pulled back into the water at speed. Here was a craft far superior to anything else the marines had found to date.

Bizarrely, the US Navy's Bureau of Ships was reluctant to adopt a design from someone outside the service. Continuing its costly probes into making landing craft for years afterwards, it still failed to come up with an adequate rival to Higgins' model. The fiasco was roundly condemned by a Senate Committee during the war.

EYE WITNESS

Gordon Kendall, from Portsmouth, UK, served with 4 Commando.

❝British commandos were assigned to set out guns on either side of the Dieppe basin ready for a seaborne Canadian invasion force. Around 150 of us went ashore before dawn, did the job and got out.

The Canadians didn't arrive until much later. That was a mistake because they were absolutely chopped to pieces. We reckoned that of the 3,000 who went ashore, 900 died on the beach and more than a thousand were taken prisoner.

The irony is that they should never even have been there. The British Northumberland Division had been training for this operation but the Canadians were restless and took it over. It seems some of their commanding officers were hungry for action after hanging around in the UK for so long. ❞

Below: US troops emerge from the bowels of USS LSM-168 in March 1945.

That original Higgins design finally became the father of the LCP(L)s, Landing Craft Personnel (Large) used by both Britain and the Americans during World War II. Work continued throughout the war to perfect landing craft of differing capabilities; some were armed, some were ocean-going; some were tracked. They proved a formidable amphibious force.

MARINE TRAINING

The Japanese were also testing the possibilities of amphibious landing craft. The Japanese army built an early version of LSDs (Landing Ships, Dock) for their operations in China during the 1930s called Shinshu Maru. Inside its cavernous interior the vessel could house a number of landing craft which rolled up a ramp and out of the ship's open doors.

In order to land troops, they had a 46ft landing craft which they modified to bear arms for the men of the Special Naval Landing Force, the equivalent of the marines.

In Britain, only a fleeting interest was expressed in the dilemma. Recovering from its battering in World War I, the service chiefs in the main neglected to look ahead and plan for another war. It wasn't until 1937 that Admiral Sir

> *In Britain, service chiefs neglected to look ahead and plan for another war*

Reginald Ernest-Ernle-Plunkett-Drax suggested that several brigades of Royal Marines should be trained especially for amphibious landings. The eventual outcome was the establishment of the Inter-Service Training

Above: An armada of LSTs offload onto a recently captured beach.

and Development Centre based near Portsmouth, in southern England, which involved all the defence forces and developed a policy for amphibious operations.

Staff in the unit addressed the problems of specialised landing craft, navy gunfire support, floating piers to aid the disembarkation of tanks and trucks and an array of workable tactics.

TANK SHIPMENT

The ranks of the Royal Marines, standing at just 12,000 when war broke out, were substantially boosted. Their role of manning guns aboard Royal Navy ships and guarding navy shore-based establishments was expanded to man commando raiding parties.

Following the evacuation of British troops from Dunkirk in 1940, the need for armoured ocean-going craft able to carry men and machines into shallow water was once again highlighted. While there was relief at the number of soldiers who got out

Right: Motorised equipment from an LST rolls on to a 'rhino' to reach the sand.

of France, they barely managed to bring back a gun between them. The army lost every tank and major piece of artillery it had committed to France. If a suitable transport craft had been available, at least some of it might have been saved.

Until his men and tanks could be transported across the Channel, there would be no opportunity for Churchill to make up the ground he had lost in France. Tanks were a primary tool of war and shipment of them in any amphibious assault was vital.

A British prototype Landing Ship, Tank (LST) came into

being in October 1940. It was further improved when tankers made in Britain especially to traverse a troublesome sand bank in South America were converted to carry tanks. These were fitted to carry 20 tanks or 33 trucks but were unable to come close into shore.

The army lost every single tank and major piece of artillery it had committed to France

A new design was created to overcome the problem. The problems posed in getting the ships produced in Britain's shipyards was overcome when America agreed to take on the contract. Shipyards across the States became involved in producing LSTs, launching the first of the new design on 7 September 1942. Before the war was over, 1,050 more came out of US yards to see action in amphibious landings across the world. They would join the Landing

Ships, Infantry (LSI) and Landing Ships, Dock (LSD) already in service. The seeds of a successful amphibious landing force had been sown, but there was a long way to go before it would threaten the Reich.

DIEPPE LANDINGS

The Allied landings in Dieppe in August 1942 ended in almost complete disaster. The Allies referred to it as a raid while Hitler insisted it was a fully-fledged invasion.

The Allied force consisted of 5,000 Canadians, 1,057 British, 50 Americans and a few Free French soldiers. They ran into difficulty when the landing craft were swept along the beach. Armed German trawlers happened on the scene and began shooting at a British section.

The Germans greeted the arrival of 27 light tanks with a hail of gunfire. All were destroyed while the landing forces suffered appalling casualties. It was just 9am when the troops were pulled out. More than 1,500 prisoners were taken and most of the equipment was left scattered on the beach.

> **The Germans greeted the arrival of 27 light tanks with a hail of gunfire**

A clutch of Allied boats was sunk and almost 100 of the aircraft dispatched to provide aerial cover were shot down. It was the largest in a succession of raids.

The Dieppe incident led Prime Minister Churchill and other British commanders to doubt the sense of making another attempt against well-fortified German positions.

Valuable lessons were learned from the raids in time to execute the biggest amphibious landing ever, on D-Day.

EYE WITNESS

Henry 'Marty' Martin, from Chicopee, Massachusetts, USA, stormed Omaha beach in a DD (Duplex Drive amphibious tank). He landed in the first wave aboard LCT 586.

❛My job was to drop the ramp. These men trained to get out in 30 seconds but we didn't have time to check that they all got out safely. We did four drops that day.

For our first we laid off 200 yards because it was so rough. The next one, though, we went right on to the beach. We were carrying three tanks and they had to get in close.

I watched the first tank take off to the right. He made it, but the second took a direct hit as he tried to follow. The third stayed closer to the shore and looked to be OK.

As they left a US officer came up to me literally holding the insides of his stomach in his hands. He was one of the underwater demolition experts who had gone in in advance of the landings. Those guys didn't have very good luck. I think nine in every ten were killed.

He told me we were the first ship to come right on to the beach. We got him back to the hospital ship but I never knew how he made out.

Sometimes historical accounts fail to mention the disputes and the arguments that took place. There was one officer who had it in for me. After D-Day I got a ten-day leave to Kilmarnock in Scotland and the thought of going back to work for this guy meant I decided to unofficially extend that leave for another ten days.

I served 30 days in the brig at Plymouth for that. But I reckoned that just because a man's an officer doesn't mean he can't be an asshole as well!❜

***Below:** A few moment's relaxation by an empty landing craft for weary troops.*

EYE WITNESS

Ernie Marshall joined the Royal Navy at the end of 1942 aged 18. After three months training he joined a combined operations unit and was stationed on LCT554.

❝When I saw it my heart dropped. It looked pretty rough. The living quarters and the engine room were at the back while the tanks were in the front. There were 12 of us aboard. I was a stoker in the engine room. I just learnt as I went, I had no training whatsoever. Eventually we sailed to North Africa. It seemed like the whole of the Atlantic was coming up at us. Then we had to slide down these huge waves. I stayed in the engine room.

We worked every port up to Tripoli. Once we carried German prisoners of war. Then we joined the landings at Sicily. We beached at 4am when it was very quiet. Next morning the Germans really came at us. We stayed there ferrying supplies for a couple of months until we went up to Anzio. We were stuck there for three months surrounded by Germans. The beachhead was about five miles inland. Once the Germans broke through and got to within two miles of the beach. Eventually, they were pushed back again.

The long range guns were more frightening than anything. Shells just landed without warning. One morning a plane attacked us. Shrapnel from one of its bombs came right through the stern, across the mess deck, through the next steel bulk head and into the engine room. Everywhere was filled with smoke and sparks. One bloke had an injured shoulder but the rest of us survived.

That afternoon we were alongside a boat unloading supplies when a bomb from a plane went straight into the hold. We managed to get ashore. Survivors got thrown into the water and were shouting to us for help. We fished a lot out of the water but we couldn't stop because the ship was burning so fiercely. That was the worst day of the war for me.

It was two and a half years before I got home. On the whole I enjoyed the experience. The rest of the crew became like family. The captain never gave us any trouble and we had some good times. I had never travelled before so to see Arabs in their African villages was really something.❞

In the rough seas off the Normandy coast, British soldiers were instructed to carry not only their 20lb packs but also bicycles for use in France. On arrival, they were told to ditch the cycles in order to fight for their lives – and never saw the cycles again.

No amount of improvements in the technique of amphibious landings could save the infantry from being held in cramped vessels for hours, sometimes days, on end before the final moment of invasion came. The food was generally poor and home comforts were lacking. Only the lucky ones got to sleep in hammocks.

Before attacking Guam in July 1944, the US 3rd Marine Division spent weeks suffering like this at sea. The Channel weather on D-Day was awful.

Below: Australian troops boarding a beach landing ship after successful operations at Lae, New Guinea.

Specially trained civilian aircraft recognition teams from the Royal Observer Corps put to sea with the troops on 6 June 1944. This was to cut the rate of Allied aircraft shot down by jittery comrades on the ground.

The design of specialised landing craft was improved. They kept their speed and low silhouettes but were enlarged to carry more men. The armament they carried was also beefed up to provide greater support for the men they off-loaded.

The beaches of Normandy, unlike that of Dieppe, were away from major towns where the German defences were strongest.

JAPAN'S LAST GASP

When America's war horse was harnessed, it galloped through the Pacific at a thundering pace. Advances made in 1944 by the combined efforts of the Army, Navy and Marine Corps mimicked those of the Japanese three years before.

By now the US strength at sea was awesome. Since the outbreak of the war with Japan a further 21 aircraft carriers had come into service capable of holding a total of about 3,000 planes.

That was in addition to a splendid array of new battleships, transports, cruisers, destroyers and landing craft newly arrived and ready for action.

On the other hand, the Japanese had suffered severe losses at sea and were continuing to do so. Apart from naval conflicts, the Japanese ships had to contend with the numerous American submarines now patrolling the Pacific in force.

Japan, so dependent on the resources it imported from overseas, was unable to replenish the fleet, with much of its merchant fleet being sunk bringing home vital war production materials. By 1944 two thirds of the tanker fleet

bringing oil to Japan from the South Pacific fields had been wrecked by the Allies. While 40 per cent of the oil produced in those fields reached Japan in 1942, only 13.5 per cent was unloaded at Japanese ports in 1944 due to the efficiency of the submarines and fleet ships. Oil reserves were dwindling fast, threatening to grind the war effort to a halt. Hopelessly outnumbered, it seemed on paper that Japan's navy was all but finished.

When it became clear that the US was preparing to attack the Philippines in the autumn of 1944, however, Japan drew

In the autumn of 1944 Japan drew up plans for one final sea battle

up the plans for one final sea battle which could have tipped the balance in its favour. It was a simple manoeuvre by what remained of the Japanese navy

Left: *All eyes turn skywards when a Kamikaze aircraft is spotted in the vicinity.*
Below: *Vice Admiral Jisaburo Ozawa was defeated by superior US tactics.*
Bottom: *The scale of the US seapower is illustrated in this picture of Task Force 58 in the Pacific.*

Above: Vice-Admiral William Halsey looks out to sea and draws up a winning strategy for the American fleet.

but might have been enough to defend the Philippines. And it was a gamble worth risking for the Japanese. If the Americans had installed themselves on the Philippines, it would have meant the end of oil supplies

> **The arrival of Admiral Ozawa and his decoy carriers went unnoticed**

from the Dutch East Indies, now more crucial than ever before to the teetering Japanese.

After the war, Japan's Admiral S. Toyoda explained his country's actions: 'If the worst should happen there was a chance that we would lose the entire fleet; but felt that chance had to be taken . . . should we lose in the Philippine operations, the shipping lane to the south would be

completely cut off so that the fleet if it should come back to Japanese waters, could not obtain its fuel supply. There would be no sense in saving the fleet at the expense of the loss of the Philippines.'

In essence, Japan's ploy was to use what was left of the carrier fleet as a decoy to lure the main thrust of the American navy away from the Philippines. Once the large ships were out of the way, a two-pronged attack from the sea was planned on Leyte, the small island in the centre of the Philippines on which the Americans had already began an assault.

AMERICAN ATTACK

The operation began badly for the Japanese. One arm of the fleet earmarked to blast Leyte was itself fired on by American submarines on 23 October, well before it reached its destination. Three cruisers were damaged.

There was a two-fold result to this action. The strength of this attacking arm was depleted and all the American shipping for miles around became focused on this single Japanese force. Despite frantic efforts to announce his presence by uncoded radio messages, the arrival of Admiral Ozawa and his decoy carriers went unnoticed by the Americans.

Now American battleships joined the attack on the hapless Japanese detachment whose brief had been to slip unobtrusively into the Philippine Sea. Japanese land-based bombers and also from distant carriers rained bombs on the American fleet, crippling the carrier *Princeton*.

There was a high price for this success, however. The relentless onslaught by the American fighter planes finally sank the majestic *Musashi*, one of the biggest battleships in the world. It had been struck by 19 torpedoes and 17 bombs. Japanese commander Admiral Kurita finally broke off from the action and appeared to retreat.

BATTLE OF LEYTE

The absence of Japan's aircraft carriers was spotted by the sharp-witted Vice-Admiral William 'Bull' Halsey, who was in control of the American fleet. When he sent out reconnaissance planes to assess the movements of the Japanese fleet, Ozawa was finally detected. It seemed a golden opportunity to Halsey who gathered up his entire force to pursue the prized

carrier, Japan's last surviving ship of the type in action.

Almost as soon as American backs were turned, Kurita reversed his course and began steaming towards his initial target once more, Leyte.

American sea defences were badly lacking after Halsey set off with his full complement of ships. Mostly it comprised a small force protecting the landing beaches at Leyte, just six escort carriers and five destroyers. In charge, Vice-Admiral T.C. Kinkaid sent a series of urgent messages to Halsey, asking him to return at once. Halsey, however, was determined to snare the carrier once and for all. He refused to turn around until he delivered some decisive damage to the carrier force. Only time would tell if his instincts were the right ones.

Meanwhile, the destroyers were defending the vulnerable section of the US fleet as best they could. One escort carrier and three destroyers were lost, however, in its retreat.

Now Kurita was steaming

Left: *The carrier USS* Princeton *is hosed after taking a direct hit from a bomber during the Battle of Leyte.*

Above: *Devastation among Japanese shipping in the run-up to the invasion of the Philippine island of Leyte.*

towards the Leyte Gulf where a collection of US transports and men lay wide open to attack. Then he hesitated. As Kinkaid watched and waited with bated breath, Kurita finally pulled his forces to the north, away from the beach targets.

Thanks to confusion among the intercepted radio messages aboard Kurita's ship, he believed Halsey and his powerful ships were only 70 miles away when in fact there were hundreds of miles between them. He was also gravely concerned about the risk of attack by air when he himself had no air cover.

SITTING DUCKS

While the survivors of Kurita's force escaped, the fate of the carriers gave credence to Halsey's actions. All four – *Chitose, Zuikaku, Zuiho* and *Chiyoda* – were sunk, completing the effective destruction of the Japanese navy. With the long-range power of aircraft, Japan's remaining battleships were no more than sitting ducks to the enemy. There was little more

EYE WITNESS

Yasuo Kuwahara was a skilled Japanese pilot who was in a Kamikaze squadron in the final year of the war.

❝ It was New Year's Day 1945 at Hiro Air Base in western Honshu. Captain Yoshiro Tsubaki, commander of the Fourth Fighter Squadron, has just called a special meeting. A silence settled over us.

After a long while, he spoke sonorously: "The time has at last arrived. We are faced with a great decision."

Again he pauses but I feel the fear, greater than I have yet known. Death is there with us, enfolding each man, lingering, growing stronger. And the words from our captain flow strangely.

"Any of you unwilling to give your lives as divine sons of the great Nippon empire will not be required to do so. Those incapable of accepting this honour will raise their hands – now!"

Once more silence and death are almost palpable. Hesitantly, timidly, one hand goes up, then another and another ... six in all. I can choose to live or die. But somehow ... Of course, I want to live. But my hands – they remain at my sides trembling. I want to raise them but I can't. Am I a coward? I cannot do it.

"Ah so," Captain Tsubaki fixes those who have responded in his stare. "It is good to know exactly where we stand." They are summoned before us. "Here gentlemen," he points to the ashen faces, "are six men who have openly admitted their disloyalty. Since they are completely devoid of honour without spirit – it is our duty to provide them with some. These men shall be Hiro's first attack group."

The breath, held so long within me, struggled out. I want to draw in more air, to expel it with relief, but something clenches inside. Six men from my squadron have just been picked for death. Hiro's first human bombs. ❞

Above: A Japanese destroyer is smashed in two at Ormoc, Leyte, by a US B-25.

they could contribute to Japan's war effort.

From first to last, the three-day Battle of Leyte Gulf was the largest in history. In total, 282 ships were engaged along with hundreds of aircraft. It took the title of largest battle from the World War I Battle of Jutland when 250 British and German ships had met in combat, with only five seaplanes.

Those who felt disgraced would commit 'hari kiri'

At the end of it, the Japanese had lost not only four carriers but also three battleships, six heavy cruisers, three light cruisers and eight destroyers. The triumph clearly belonged to the Americans whose casualties amounted to just one light carrier, two escort carriers and three destroyers.

Had the Japanese Admiral Kurita been different on the day and had he chosen to bombard the American beach positions, history might have had a different story to tell.

SUICIDE SQUADS

The Battle of Leyte Gulf is not only remembered as being the biggest naval battle ever. It was also the first to see the co-ordinated use of kamikazes – Japanese suicide squads.

Among the Japanese there was a strict code of honour, instilled in them for centuries, that death was better than dishonour or defeat. The first form of ritual suicide in Japan, called 'seppuku', was reserved by law for the samurai and was considered a privilege. Suicides could equally be carried out as a mark of respect.

Centuries later, those who felt disgraced in some way would commit 'hari kiri', literally translated to 'a cut to the stomach'. The aim for the person was to disembowel themselves by using a ceremonial sword, an agonising process. As the years wore on, many made a symbolic cut in the stomach before turning a gun on themselves.

Surrender was abhorred by the Japanese, particularly among the troops, which explains the antipathy they displayed towards their own prisoners of war. Many Japanese servicemen

Allied soldier stopped to help a wounded or dying Japanese victim, the latter would devote his last burst of energy to pulling the pin from his final grenade, killing both men outright.

DESPERATE ACTS

Others would strap explosives to their bodies and hurl themselves at tanks or enemy positions to cause as much devastation as

possible. Until now, these acts were committed very much on an individual basis. But by 1944, staring into the jaws of defeat, the Japanese commanders decided to orchestrate suicide missions to cause the maximum hardship and loss of life to their enemies. Behind the enterprise was Vice-Admiral Takijiro Onishi who himself committed 'hari kiri' at the end of the war.

> ### Japanese commanders orchestrated suicide missions to cause maximum loss of life

Kamikaze pilots in small planes would target the deck of an enemy ship. While bombs dropped from planes often missed their target, the kamikazes' aim was very accurate. British ships with often more deck armoury than their American counterparts were better defended against such attacks.

There were plans for suicide

Above: USS St Lô *takes a direct hit from a kamikaze.*
Right: USS Suwanee *gets running repairs after sustaining damage from a kamikaze.*

readily chose suicide rather than shame. High ranking officers also used to inspire courage and commitment among their men by killing themselves.

This made the Japanese difficult enemies in the field. They were reluctant to be rescued if their missions went awry. At sea, Allied sailors watched as the survivors of a wrecked ship tried to drown themselves or cut their own throats if they were armed. For if any unfortunate motorboats to target major ships. Beneath the waves there were one-man midget submarines which would set themselves on a collision course with a much larger vessel. These were difficult tactics to counter.

Stepping forward for these 'special' one-way missions were upright, traditional, fervent and deeply patriotic young men who

Those without the necessary iron nerve were just as likely to plunge themselves and their aircraft into the sea instead of a ship, representing a waste of valuable resources. In a panic, many chose the first ships they saw to descend on. These were generally strategically less important than others in the fleet, once again wasting man and

Lieutenant-General Torashiro Kawabe explained the reasoning behind kamikaze attacks. 'We believed that our spiritual convictions and moral strength could balance your material and

---

Those without the necessary iron nerve were just as likely to plunge into the sea

---

scientific advantages. We did not consider our attacks to be 'suicide'. The pilot looked upon himself as a human bomb which would destroy a certain part of the enemy fleet ... he died happy in the conviction that his death was a step towards the final victory.'

At the Battle of Leyte Gulf, six aircraft took off from Cebu in the Philippines on 25 October 1944. Two hours later when they arrived at Leyte the planes deliberately rammed the US carriers *Santee* and *Suwanee*, causing extensive damage. The next day one American ship, *St Lô*, was sunk by use of kamikaze.

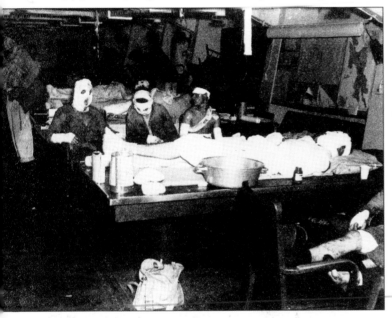

Above: *Wardroom of the carrier USS* Suwanee *becomes an emergency sick bay after the kamikaze attack during the Battle of Leyte Gulf.*

thought little of laying down their lives for their country. Despite the glory heaped on such pilots in domestic propaganda, the volunteers for the kamikaze ('divine wind') squads were drying up. The Japanese commanders had no choice but to brand units as kamikaze squads whether the men were willing to die or not.

machine. Others would fly off in search of a specified target and return claiming the ship they were after could not be found. There were many accidents as the fuel-starved Japanese economised on oil and stoked up the kamikaze aircraft with 50 per cent alcohol. If the aircraft engine failed, it was impossible to restart.

Commanders had no idea about the kamikaze success rate as there was no one left to report a result.

Following the war, Japan's

BEST DEFENCE

In the next three months, 22 Allied naval vessels were sunk by kamikaze pilots against 12 holed in conventional air attack. A further 110 kamikaze strikes damaged shipping.

They were a hazard which was to plague the Americans, Australians and British for the rest of the war. The best defence against kamikaze was interception by fighter planes or a volley of anti-aircraft fire, but it was not always successful. One Japanese pilot could still destroy many lives.

BATTLE FOR THE SKIES

BATTLE OF BRITAIN

When France was overrun, Führer Adolf Hitler cast his eyes across the English Channel and set his sights on Britain.

Although he never had an appetite for war with the island, he now saw it as the next jewel in his crown. He believed its government and people would choose to make peace after the unstoppable power of the Reich had been so amply illustrated in France.

He was, of course, wrong. A peace offer made to Britain in July 1940 was rebuffed – even though the remnants of its army, hounded out of Europe via Dunkirk, were in disarray. Hitler made up his mind to invade and began gathering the necessary invasion forces in the newly acquired Channel ports of Holland, Belgium and France.

Göring pledged to the Führer that the Royal Air Force would be banished forever

---

Yet while the Germans were veterans of waging attacking wars on land, they had never tackled the sea before. Nor was Germany a great seafaring nation. Hitler believed the arrangements for taking war across the water could be made in a matter of weeks. Given that 'Operation Overlord', carried out from Britain in 1944 to free France, took upwards of a year to plan, he was very shortsighted.

It was clear even to Hitler that an invasion could not go

ahead until his air force had charge of the skies. It was one of the few issues that united his warring chiefs of staff, too.

'The British Air Force must be eliminated to such an extent that it will be incapable of putting up any substantial opposition to the invading troops,' Hitler announced to his generals. Göring, the supremo of German air power, was all ears. He pledged to the Führer that the Royal Air Force would be banished forever.

IN EASY REACH

On paper, Göring had good reason to be confident. The Luftwaffe had a three-to-one numerical superiority against the RAF. German pilots were experienced, having flown missions throughout the Spanish Civil War. Now they were based in airfields in France, the Low Countries and Norway, within easy reach of Britain.

Göring believed his men would smash the Royal Air Force.

'Operation Sealion', Hitler's planned offensive against Britain which would bear him triumphantly to London, was set for 15 September 1940. The German navy chief Admiral Raeder had convinced Hitler his forces could not be prepared any sooner. Nor could it happen much later than that for fear of the invasion force falling foul of autumn storms.

Timing was crucial – but this did not unduly concern the Luftwaffe chief. When operations began against Britain in July,

---

Left: *Spitfires proved the saviours of Britain.*
Top right: *Göring believed the Luftwaffe aircraft could finish the RAF.*
Right: *Air crews were scrambled at a moment's notice when attacks came.*

Top: Formations of Messerschmitt 110s became a familiar sight in the skies.

Above: Britain and the Common- wealth countries were recruiting air crews.

Göring was sure he had time enough to fulfil his part of the bargain. Privately, he thought four days would be sufficient to virtually destroy his opposition. Events proved his optimism to be wildly misplaced.

For its part, Britain waited in anticipation during the summer of 1940 for the start of a battle for its very existence. Air reconnaissance teams spotted the gathering German forces. Hitler's intentions were clear.

Many of the men plucked from the beach at Dunkirk were redeployed on coastal defences. The Royal Navy played its part by attacking the collection of landing craft gathering at the occupied ports. Airmen joined the action and laid still more mines in the Channel to hamper a seaborne force destined for Britain.

There was a new evacuation among the children of London and the south east. As tension and expectation mounted on the home front, production doubled during June in factories working round-the-clock in a bid to help Britain's defenders meet the foe on equal terms. Lord Beaverbrook, Minister of Aircraft Production, appealed to the public to donate its metal scrap to build fighters. The result was mountains of old iron which could not be transformed into Spitfires or Hurricanes. But in terms of a morale-boosting exercise, it was a runaway success.

CONVOYS ATTACKED

As the German victory parades and celebrations died down in France there came the opening salvos of the Battle of Britain. They were quite tame by comparison with what was to come, a bid to 'soften up' Britain.

Lord Beaverbrook appealed to the public to donate its metal scrap to build fighters

---

The targets were Britain's lifeline convoys as they reached home waters and the coastal ports, most notably Portsmouth and Dover. Both sides suffered losses in the air, with the English pilots, ground controllers and radar operators learning some valuable lessons.

Germany began with about 2,600 aircraft ready for action. They were in the main Messerschmitt fighters and Dornier, Heinkel, and Junkers bombers. Well-organised into groups – Luftflotte 2 flew from Belgium, Luftflotte 3 from northern France, and Luftflotte 5 was based in either Norway or Denmark.

FIGHTER COMMAND

Lining up against them were fewer than 700 operational aircraft for the Royal Air Force. There were the legendary Spitfires and Hurricanes and some outdated Bleinheim bombers.

Britain's aerial defences were divided into four groups. Fighter

FINEST HOUR

'Let us brace ourselves to our duty and so bear ourselves that if the British Commonwealth and Empire lasts a thousand years men will still say, "This was their finest hour".'

(Winston Churchill after the fall of France.)

In the middle of August Göring opened phase two of the Battle of Britain

---

some 217 planes. The losses by Fighter Command were fewer than 100 but its outlook was bleaker than that of the enemy. British aircraft reserves were tiny. Yet it was the loss of experienced pilots either by death or injury that began to concern Air Chief Marshal Sir Hugh Dowding most. Despite the acute pressure of his position, Dowding, a master tactician, did a first-class job of keeping the marauding German planes at bay during those hectic months of summer and autumn 1940.

Above: Göring and his staff officers survey England across the Channel, convinced the island would easily fall.

Command 10 Group covered south west England, Fighter Command 11 Group oversaw the south east including London, Fighter Command 12 Group patrolled the airspace over the Midlands, while Fighter Command 13 Group was based in northern England and Scotland.

Britain was not standing entirely alone, as the line-up for the ensuing battle proved. Although more than 2,500 of the men who took part were British, there were also 147 Poles, 101 New Zealanders, 94 Canadians, 87 Czechs, 29 Belgians, 22 South Africans, 22 Australians, 14 Free French, ten Irish, seven Americans, two Rhodesians, one Jamaican and a Palestinian.

Now Germany was down by

Yet Churchill unceremoniously replaced him once the threat of 'Operation Sealion' had passed.

In the middle of August, Göring opened phase two of the Battle of Britain. His target now was RAF Fighter Command itself. Daily attacks were made on the airfields of southern England. Unlike the unfortunate air forces of crushed Allies Poland and France, the British planes were not caught on the ground. Britain's radar system, to waste vital manpower and resources, ground control never scrambled pilots until the last moment when they were sure a raid was imminent. It gave them little time to plan the most effective attack.

Both sides fell victim to erroneous propaganda. The RAF airmen were buoyed to hear that German air force losses were running at three or four times their own. In fact, vastly inflated German casualty figures were

Left: Air crews at Biggin Hill, Kent, enjoy a few moments' respite.
Below: Pilots and crews always appeared relaxed.

the most advanced in the world, gave early warning after seeing incoming formations of enemy bombers. There was just enough time to scramble the pilots and bring the valuable men and planes into the air.

Smoke from planes embroiled in dog-fights was scrawled across the sky

For now the heroes of the battle were the ground crews. It was their job to patch up not only the planes which were battered during aerial spats but also the hangars and runways damaged by bombs, to keep the Royal Air Force working.

Göring earmarked 13 August as 'Eagle Day' when a preponderance of German planes would swarm over the British skies and finally subjugate the stubborn RAF. Despite wave upon wave of Luftwaffe planes, his plan failed. Smoke from planes embroiled in dog-fights

was scrawled across the sky. The British fighters held their own.

NIMBLE SPITFIRES

German bombers were at a disadvantage against the nimble Spitfires. Laden with bombs, they were no match for the British planes. But the RAF fighters were struggling to achieve the best height and position to carry out attacks on the German formations as they crossed into Britain. Not wishing

broadcast, some of which were not rectified until after the war. Göring, meanwhile, was happily convinced during the early stages of the Battle of Britain that many airfields were out of action and scores of British planes were destroyed, estimates which were grossly exaggerated.

On 15 August nearly 1,800 sorties were flown by the German airmen, attacking targets from Newcastle to Hampshire. Britain was forewarned by radar,

BATTLE OF BRITAIN

In the Battle of Britain, RAF Fighter Command was divided into groups distributed throughout the country. The south west of England was the responsibility of 10 Group, London and the south east was covered by 11 Group, the Midlands region was patrolled by 12 Group, northern England and Scotland was the beat of 13 Group. Against these forces were three Luftwaffe formations – Luftflotte 2, Luftflotte 3 and Luftflotte 5.

NORTH SEA

Luftflotte 5
from Norway
and Denmark

Fighter
Command
13 Group

Chain
Home
High
Radar
Range

Chain
Home
Low
Radar
Range

LIVERPOOL

MANCHESTER

Fighter
Command
12 Group

BIRMINGHAM

ROTTERDAM

Fighter
Command
10 Group

LONDON

Fighter
Command
11 Group

SOUTHAMPTON

PORTSMOUTH

CALAIS

PLYMOUTH

ENGLISH CHANNEL

Luftflotte 2

CHERBOURG

LE HAVRE

Luftflotte 3

PARIS

F R A N C E

and each flight was attacked from the ground and the air and there were 75 German losses against Britain's 34.

The following day 1,700 sorties were made over Britain, with Göring confident the RAF would be left in tatters. Yet on that day, the German pilots found themselves confronted with healthy numbers of British planes and pilots.

Göring was left fuming at the apparent inability of his men to finish off the RAF. In addition, he was counting the cost of 363 lost aircraft and crew.

Of course, the incessant demands on each and every British squadron were causing immense difficulties by mid-

Above: *A Heinkel 111 over the Thames, taken from another German plane.*

August. Britain had lost 181 fighters in the air and 30 more on the ground. Only 170 replacement aircraft had thus far been manufactured, while just 63 new pilots had been brought up to replace the 154 turn to be furious. He pledged in turn to annihilate London, abandoning his deeply held wish to occupy the city unscarred by bomb damage. With the German campaign to obliterate the RAF clearly failing, he thought it was time for a new and different tactic. The wholesale bombing of London would not only hit at the heart of the British government but would demoralise its people. 'Sealion', he believed, would still go ahead as planned. The gloves were now off. It was the start of an arduous period of bombing raids which would test the

lost in battle. The raiders had succeeded in knocking out a radar station at Ventnor on the Isle of Wight, which was a serious blow, although their main aim of wrecking airfields had been frustrated. How long could the casual, seemingly cheery young men in silk scarves and leather jackets who laid their lives on the line several times a day without an outward trace of anxiety hold out?

Dowding, by skilful management, contained the mounting problems. Yet he was wearied by the effort and certain in the knowledge that Fighter Command could not cope with many more all-out raids. Another change in German tack saved the force from certain defeat.

Stage three of the Battle of Britain was sparked in part by accident. On 23 August a German pilot ditched his bombs over London, not to cause mayhem in the capital, but rather to speed his flight home. Churchill was outraged. In retaliation, he ordered the bombing of the German capital, Berlin. Now it was Hitler's

Below: *The unmistakeable shape of St Paul's Cathedral stands firm among the bomb damage in the City of London.*

strength of the RAF and also the people of Britain to the very limit.

Now the German forces were throwing their entire weight at Britain. With their losses amounting to 60 planes on 15 September, the decision to undertake mostly night bombing raids was made.

Searchlights in London were unable to track the fast-moving attackers. Night fighters in the RAF squadrons badly needed airborne interception radar to hit back, which took valuable time to provide. The demands on the men of the RAF, already weary from their exertions, were enormous, and their ability to strike back under cover of darkness was limited. They were sleeping for just a few hours in every 24 before being scrambled once more. The casualties among them continued to mount and, for the first time, their losses exceeded those of the enemy.

It took hours, some times days, to find bodies trapped in their wrecked homes

---

On the ground, the conditions for residents of London and, eventually, other main British cities were appalling.

The London docks were among the first targets in a daring daylight attack on 7 September. Residents watched in horror as scores of German bombers sparked a ferocious blaze. It took just an hour for the Luftwaffe to drop 300 tons of high explosives and countless numbers of incendiaries.

EYE WITNESS

Fred Graves, of Swindon, Wiltshire, served in the RAF ground crews which worked on Hurricanes and Spitfires during the Battle of Britain. Later in the war he serviced Lancasters of Bomber Command and was based near Newmarket.

❝ I remember the Battle of Britain as a non-stop series of dog-fights in the skies above us. Our pilots knew they had a very low life expectancy. I lost an awful lot of friends.

I was particularly impressed by the Polish airmen serving with us. Every time there was a scramble alert they would race out, usually still in their shirt sleeves, jump into a plane and take off. They were very highly motivated to hit back at Germany.

Airmen rarely if ever showed they were scared. Even the Lancaster bomber crews assigned to missions over the Ruhr somehow coped with the pressure. You could detect a reluctance among them – simply because the Ruhr industrial region was so heavily defended – but they did their duty.

I think teamwork helped beat the fear. Bomber air crews were teams. If one of them wasn't fit or well then the whole crew was grounded until he was. They also had to have faith in their aircraft and in us as ground crew. We were the last friendly faces they saw before they flew east.

Looking back it is a miracle some of these men ever made it home. Their aircraft were so shot up they were almost unrecognisable. ❞

At night the raging fires burned like beacons, guiding Luftwaffe pilots to their target.

Soon London Underground stations became shelters for frightened city folk despite an immediate ban on such a use. People slept end to end in close proximity to friends, neighbours and complete strangers. Those lucky enough to have gardens and shelters in their gardens became accustomed to retiring to them in time for tea and staying put until daybreak. It was soon

clear that the option of sheltering under a sturdy wooden table was dangerous as homes were reduced to rubble by the bombs.

It took hours to find bodies trapped in their wrecked homes. If bombs had failed to explode, there was still danger for the residents of London after the planes were long gone.

Fire-watchers, full-time fire-fighters and auxiliaries, air raid wardens and the Home Guard did their best to combat the terrible ravages of the raids.

Above: Coventry was blitzed in a raid code-named 'Moonlight Sonata'. The raid claimed 568 lives.

Despite all this, the mood in London was far from one of defeatism. The spin-off planned by Hitler of grinding the British public into the ground with the incessant bombing raids was failing miserably. In the tube stations there was impromptu entertainment from singers and musicians. Cups of tea were passed around and soon people learned to pay little heed to the sound of pounding bombs above.

BUSINESS AS USUAL

Instead of people weeping and wailing on the streets when the harsh light of day revealed the full extent of the night raids, there was a camaraderie which no one could have foreseen. Business went on as usual in daylight hours, despite broken windows, fractured gas and water pipes. The spirit of the people of London was ultimately symbolised in the great cathedral of St Pauls, which stood intact overlooking the battered city

while smoke from incendiary fires plumed around its dome.

If anyone was demoralised by the successive and apparently fruitless attacks it was the German pilots who were patently failing in their task of bringing Britain to its knees.

The attacks came in earnest from 15 September as Göring tried to ground the British air force in time for 'Sealion'. That day a record 56 Luftwaffe planes were brought down. Hitler twice postponed making a final decision on whether or not to go ahead before making his decision day 17 September. As the day dawned, London was smoking. But the Luftwaffe had paid a heavy price for the privilege of setting alight this historic capital, and the planes of the Royal Air Force were not only still challenging their fighters but also found time to bombard

FINEST HOUR

'Never in the field of human conflict was so much owed by so many to so few.'

(Winston Churchill after the Battle of Britain.)

the Channel ports where the German invasion fleet was based.

Hitler had no option but to call off 'Sealion' indefinitely. The Battle of Britain was won and the little island was safe from invasion. That meant renewed hope for occupied Europe, for without Britain from which to mount an attack on Hitler's Nazi empire there would have been barely a flicker of opportunity for liberation. Churchill's words of praise and thanks for the gallant RAF, spoken back in August, echoed through the free world. 'Never in the field of human conflict was so much owed by so many to so few.'

Yet the ordeal went on for both the men of the RAF and the people of Britain. Luftwaffe attacks continued unabated. London was attacked for 76 nights in succession and enjoyed little more than a few hours of eerie peace until the middle of 1941.

Anti-aircraft guns boomed in answer to the rain of bombs. There was little chance of them hitting their target. Only 75 air-craft were brought down by anti-aircraft shells – when the

RUDOLPH HESS

The Führer flew into a three-day rage when his deputy, Rudolph Walter Richard Hess, flew to Britain to make peace. A full day after the flight from Germany in a Messerschmitt 110 fighter aircraft, German radio explained away the demoralising desertion by claiming Hess was suffering from hallucinations.

British intelligence chiefs, meanwhile, were similarly at a loss to know what to make of the ace pilot who had been a loyal member of the Nazi party since 1920. On 10 May 1941, when he came down to earth at the end of a parachute and suffered a broken ankle, he claimed he had an important message for the Duke of Hamilton. This message was, apparently, a peace formula which would end the conflict between Britain and Germany.

High-ranking British officers and Churchill himself would not hear of making peace by the back door. Nevertheless, they were reluctant to trumpet the capture of such a key Nazi. Were they being duped by Hitler? Was there a further dimension to this unexpected prize which had fallen into their laps?

Even today, no one can tell whether Hess was demented at the scale of the bloodshed and hatched his plan to end the war accordingly; whether he discussed the plan with Hitler who wished to secure peace with Britain before invading Russia; or whether it was in fact the real Hess who carried out the madcap caper. Years later there were claims that the man held by the Allies was in fact an imposter, dispatched by Himmler or Göring after the murder of Hess.

What remains certain is that the man who fell to earth that night in 1941 was tried as a war criminal at Nuremberg, sentenced to life imprisonment and incarcerated at Spandau prison in Germany for 46 years until his death, apparently by suicide.

Luftwaffe flew about 12,000 sorties over Britain. Post-war investigation proved that for every bomber shot down by an anti-aircraft gun in September 1940 the gun had to expend an enormous 20,000 rounds. By February 1941 the figure was down to 3,000. The knowledge that something was being done was at least a small comfort to the population.

Göring also turned his attention to other British cities. Perhaps his intention was to eliminate great industrial centres and not simply to mete out punishment to British civilians. In fact, the lack of accuracy among bombers, ensured that civilians were foremost among the casualties.

In Coventry, 568 people were killed on 14 November 1940 when German bombers opened their doors and let 450 tons of bombs drop on the city and destroyed its historic cathedral. Birmingham, Cardiff, Exeter, Manchester, Southampton, Liverpool, Norwich, Swansea, Plymouth, Ipswich, Bath, Sheffield, Sunderland, Hull, Canterbury and Middlesborough all received a battering.

BITTER TRUTH

Thousands of people were made homeless by these air raids. During the worst of them which occurred in December 1940 and May 1941 in London, the firefighters ran out of water as they fought hundreds of blazes and were left with little option but to let them rage on. On 10 May 1941 550 German bombers unleashed 700 tons of high explosives and thousands of incendiaries, killing 1,436 people and destroying 700 acres of city. Just 14 of the attackers were brought down.

From August 1940 to May 1941, 44,000 civilians died and 103,000 were injured. The destruction and misery was merely a camouflage for Hitler's real intentions, to expand eastwards across the Russian borders, to Moscow and beyond. Only when Luftwaffe planes were pulled out of France to concentrate on the Russian front did the attacks on Britain subside.

Left: As dawn breaks, the destruction of the previous night's raid on London's docklands is revealed.

AIR BATTLE –
BALKANS

Both Axis and Allied powers saw benefit in opening a battle-front in the Balkans.

For Hitler, there was a chance of mopping up a potentially troublesome southern flank before mounting 'Operation Barbarossa', the invasion of Russia.

Churchill and his top brass saw a successful campaign in Greece or Yugoslavia offering a possible back-door entry into Germany when no access seemed available at the front.

In the event, the short and bloody campaign in the region left both sides as losers when it illustrated both the advantages – and drawbacks – of an airborne campaign.

Mussolini had opened hostilities when he invaded Greece on 28 October 1940. It was an impetuous decision which he lived to regret. Not only did it infuriate his ally Hitler, who had fostered an amenable relationship with Greece's ruler General Metaxas and considered the country in the bag. But it served to further humiliate Mussolini and his troops in addition to their inept showing in North and East Africa.

For the Greeks, although poorly equipped for modern warfare, were imbued with fighting spirit and managed to see off the Italians, pushing them back behind their lines in occupied Albania.

Britain was determined to stand by pledges of aid made to Greece – even though it had been unable to honour promises made to Romania, which was occupied by German troops at the start of October 1940.

ALLIES IN GREECE

Hitler had no option but to intervene in the action. However, for a few months he bided his time.

Having dispatched several thousand men, the British were keen to send even more of their contingent presently in North Africa to the aid of the Greeks. Metaxas was unsure. Although the presence of air support was welcomed, his own men were putting up an adequate performance and the presence of Allied ground troops would only succeed in drawing the

awesome firepower of an irate Hitler whose soldiers were suffering greatly due to the inadequacies of their footwear.

By the end of November 1940 three squadrons of Blenheim bombers and fighters had been stationed in Greece. Their brief, to defend Athens.

The political outlook changed at the end of January 1941 when Metaxas died suddenly and was replaced by Emmanuel Tsouderos who was well-disposed towards the Allies.

At a meeting in February, it was agreed the 1st Armoured Brigade, the 6th Australian Division and the 2nd New Zealand Division would be stationed in Greece to repel possible German aggression. With Bulgaria to the east rapidly

> *The Greeks were imbued with fighting spirit and managed to see off the Italians*

falling under the influence of Germany, and with Italy in the west, the fresh troops could plug defensive gaps left open by the Greeks fighting in Albania.

Neighbouring Yugoslavia, a country Britain failed to support, was feeling the Nazi pressure. The government were given an invitation-ultimatum in March 1941. Yugoslavia was to join the Axis powers. Prince Regent Paul was unable to secure aid from the British. With a heavy heart he finally gave his consent

Far left: A ship unloading supplies for the Allies in Suda Bay comes to grief.
Left: Italian soldiers were held at bay when trying to invade Greece.

EYE WITNESS

Howard Ganly was in the US 82nd Airborne Division. He was dropped behind enemy lines before D-Day to act as a pathfinder.

❝I was a little lost. They gave us the wrong maps. I made a few mistakes. I was shot at by my own men. They had got hold of some farmers' clothes and put them on, thinking they would be good disguises in German territory. Some of them were from my own company. I could have had them court martialled but I didn't. They stuck to me close for the rest of the war.

I was looking for open fields that weren't mined and didn't have big stumps stuck in the ground so they would be suitable for landing gliders. I would signal the gliders if it was OK to come in, with special lights and flares. We didn't dare use radios too much. I was very scared, I was just 19 years old. I came into the service when I was 17. The army kept pushing me around from one place to another. I didn't have any family, I spent most of my childhood in orphan asylums. I joined up to get a job and the money was good.

I survived D-Day but ran into trouble later on in Europe. I baled out in Holland behind enemy lines. A young Dutch girl put me in a barge and hid me from the Germans. She probably saved my life. I looked for her a few times after the war but never found her. I broke my leg and back in the fall. I have been disabled ever since. I was hospitalised for two years. I worked on and off but most of the time I have been crippled up.❞

and the Tripartite Pact was signed on 25 March.

Fury against the agreement among the Yugoslav people erupted immediately. There was an internal revolt which unseated the Prince Regent and put 17-year-old King Peter II in his place. On 27 March the pact signed with Hitler was ripped into pieces. The sombre mood in Belgrade was suddenly lifted, to be replaced with rejoicing.

HITLER OUTRAGED

The outbreak of anti-Nazism outraged Hitler. He resolved to teach the people of Yugoslavia a lesson. German commanders were told: 'Politically it is very important that the blow against Yugoslavia is carried out with pitiless harshness.' It made sense to combat the Greek problem at the same time so 'Operation Strafgericht' (punishment) against

Right: *Germany soon won command of the skies over Greece, and this tipped the balance of the battle in their favour.*

Yugoslavia and 'Operation Marita' against Greece were co-ordinated to begin on 6 April.

Hitler's campaign to break Yugoslavia into submission started with a dawn raid by the Luftwaffe. The sole declaration of war was the shower of bombs which hit Belgrade at 6am. The day-long assault claimed 17,000 lives and the grand buildings of the capital crumbled.

The day closed with another disaster, this time for Greece. The Luftwaffe wreaked havoc on Piraeus, the harbour of the Greek capital, which was crowded with ships from an incoming convoy. As the German bombs rained down destruction, one ship at anchor, SS *Glen Fraser*, had its 250-ton cargo of explosives ignited by a direct hit. The explosion that followed flattened much of the harbour, sank yet more vessels and even shattered windows in Athens some seven miles distant.

German armies began driving into both countries at the usual alarming rapid Panzer pace. Yugoslavia, which had a small army, held out for just 11 days. Much of its air force was knocked out on the ground by Luftwaffe attacks. The inglorious fortnight was compounded when Royal Yugoslav Air Force Hurricanes became embroiled in a dog-fight over Belgrade with some GBF-109s which unfortunately belonged to the very same air force.

Above: *Serbs in Yugoslavia were no friends of the Germans. Many fought as guerrillas against the invaders.*

RETREAT TO CRETE

The Greek army, too, was having difficulty fending off the advance. The fighting was gruelling. British commander General Sir Henry 'Jumbo' Maitland Wilson soon saw the hopelessness of the situation and ordered evacuation to the south. On 22 April Greece capitulated also. The initial destination of the fleeing Allied troops was the Peloponnese islands linked to mainland Greece by a bridge at Corinth. Then it was onwards to the island of Crete.

Under fire from the Luftwaffe above, the Royal Navy came in to the southerly beaches on 26 and 27 April to hoist 26,000 men to safety. Left behind were 900 dead, 1,200 wounded and something in the order of 10,000 men who had fallen prisoner to the Germans. Then there was the abandoned weaponry, amounting to more than 100 tanks, 400 guns, 1,800 machine guns and 8,000 vehicles. The RAF had lost more than 200 aircraft in total

> ## *On Crete there was chaos with hundreds of leaderless men awaiting an uncertain future*

while the Royal Navy had had two destroyers and about 25 other ships sunk.

On Crete there was chaos with hundreds of leaderless men awaiting an uncertain future. The only thing of which they could be sure was that Hitler's men would not rest until Crete too fell into their grasp.

In command was Major-General Bernard Freyberg, a pugnacious New Zealander who was ready to refuse the mantle of leadership until he discovered there was a sizeable number of his own men on the island – troops he believed had been taken back to Egypt.

His force amounted to two New Zealand brigades, about 7,750 men, plus an Australian brigade, two further battalions of Australians and a field regiment of artillery, with a combined total of 6,500. There were 15,000 British troops, too, comprising a brigade of infantrymen and part of the 1st Armoured Brigade, complete with two light tanks. Also at his disposal were about 10,000 Greeks. The Allies also had the support of

Above: A Panzer division parades its might before the centuries-old Acropolis in Athens, after the city was overrun.

the local population, many of whom would take up arms against the incoming Germans.

Freyberg, who won the VC in World War I, set about defending the island as best he could. He focused his forces at the three airfields, Maleme, Retimo and Heraklion, and the easily accessible Suda Bay.

From North Africa he received some tanks – less than two dozen but welcome nonetheless – and some rather war-worn artillery. There was a further injection of men, the 2nd Leicesters, who arrived on 16 May.

Crete – 136 miles long and an uneven 40 miles wide, and full of mountainous terrain – could hardly be adequately defended given the small number of men. Yet Freyberg was determined his men would give it their best shot.

From North Africa Freyberg received some tanks – less than two dozen but welcome

---

For Germany, the invasion of Crete posed some difficulties, not least in how to transport troops to the island. The Royal Navy had established a command of the seas. Already the shortcomings of the Italian navy had been shown up and the German command did not trust its ally's sailors with the lives of crack soldiers of the Third Reich. So an all-out amphibious assault was deemed too dangerous.

Yet in the air the Luftwaffe was unrivalled. By 18 May only seven RAF aircraft were left on Crete, and these were promptly withdrawn to Egypt. An airborne assault might work. Airborne forces had been in existence since 1927 when the first was formed by Italy. The Soviet Union soon followed suit and the value of these sky-fliers was clear. They could be dropped into enemy territory either in small numbers for the purpose – of sabotage or in large numbers to begin an invasion.

There were, of course numerous hazards inherent in airborne operations, but until now the Germans had known only successes. Their use of paratroopers in Norway, Belgium

EYE WITNESS

Morley Pence, 71, from Los Angeles, served with the 26 Mobile Reclamation Squad of the 442 Troop Carrier Command. Based at Thatcham, near Reading, he built and tested CG4A canvas and wood gliders (capable of carrying six men or two men and a Jeep) for 'Operation Overlord'.

❛Before the invasion the whole of southern England was one big military camp. Everything was either painted green or under green canvas. It was like the civilians had all left for the summer.

It was such an unreal time. I remember us bringing aero-planes through the centre of London on 40ft flat-bed trucks. There was absolutely no room for us to get round the corners so we just made room. No one seemed to mind. Actually, no one seemed to even notice.

When I see London now, this huge, busy bustling city, it brings it all back. I marvel at how the hell we drove those trucks anywhere.❜

and Holland during 1940 had brought striking results. The 55 men from the 'Granite' assault team who parachuted into Eben Emael, the strongest fortress in the world, on the Belgian-Dutch border, in May of that year,

---

The use of paratroopers in Norway, Belgium and Holland during 1940 had brought striking results

---

defeated 700 defenders in less than a day.

The Luftwaffe's airborne supremo was Kurt Student, a World War I fighter pilot and squadron leader. He had keenly studied the potential of airborne

techniques in Russia during the 1930s and saw 'Blitzkreig' as an excellent opportunity to put theory into practice.

Not only did he have troops leaping from flying aircraft but also equipment-bearing soldiers carried in gliders, and 'air mobile' forces, men trained in the art of going into action straight from the door of a landed plane. He sought to use all types in the invasion of Crete.

'MERKUR'

'Operation Merkur', the German attack on Crete, was to be launched following days of heavy aerial bombardment, with the landing of 36 gliders whose elite troops would knock out anti-aircraft guns and capture key locations.

The men of XI Air Corps' 1st Assault Regiment were the next penned in to see action, capturing an airfield and other key locations. At the same time, men of the 3rd Parachute Regiment would drop further up the coast and the aim was for both prongs to battle to a reunion.

Then a second wave was planned in which the 1st and 2nd Parachute Regiments were introduced with heavier arms, while two further battalions arrived by sea in fast motor-cutters. More amphibious activity was planned when the island was in German control.

Right: General Kurt Student was the mastermind behind German paratroopers' triumphs – and their failures, like the ill-fated assault on Crete.

First hitch for the Germans came when too few planes were provided, forcing the commanders to cut the size of the airborne assault.

Student and his men believed only a few thousand men would be there to meet them when the attack on 20 May got underway. It was a catastrophic miscalculation.

As a swarm of aircraft receded into the distance, hundreds of parachutes billowed in the breeze. The troops on the ground had plenty of time to take aim and fire, relishing a chance to get revenge on the men who had so recently chased them out of Greece. The helpless paras were picked off one by one as they all fell virtually on

Above: German paratroopers were confident as they embarked for Crete, with good reason. Until then, they had only known success.

top of the defending Anzac and British forces. Olive groves and rocky escarpments were littered with bodies, many still strapped into 'chutes.

Some parachutists didn't even make it out of their planes. Ground fire penetrated the hulls of the low-flying aircraft, killing or wounding men while they were still inside.

The few that survived were compelled to seek cover and join up with their comrades as soon as they could. Only those who dropped away from their targets – and thus away from defensive fire – escaped being cut down. It was for them to fight their way across the rocky landscape and unite with other groups.

Communications were poor on both sides. With telephone lines down and radios suffering patchy reception, the Allied groups felt equally isolated from assistance and exposed to the enemy. It caused one New Zealand commander to withdraw his men from a commanding position in the heights above an airfield, leaving a vital foothold open to the attackers.

Groves and escarpments were littered with bodies, many still strapped into their 'chutes

There followed more bitter fighting, often at close quarters, with many Allied soldiers claiming victims at the point of a bayonet. Both sides vied for the airfields. There was an uncomfortable stalemate as both Allied and German commanders tried to land reinforcements. The Royal Navy sank the German transports while the Luftwaffe holed the British ships.

GERMAN VICTORY

At Maleme airfield brave German pilots began to land their transport planes, some coming to grief on the runway, others colliding with planes that had preceded them. Inside were well-trained, well-armed soldiers fresh and ready for the fight.

The New Zealanders at Maleme were finally overwhelmed. Germany had scored the first Victory in the battle for Crete.

It was a key triumph, for now that the attacking troops had control of Maleme airfield, the gateway was open for supplies and still more troops to be transported in.

OTTO SKORZENY

A scar-faced German captain called Otto Skorzeny was the action-man asked by Hitler to rescue Mussolini from imprisonment in September 1943. Skorzeny, who was frustrated in earlier plans to snatch the Duce to safety by the diligence of the Italian authorities who kept their prized prisoner on the move, planned for a German plane to land on a precarious mountain plateau while he in the company of other troops parachuted into the hotel hideaway where Mussolini was held. Italian guards at the mountain village of Assergi abided by his requests not to resist the bold German move. Mussolini was flown off in the tiny plane which battled to ascend from the plateau. On reaching Rome he was transferred to a Heinkel 111 for a flight to the safety of Vienna.

In less than a week, Freyberg assessed the situation as hopeless. He ordered the Allied troops, by now mentally and physically exhausted, to withdraw to the south where an evacuation was being launched by the Royal Navy.

Between 27 May and 31 May, about 16,500 Allied men were taken off Crete. Germany had sealed its Balkan front.

BALANCE SHEET

Both sides were left counting the cost, however. Left on Crete were 1,750 Allied soldiers killed in action, two thirds of them Anzacs, and 13,500 men now held as prisoners of war. The Royal Navy lost three cruisers and six destroyers in the rescue bid, along with about 2,000 sailors killed or taken prisoner. Also left behind were Greek, British and Anzac soldiers who turned guerrilla to fight a cloaked campaign against the occupiers. It was another inglorious rout for the Allies.

As for the Germans, nearly half the initial force were killed on Crete, amounting to some 3,700 men. Among them were

high-ranking officers including a divisional commander, and a colonel. The number of aircraft shot to smithereens by the Allies or junked on the island airstrips was also immense.

Hitler surveyed the results – and decided the price was too high. Matter-of-factly, he told Student afterwards: 'Of course you know, General, that we shall never do another airborne operation. Crete proved that the days of parachute troops are over.'

It was a gross over-exaggeration. Germany continued to employ parachute troops although never again in such numbers. Nevertheless, Hitler did decide to abandon plans to parachute men into Malta, the stepping-

stone island in the Mediterranean. Had he won Malta, Hitler may have found victory in the North African campaign, and pushed into the Middle East and India to join hands with Germany's ally Japan.

The Allies observed the German experience on Crete but also decided in favour of using airborne troops in future engagements. Paratroopers played a pivotal role in the success of the D-Day operations in 1944.

> ### 'Of course you know, General, that we shall never do another airborne operation.'

Theirs was a precarious job, dropping behind enemy lines in darkness to act as pathfinders for the incoming gliders. Men of the US 82nd and 101st Airborne Divisions were charged with hindering the enemy advance towards to the coast. But the landings did not go as planned.

A combination of mistakes in navigation and inexperienced piloting had men dispersed over a huge area instead of being in a

Right: Captured Australian servicemen are a source of curiosity for their German guards.

Left: 'Pathfinder' parachutists are briefed before dropping into France, their task to direct airborne forces to landing points.

and unseen troops. One regiment in the 82nd Airborne Division managed to capture the town of Ste Mère Église.

British airborne troops were also seeing action as they seized vital bridges and knocked out a battery of guns aimed at the coast. For the British paratroopers, the ultimate test of endurance was to come later in the year at Arnhem in 'Operation Market Garden'.

concentrated group. Parachutists found themselves landing in some of the many engorged rivers in the region. Weighed down by their equipment they floundered for hours trying to get out. Others drowned in the struggle. Both Divisions were literally thousands of men short when they went into action. All

Weighed down by their equipment they floundered for hours trying to get out

the hazards of airborne operations, particularly those carried out at night, appeared to be coming in at the Americans.

Yet success bred out of disaster. Undoubtedly, the German defenders were thrown into confusion by the unexpected

Right: Horsa gliders lie in pieces after landing men in northern France in 1944. On these gliders the fuselage is split from the wings to unload.

ALLIED SUCCESS

Air superiority during D-Day became the key to Allied success. While it was thought that the Luftwaffe would sent up some 900 aircraft to make 1,200 sorties on D-Day, in fact only 100 were made in daylight and a further 175 after dark. By contrast the RAF alone flew 5,656 sorties on D-Day, about 40 per cent of the total made by the Allies.

Allied aircraft dropped a total of 4,310 paratroops and towed gliders containing 493 men, 17 guns, 44 Jeeps and 55 motorcycles without suffering harassment from enemy bombers.

As well as protecting troops and ships, Allied aircraft dropped 5,267 bombs against the coastal gun batteries.

The first German plane to fall victim on D-Day was a Ju 88, brought down by New Zealand Flying Officer Johnnie Houlton, one of 2,000 pilots in the Second Tactical Air Force who was in a Spitfire.

In the months which followed, three times as many bombs were dropped on Germany than in all the previous years.

Montgomery was eager to persuade Eisenhower of the wisdom of committing the ground troops to one hammer-blow into northern Germany. Eisenhower, however, favoured a fan-shaped attack instead.

'MARKET GARDEN'

'Operation Market Garden' was designed to capture key bridges in Holland through which Allied troops could be funnelled into Germany. The US 101st Airborne Division was charged with gaining land north of Eindhoven, the US 82nd Airborne Division was allocated two big bridges over the Meuse and the Wall rivers, while the British 1st Airborne Division had to seize bridges over the lower Rhine at Arnhem.

The men were carried to their targets in a total of 1,068 aircraft and 478 gliders. While the Americans experienced considerable success on their fronts, the British met enormous

Right: Troops taken by gliders into Arnhem in a bid to short-circuit the route to Berlin. The Britons had a grim fate in store.

German resistance en route to their target. Just one battalion, the 2nd, reached the bridge at Arnhem. Soon after, they were cut off.

Unfortunately for the British paratroopers, the Germans picked Arnhem as a focal point

of defence and reinforced their lines with troops, including an SS Panzer corps containing two armoured divisions. All efforts by the British to reach the men isolated at Arnhem were repelled after fierce clashes.

At the bridge, the paratroopers were pushed back into a defensive margin. It took nine days for the men to establish an escape route across the Rhine. Just 2,200

It took nine days for the men to establish an escape route across the Rhine

---

men got out from a force which began with a strength of 10,000. Montgomery's plan to by-pass Germany's defensive Siegfried line had failed. The thrust continued as before.

WINGS OVER THE DESERT

The Western Desert Air Force was officially born on 9 October 1940 at Maaton Bagush in North Africa.

H ere in the African desert, the theories of modern air warfare were established. For it was in North Africa that the principles of 'partnership' between air, sea and land forces were tried and tested for the first time, helping to put an end to decades of overt inter-service rivalry.

Co-operation of the kind enjoyed by air, sea and naval personnel among the Allies was unthinkable for their German and Italian counterparts, who not only fought a common enemy but were constantly embroiled in sniping against different factions on their own side. Indeed, there were plenty of hiccoughs along the way among the Allies with soldiers convinced the only worthwhile aeroplane was the one that flew protectively above their heads, regardless of the risk to the pilot and his inability to achieve results from that vulnerable spot.

The initial trials of tactical airborne operations were honed by the men of the Desert Air Force until they finally became adopted everywhere.

Lessons learned in the Desert Air Force now seem rudimentary and even naive. Yet aerial combat was still in its infancy when the war commenced. Fliers in World War I had the opportunity to make only elementary trials and errors. Little was done to advance the theory of warfare in the air after 1918 as most nations were concentrating on peace.

And until the conflict in the desert got underway, the Royal

Above: Mussolini believed his air force could win the skies over Africa.
Left: Stalwart Beaufighters played a key role in the North African campaign.

Air Force was from necessity concentrating primarily on defence.

To call it simply a Desert Air Force is to vastly over-simplify the case. The men who worked under its umbrella saw action in the skies above Egypt, Libya, East and West Africa, Greece, Yugoslavia, Palestine, and Italy.

This tremendous fighting force grew from an original nucleus of some 29 squadrons – a total of 600 aircraft. These were all that were available to Middle East Commander Air Chief Marshal Sir Arthur Longmore when hostilities with Italy commenced in 1940. Included in this total were a number of outdated biplanes and obsolete Blenheim bombers. That summer saw the Battle of Britain reach its momentous heights. So the chances of getting quality replacements were slim.

In addition, the airmen faced the same shortages that cursed the soldiers on the ground, those of water, fuel and spare parts to replace those worn by the inhospitable terrain.

Against them was the Regia Aeronautica, the Italian air force, which had proved itself already in the Spanish Civil War and Mussolini's Ethiopian campaign in the mid-1930s. The Italians were flying home-produced planes like Capronis and Fiats. Unfortunately for the Italians, their early promise was soon dashed by the Desert Air Force.

MALTA ATTACKED

The Regia Aeronautica went into action for the first time on 11 June 1940, with 35 Savoia-Marchetti bombers attacking Malta. Pitted against them were four Gloster Sea Gladiators. By the end of the day, the Italians had launched seven attacks.

Responding to this, 26 RAF Bristol Blenheims attacked an Italian airfield in North Africa, eventually destroying 18 enemy aircraft on the ground.

Above: Despite their years of experience, Italian aircraft and pilots proved no match for the Desert Air Force.

There followed a number of skirmishes. Prime targets for the Italians were Malta, Gibraltar, the British base at Alexandria in Egypt and the British Mediterranean Fleet.

The action in Africa then forked, with General Graziani leading his contingent of Italians in the Western Desert against Wavell, while the Duke of Aosta led some 215,000 troops out of Italian East Africa and into a British dominion. To meet Graziani's men were the British 7th Armoured Division, soon to be joined by the 6th Australian Division. Meanwhile, the 4th Indian Division was dispatched to meet the threat in East Africa.

It was in the East African campaign that vital steps towards an orchestrated plan for close air support were made. At the outset in October 1940, the Italians in East Africa

were a formidable enemy. Their spirits were high, their maturity in desert warfare a major advantage. But much of their buoyancy could be put down to the fact that they enjoyed air superiority. Italy had 14 bomber squadrons or gruppi in East Africa, and five supporting fighter gruppi. The over-stretched British forces, comprising nine squadrons, were reinforced by a further eight squadrons from South Africa, flying Hurricane aircraft.

Soon the battle to win supremacy of the skies began to swing in favour of the Allies

Soon, the battle to win supremacy in the skies began to swing in favour of the Allies. Both sides fought bitterly, both on land and in the air, for command of Keren, a fortified hill top in Eritrea. At the end of eight weeks, however, the Italians were turfed out of their strong-

hold and, by April 1941, a corner in the war of East Africa had been turned. As the campaign toiled on, the South African Air Force formed a first Close Support Flight to co-operate with ground troops, achieving a good measure of success.

FIVE LESSONS

After the battle of Keren, one British observer noted five lessons to be learned. They were: the need for transport planes; the need for supplies to be dropped by air (which was to prove crucial in the jungle wars of Burma and the Pacific); the advantage lent by long-range fighters which could destroy the enemy's aircraft before they lifted off; the need for Red Cross air ambulances to evacuate the wounded; and the preference for dive bombers.

These were all points which would be brought home to subsequent senior air force officers. For now, only the immediate achievement of winning an

EYE WITNESS

Ern Stanton, from New South Wales, was 18 when he joined the Royal Australian Air Force and qualified as a flier on the Empire Air Training Scheme.

❝Of our EATS course in Canada, about 40 per cent were later killed. It was very sad and disheartening to hear about your mates dying in action but I was really too young and conditioned too much to death to realise the more serious aspects of war

I do particularly remember one little bloke in our squadron who would give away all his personal effects before he went on a mission because he was convinced he wasn't going to come back. When he did return safely, he would go around and get them all back. But he did finally get killed.❞

Below: *Hurricane pilots of 73 Squadron line up before a desert-worn aircraft in North Africa during 1941. The Hurricane was the RAF's first monoplane fighter.*

important initial victory was noted. As the Allies took greater command of the action, Italian commanders found themselves battling not only against the Allies but also against a sapped will among their own men. A proportion of their troops were native Africans whose loyalty was suspect.

The campaign in Eritrea was to end in a complete and resounding victory for the Allies by the middle of 1941. Yet short on success though the Allies were at this stage, there was little chance to celebrate. Much as the British commanders had feared, Hitler had sent German forces into the region to assist his floundering fascist soul-mate.

Early in 1941 it was clear the Luftwaffe were installing units of Fliegerkorps X in Sicily, a specialist branch of the air force which had cut its teeth in the Norwegian campaign and

specialised in picking off ships. The Mediterranean Fleet first felt its presence on 10 January 1941 when up to 40 aircraft attacked a convoy. In aerial warfare, the Luftwaffe quite simply outclassed the Italians.

At the same time, the conflict in Greece was intensifying. The

Early in 1941 it was clear that the Luftwaffe were installing units of Fliegerkorps X in Sicily

only assistance actively required by the Greeks at the start was an injection of air power. The expanding Allied air strength had little problem asserting its authority. In one battle which took place on 28 February 1941, 16 Hurricanes and 12 Gladiators were patrolling at 14,000 feet when they were attacked by 50 Italian Fiat planes. In the two-hour clash which followed, the Royal Air Force fighters claimed 27 enemy planes for just one Gladiator lost.

The string of successes was a tribute to the ground crews who faced appalling winter conditions in the most primitive of airfields in order to keep the planes airborne. Spring saw further aerial reinforcements sent in by the British but the leaders in the field were uneasy. It was surely only a matter of months before Hitler made that battleground his own as well.

LUFTWAFFE ARRIVES

In April those grim predictions became reality. The Royal Air Force found its forces and those of its Greek and Yugoslav allies suddenly dwarfed by the arrival of the Luftwaffe. Its ranks included 430 bombers, 180

fighters, 700 transport planes and 80 gliders.

By 19 April the four Hurricane squadrons in Greece could rally just 22 operational aircraft between them. All were pulled down to Athens to lend air support to the evacuation of troops from Greece to Crete and North Africa. In the end there were only seven Hurricanes left.

On Crete they were joined by four Sea Gladiators and three Fairey Fulmars of the Fleet Air Arm. The abysmally small fighting force was virtually wiped out on the ground by the marauding Germans.

Added to the boiling pot was the Iraqi uprising against the British in May 1941. The Desert Air Force was by now staffed with Australian, New Zealand, Rhodesian and Free

Above: *German aircraft and pilots suffered the same difficult conditions as their Allied enemies.*

French units, as well as British and South African. But the ceaseless demands took their toll of its strength. And the menace from the Third Reich in

By April the four Hurricane squadrons in Greece could rally just 22 operational aircraft

the region did nothing to recede during that period. In fact, it gained momentum. Hitler was dallying with the idea of invading Malta. The little island which had found some relief when attacking forces were diverted to assist in the invasion of Greece, was once again at the top of the agenda for the Luftwaffe.

MALTA REPLENISHED

Its defences amounted to just four fighter squadrons as well as bombers and Fleet Air Arm forces based off the island. The succession of raids both by the Italians and increasingly by the Germans pared down the number of fighters. But the ranks were replenished on 15 June 1941 when 47 flew from the deck of the *Ark Royal*, and a further 64 were dispatched by similar means before the month had ended.

Below: SS Talbot *was one of scores of ships to fall foul of enemy planes in Malta's Grand Harbour.*

The hectic months ahead, saw the Malta-based fliers toiling to keep the convoys safe, and so deprive Hitler and Mussolini of the toe-hold they both sought. In addition, they attempted to destroy enemy convoys and hit targets in Italy – particularly Naples where, on 16 December 1941, 16 Wellingtons showered a torpedo factory with 4000lb bombs, the largest used in the Mediterranean to that date.

Between June and October 1941, 220,000 tons of Axis shipping was sunk en route to Libya, of which 115,000 tons could be marked down to the Desert Air Force, especially its Maltese division.

The fruits presented to Churchill by the frustrated Longmore were too few and far between to impress. Friction

---

On 16 October 1941, 16 Wellingtons showered a Naples torpedo factory with 4,000lb bombs

---

between the ground and air forces was still in evidence, never more so than when a reconnaissance flight reported enemy troops approaching a vital petrol dump in the North African desert. The dump was destroyed before it was discovered – the troops in question were in fact, British. Never mind

Above: *On Malta, air strips like this one provided constant targets for Luftwaffe pilots.*

EYE WITNESS

Post Office worker Arthur Helm was one of the first New Zealanders to sign up and fight for Britain following the outbreak of World War II.

❝ I had read a lot about the Germans and I knew how despicable they were. And I knew what I was letting myself in for.

I was a member of the First Echelon, the 6,607 men who first left New Zealand for Egypt. Later I was in northern Greece as a member of 4th Brigade Signals. After the invasion of the Germans, we moved to fight a rearguard action at Thebes. I saw the Acropolis about four hours before the Swastika was raised over it. At Port Rafti we held a two-mile stretch of coastline and two miles inland during the evacuation. We had to throw everything overboard except for our rifles, the clothes we stood up in and a small haversack.

Author Lawrence Durrell wrote that when everyone arrived in Crete they were dishevelled, dispirited and defeated – except the New Zealanders. They came up the beach with their rifles poised, their hats on and every one had a book under his arms. He was wrong – I had two books, a book of poetry and a Bible.

Spirits were high among the New Zealanders. We simply felt sorry for the Greek soldiers we left behind.

We expected the arrival of the Germans. I had just knocked off after 24 hours on duty and was having my breakfast when the first parachutes appeared.

There was a lot of deer-stalking and rabbit-shooting in New Zealand so most of us could shoot pretty straight. You knew when you had hit a parachutist coming down. He retracted his legs up as an automatic reaction.

Later I got involved at Galatas where we went in with bayonets after dark and drove out a bunch of Germans from the houses there. It was very nerve-racking but we got rid of them – even if we did have to retreat the next day.

I got out over the mountains to the harbour for evacuation. I met an English soldier at the side of the track and pointed out the way. He said: "I'm not going any further." I gave him some water and he told me he had been through Dunkirk but it wasn't a patch on this.

He just laid down on the hillside and died. He was done for, absolutely exhausted, and he had no will to live.

We lost Crete because the Germans had planes and we didn't. But we never lost heart. After being evacuated from Crete we went to Sidi Rezburgh. That was probably the worst campaign of the lot. ❞

that it was notoriously difficult to positively identify the nationality of soldiers from the air. The fighters on the ground had been deprived of valuable fuel for no reason. Longmore's repeated requests for more aircraft did little to endear him at home, either. Duly, Longmore was replaced by Arthur Tedder in May 1941.

AIR FLEET ENLARGED

The following month, Wavell was dispatched from North Africa by an irate Winston Churchill. Happily, his replacement, General Sir Claude Auchinleck, struck a harmonious note with Tedder which helped to end the bubbling army-air force discord.

Tedder, with support from the Air Ministry, helped to overhaul the repair and maintenance operations in the region which were proving so inefficient and therefore costly to the service.

Once he had enlarged the fleet of aircraft available to the Desert Air Force to beyond 1,000 in November 1941, Tedder turned his attention to the quest for new, well-trained recruits. There was a chronic shortage of training facilities in the Middle East. Tedder fell back

Two operations to relieve Tobruk, 'Brevity' and 'Battleaxe', had failed in the early summer of 1941

on his usual standpoint, which was to employ an expert – in this case Air Commodore B. Embry – who could devote his time and attention to the problem.

CO-ORDINATED ACTION

Two operations to relieve Tobruk, 'Brevity' and 'Battle-axe', had failed in the early summer of 1941 and once again it seemed that the relations between army and air force would be strained. It was in September 1941 that an adequate blueprint for co-ordinated action was finally drawn up to at last eliminate this problem. Drawing on the illustrations of the East African campaign, it set out the principles of close support of land forces by air forces, including pre-arranged and impromptu attacks on the enemy. Indirect air support was

Above: *Air Chief Marshal Sir Arthur W. Tedder, Deputy Supreme Commander, Allied Forces Western Europe.*

defined as attacks on objectives other than the enemy forces in the battle proper.

An Air Support Control headquarters was created for each army corps. These were information exchanges linked by two-way radio to brigades in action. Representing the RAF at brigade was a team called a Forward Air Support Link. The RAF team could assess the action at close quarters and request air support if necessary. On receiving the request, the staff at the Air Support Control

team headquarters could work out where best to send its aircraft during a battle for the most effective results.

The principles had already been put into practice on exercises in Northern Ireland as early as September 1940. A developmental Army Co-Operation Command had been set up by the RAF following Dunkirk when the air force received flak for not coming more visibly to the aid of evacuating soldiers.

In Africa, these close-support principles were put into action and adopted thereafter to the satisfaction of everyone involved.

THE END OF THE BEGINNING...

'This is not the end. It is not even the beginning of the end. But it is, perhaps, the end of the beginning.'

(Winston Churchill after the Allied victory in North Africa.)

REDS IN THE SKY

No one in Russia was ready for war when it came in June 1941, least of all the unwieldy air force.

Stalin boasted of a large body of planes. But like the sizeable French air force of 1940, the Red Air Force was ineffectively used and no match for the skill and experience of the Luftwaffe. Its sole four-engined bomber at the outset of the war was the TB-3, slow, under-powered and inadequately armed. It had ten squadrons of MiG, Yak and Lagg fighters. Yet these were far inferior to the Messerschmitts so elegantly handled by German pilots.

In addition, the Russians were part-way through a modernisation plan in which their outdated planes would be replaced by more competitive models. The Russian air force, like all branches of the establishment, had suffered its fair share of losses in the purges which Stalin organised to rid himself of potential opponents.

AID FROM BRITAIN

The pilots of the Red Air Force were trained to support the troops on the ground rather than enter into combat with

Above: Britain provided Hurricanes and know-how to the Russian air force, following the German invasion.

other aircraft. Many ended up frantically helping to evacuate Russian industry to the east, to save it from falling into German hands – reducing the aircraft available for other duties still further. Indeed, its fighter arm had never been put to the test. The summer and autumn of 1941 brought a succession of disasters for the Red Air Force.

Still punished by the Germans at home, the RAF still found the resources to send several squadrons of Hurricanes

to the aid of the Russians.

It was Churchill's wish that as much aid should be devoted to the beleaguered and reluctant new ally as possible – despite the fact he was a lifelong critic

> ### The summer and autumn of 1941 brought a succession of disasters for the Red Air Force

of communism. In a broadcast shortly after Hitler's 'Operation Barbarossa', he explained how the hatred of fascism remained uppermost in his emotions.

'The Nazi regime is indistinguishable from the worst features of Communism. It is devoid of all

Left: Much of Russia's air power was devoted to shipping industry east.
Far left: The TB-7 bomber that brought Russian minister Molotov to Britain.

theme and principle except appetite and racial domination. It excels all forms of human wickedness in the efficiency of its cruelty and ferocious aggression. No one has been a more consistent opponent of Communism that I have for the last 25 years.

'But all this fades away before the spectacle which is now unfolding. The past, with its crimes, its follies and its tragedies, flashes away. I see the Russian soldiers standing on the threshold of their native land, guarding the fields which their fathers have tilled from time immemorial. I see them guarding their homes where mothers and wives pray ...

'I see advancing upon all this in hideous onslaught the Nazi war machine with its clanking, heel-clicking, dandified Prussian officers, its crafty expert agents fresh from the cowing and tying down of a dozen countries...

'I see the Russian soldiers standing on the threshold of their native land'

'I see the German bombers and fighters in the sky, still smarting from many a British whipping, delighted to find what they believe is an easier and safer prey.

'. . . if Hitler imagines that his attack on Soviet Russia will cause the slightest divergence of aims or slackening of effort in the great democracies who are resolved upon his doom, he is woefully mistaken.'

BRITISH TEACHERS

A British unit was sent with the aircraft to the Soviet Union to teach the Russians how to make and fly Hurricanes and to pass on tactical tips about the escort of bombers and general air operations.

Soon, the lessons of the visiting Britons and that of bitter experience began to sink in. Until the Russians became fully conversant with combat know-how and were better equipped,

Below: *Royal Air Force Hurricanes pictured in the air over the Russian countryside on their way back to base from escort duty.*

EYE WITNESS

Alexander Pokryshkin, the son of a bricklayer in Novosibirsk in Siberia, emerged as one of Russia's air aces. He flew 550 operational flights, fought 137 aerial battles and had 59 victories to his credit. He became the first member of the Soviet armed forces to be awarded the title 'Hero of the Soviet Union' three times, receiving his third Hero's Gold Star Medal in August 1944.

❛I was out with pilot Semyonov as my partner flying on a reconnaissance mission to Jassy where the Germans had an aerodrome. As we approached the town I espied five Messerschmitts flying towards us, three below us and two above. Here, at last, were live Germans. They spotted us. I rocked my wings as a signal to Semyonov that I was going to attack. There were five of them and only two of us.

I was flying a MiG-3. It is a sturdy machine and well armed. It behaves wonderfully at high altitudes when its speed and manoeuvrability increase. I had my plan of action all worked out in an instant. Semyonov was to cover me as we had previously arranged on the ground. I shot up into the clouds and kept on climbing until I ran into one of the two Messerschmitts coming towards me. The German zoomed almost in my face. I did a stall-turn and found myself on the tail of the yellow, blunt-winged craft. I fired at short range. The Messerschmitt burst into flames and plunged downwards. I watched it as it fell and that almost cost me my life. The other German had crept up behind me. White ribbons of his tracers shot by and then my plane shuddered. Its port wing had been torn by bullets.

I dived to zero feet and hedge-hopped all the way home and, feeling that my aircraft was losing stability all the time, with great difficulty got back to the airfield. I made a normal landing, taxied to a stop, shut off the engine and slumped against the armoured back of the seat. I needed a drink. My throat was parched. That was the first German I had bagged.❜

a glider pilot and instructor, Hartmann then joined the Luftwaffe aged 18.

He revealed the secret of his success: 'My only tactics are to wait until I have the chance to attack the enemy then close in at high speed. I open fire only

During World War II Hartmann scored a record 352 kills, all of which were validated

when the whole windshield is black with the enemy. Then not a single shot goes wild. I hit the enemy with all my guns and he goes down.'

In his beloved Me-109, he knocked out seven Red Air Force planes above the Battle of Kursk on 7 July 1943. It wasn't unusual for him to return from a sortie with more than one kill to his credit. No Allied pilot even approached such a mighty score.

HARTMANN ESCAPES

Operating over Russia, his plane was once shot down. Although he was unhurt, he was taken prisoner by Russian soldiers – a fate dreaded by German airmen at the time.

He pretended he was injured and was placed on a stretcher in a truck. En route to find a doctor he sprang up, overpowered his guard and leapt under fire from the lorry into a field of sunflowers. Sleeping by day and walking by night, he finally reached the German lines where he was almost shot by one of the sentries.

His outstanding success and distinctly Aryan features made him a favourite with Adolf Hitler

however, a handful of German pilots had a field day.

King of the skies at that time was Erich Hartmann, otherwise known as 'Bubi' Hartmann or the 'Blond Knight'. During World War II he scored a record 352 victories, or kills, all of which were validated, making him an 'ace of aces'. Most were

made on the Eastern front.

Hartmann was born in Weissach, near Stuttgart, on 19 April 1922. As a boy, he lived in China where his father was a doctor. When the family returned to Germany Hartmann was encouraged by his mother, herself a pilot, to sample the joys of flight. First qualifying as

Above: Russian pilots are congratulated by their major after completing a mission on the Eastern front.

Below: Erich Hartmann was one of the most successful pilots of the war, scoring most of his victories over Russia.

Once he was even drunk enough to begin juggling with the Führer's hat but still remained a 'golden boy'.

HARD LABOUR

Erich Hartmann scored his last victory on the final day of the war, having flown 1,400 missions. He then came down to earth with a jolt, being captured by Russians. His sentence following the war was 25 years' hard labour – although he was offered freedom if he agreed to settle in East Germany and train their air force. He refused the deal and was finally released in 1956 following negotiations by Chancellor Adenauer of West Germany.

who awarded him the Knight's Cross and later added the prestigious German military decorations of Oak Leaves, Swords and, then finally, Diamonds. Courageous not only in the air, he frequently had cross words with his German superiors.

Hartmann resumed his air force career and learned to fly jets under the auspices of the

ACE PILOTS

In the league table of wartime ace pilots, the first five places are occupied by Germans followed by two Japanese and a Finnish pilot. The first pilot from the West to appear in the league comes in 27th place, South African J. Pattle, who is followed by Richard Bong (below) and Thomas McGuire of the US and J. Johnson of Britain.

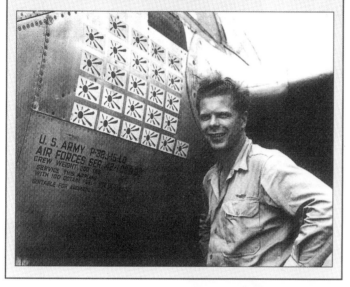

the conflict with Russia dragged on, and a final total of 200,000 men abandoned their air duties to become infantrymen. They were also to suffer from lack of aircraft and fuel and a diminishing training programme.

Worse was to come for the German air forces remaining on the Eastern front

Russian industry which had moved to the safety of the east produced supplies for the Red Air Force – which was further bolstered by American aircraft through the Lend-Lease Act.

Below: With much of Russia's powerful industrial muscle in the safety of the east, Stalin was able to provide his air force with vital replacement planes and components when Hitler could not.

Americans. He was married in 1944 to his wartime sweetheart Ursula Puetsch, and the couple had a daughter. Hartmann died in 1993, aged 71.

As 1941 closed, the prospects improved considerably for the Russians in the air war. The Luftwaffe having deployed the majority of its air power in the opening stages of 'Operation Barbarossa', its strength on the Eastern front soon waned as it became overstretched and struggled to maintain its operations on three fronts.

LUFTWAFFE SUFFERS

Worse was to come for the German air forces remaining on the Eastern front. Luftwaffe field divisions were created to back up the ground forces as

TIGER, TIGER, TIGER

By 1941, tensions were running high between the Americans and Japan. The United States government looked on uncomfortably as Japan sought to expand its empire by waging a brutal war on China.

Although Japan's leaders had pledged neutrality in the European war, alarm bells were sounding out across the Western world. Both America and its future allies aided the hard-pressed Chinese.

Seizing an opportunity in September 1940, the Japanese, pushed the boundaries of their empire back by moving into Indochina at the expense of Vichy France, the colonial rulers of the country. This was a move the European puppet state was powerless to resist. In retaliation the anxious and angry United States and Britain broke off trading relations, which meant a halt to the supply of vital oil to Japan. The exiled Dutch government did likewise. Australia was by now viewing the aspirations of Japan with trepidation.

Without oil, Japan could only survive for 18 months at the most despite the huge stockpiles it had imported during the 1930s. At stake was its considerable economic might. The hawks among the Japanese hierarchy quickly argued that time was running out for Japan and that a military strike to consolidate its position was needed sooner rather than later.

TRIPARTITE PACT

In the same month as the threatening manoeuvres in Indochina, Japan joined with aggressors Germany and Italy in the Tripartite Pact, which set out a code of co-operation between the three. There could be little doubt now that the Land of the Rising Sun was poised on the brink of war. But the question which troubled the

Americans was, just how would the inevitable conflict begin?

Japan had sound reasoning behind the desire to enlarge its lands. In 1939, its population reached 99 million and was increasing at the rate of five million a year. Its home islands were becoming overcrowded and overstretched. Britain, France and Holland all enjoyed the benefits of colonies. America, although ideologically opposed

> ### *In September 1940 Japan joined with aggressors Germany and Italy in the Tripartite Pact*

Left: An aerial view of the US Pacific Fleet's base at Pearl Harbor. *Below:* Japan's foreign minister Matsuoka talks with Ribbentrop in early 1941.

to colonialism, had its spheres of influence. Japan felt entitled to the same. It was not unreasonable, the Japanese felt, for their country to hold sway over the Pacific and China. Japan's transformation from feudal backwater to a burgeoning world power had been rapid. It was only in the latter half of the 19th century that Japan had come out of isolation. After that, the Japanese followed the British and American examples

The Japanese felt cheated, unable to trust the countries they had known as friends

and were set on a programme of industrialisation. This new breed of manufacturers struggled to compete on the same terms as the Westerners. Britain had tariffs which discouraged overseas trade while America also followed a policy of protectionism. Japan joined the Allies during World War I. Afterwards, the Japanese were anxious to be accepted as part of the New World

Right: Japanese pilots were hailed as heroes back home after their unannounced attack on the US Pacific Fleet's base at Pearl Harbor.

Order on equal terms with other nations. Failure was in store.

At the Paris peace conference, the Japanese proposed a clause of racial equality, with the aim of removing the discrimination they had felt. The emissaries from Japan assumed that there would be no controversy over the clause's acceptance.

JAPANESE ANGER

In the event, it was barred by none other than American President Woodrow Wilson, who went on to place a ban on Japanese people entering the US when immigration by other nationalities was rife. Australia, too, had a 'whites only' immigration policy. The Japanese felt cheated and angry, unable to trust the countries they had hitherto known as friends. Western powers seemed more fraudulent than ever when the Washington Treaty of 1922 was drawn up, limiting Japan to just three capital ships for every five run by both the US and Britain.

Left: Admiral Isoroku Yamamoto was the architect of the strike against Pearl Harbor. Yet he feared he had 'awakened a sleeping giant'.

The Japanese largely followed Western models of democracy. Although there was an emperor, he was bound by the decisions of his ministers. Its civilian ministers ran civil affairs. But there were ministers from the army and navy entirely responsible for military matters. Without the co-operation of those ministers from the armed services, the government fell. It meant they wielded huge power. To further complicate matters, there was an enormous degree of rivalry between the army and the navy and the two services could rarely agree.

Aside from these wranglings, there was also the sinister threat of assassination. It became a political tool increasingly used by young patriots. Those in power became cautious, corrupt and sly. There came a feeling among the Japanese that politicians could

PEARL HARBOR

On the morning of 7 December 1941, the Japanese attacked on Pearl Harbor. As the US naval base prepared for its day, Japanese carrier aircraft swept in and tore into the US Pacific Fleet at rest. The fleet's carriers were at sea, but the battleships were in. *Arizona*, *West Virginia*, *California* and *Oklahoma* were destroyed; *Pennsylvania*, *Nevada*, *Tennessee* and *Maryland* were damaged. The Japanese lost nine Zeroes, 15 'Vals' and five 'Kates'.

wealthy, precisely why they were incorporated into empires in the first place. Japan would become stronger than ever if only it could avail itself of the assets there.

With Japan's vast military might, the islands were easy enough targets. But the Japanese leadership rightly guessed that America was unlikely to sit back and watch as it established a thriving Pacific or Asiatic powerbase. It would send its big ships to trouble-spots. The answer, it seemed, was to knock out the American navy to obtain the freedom of the seas.

The answer, it seemed, was to knock out the mighty American navy

The pride of the US fleet was based in Hawaii, closer to Japan ·than the inaccessible mainland of the United States. And so the infamous attack on Pearl Harbor was conceived.

It was a brilliant short-term strategy drawn up by Admiral Yamamoto. Key to its success was the element of surprise. There was a summer of training for the pilots of the fighters, dive-bombers and torpedo-bombers which were to be shipped in for the pre-emptive strike. Most Japanese pilots had seen action in the war with China.

To ensure the action, code-named 'Operation Z', was effective, powerful six-inch naval shells were adapted for use by the aircraft, sufficient to plough through the armour of the US battleships. The Japanese also had a 24-inch torpedo known as the 'Long Lance', containing

not be trusted. Not only that, there was widespread fear about the encroachment of communism. Together with a growing admiration for the achievements of Nazi Germany, Japan swung towards militarism.

Japan, still cut out from overseas trade by the policies adopted by key trading partners Britain and America, began to feel the pinch during the Great Depression of the 1930s. Japan spent much of the 1930s meddling in internal Chinese affairs. When China became unwilling and belligerent, the two countries

finally went to war. In 1937, Japan withdrew from the League of Nations and denounced the Washington Treaty, privately planning to increase its naval strength to compare with that of Britain. And she sought to boost her empire.

YAMAMOTO'S PLAN

Japanese Military leaders realised the colonial outposts were now vulnerable, with the mother countries being embroiled in problems thousands of miles away. The remote islands were economically

Right: Japanese aircraft warm up on the deck of the carrier Hiryu before delivering their stunning blow to the US Navy at Pearl Harbor.

Right: Japanese aircraft warm up on the deck of the carrier Hiryu before delivering their stunning blow to the US Navy at Pearl Harbor.

1,000 pounds of explosives; it was among the most powerful weapons in the world.

As early as 26 November 1941 the Japanese navy set off from its base, using an obscure route and maintaining complete radio silence. By 7 December it was in position, 270 miles north of Pearl Harbor in the Kurile Islands.

'TIGER, TIGER, TIGER'

The fleet, under Vice-Admiral Chuiki Nagumo, comprised six aircraft carriers, with a capacity of 423 planes. In the attack 360 were used, the force comprising 104 high-level bombers, 135 dive-bombers, 40 torpedo bombers and 81 fighters. In addition, the escort force consisted of two battleships, three cruisers, submarines and supply ships.

In dock at Pearl Harbor were 96 American ships. Fortunately for the US, the base's two aircraft carriers were at sea. Their destruction may have altered the course of the war.

At Pearl Harbor, a new day day was beginning, clouded only by a general fear of war. Still, the beaches were silvery, the sun was warm and the majority of the servicemen based there were looking forward to a day of relaxation. Many were still in bed when the storm broke.

Although America had been forewarned that Japan was planning a major strike, it didn't

The ships in Pearl Harbor were undefended, their ammunition in lockers

know where or when it would take place. Most thought the Philippines the obvious target for Japanese aggression. The ships in Pearl Harbor were undefended, their ammunition safely held in lockers.

The only clue to the carnage to come came in the early hours when a periscope was spotted in the harbour mouth. A destroyer

Left: Pearl Harbor explodes under the onslaught of Japanese bombs. Fortunately, key fuel installations were left intact, so averting utter disaster.

PEARL HARBOR

US Losses
18 ships, including 8 battleships, sunk or badly damaged; 164 aircraft destroyed and 124 aircraft damaged; 2,403 men dead and 1,178 men wounded.

Japanese Losses
29 aircraft downed; 5 midget submarines sunk; 64 men dead or missing; 1 prisoner taken.

Below: US servicemen at Pearl Harbor were staggered at the sight that greeted them. Japanese aggression was dubbed 'treachery' around the Allied world.

duly went out to sink the unidentified submarine.

In fact, few people outside the navy top brass in Tokyo knew what was going on. Unwilling to announce its intentions and give its game away, Japan didn't deliver its declaration of war to America until Pearl Harbor was smoking.

At 6am the first wave of aircraft took off and headed to Hawaii. As they came within sight of Pearl Harbor Captain Mitsuo Fuchida, in command of the first wave, broadcast to his men, screaming 'Tora, Tora, Tora' – 'Tiger, Tiger, Tiger',

literally translated. The message informed them that the Americans were still unaware of what was to come. At 7.56am the first shots rang out.

As they came in sight, Fuchida broadcast to his men, screaming 'Tora, Tora, Tora'

In neat formations, the skilful, well-practised pilots made runs over the lines of vessels anchored along 'Battleship Row', the section of the harbour where the capital ships lay.

Far below them, braving the

tell-tale shallow waters of the harbour, were Japanese midget submarines, each one hoping to bag a battleship.

A stunned commander ordered them to take action, bellowing 'This is no drill!'

Ship after ship was blasted and soon the air was filled with thick, oily black plumes of smoke. As the flaming oil from one stricken vessel spilled into the sea, it set light to another. The second wave of Japanese bombers had difficulty locating targets through the smoke.

The *Arizona* was hit and exploded – 1,200 members of her crew died. The battleships *West Virginia*, *Oklahoma*, and *California* were also destroyed, and *Nevada*, *Maryland*, *Tennessee*, and *Pennsylvania* were damaged. Further casualties included the cruisers *Honolulu*, *Raleigh* and *St Helena*, and the destroyers *Shaw*, *Cassin* and *Downs*. These ships, all symbols of America's greatness, were left tattered wrecks.

In the midst of the chaos a contingent of American aircraft arrived. Their pilots must have gaped in disbelief at the scenes before them. What once was a landing strip had been set ablaze, along with most of the aircraft on it. Then they too were attacked. The same fate applied to the crews of dive-bombers from the absent carrier *Enterprise* returning to base during the attack.

29 PLANES DOWNED

At times the Japanese pilots screeched in so low they were clearly visible to the frantic Americans.

The men at Pearl Harbor responded to the onslaught with considerable zest. A stunned commander ordered them to take action, bellowing the words: 'This is no drill!' Despite the shock and disbelief, the Americans soon manned the guns as they had done before in training and claimed Japanese planes. Others raced to rescue comrades trapped in blazing ships or operated fire-

Below: 'Battleship Row' Pearl Harbor provided rich pickings for the carrier-borne aircraft of Yamamoto's strike force.

Above: Despite the suddenness of the strike, troops rushed to man the guns. A total of 29 Japanese planes – 9 Zeroes, 15 'Vals' and 5 'Kates' were downed.

fighting equipment. Finally, there was calm. The surviving servicemen set about their grim tasks with one ear open for the return of the Japanese.

While the Pacific Fleet's base was extensively damaged, it was not crippled, since the fuelling and repair depots had escaped unscathed. However, it would take months, and in some cases years, to refloat and repair the shattered bodywork of the damaged ships.

The Japanese did not return to finish off the base, as was widely feared among US servicemen and their families. Well satisfied with the results of the operation, which went better than any of the Japanese commanders dared hope, Vice-Admiral Nagumo decided a quick, getaway was now in order, particularly as fuel was

running dangerously low, and the US carriers *Lexington* and *Enterprise* might appear.

In America there was outrage and horror at the loss of life. US Secretary of State Cordell Hull was still in conference with Japanese negotiators when news of the attack reached him. They had already presented him with a document purporting to set out the area of debate.

A REPEAT OF 1904

Mr Hull furiously declared: 'In all my 50 years of public service I have never seen a document that was more crowded with infamous falsehoods and distortions on a scale so huge that I never imagined until today that any government on this planet was capable of uttering them.'

Although some took the opportunity to condemn President Franklin Roosevelt for his lack of readiness, most US citizens were determined to pull behind him in their fury at the

Japanese action.

Ironically, the attack on Pearl Harbor mirrored a military move made by the Japanese against the Russians in 1904. Once again, without an official declaration of war, the Japanese navy carried out a surprise attack on a key Russian base. Back then, *The Times* of London hailed it as 'an act of daring' and praised the Japanese for their initiative and vigour.

In Britain, the *Daily Mail* now voiced the venom of many when it wrote: 'Not even Hitler has yet achieved the infamy of a stab in the back while his envoys were still ostensibly negotiating terms of agreement with his intended victim.

'This is an act which the world will never forget so long as the records of history are

---

On 8 December, both America and Britain officially declared war on Japan

---

read. It will stand for all time as an example of the ultimate depths of deceit to which it is possible for any nation to descend.'

On 8 December, both America and Britain officially declared war on Japan. In response to the declaration and the wave of Japanese attacks around the region, the Royal Navy battleship *Prince of Wales* and battlecruiser *Repulse* sailed out of Singapore with an escort of four destroyers. Disastrously, 'Force Z', as it was known, ignored the threat of airborne action and left without the protection of an aircraft carrier.

EYE WITNESS

Kazuo Sakamaki was the commander of a midget submarine, one of five which was sent into action at Pearl Harbor.

❛Something went wrong. At the moment of release my submarine nearly toppled over into the water. The trim had not worked well. I feared that it we attempted to emerge hastily, enemy observers might spot the ship. I remembered that the opening of hostilities was to follow the handing of the notice of war to the US government. If by my own mistake the presence of the Japanese forces should be discovered it would create a grave problem. It would spoil the air attack and every other detail of the carefully worked-out plan. I could not cause such a blunder. No matter how dangerous the condition of my ship I could not let it emerge to the surface.

My aide and I crawled back and forth inside the submarine removing the lead ballast and filling the tanks with water to correct the trim of the craft. It had been our plan that by midnight all five submarines would be inside the harbour and would sink to the bottom and wait for the dawn. But when I looked at the watch it was midnight already. The ship righted itself.

I figured that as long as we entered the harbour during the night no damage would have been done. I drank a bit of wine and ate my lunch.

"Let's do our utmost." My comrade and I held each other's hands and pledged success. I took my position and moved forward with minimum speed.

After ten minutes I lifted the ship slightly to see through the telescope where we were going. To my horror, the ship was moving in the wrong direction.

Moving blindly because my gyrocompass was not working, the ship had gone 90 degrees off her course. If I could manage the ship with the help of the telescope we could get back on our course but this was clearly impossible.

"We must get to the mouth of the harbour" I repeated to myself. My hands were wet with cold sweat. I changed the direction three or four times, hoping against hope that somehow the ship would get going where I wanted to go. The speed was maintained at the minimum as before.

Time ticked away in complete indifference to my predicament. It was almost the moment for attack.

As we came nearer to the enemy ships guarding the entrance I was able to see the white uniforms of the sailors aboard. I concluded they were destroyers.

I pushed the midget submarine toward them, Suddenly I heard an enormous noise and felt the ship shaking. I was hit on the head and lost consciousness. This was my first contact with war.

I came to myself in a short while and saw white smoke in my submarine. I changed the speed to half gear and turned the ship around. I wanted to see if any damage had been done. My comrade was all right. My two torpedoes were all right. I did not want to waste my torpedoes on those destroyers which began again to charge against me. They threw depth charges at us. They fell near us but not as close as the first time.❜

Their aim was to prevent the Japanese making landings on British-held territory in South East Asia. But the mission went wrong when the two British giants became targets for the Japanese Naval Air Arm flying out of Indochina.

The *Prince of Wales*, able to fire 60,000 shells every minute from its 175 anti-aircraft guns, was thought to be impregnable. Japan's pilots didn't think so.

On 10 December, both ships were sunk off the coast of Malaya within an hour of each other and 800 crew members were killed, although 2,000 were saved by the accompanying destroyers. Among the dead was the leader of the ill-fated squadron, Admiral Tom Spencer Vaughan Phillips. There were 34 high-level bombers and 51 torpedo-bombers coming at the ships from all directions. Winston Churchill heard the news by telephone from the Chief of Naval Staff.

'I never received a more direct shock,' he commented.

As militarily admirable as it might have seemed to the Japanese at the time, the long-term consequences of the attack on Pearl Harbor were clearly ill thought-out. Japan had a superb

Below: *Both Roosevelt and Cordell Hull were disgusted by the Japanese attack.*

navy, powerful enough to compete with that of America or Britain, with the most modern aircraft carrier fleet in the world.

A GIANT AWAKENED

Japan could not have hoped for an occupation of the US. It was a geographical and numerical impossibility. If the leaders of Japan hoped the action at Pearl Harbor would encourage the Americans to capitulate, they sorely misjudged their foe. The aim seems to have been merely to cause enough damage to keep America at bay while Japan built up its strength in the Pacific.

It is likely they were then hoping for a war of attrition in which America would compromise. Admiral Yamamoto clearly had

an inclination of what lay ahead when he said: 'I fear we have only awakened a sleeping giant and his reaction will be terrible.'

Above: British newspapers joined the wave of indignation against the war-mongering Japanese after their opening strikes in the Pacific.

EYE WITNESS

A correspondent for the National Broadcasting Corporation gave this account of the bombing of Pearl Harbor.

❛The most thickly populated air base was attacked by Japanese planes a little after 8am local time.

After machine-gunning Ford Island the Japanese planes moved to Hickman Field. Observers say that considerable damage was done there but a number of planes were brought down.

Three ships of the United States Pacific Fleet based at Pearl Harbor were attacked and the 29,000-ton battleship *Oklahoma* was set on fire.

All lines of communication appear to be down between the various Army and Navy aerodromes and the Army in the field. The Army has issued orders for all people to remain off the streets.

The first raiders carried torpedoes and did considerable damage to shipping in Pearl Harbor and off Honolulu. They came in squadron formation over Diamond Head, dropping high explosives and incendiary bombs. They came over Honolulu itself and were at once met with anti-aircraft from Pearl Harbor, Ford Island, Wheeler Field, Honolulu Municipal Airport, Hickman Field and the new Navy repair base. A terrific barrage was put up but all the points I mentioned appear to have been attacked.

The chief of fire services has reported that the fires were under control and were not as bad as expected. ❜

FIRES IN THE NIGHT

While German bombers werc pounding Britain during 1940 and 1941, the British people huddled night after night in stuffy, cramped shelters and comforted themselves that Royal Air Force bombers were delivering similar punishment to the citizens of the Third Reich.

S adly, they were mistaken. While British bomber crews were full of sterling young men with an iron resolve, their success rate in the first half of the war was low – and for sound reasons.

Night bombing was far safer for the aircraft and crew, as the Germans had illustrated in their raids over London. RAF Bomber Command was keen to conserve these valuable assets too and favoured night-time bombing raids instead of exposing its forces to daylight risks.

But the Luftwaffe was operating from occupied airfields a short hop over the English Channel. For the Royal Air Force to strike at the heart of Germany, its pilots and planes had to fly many more miles than their German counterparts, in aircraft that were ill-equipped for long-distance flying or bombing. It took time and investment for new, heavier bombers to be commissioned for the task.

The limited resources of Bomber Command were stretched in many different directions. Not only were there the demands of bombing raids over enemy territory but Coastal Command was in constant need of planes to combat the U-boat menace in the Battle of the Atlantic. With Britain under threat of isolation if the U-boat peril was not seen to, the need to have planes available for maritime duties was paramount in 1940. In addition, the Middle East and North Africa required a quota of bombers, together with crews and parts – all of which required regular replacements. For a while, night bombing raids over Germany were abandoned so the force could focus on its duties elsewhere.

EARLY PROBLEMS

Operational shortcomings put the RAF at a disadvantage, too. For the first sorties were flown, rather informally, on an almost

individual level. Following a joint briefing, each aircraft would depart at five-minute intervals following a course chosen by its own navigator to the target. Often, the crews would not catch sight of another plane until after their return. The effect of single bomb drops on

For a while night bombing raids over Germany were abandoned altogether

the ground were, of course, much less than an orchestrated raid involving greater numbers.

Added to this, the navigational aids available on planes at the time were wildly inaccurate. Crews conforming to their instructions were sure their bombs were away right on top of the targets. It was not the case. While bomber crews scored hits on clear nights in easily located target areas, bombs dropped on blacked-out Germany often as not fell short. After the war it was discovered that 49 per cent of the ordnance released by British crews between May 1940 and May 1941 exploded in open countryside.

Navigators used maps, a sextant and a procedure of 'dead-reckoning' to work out their position, all of which could be fouled up by poor weather conditions. Precision bombing by the RAF at night could be successful only on clear, bright,

Left: German planes on a daylight raid of London before night-time tactics were introduced.
Far left: The Renault works at Billancourt after bombing by the Allies.

Above: A Wellington bomber and its crew prepare for an arduous night's work over Hitler's 'Fortress Europe'.

windless nights of which there were few. It took many months before the difficulties of finding targets under cover of darkness were resolved.

Bomber Command was bearing losses from the missions over Germany, in exchange for few results. It soon became clear a new tactic was in order.

The principles of precision bombing – almost impossible to execute successfully given the constraints of the era – were abandoned for 'area bombing'. A large factory making vital components in open countryside would be overlooked in favour of a smaller factory among other small factories and industrial workers' housing.

That way enormous damage could be caused for the same amount of effort and risk as was required in precision bombing. Not only was there the clear-cut

intention of halting Germany's industrial output, but the chance to demoralise the people by bringing the war to their doorstep, making them homeless or otherwise hampering their daily existence.

The concept was fostered by Air Marshal Sir Richard Peirse, in charge of Bomber Command during 1941. The failure of his forces to destroy three German warships, *Scharnhorst*, *Gneisenau* and the heavy cruiser *Prinz Eugen*, while they were in dock at Brest, northern France, did little for the reputation of the force.

BREST RAIDS

While these three sea monsters roamed, the British suffered terribly. Between them they were responsible for the loss of HMS *Glorious*, HMS *Ardent*, HMS *Acasta* and the armed merchant cruiser *Rawalpindi* and something in the order of 115,600 tons of merchant shipping.

In the spring of 1941, Bomber Command flew 1,161 sorties against the ships, scoring just four direct hits, none causing substantial damage. All this for the loss of 43 bombers. Even when the three ships left the dockyard to slip back to home

Below: Air Chief Marshal Sir Arthur 'Bomber' Harris, Commander of the RAF's Bomber Command.

ports, the 242 planes sent to destroy them failed to dent the pride of the German navy.

It signalled the departure of Peirse and the arrival of Air Chief Marshal Arthur Harris, who adopted the idea of area bombing as his own.

Afterwards, Harris summed up his position. 'I had to prove quickly, to the satisfaction of those who mattered that the bomber force could do its work if it was large enough and if its efforts were not frittered away on objectives other than German industry as a whole.'

The historic town was engulfed in a firestorm which swallowed up 200 acres

---

His first priority was to bolster the stocks of planes available to carry out attacks, particularly heavy bombers of which there were fewer than 70.

An opportunity to prove the ability of himself and his men came just a matter of weeks after he was installed at Bomber Command. On 3 March 1942, Harris sent a force of 235 bombers across to Billancourt, France, where a giant Renault factory was turning out tank components for the German war effort.

The planes set off in three waves and now Harris mimicked a successful German tactic. The first wave carried not only bombs but a large number of flares which would light up the target for subsequent attackers. With the River Seine acting as a brilliant marker, 223 of the aircraft found their targets within

the space of two hours. Enough machinery was put out of action to stop the factory working for several months.

Harris felt that Germany's industrial heartland of the Ruhr was his for the taking.

Five days after the Renault raid, 211 bombers took off and headed towards the city of Essen. Once again, the technique of using flares and incendiaries was employed. But this time, many had burnt out before the second wave of bombers had got the measure of the area. It finally bore the hallmarks of the haphazard raids which Bomber Command were now known for. Another three attacks made on ensuing nights also failed to produce the spectacular results Harris yearned for although there was widespread damage caused in the city.

Harris had to wait until the end of the month for the next feather in his cap, a raid carried out against Lübeck, a Baltic port comprising many ancient timbered buildings.

When almost 200 aircraft dropped 300 tons of high explosives plus 144 tons of incendiaries on the night of 28/29 March, the historic town was engulfed in a firestorm which swallowed up 200 acres.

ROSTOCK RAID

At the end of April another Baltic port, Rostock, was given similar treatment. The targets for the bombers were specifically a factory which produced the Heinkel 111 aircraft and the town itself. An estimated 70 per cent of the old town was turned to rubble with direct hits being scored against the factory too. Of the 168 bombers that set off for the mission, all but 12 returned safely.

Harris noted that, yard for yard, the destruction wrought in Germany by Bomber Command in those two raids equalled that caused by the Luftwaffe in Britain in 1940 and 1941.

Below: The Renault works at Billancourt was destroyed by Bomber Command.

The Nazi hierarchy was riled by the savage encroachment into the Fatherland. In a fury, Hitler ordered raids against Britain's historic cities to even the score. He picked the targets from a tourists' book of Britain called the *Baedeker Guide*. Among them were Bath and Exeter.

'MILLENNIUM'

For one daring raid against a factory producing U-boat parts, Harris was persuaded to return to daylight attack. New Avro Lancaster heavy bombers were brought in for the assault on Augsburg in southern Germany. Together with their fighter escorts they flew in low over enemy territory to avoid radar detection and then began a breathtaking roof-top scrap with Luftwaffe fighters before hitting their target. The cost was high. Seven out of 12 bombers were lost. The crews of the

returning battle scarred aircraft were decorated for their bravery.

It confirmed the view that daylight raids were too risky given the aircraft available. In any event, Harris became far too preoccupied with his latest tactical trailblazer to consider further daylight sorties. The continued all-out efforts to obliterate the Ruhr were proving frustrating. With the lack of truly efficient navigation and the industrial smog it was impossible to co-ordinate a successful mission. He had pondered about pulling off a single operation which would earn the admiration of those doubters at home and the trepidation of the Germans.

The answer, he decided, was a thousand-bomber raid against a prime target in Germany. But, given that the most he had been able to rally for an attack to date was 235 bombers, it seemed this was nothing more than a

flight of fancy. That was until Harris's deputy Air Vice Marshal Saundby got to work.

With the use of borrowed aircraft from Coastal Command and the entire stock of his reserves flown by trainee pilots and instructors alongside existing crews, it was conceivable that 1,000 bombers could be gathered for an epic raid.

Code-named 'Operation Millennium', the first thousand-bomber raid took place against Cologne on 30 May 1942. All the planes were to strike within an hour and a half.

The raid represented a new departure in aerial warfare. The largest force of aircraft dispatched to Britain at any one time had numbered 487 while the British had never been able to gather together more than 235 bombers at any one time.

Churchill was captivated by the idea of such a mighty strike. He

Below: *An RAF Wellington bomber is loaded with bombs before setting off on another mission.*

was under pressure from fellow politicians who saw the largely inconclusive night raids against Germany as a waste of time and effort. Stalin was also waiting in the wings, always demanding a decisive attack by the British against Germany. It was realised that there would be too

> ## Ground crews worked flat out on damaged aircraft to furnish Harris with the required number

few German fighters in the air to halt the impact of the raid. The possibility of collision was to be diminished by dividing the planes into three groups operating in parallel lines against different targets. Despite the immense commitment, it seemed the risks were calculated. The raid could not end up as the swan-song of Bomber Command.

1,046 BOMBERS

For some time, 'Operation Millennium' was under threat as Coastal Command refused to release the 250 planes it had promised. Its chiefs had got cold feet. They decided the risk of releasing their aircraft was too

great. A spell of poor weather which caused the operation to be postponed proved a saving grace. Ground crews worked flat out on damaged aircraft to furnish Harris with the required number. On the morning of 30 May the magic 1,000 was surpassed.

The 1,046 bombers departed from 53 airfields across Britain and assembled in a 70-mile convoy across the North Sea. Before them went 50 fighter planes ready to duel with the defending Luftwaffe.

Mechanical difficulties would account for 100 planes in the force even before it had reached the target and they turned back to base.

Still, the first bombs and incendiaries were dropped at 12.47am on 31 May. The rest of the operation went according to plan. Land-based defences and intercepting Luftwaffe fighters were overwhelmed and the last bomber dropped its load over Cologne at 2.25am.

As they flew homewards, rear gunners could see the city burning from 150 miles away. The night's work destroyed 18,432 buildings, killed nearly 500 people, injured 5,000 more

Above: *Sir Barnes Wallis, inventor of the bouncing bomb, which proved a huge morale-booster in Britain.*

and left almost 60,000 homeless. Forty bombers did not return, which meant the loss of 40 instructors and 49 pupils.

It was hailed as a triumph at home but the success in itself put pressure on Harris to produce more of the same. Now the British public expected many more raids of similar dimensions to lambast the enemy.

An attack on Essen on 1 June involving 956 bombers left key industrial centres unscathed.

It wasn't until 25 June that another large-scale attack was attempted, on Bremen. For the 1,046 bombers, it was a great success except for the higher number of casualties claimed by Germany. This time 49 aircraft didn't return.

The Luftwaffe quickly realised the intention of Bomber Command. It set about denying the British an opportunity to destroy German industry.

To combat the upsurge in Luftwaffe fighters and improve

EYE WITNESS

Dennis Golding, of Gosport, near Portsmouth, England, was a British rifleman with the King's Royal Rifle Corps. As a light infantryman he was engaged in hand-to-hand combat with German troops throughout the 1944 advance across Western Europe.

❝On VE day we marched into Hamburg to find everything devastated except the roads. The Germans had cleared them and stacked up all the re-usable bricks they could salvage. It was typical German efficiency and I suppose it also helped improve their morale.

The civilians were more or less glad to see us. There was certainly no hostility and, like our own people, they were just glad it was all over. We weren't allowed to fraternise with them at first. It you were caught you were put on a charge. That rule soon broke down. When they spoke to you you felt you had to talk back.❞

EYE WITNESS

George Funnell joined the 55th Kent Regiment in 1939 aged 17, after lying about his age. He witnessed the Blitz in London when he was stationed at an anti-aircraft battery – and later saw the destruction caused by air raids in Germany after fighting his way through Normandy, Belgium and Holland to Hamburg in 1944.

❛In Hamburg there was mile after mile of devastation. I lived through the London bombing but it was nothing like as bad as that over Germany.

Even when we got to Hamburg, long after the air raids had taken place, there was still the stench of death coming from crumbled buildings. It took ages to find some of the buried remains.

On the streets we only found a few old men and young boys. The rest of the male population had been called up into the army. The vast majority of the people we met were women struggling to survive as best they could.❜

most successful in capturing the public's imagination in terms of a morale-boosting coup and depriving the Atlantic Wall in northern France of some labour.

Harris continued his bombing campaign, targeting Hamburg. 'Operation Gomorrah' began on 24 July with the first use of aluminium foil, which was able to fog radar screens. The Air Ministry refrained from using as the same device could be used in retaliation. Germany also refrained from using it, for the same reason. Called 'Window', it was brought in to play on the orders of Churchill in a bid to counter the Luftwaffe defences.

HAMBURG HORROR

At midnight 740 bombers dropped 92 million strips of tin foil, blocking radar systems. The planes went on to deliver almost 3,000 tons of bombs. Subsequent attacks made by night and day virtually devastated the city's defences. Fine weather had left the city dry as paper. As new fires were sparked by existing blazes, the perpetual heating of the air which funnelled into the sky caused a firestorm, akin to a

tornado with wind speeds of 150 miles per hour. Delayed detonators on some of the bombs wrought havoc among the rescue workers.

The melting temperatures achieved in the raid scorched buildings and bomb shelters, water mains and electric cables. Hamburg endured the horror for nine days by which time ten square miles of the city was laid waste. In total 2,630 bombers unleashed more than 4,300 tons of incendiaries and a similar amount of high explosives, creating three firestorms. The death toll was estimated at 42,000.

Harris continued to work through the list of German cities he hoped to destroy. His armoury now included a 12,000lb bomb and excellent new navigational aids and target-finders. Now his sights turned towards Berlin. The German capital was a far-distant target from British airfields across hostile territory. The Battle of Berlin opened in November 1943 and a further 15 attacks were launched against it. The demands on the participating crews of Bomber Command eased when airfields were opened in Europe following D-Day. Those raids cost no less

than 587 aircraft together with 3,640 men killed or missing. When reconnaissance photographs proved little was being gained from the attacks, they were suspended.

If Harris had hoped to end the war with his tactics bathed in a blaze of glory, he was to be disappointed. Public opinion both in Britain and overseas began to question the wisdom of saturation bombing.

On 30 March 1944 a night raid by Halifaxes and Lancasters was sent awry by a strong wind which sent them into the arms of defending Luftwaffe fighters. Out of the 795 aircraft that set off, 95 failed to return and another dozen crashed in England. Night bombing raids afterwards came to an end.

Below: A reconnaissance photograph reveals the damage done to the Möhne Dam by Wing Commander Guy Gibson and his Dambusters.

the success of the night bombing raids, a Pathfinder force was created, led by Australian Group Captain D.C.T. Bennett, a first-class pilot and skilled navigator.

Their aim was to fly 'finder' aircraft over the target on parallel tracks two miles apart dropping flares, creating a 'runway'. Behind them came 'Illuminator' aircraft, dropping further flares picking out the target area precisely. Then came the 'marker' group starting fires with incendiaries to pinpoint the targets for following bombers. When it was cloudy the Pathfinders dropped 'sky-markers', parachute flares which lit up the target beneath the cloud cover. In response the Germans used fires on the ground as decoys in much the same way as the British did during the Battle of Britain. The Pathfinders proved a huge boon to the night bombing raids, with the additional attraction that their loss rate was a smaller-than-average three per cent.

At the end of 1942 Bomber Command diverted resources to the 'Torch' landings in North Africa and provided valuable support. At the same time it carried out some successful raids over Italy, finding the air defences there far lighter than those in Germany.

Still, Harris was determined to kill off German industry in the Ruhr. By March 1943 he was set upon a concerted attack on the region. The Battle of the Ruhr got underway on the night of 5 March with a 442 aircraft raid and continued for six weeks more or less none stop. During the battle the

Above: A Lancaster of 617 Squadron, loaded with its 'bouncing bomb' before heading for the German dams.

famous Dambusters raid was carried out. Although Harris himself was opposed to it, the Air Ministry favoured a plan to knock out three giant dams which would deprive the region of vital hydroelectric power. To succeed, Wing Commander Guy Gibson and his squadron had to drop new 'bouncing bombs', designed by engineer Barnes Wallis.

DAMBUSTERS

Each bomb weighed five tons, measured five feet in length and four feet across. Carried in a special cradle beneath a Lancaster bomber, it went into action with backspin imparted, which would cause it to skip along the surface of the water until it met the dam wall.

The targeted dams – the Möhne, the Eder and the Sorpe – were 150 feet high and their concrete walls were almost the same again in thickness. The skill required by Gibson and his crews was enormous. They had to fly in at low altitude to evade

German radar and drop their bombs at precisely 60 feet above the water and exactly 425 yards from the perimeter of the dam.

On the night of 16 May 1943 the 19 Lancasters took off in three waves. In the first wave of nine planes, headed by Gibson, one plane was lost to flak before three explosions ripped through the Möhne Dam and a flood poured down the valley.

In the second wave just one of the five Lancasters reached the Sorpe Dam, under the guidance of Flight Lieutenant McCarthy, an American serving with the RAF. His bomb load damaged the dam but failed to breach it. The third wave scythed a gap in the Eder Dam.

Eight of the Lancasters together with their 56 crew members failed to return. And, although it was a feat of undoubted heroism, the damage took the Germans just three months to repair. Perhaps it was

CARRIERS AND KAMIKAZES

Americans were down in the dumps following the raid on Pearl Harbor. With the Imperial Japanese Army and Navy riding roughshod over the Pacific and South East Asia, there was no glimmer of optimism as the nation became preoccupied with the sight of its young men marching off to war.

Finally, on 18 April 1942, there came some small consolation for the folks back home. It was provided by a daring air raid into the heart of Japan itself. American airman Lt-Colonel Jimmy Doolittle, a veteran of glamorous pre-war air races, delivered a small but significant strike back against the aggressor.

The newly commissioned aircraft carrier *Hornet*, bearing 16 army bombers, in the company of fellow carrier *Enterprise* and a body of cruisers set off from Midway Island towards Japan. Some 650 miles short of the Japanese coastline, the fleet stopped so the B-25s could be launched. Despite the stiff wind, the planes took off at dawn, heading for Tokyo and other major cities.

At noon, 13 of the aircraft unloaded their cargoes of bombs over Tokyo. The other three dropped incendiaries on Nagoya, Osaka and Kobe. In fact, little was achieved in the

exploit and many Japanese people remained unaware that it had even taken place at all. Its main effect was to shock the Japanese commanders who had until now considered themselves somewhat impregnable.

It now seemed vital to the Japanese to take control of Midway Island, a gap in the extended front line they had created in the Pacific. Those who had doubted the wisdom of pushing Japanese lines still further were persuaded that the vulnerability of the home islands warranted the new push.

As for the attacking American B25s, they did not have the range to return to the aircraft carriers which were by now high-tailing it for home. Their orders were to seek out friendly airstrips in China.

JAPANESE REPRISALS

All made it out of Japanese air space without a problem although one crash-landed in Russian Vladivostok. Only four

of the planes actually touched down while the rest ditched after their crews baled out. Three of the men were captured by Japanese troops operating in China and shot.

A further five died but 72, aided by Chinese peasants, made their way to Chungking and eventual freedom.

When Japan realised the escape route taken by the fliers, troops exacted revenge against the native Chinese, slaughtering anyone suspected of aiding the airmen.

It was 30 months before Japan was once again in range of American bombers. This time the aircraft were far more fearsome, their capacity for wreaking terror far greater than in 1942.

Even from airfields in India and China in the summer of 1944, the American fliers found it difficult to carry out effective missions over Japan. The only island within their range was Kyushu, the southernmost Japanese home island.

It took victory in Saipan, freeing the Marianas Islands and their airfields, before a more comprehensive bombing campaign could begin. On 24 November 1944, 110 B-29s took off with the aim of knocking out Japan's aircraft industry in Tokyo, Nagoya, Kobe and Osaka. They were to drop 500lb bombs from high altitudes. But cloud cover obscured the targets and only one factory out of nine was struck.

Left: Lieutenant-Colonel Doolittle ties a medal to a bomb bound for Japan.
Far left: US Navy pilots receive a final briefing before a raid on Tokyo.

At the start of 1945 Major-General Curtis LeMay was brought into 21st Bomber Command. He had an inkling that the flimsy wooden shacks which filled Japanese cities were a major fire hazard. He pinpointed incendiaries as the best weapon with which to attack them.

On 4 February his theories were proved correct when a force of 70 Boeing B-29 Superfortresses dropped 160

To add to the effect of the bombs a fresh wind fanned the flames

tons of incendiaries on the centre of Kobe. A tenth of a square mile was burnt out and that included several factories.

The ploy was repeated on 25 February, this time against Tokyo. 172 B-29s dropped nearly 450 tons of incendiaries, devastating a square mile. An estimated 28,000 buildings were razed.

Right: Kobe, Japan's sixth-largest city, comes under attack with incendiaries dropped by US B-29s. Fires have already been sparked in the industrial areas.

Left: A B-25 heavy bomber takes off from the USS Hornet to deliver its load to Japan. The Doolittle Raid sparked Japanese reprisals in China.

Interrupted by the call for aid in Okinawa, LeMay had time to consider his options. The use of incendiaries had proved itself beyond question but the effect was far more widespread when the bombs were dropped from lower altitudes. It pointed to the need for night raids.

In advance, a single plane would pinpoint targets with marker bombs and the rest of the bombing party would follow at intervals of every couple of minutes.

On the night of 9 March 334 B29s took off and showered a 12-square-mile industrial area of Tokyo with 1,700 tons of oil incendiaries. To add to the effect of the bombs, a fresh wind fanned the flames until it seemed the entire city was on fire.

RAIDS CONTINUE

Anti-aircraft fire claimed 14 of the planes but their mission was an outstanding success. No less than 16 square miles of the city had been burned out, with 267,000 buildings flattened and 84,000 people killed. An official Japanese report noted: 'People were unable to escape. They were found later piled upon the

EYE WITNESS

Masuo Kato was a reporter in Japan throughout the war and detailed the terror by fire inflicted by US bombers.

❝For more than three years my small nephew Kozo Ishikawa, who was about five years old when the war began, held an unshakeable faith in Japanese victory. To his small world it was unthinkable that the Emperor's armies could suffer defeat or that the Japanese navy should endure any fate other than glorious victory.

After his home was burned to the ground during a B-29 raid, destroying almost every familiar material thing that had made up his existence, he told me with great gravity. "We cannot beat the B-29." The psychological effect of the loss of his home went deep. He had been one of the happiest and most carefree of children. He became thoughtful and serious and it was seldom that he laughed. He became ill and died shortly after the war was over. A nervous breakdown, the doctor called it.

The B-29s had brought the war to the Japanese people in a real and personal sense and each man had begun to form his own opinion on whether Japan was winning or losing. My nephew's experience was repeated many thousands of times in every part of Japan. To each family that watched its home and belongings go skyward in a rush of smoke and flame, the news from Okinawa, true or false, meant little. For them, their personal war was already lost.❞

bridges, roads and in the canals. We were instructed to report on actual conditions. Most of us were unable to do this because of horrifying conditions.

Two nights later 285 aircraft dropped 1,800 tons of incendiaries at Nagoya. Without the wind, the fires were more contained. One aircraft was lost and two square miles of the city destroyed.

On 13 March Osaka was the target for 274 B-29s. 13,000 people died, 135,000 homes were

Below: A large area of Osaka was levelled by sustained fire-bomb attacks carried out by the Americans.

Above: Tokyo became a patchwork city following the destruction delivered by the incendiary raids, with much of its industry and housing flattened.

burned down and 119 factories were knocked out. American losses were light, with just two aircraft lost and 13 damaged by anti-aircraft fire.

The heaviest attack was made against Kobe on 16 March, using 2,355 tons of mixed oil and thermite bombs. More than 300 planes launched the onslaught and three were lost. At Kobe 2,669 people were killed, with 66,000 houses and 500 industrial centres eradicated. A fifth strike was made against Nagoya three days later, in which high-explosive bombs were among those used.

In 11 days 21st Bomber Command had notched up

Right: Major-General Curtis LeMay (left) believed the policies of 21st Bomber Command – obliterating key centres – would bring about Japan's defeat.

1,595 sorties and dropped in excess of 9,000 tons of incendiary bombs, proving that Japan was exposed to complete devastation. Equally as important to the Americans was the low level of losses the bomber command had sustained. Only 20 aircraft were destroyed, mostly by anti-aircraft fire and only one per cent of the crews were lost.

The rate of attacks was kept up, some made by day but those against Tokyo were at night. LeMay became involved

in psychological warfare, too, with the dropping of thousands of leaflets prior to the raids, naming 12 cities which were going to be hit and urging the civilian population to evacuate. This not only spread confusion but helped to demoralise the battered, war-weary population.

At the same time, 21st Bomber Command was involved in a minelaying programme to complete the blockade of Japan. Between the end of March and the middle of August about 12,000 mines were dropped into the waters around the islands. It meant that in May, mines were responsible for more losses to Japanese shipping than submarines were.

LEAFLETS DROPPED

Submarines were then able to move into the Sea of Japan, looking for the occasional ship which had escaped the blockade and also organising lightning sabotage raids.

With the Japanese Imperial Navy now completely impotent and the majority of surviving Japanese aircraft in hiding, American aircraft carriers also

EYE WITNESS

Geoff Michael, from Perth, was 18 when he joined the Royal Australian, Air Force in 1942 and trained under the Empire Air Training Scheme, launched in 1939 to train Allied pilots. He went on to complete 32 missions with Bomber Command and retired from the RAAF after 37 years' service, as Air Commodore.

❝Even though it was a hectic and sad time, one is inclined to remember most of the good things – the great time I had on leaves etc.

But I also recall vividly having my aircraft shot up by ground fire and fighters. The fortunate part was that I was never wounded and never lost a crew member.

However, I did lose a close mate who was killed in a daylight raid over Germany. I saw the plane go down but didn't realise at the time it was my mate's plane.

It was a time when we were conditioned to death. Every morning you expected not to see the next one. So all you did was to read the operations board, see if you had been metered on a mission and, if your weren't, go out and relax and have a good time.❞

DEVASTATION

In Japan itself the people were enduring appalling hardship. Homelessness caused by the effective incendiary strikes left many in dire straits. If their factories had also been destroyed they were in an even worse situation. There were few building materials on hand in the devastated city and little food. Inadequate rice rations were sometimes being boosted by sawdust. The wounded were also receiving scant attention. But if the population went to the countryside to scavenge food where it could, who would man the remaining factories and workplaces?

By August, Japanese ministers called for a collection of acorns to turn into food

Natural disasters, including extensive flooding, added to their problems. By July 1945 an estimated 25 per cent of all housing in Japan had been destroyed, leaving 22 million people homeless.

By August, Japanese ministers had called for a collection of acorns to turn into food. Yet, the people spoke of surrender only in whispers. An inherent will to serve the Emperor prevented an uprising. The Japanese would struggle on regardless.

LeMay was delighted with the success of his aerial bombing campaign and was convinced that it alone would bring Japan to the point of surrender. His confidence was somewhat premature.

sailed close to the home islands, their aircraft launching attacks at regular intervals. Freed by the end of the war in Europe, Royal Navy warships joined the US Navy in the waters off Japan, and combined attacks were launched, before the typhoon season made any air attack impossible.

In August a Japanese plan to launch 2,000 kamikaze planes on the 21st Bomber Command bases in the Marianas was discovered. The carrier fleets moved to within range of the airfields on the northern island of Honshu where the heavily camouflaged planes were being gathered for the covert operation. For the first time since the end of the Okinawa campaign, a Japanese fighter counter-attacked and a kamikaze aircraft struck at an American destroyer. Still, Japanese airfields came in for heavy bombing.

DAYLIGHT RAIDING

By the time America entered the war, the British had some fixed ideas about aerial combat.

The Royal Air Force had learned the hard way that aircraft employed on daylight raids were more vulnerable to the enemy, that bombers had a better survival rate when they were accompanied by fighters. Harris and the other British air supremos thought it best that the US fliers reinforced the existing night bombing expeditions being carried out by the RAF.

Novices at warfare in the air they may have been, but the Americans had thoughts of their own on the issue. US pilots were untrained for night missions. Not only that, they had a different bombing philosophy from that of their British counterparts, that of precision bombing.

FIRST ACTION

Given that their Flying Fortresses were, in their opinion, well defended and that the aircraft were equipped with a revolutionary new bombsight called the Norden which 'could drop a bomb into a pickle

barrel from 20,000ft', it was their preferred plan to fly during the day. No amount of friendly persuasion from the British could dissuade the US air chiefs from their stated aims.

The Royal Air Force held Flying Fortresses in low regard. During experiments with the new aircraft in 1941, pilots felt they became large targets for German defences. For their part, the US air chiefs believed the RAF had used the Fortresses wrongly, sending them out in twos and threes instead of in a large formation when they performed best.

First taste of action for the US pilots came on 17 August 1942 when a dozen Flying Fortresses flew out of Grafton Underwood aerodrome, heading for Rouen, northern France.

With protection from four squadrons of RAF Spitfires, they made the flight, dropped the 18.5 tons of bombs on railway targets and returned home intact but for slight damage on two Fortresses caused by flak.

On the mission was Ira

C. Eaker, a Brigadier-General, and superb pilot, who set up the headquarters for the US 8th Air Force in Britain and was soon given command of its European flight operations.

There followed a succession of small-scale bombing raids. The success of precision bombing was trumpeted by Eaker although, like the number of victories claimed against the Luftwaffe on such outings, the statistics had to be treated with caution. Nevertheless, in 13 missions, just two planes were lost – an enviable record.

The Norden bombsight 'could drop a bomb into a pickle barrel from 20,000 ft'

Still, their operations had been strictly 'local' on missions regarded as workaday 'milk runs' by the British pilots.

Left: A US Flying Fortress carries out daylight bombing raid over Germany. *Below:* By 1942, US aircraft were a familiar sight in Britain.

Above: US B-17s plough on towards their targets while fighter escorts fend off marauding enemy interceptors. The range of escorts increased during the war.

Then poor weather began to not only hamper the efficiency of the Norden bombsight – which had earned its colours in the cloudless skies above New Mexico and struggled in the cloud – and smog-filled heavens above Germany – but brought about the wholesale cancellation of planned raids.

Like the RAF, the USAAF had to do its bit for the 'Torch' landings in North Africa in late 1942, which cut aircraft and crew stocks by a third.

Then the Luftwaffe hit on a new tactic which took its toll among the American fighters. German pilots spotted the Achilles heel of the Flying Fortresses, which was head–on attack. There were no defences on the nose of the plane and the

Germans had enough guts to mount daring frontal assaults despite the obvious risk of a collision.

Churchill was among those who strongly objected to the Americans going their own way. He believed that precision bombing being executed by the Americans, which needed daylight to succeed, was the height of folly. Area bombing under the cover of darkness appeared a far better bet and might encourage the Americans to venture for the first time over German territory.

At the Casablanca Conference of January 1943, Churchill hoped to persuade Roosevelt that daylight bombing raids should be dropped in favour of night bombing operations by both air forces.

Eaker had one chance beforehand to convince Winston Churchill otherwise. Finally, it only took one sentence. His proposal in favour of the

continuation of daylight raids contained the words: 'By bombing the devils around the clock we can prevent the German defences from getting any rest.' The idea instantly caught Churchill's imagination. He vowed to give Eaker the opportunity to prove his point.

THE B-24 ARRIVES

The Casablanca Directive, backed orchestrated day- and night-time bombing raids and listed top targets, namely the centres of German industry.

On 27 January that year the US airmen were at last sent to Germany to produce the goods. Their target was Wilhelmshaven on the North Sea, where U-boats were made. By now B-24 Liberators had joined the Flying Fortresses in the ranks. Of the 53 which left for Wilhelmshaven, three were lost and the remainder had to battle at close quarters with Luftwaffe fighters while achieving only moderate success in their mission. The difficulties of daylight raids over hostile territory were crystallised for the Americans.

Danger from flak and enemy fighters was not the only problem to be faced by the Americans on their daylight raids. To stay out of reach of the enemy, they flew at high altitudes, usually above 20,000 feet. The chill of the air numbed their faces, crammed as they were in small cockpits. Tension mixed with boredom as another lengthy mission got underway. For a while each member of the crew remained vigilant for the enemy, but there were long hours when the Luftwaffe didn't

EYE WITNESS

Burdsall D. Miller, from Sacramento, California, joined the US Army Air Force, aged 24, following the Japanese raid on Pearl Harbor. Based in Sudbury, England, he became a colonel and flew 32 missions.

❝I flew ten missions in a B-24 Liberator and then switched to B-17s for a further 22 raids. Most of them were daylight raids over Germany although we also hit Italy and Noway. I got shot up but never enough to bale out or crash land.

As command pilot, I sat in the co-pilot's seat and made all the decisions as far as the group or squadron were concerned that day. I was scared but I was trained to do a job. The thing that made the biggest impression on me was flying in formation and seeing a wing man shot down in flames. It was very upsetting.

But we all got fatalistic and figured when our time came we were going to get it. Perhaps that made us seem like we had nerves of steel. Otherwise we would not have lasted. We had some men who didn't last. They refused to fly, but It was very few out of a considerable number of men.

As soon as we dropped our bombs, we got out of the target area as most were heavily defended. As we turned we could see bombs hitting and we could usually tell if we had hit the target.

I have a big picture at home. It was taken on a raid over Germany on one of the most heavily defended targets. We had turned to start our bombing run. We just opened our bomb bay doors. To the left of us, another plane was doing the same when some flak went right into the bomb bay. The plane just exploded. Nobody got out alive. At the moment the plane blew up, my waist gunner took the picture.❞

appear in which there was little to do but study the clouds.

Every US airman wore a steel chain vest to protect himself from flak. His flight suit was thick to protect him from the cold. Each wore a parachute and an oxygen mask, itself deeply uncomfortable. Despite the elaborate precautions, there

was at least a one in ten chance of dying.

Americans adopted different flying patterns to suit the daylight nature of the raid. Up to 21 planes would form a box which was staggered vertically and horizontally for protection. Three boxes lined up in the air to form a combat wing.

To improve the accuracy of bombing, the most skilful men were placed in the lead planes and gave the signal for the rest of the aircraft in the box to drop their bombs.

Historically the US Army Air Corps was treated as the poor relation by the White House

On the ground, Eaker had his own problems. The US Army Air Corps, as it was first known, was treated as the poor relation by the White House. Priorities changed only slowly during the war and Eaker spent many fruitless hours harrying his bosses in America for extra planes and crews. It wasn't until mid-1943 that his efforts paid off. The US 8th Air Force could at last increase the size and effectiveness of its attacks.

DANGEROUS GAME

Perhaps the biggest bonus of all to the US airmen was when fighter aircraft increased their range, although it was late in the conflict when a combat aircraft, which could escort bombers into the heart of Germany and back, came into use.

Daylight missions were stepped up in 1943 and the heavy bombers recorded some admirable successes. Assisting their cause was the decision to scale down Luftwaffe defences in France by withdrawing two groups back to the Reich to improve air security there. The

Left: *Despite damage from a German rocket in the Battle of Berlin, this US B-17 still managed to land safely.*

Allies were now making a concerted effort to draw the Luftwaffe aircraft into the sky at every opportunity, trying to shoot down as many as possible. A considerable number of Allied planes fell victim while playing this dangerous game.

PLOESTI RAID

The US medium bombers fared less fortunately. A flight of B-26C Marauders which set off from Great Saling on 17 May was virtually wiped out during a raid on Haarlem.

And raids later in the year proved yet again the perils of daylight raiding. On 1 August 1943 the target was Ploesti, the oilfields in Romania which fed Germany's war machine.

The Americans had planned a surprise attack, keeping radio silence and flying at low altitudes to avoid radar detection. Their approach was to be over a lightly defended sector and their escape route was to North Africa. Alas, the planes were picked up in Germany as soon as they left the runway.

Navigational errors brought them in over the thickest of the anti-aircraft gunfire. Fifty three of the Liberators on the raid were shot down in enemy territory. A further 55 reached Libya in such appalling condition that they were fit only for scrap. The results were disappointing, with only a small dent being made in the oil production levels.

In the same month, the Americans tackled Regensburg and Schweinfurt, key centres for aircraft manufacturing and the production of that tiny but indispensible engineering component, the ball bearing. The raids would be without fighter escorts. So deep were the targets inside Reich territory the existing fighters did not have the capacity to fly there and back.

When the 146 Flying Fortresses dispatched for Regensburg crossed over the German border they met a hail of fire from a host of defending Luftwaffe planes. The German pilots were under no illusions. They were no longer the favoured elite. Hitler was once

Above: A German tank factory is ruined and its new stock in tatters following a daylight raid by the United States Army Air Forces. The Americans specialised in precision bombing by day.

again frustrated at the lack of success brought home by the Luftwaffe which once had seemed invincible. Now fewer resources were being ploughed into aircraft manufacture and the training of crews. Without this investment, the entire force would surely be strangled. Luftwaffe production chief Ernest Udet had committed suicide in despair at the plight of the force. The pressure was on to prove the worth of the air force before the unpredictable Führer sought his own revenge against it.

Those Flying Fortresses that had survived the arduous 90 minute flight to Regensburg dropped their bomb loads and made off in haste towards Algiers, saving themselves a possibly fatal return journey.

Now it was the turn of 230 Flying Fortresses to run the

gauntlet across Germany en route to Schweinfurt.

The fierce firepower of 300 Luftwaffe fighters battered the American planes. The Germans lost 25 fighters that day, the US bombers lost 60 and another 47 planes could not be salvaged.

The figures were bleak for the USAAF. In October 1943, 153 aircraft were lost in a single week. It led to the halt of bombing raids without fighter escort.

DROP TANKS

Fortunately the drop tank appeared, a suspended fuel tank which could be jettisoned when empty. This was attached under the wing to vastly increase the range of fighters. Hot on its heels came the P-51 Mustang, a fighter with an 850-mile range. It helped tip the balance of the air war over Europe in favour of the Allies.

By 1944 the Allies were producing twice the number of aircraft as the Reich was. The Luftwaffe's difficulties were compounded by the damage each fighter was sustaining which wasn't being repaired. Hitler was punishing the disappointing Luftwaffe by depriving it of essential materials to stay alive.

Yet the theories adopted by 'Bomber' Harris for the RAF and Eaker for the USAAF cannot be said to have been an outright success. Harris hoped to defeat the Third Reich by saturation bombing, destroying the will of the German people. The question of the morality of carpet-bombing civilian centres, including the ancient city of Dresden late in the war, raged long after the conflict had ended.

Eaker targeted industrial centres, certain that concerted bombing raids would cause Hitler's regime to topple. The principles were flawed. Hitler illustrated only too well over Britain in 1940 that air power by itself was not sufficient to win a war. Bombs from above failed to break the will of the Germans in just the same way as they had failed to crack the British. And damage sustained by industry could inevitably be repaired – particularly in Germany with the use of forced labour.

The liberation of Europe came with the arrival of the ground troops, albeit with priceless assistance from their colleagues in the air forces.

EYE WITNESS

Lieutenant Harmon Cropsey, a former state senator from Decatur, Michigan, served with VB110, a US Navy squadron, navigating, Liberators on 12-hour anti-submarine patrols into the North Atlantic. He was based at Dunkeswell in Devon under RAF Coastal Command.

❮One of my fellow officers was Joe Kennedy, John's elder brother. We used to moot quite regularly in the mess and swap notes He was flying the same aircraft as me.

It was Joe who volunteered for one of the most dangerous missions of the war. The idea was to strip everything out of one of the Liberators and pack it full of TNT. He was to fly this out over the North Sea to a prearranged navigational point and bale out. The plane would then be radio controlled to crash-land on its target – a 40-foot layer of reinforced concrete around some U-boat pens in Holland.

But something went wrong and the plane exploded in mid-air over England. We never found out what the problem was, and obviously there was nothing left of his body. He was a very brave man.

Our base lost a many airmen. The other two squadrons, 103 and 105, had around two-thirds of their crews killed in the first few months of our arrival in 1943. There was a German advanced training base at Brest and they were sending up the twin-engined Junkers 88 which had a 50-knot advantage on our planes. If you got caught out over the sea on a clear day you were a dead duck. Your only hope was to find cloud cover.

I know of only one plane, flown by a Free Czech crew, which made it home after being attacked. We were just fatalistic about it.

Every mission you were handed a top secret chart showing where all the Allied subs and ships should be. One day I'd got this thing spread out inside the plane with the door still open. Suddenly the engines start and the chart blows right out into a field. I chase after it and my flight suit gets caught on some barbed wire. As a result, I fall and dislocate my shoulder.

That incident extended my war. You could go home after 25 missions but due to my injury I stayed behind when all my chums left. Then they decided they needed an experienced navigator to show the new crews what to do. I ended up flying 42 missions. ❯

THE ULTIMATE WEAPON

In Japan, the people were preparing for all-out war against invading Americans.

As early as November 1944 all Japanese men aged between 14 and 61 were conscripted. Women between the ages of 17 and 41 were on standby for military service. They were schooled in beach defences and guerrilla warfare. Those that were left unarmed – the vast majority – were told to practise martial arts skills as a form of defence. The message from the rulers of Japan was to be seen on giant posters hung around towns and villages. 'One hundred million will die for Emperor and nation!'

Key installations in Japan had been destroyed by the American bombing campaign. Much of the Japanese shipping had been sunk already by US ships, aircraft and submarines, which were now operating a blockade of the island coastlines. Japan was being starved of everything she needed to survive – yet still there was no sign of surrender.

The Japanese had explored

through neutral sources for a negotiated peace, all cloaked in secrecy. Finally, the Japanese foreign ministry approached Russia to act as an intermediary. But Japanese demands were unacceptable to the Allies who would agree to nothing less than an unconditional surrender.

The lack of a cohesive war leader in Japan was keenly, felt. Emperor Hirohito was a figurehead who could apparently do little without the say-so of his government. Prime Minister Admiral Suzuki was eager to sue for peace but there remained in opposition hardliners who were willing to fight to the death. No one, it seemed, was in outright control and nobody dared utter the word 'surrender' without the prospect of assassination, political retribution or military uprising looming large. Japan struggled on in a vacuum of indecision.

The losses among the American troops in the landings around the Pacific islands had horrified and shocked the commanders. By now painfully

aware of the Japanese resilience to attack and their reluctance to surrender, they viewed invasion of the home islands as a tall order. The estimates for the number of US casualties appeared virtually open ended.

When Truman met with Churchill and Stalin in Potsdam in July 1945, they discussed the inadequate peace overtures from the Land of the Rising Sun. Later, Truman confided that America had developed a new bomb which could finally end the war.

ATOMIC POWER

He was referring to the end result of the Manhattan Project, begun back in 1942, in which a band of élite scientists, the most admired brains of the free world, had got together to probe the possibilities of atomic power.

By December of that year, scientists under the leadership of Professor Enrico Fermi had made a significant breakthrough in understanding how to spark a man-made chain reaction.

At two big plants – Oak Ridge, Tennessee, and Hanford, Washington – work continued in the bid to extract the essential substance known as U-235 from uranium for the manufacture of plutonium.

It wasn't until 5.50am on 16 July 1945 that the theory was finally put into full-scale practice. In the scorched sands of the New Mexican desert the

Far left: Scientists knew they had created the ultimate weapon when it was tested.
Left: Truman confided in Churchill about the bomb at Potsdam.

Above: A weapon similar to that detonated at Nagasaki. Its weight was 10,000 pounds and it was equivalent in power to 20,000 tons of TNT.

Below: Dr Albert Einstein (left) was the initial innovator. Dr Robert Oppenheimer (right) took up his theories and made them reality.

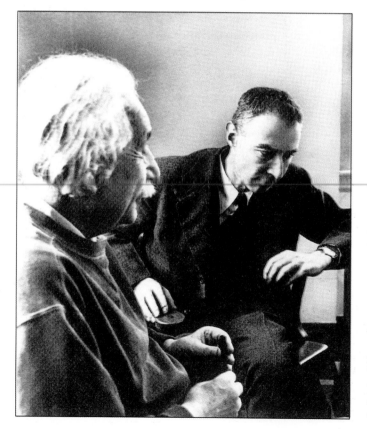

plutonium bomb called 'Fat Man' was detonated. (It won the name by having a passing resemblance in profile to Churchill.) Observing scientists could barely hide their awe at the intense power man had created.

Dr Robert J. Oppenheimer, the physicist directing the project, instantly realised the shattering effect it would have on the world.

TRUMAN INFORMED

A telegram detailing the precise results of the 'Fat Man' experiment was sent to the Potsdam Conference for the consumption of President Truman – who himself had only found out in April the full scope of the Manhattan Project.

Two further atomic bombs were made and dispatched to the Pacific while the politicians pondered. Was the world ready for the atomic age? Once unleashed, would this mighty new force return to act as a Sword of Damocles poised over the heads of free and fair countries?

Churchill for one was in no doubt that it should be used. Afterwards, he wrote: 'To avert a vast, indefinite butchery, to bring the war to an end, to give peace to the world, to lay healing hands upon its tortured peoples by a manifestation of over-whelming power at the cost of a few explosions seemed, after all our toils and perils, a miracle of development.

'British consent in principle to the use of the weapon had been given on 4 July before the test had taken place. The final decision now lay in the main with President Truman, who had the weapon. But I never doubted what it would be nor have I ever doubted since that he was right.'

In his memoirs, Truman wrote: 'Let there be no mistake about it. I regarded the bomb as a military weapon and never had any doubt that it should be used.'

Still, there was debate about whether Japan should be warned about its terrible fate. A chain of events finally overtook these talks.

The Potsdam Conference finally closed on 26 July with an ultimatum for Japan. It called for unconditional surrender. In the absence of such a surrender, Japan would face complete destruction. Just two days later, Premier Suzuki announced his country would be ignoring the Allied threat.

Such belligerence was enough to confirm an order sent to Lieutenant-General Spaatz, Commanding General of the US Army Strategic Air Forces to prepare a B-29 to carry the newly fabricated atomic bomb.

On 6th August 1945 the first atomic bomb, called 'Little Boy', was released over Hiroshima.

Below: Smoke rises more than 60,000 feet into the air following the explosion of the atomic bomb at Nagasaki.

EYE WITNESS

Dr Michihiko Hachiya was at home when the first atomic bomb – 'Little Boy' – fell on Hiroshima from the bomb bay of B-29 'Enola Gay'. He recalls the moment of impact in his eye witness account Hiroshima Diary.

❛The hour was early, the morning still warm and beautiful. Shimmering leaves reflecting sunlight from a cloudless sky as I gazed absently through wide-flung doors opening to the south.

Clad in vest and pants, I lay on the living room floor exhausted because I had just spent a sleepless night on duty as an air raid warden in my hospital.

Suddenly a strong flash of light startled me – and then another. I remember vividly how a stone lantern in the garden became brilliantly lit and I debated whether this light was caused by a magnesium flare or sparks from a passing tram.

Garden shadows disappeared. The view where a moment before all had been so bright and sunny was now dark and hazy. I could barely discern that a wooden column that had supported one corner of my house, was leaning and the roof sagged dangerously.

I tried to escape but rubble and fallen timbers barred the way. By picking my way cautiously I managed to reach the roka and stepped down into my garden. A profound weakness overcame me so I stopped to regain my strength. I discovered that I was completely naked. Where were my vest and pants. What had happened?

All over the right side of my body I was cut and bleeding. A large splinter was protruding from a wound in my thigh and something warm trickled into my mouth. My cheek was torn, I discovered, as I felt it gingerly with the lower lip laid wide open. Embedded in my neck was a sizeable fragment of glass which I matter-of-factly dislodged and with the detachment of one stunned and shocked I studied it and my blood-stained hand. ❜

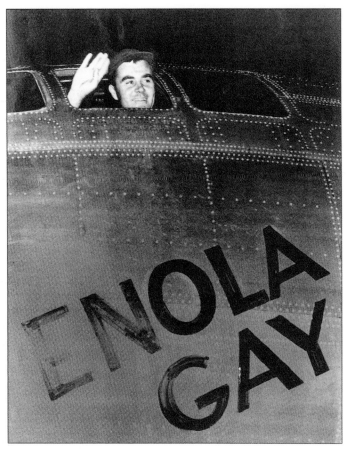

any other description I can give it. It was black and boiling underneath with a steam haze on the top of it. Arid, of course, we had seen the city when we went in and there was nothing to see when we came back.'

On 8 August further pressure was exerted on Japan when the Soviet Union declared war and launched an invasion of Manchuria.

'We had seen the city when we went in and there was nothing to see when we came back'

A day later a further atomic bomb dropped, this time on Nagasaki. It came from the bowels of another B-29, this one christened 'Great Artist', under the command of Major Charles Sweeney. About 40,000 people died this time with a further 60,000 injured.

It is doubtful whether the introduction of atomic weapons had a huge effect on the people of Japan. The scale and horror of the previous bombing campaigns had claimed victims by the thousand and caused acres of destruction. Wholesale killing, burns and homelessness was nothing new for them. The only new aspect was the radiation sickness among the survivors, the wide-ranging effects of which were not immediately apparent.

For the rest of the world, the double bombing was like a

A mammoth 120 inches long and weighing 9,000 pounds, beneath its shell it contained the power equivalent to 20,000 tons of TNT. It was carried to its target in a B-29 called 'Enola Gay' which took off from the Marianas. In command was Colonel Paul Tibbets.

The uranium bomb exploded 2,000 feet above the centre of Hiroshima. Four square miles of the city was instantly wiped out. Those at the epicentre of the bomb were reduced to ashes along with buildings and cars. Beyond that immediate area, many more died and tens of thousands were horribly burned.

SHOCK WAVES

The authorities could only estimate the numbers of people who had perished in the ferocious cauldron. The final figure was put between 70,000 and 80,000 persons. Colonel Tibbets later described how his plane was shaken by the shock waves as it sped away and told of the scene of devastation he left behind: 'There was the mushroom cloud growing up and we watched it blossom. And down below it the thing reminded me more of a boiling pot of tar than

EYE WITNESS

Tsutomu Yamaguchi worked in the Hiroshima yard of the Mitsubishi shipbuilding company and was on his way to work when the bomb dropped more than a mile away.

❝Suddenly there was a flash like the lighting of a huge magnesium flare. As I prostrated myself there came a terrific explosion. I was lifted two feet from the ground and I felt a strong wind pass my body.

How long I lay in the road dazed, I don't know, but when I opened my eyes it was so dark all around me that I couldn't see a thing. It was as if it had suddenly become midnight in the heat of the day. When my eyes adjusted to the darkness I perceived that I was enveloped in an endless cloud of dust so thick it was black.

As the dust blew away and my surroundings became visible I saw what seemed to be thousands of tiny, flickering lamps all over the street and in the fields. They were little circles of flame, each about the size of a doughnut. Myriads of them were hanging on the leaves of the potato plants.

I looked toward the city and saw a huge, mushroom-shaped cloud rising high into the sky. It was an immense evil-looking pillar. It seemed to be reflecting every shade in the spectrum turning first one colour then another.

Feeling terribly weak and suffering intense pain from the deep burns on my face and arm, I stumbled into the potato field. There was a big tree out in the field and I headed for that. Sometimes I could only crawl, creeping from bush to bush. When I finally reached the tree I had no more strength to go on. And I had acquired a terrible thirst.

I saw a group of teenage boys unclothed except for torn underpants. As the boys came near I saw that they were pale and shaking severely. I had never seen such a horrifying sight as those five shivering boys. Blood was pouring in streams from deep cuts all over their bodies mingling with their perspiration and their skin was burned deep red like the colour of cooked lobsters.

At first it seemed strangely that their burned and lacerated backs and chests were growing green grass. Then I saw that hundreds of blades of sharp grass had been driven deep into their flesh, evidently by the force of the blast.❞

macabre sideshow with people riveted by the footage and photos of the vast mushrooming cloud that rose up some 20,000 feet as the bomb was detonated.

JAPAN SURRENDERS

In any event, it was clear that Truman's pledge to 'obliterate' Japan was no empty threat. Hirohito himself was sickened by the suffering among his people. Finally, he found the leverage inside his government to bring the conflict to an end.

The day after Nagasaki was bombed, Japan broadcast a willingness to surrender 'on the understanding that it does not comprise any demand which prejudices the prerogatives of the Emperor as Sovereign ruler.'

Yet still the hawks in the regime dragged their feet. A flight of US Navy carrier-borne planes flew over Japan on 13 August dropping leaflets which spelled out the surrender so the people would understand that it was all over.

The following day at 11pm the Emperor himself told his people the war was over. Even at this late stage, 1,000 militant soldiers stormed the Imperial Palace in a bid to prevent the surrender. They were beaten off by the Emperor's own guard.

VJ day was then declared on 15 August. The pockets of Japanese resistance around the Pacific and South East Asia surrendered through the following month, ending with Hong Kong on September 16th.

Left: *The atomic bomb scarred the landscape of Nagasaki so deeply it was beyond recognition.*

Left: The luckier victims of the atomic bomb blasts suffered burns to their bodies. The remains of many of the victims were never found.

battlefields of the world and hence are not for our discussion or debate.

PRAYER FOR PEACE

'Nor is it for us here to meet representing as we do a majority of the people of the earth in a spirit of distrust, malice or hatred. But rather it is for us both victors and vanquished to serve, committing all our peoples unreservedly to faithful compliance with the understandings they are here formally to assume. It is my earnest hope... that from this solemn occasion a better world shall emerge... a world dedicated to the dignity of man... Let us pray that peace be now restored to the world and that God will preserve it always.'

In the meantime the official ceremony marking the outbreak of peace came on 2 September aboard the USS *Missouri* in Tokyo Bay. The Japanese delegation was led by the one-legged

'Let us pray that peace be now restored to the world'

Foreign Minister Mamoru Shigemitsu, who wore a top hat for the occasion. The military wing of the country was represented by General Yoshijiro Umezu. There to receive them were dignitaries from all the countries that had taken part in the war against Japan – America, Britain, Australia, New Zealand, Canada, China, France and Holland. Sailors squeezed into every available inch of the deck to witness the historic moment.

After the signing was over, General MacArthur gave a

stirring speech opening the door to a new order.

'We are gathered here, representatives of the major warring powers, to conclude a solemn agreement whereby peace may be restored. The issues involving divergent ideals and ideologies have been determined on the

Right: Servicemen greeted news of the atomic explosions with relief. The blasts probably saved thousands of US troops.

GREAT AIRCRAFT
OF WWII

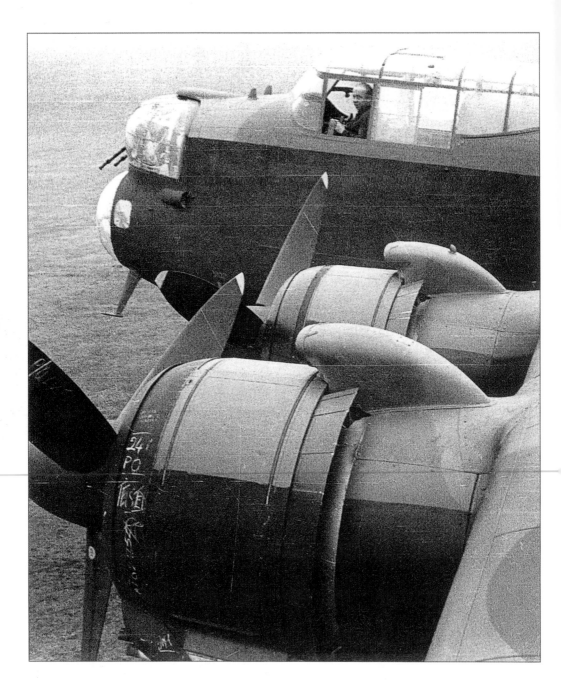

THE SUPERMARINE
SPITFIRE

Supermarine Spitfire VB

1 Aerial stub attachment
2 Rudder upper hinge
3 Fabric-covered rudder
4 Rudder tab
5 Sternpost
6 Rudder tab hinge
7 Rear navigation light
8 Starboard elevator tab
9 Starboard elevator structure
10 Elevator balance
11 Tailplane front spar
12 IFF aerial
13 Castoring non-retractable
   tailwheel
14 Tailwheel strut
15 Fuselage double frame
16 Elevator control lever
17 Tailplane spar/
   fuselage attachment

18 Fin rear spar
   (fuselage frame
   extension)
19 Fin front spar
   (fuselage frame
   extension)
20 Port elevator tab hinge
21 Port elevator
22 IFF aerial
23 Port tailplane
24 Rudder control lever
25 Cross shaft
26 Tailwheel oleo access place
27 Tailwheel oleo shock-absorber
28 Fuselage angled frame
29 Battery compartment
30 Lower longeron
31 Elevator control cables
32 Fuselage construction
33 Rudder control cables
34 Radio compartment
35 Radio support tray
36 Flare chute
37 Oxygen bottle
38 Auxiliary long-range fuel tank
   (29gal/132l)
39 Dorsal formation light
40 Aerial lead-in
41 HF aerial
42 Aerial mast
43 Cockpit aft glazing
44 Voltage regulator
45 Canopy track
46 Structural bulkhead
47 Headrest
48 Plexiglass canopy
49 Rear-view mirror
50 Entry flap (port)

51 Air bottles (alternative rear
   fuselage stowage)
52 Sutton harness
53 Pilot's seat (moulded Bakelite)
54 Datum longeron
55 Seat support frame
56 Wingroot fillet
57 Seat adjustment lever
58 Rudder pedal frame
59 Elevator control connecting tube
60 Control column spade grip
61 Trim wheel
62 Reflector gunsight
63 External windscreen armour
64 Instrument panel
65 Main fuselage fuel tank
   (48gal/218l)
66 Fuel tank/longeron
   attachment fittings

67 Rudder pedals
68 Rudder bar
69 King post
70 Fuselage lower fuel tank (37gal/168l)
71 Firewall/bulkhead
72 Engine bearer attachment
73 Steel tube bearers
74 Magneto
75 'Fishtail'/exhaust manifold
76 Gun heating 'intensifier'
77 Hydraulic tank
78 Fuel filler cap
79 Air compressor intake
80 Air compressor
81 Rolls-Royce Merlin 45 engine
82 Coolant piping
83 Port cannon wing fairing
84 Flaps
85 Aileron control cables
86 Aileron push tube
87 Bellcrank

88 Aileron hinge
89 Port aileron
90 Machine-gun access panels
91 Port wingtip
92 Port navigation light
93 Leading-edge skinning
94 Machine-gun ports (protected)
95 20mm cannon muzzle
96 Three-blade constant-speed propeller
97 Spinner
98 Propeller hub
99 Coolant tank
100 Cowling fastening
101 Engine anti-vibration mounting pad
102 Engine accessories
103 Engine bearers
104 Main engine support member
105 Coolant pipe
106 Exposed oil tank
107 Port mainwheel

108 Mainwheel fairing
109 Carburettor air intake
110 Stub/spar attachment
111 Mainwheel leg pivot point
112 Main spar
113 Leading-edge ribs (diagonals deleted for clarity)
114 Mainwheel leg shock-absorber
115 Mainwheel fairing
116 Starboard mainwheel
117 Angled axle
118 Cannon barrel support fairing
119 Spar cut-out
120 Mainwheel well
121 Gun heating pipe
122 Flap structure
123 Cannon wing fairing
124 Cannon magazine drum (120 rounds)

125 Machine-gun support brackets
126 Gun access panels
127 .303in machine-gun barrels
128 Machine-gun ports
129 Ammunition boxes (350rpg)
130 Starboard aileron construction
131 Wing ribs
132 Single-tube outer spar section
133 Wingtip structure
134 Starboard navigation light

A FIGHTER IS BORN

The story of the Spitfire began almost ten years before Dick Audet's famous action, in December 1934. Then, at the Supermarine Aviation Company's works at Southampton, Reginald Mitchell and his team finalized the layout of their new high-speed fighter for the RAF.

Mitchell had established his name as a highly successful designer of racing floatplanes for the Schneider Trophy competition. One of his designs – the Supermarine S.5 – had won the Schneider Trophy competition in 1927. The S.6 won it two years later in 1929. After another two-year gap the Supermarine S.6B won the trophy outright for Britain in 1931 and later went on to raise the World Air Speed record to 407mph (655km/hr).

These had been magnificent achievements but the market for high-speed racing seaplanes was extremely limited. The Supermarine company's main 'bread and butter' products were its big Southampton and Scapa flying boats which now equipped seven RAF maritime patrol squadrons.

In 1934 the fastest fighter in the Royal Air Force was the Hawker Fury, which had a maximum speed of 207mph at 14,000 ft (333km/hr at 4,270m). At that time, Air Vice Marshal Hugh Dowding was responsible for issuing to manufacturers the specifications for new aircraft required for the Royal Air Force. Dowding was what we would now call a 'technocrat'. He saw the vital need for a new fighter to bridge the huge gap in performance between the Schneider Trophy racers and the biplanes that were then in service.

MITCHELL'S FIRST FIGHTER

In February 1934 Reginald Mitchell's first fighter design appeared, the Supermarine Type 224.

Far left: Production of wings at Woolston, early in 1939.

THE SCHNEIDER TROPHY AND THE SPITFIRE

The Supermarine S.6B, Reginald Mitchell's final racing floatplane design, gained the Schneider Trophy outright for Great Britain in 1931. Later that year it raised the world absolute speed record to 407mph (655km/hr). One common myth about the Spitfire is that it was 'developed from' the Supermarine S.6B. This is simply not true. The two aircraft were quite different designs, intended for quite different roles.

Type Single-seat racing floatplane.
Power Plant One Rolls-Royce 'R' engine developing 2,350hp.
Dimensions Span 30ft 0in (9.14m), length 28ft 10in (8.79m).
Weight Maximum loaded weight 6,086lb (2760kg).
Performance Maximum speed 407mph at 245 ft (655km/hr at 75m), a World record.

Right: The Supermarine S.6B racing floatplane won the Schneider Trophy for Great Britain in 1931. Later that year it captured the world absolute speed record at 407mph (655km/hr).

THE SUPERMARINE TYPE 224

REGINALD MITCHELL'S FIRST FIGHTER DESIGN

This single-seat interceptor fighter used a novel type of evaporative cooling for the engine, employing a steam condenser built into the leading edge of each wing. The system gave continual trouble and would probably have precluded the fighter being ordered for the RAF even if its performance had been more impressive.

Type Single-seat interceptor fighter.
Armament Four Vickers 0.303in (7.7mm) machine guns synchronized to fire through the propeller arc.
Power Plant One Rolls-Royce Goshawk developing 680hp.
Dimensions Span 45ft 10in (13.97m)

length 29ft 5^1/4in (8.97m).
Weight Maximum loaded weight 4,743lb (2,151kg).
Performance Maximum speed 228mph at 15,000ft (367km/hr at 4,575m); time to climb to 15,000ft, 9^1/2 minutes.

Above: The Supermarine Type 224, Reginald Mitchell's unsuccessful first attempt at designing a fighter aircraft.

Right: The Hawker Fury, the fastest fighter type in the RAF in 1934, had a maximum speed of 207mph (333km/hr).

The aircraft took part in a competition to select a new fighter type for the Royal Air Force. The Type 224 proved a flop. Its maximum speed was only 228mph (367km/hr) and it took 9^1/2 minutes to reach 15,000 ft (4,575m). The cooling system for the engine, gave continual trouble. The winner of the competition, the Gloster entrant later named the Gladiator, had a maximum speed of 242mph (390km/hr) and it climbed to 15,000 ft in 6^1/2 minutes.

Having learned that painful lesson, Reginald Mitchell persuaded the company to allow him to design a smaller, and more streamlined fighter. This time he would use the new 1,000 horse power V-12 engine, later named the Merlin, then under test at the Rolls-Royce company in Derby. When Air Vice Marshal Dowding saw details of the proposed new fighter he gave it his full support, and issued an official Royal Air Force specification so that the government would meet most of the cost of building a prototype.

The new fighter made its maiden flight on 5 March 1936, with Chief Test Pilot 'Mutt' Summers at the controls. the Air Ministry allocated a name to the new fighter – 'Spitfire'.

FASTEST FIGHTER

'It is claimed that the Spitfire is the fastest military aeroplane in the world. It is small and light for a machine of its calibre (the structural weight is said to have been brought down to a level never before attained in the single-seat fighter class), and its speed and manoeuvrability are something to marvel at.

'Tight turns were made at high speed after dives, and the control at low speeds was amply demonstrated. The demonstration was cramped by low clouds, but after the main flying display the machine was taken up again and gave one of the smoothest displays of high-speed aerobatics ever seen in this country.'

FLIGHT MAGAZINE 3 JULY 1936

When Mitchell learned of the official choice of name, he was heard to comment: 'It's the sort of bloody-silly name they would give it!'

During flight tests the new fighter attained a maximum speed of 349mph at 16,800 ft (562km/hr at 5,122m), and in the climb it reached 30,000 ft (9,145m) in 17 minutes. It was one of the most heavily armed, fighters, designed to carry eight Browning .303in (7.7mm) machine guns in the wings.

LARGE ORDER

The Spitfire became available at exactly the right time for the Royal Air Force. In Germany the Luftwaffe was building up its strength rapidly. Its new monoplane fighter type, the Messerschmitt 109, was on the point of entering large-scale production. To meet the mounting threat, in June 1936 the British Government signed a contract for 310 Spitfires.

The Spitfire first appeared on 18 June 1936, at Eastleigh. With press photographers snapping away, Jeffrey Quill started the Spitfire's engine and taxied to one end of the runway. As he pushed open the throttle to begin his take-off run, the pilot made a brief scan of his instruments, and noticed the needle of the oil pressure gauge suddenly drop to zero. That left him in an unenviable position. He had no room to stop before reaching the airfield boundary. The pilot eased the aircraft into the air and reduced power. He eased open the throttle for one last burst of power, the engine responded and he made a safe landing.

Above: The prototype Supermarine F.37/34, serial number K 5054, pictured at Eastleigh shortly before its maiden flight. The metal parts of the aircraft were unpainted, the aircraft carried no armament and the undercarriage was locked in the down position.

PROTOTYPE SPITFIRE

Type Single-seat interceptor fighter.
Armament Eight-.303in (7.7mm) Browning machine guns with 350 rounds per gun.
Power Plant One Rolls-Royce Merlin Type C liquid cooled V-12 engine with single-speed supercharger developing 990hp.
Dimensions Span 40ft (12.1m); length 29ft 11in (9.17m).
Weight Maximum loaded weight 5,395lb (2,446kg).
Performance Maximum speed 349 mph at 16,800 ft (562 km/hr at 5,122 m). Service ceiling 35,400ft (10,790m).

Below: *The Supermarine works at Woolston near Southampton.*
Above: *Close to disaster! Jeffrey Quill taking off in the prototype Spitfire at Eastleigh on 18 June 1936. A few seconds before this photograph was taken, an oil pipe had come adrift. In the background is the Southern Railway works over which the aircraft had to pass before it returned to the airfield. By skilful flying, Quill landed before the engine seized. Had the prototype been lost that day, it is possible that the RAF might have cancelled its order in which case the Spitfire would not have gone into production.*

Examination of the engine revealed that an oil pipe had come adrift, allowing the lubrication system to run dry. The engine was changed and sent to Rolls Royce for examination, but it had suffered remarkably little damage. Had the prototype been lost during its first air display, the consequences to the nation hardly bear thinking about. Only the one Spitfire existed and it had not completed its initial performance trials with the Royal Air Force. If it had crashed the Royal Air Force would probably have cancelled the contract and ordered other fighters instead. That would have had a disastrous effect on the capability of Fighter Command during the Battle of Britain, four years later.

Five days later the Spitfire resumed flying with a new engine. On 27 June Flight Lieutenant Hugh Edwardes-Jones demonstrated the aircraft at the Royal Air Force Pageant at Hendon. Two days later 'Mutt' Summers flew it at the Society of British Aircraft Constructors' air display at Hatfield. The demonstrations aroused enormous public interest in the fighter, and drew lyrical descriptions in the press.

ON DISPLAY

The prototype completed its initial service trials at Martlesham Heath in July 1936, and returned to Eastleigh for modification. The fighter received a newer version of the Merlin, giving slightly greater power, and eight machine guns were fitted in the wings.

One of the most serious problems was that the fighter's guns did not work reliably at high altitude. During the initial firing trials in March 1937, all eight guns fired perfectly at 4,000 ft (1,220m). A few days later, when an RAF pilot climbed the Spitfire to 32,000 ft (9,755m) over the North Sea for the first high-altitude firing, it nearly ended in tragedy. One gun fired 171 rounds before it failed, another fired 8 rounds, one fired 4 rounds and the remaining five guns failed to fire at all. When the Spitfire touched down at Martlesham Heath after the test the shock of the landing released the previously frozen-up breech blocks. Three of the weapons loosed off a round in the general direction of Felixstowe, fortunately without hitting anyone.

'...the Spitfires will be useless as fighting aircraft...'

During the next 18 months Supermarine engineers tried various schemes to solve the problem of gun freezing, but the guns were still not function-ing reliably in July 1938 when the first Spitfires were delivered to the Royal Air Force.

It took until October 1938 to resolve the problem. Then on the 14th, a service pilot took the prototype to high altitude and fired off the entire contents of the ammunition boxes. The gun-heating modification was then incorporated in all Spitfires on the production line.

During the test programme the prototype Spitfire survived two serious accidents. During March 1937, it made an emergency landing with engine failure.

Later it suffered an undercarriage collapse, after a fatigue fracture in one of the main wheel legs. On 4 September 1939, the aircraft suffered serious damage in a fatal landing accident. Since there was no further use for it the machine was scrapped.

The prototype Spitfire had cost the public purse a mere £15,776.

Below: The prototype Spitfire wearing military camouflage, in 1938. The muzzles of the two outer machine guns can be seen protruding from the wing.

MY GOD, IT'S MADE OF TIN

Whenever the prototype Spitfire landed away from its base, it was the subject of great interest. At that time most airframes comprised a wood or light metal framework with a covering of linen fabric. The streamlined all-metal monoplane Spitfire with its enclosed cockpit and retractable undercarriage made every other aircraft in the Royal Air Force look positively prehistoric!

During a test flight in December 1936 Jeffrey Quill ran short of fuel, and landed his Spitfire near Chichester. As he taxied in, a crowd of RAF ground crewmen gathered to meet it. Then, Quill recalled:

'I taxied to a standstill and shut down, and could hear a tapping sound. I checked I had shut everything down, but the tapping sound continued. Then as I climbed out I saw the reason. Several mechanics were standing around the rear fuselage, tapping it with their knuckles disbelievingly. "My God, one of them exclaimed, It's made of tin!"'

SPITFIRE IN ACTION

The initial order for 310 Spitfires placed the Supermarine Company in a difficult position. They had previously built small batches of flying boats for the Royal Air Force and its work force numbered only about 500. The new all-metal fighter required specialized manufacturing techniques, and at a time when the aircraft industry was expanding it was difficult to recruit workers with the necessary skills. As a result there were delays in getting the fighter into production.

In August 1938, No. 19 Squadron at Duxford received the first Spitfires. It took until December for the unit to get its full complement of aircraft, then other squadrons began to re-equip. By this time Hugh Dowding had been promoted to Air Chief Marshal and held the post of Commander-in-Chief RAF Fighter Command. By a quirk of history, the man who had done so much to bring the Spitfire into being was now to direct these fighters into action.

When Great Britain declared war on Germany in September 1939, RAF Fighter Command possessed 187 Spitfires in front-line units.

Spitfires first saw action on 6 September 1939, during the so-called 'Battle of Barking Creek'.

Because of a technical fault at the radar station at Canewdon in Essex, aircraft flying west of the station appeared on the screen as if their position

Left: Cockpit of early Spitfire I.
Inset: Spitfires of No. 19 Squadron.

SPITFIRE I

Type: Single-seat interceptor fighter.
Armament: Eight Browning .303in (7.7mm) machine guns with 350 rounds per gun.
Power Plant: One Rolls-Royce Merlin II liquid cooled V-12 engine with single-speed supercharger developing 1030 horse power.
Dimensions: Span 36ft 10in (10.98m); length 29ft 11in (9.11m).
Weight: Maximum loaded weight 5,819lb (2,639kg).
Performance: Maximum speed 362mph at 18,500ft (583km/hr at 5,640m).

Top and overleaf: The 600th production Spitfire during its testing in April 1940. During the Battle of Britain this aircraft served with No.64 Squadron.
Above: Spitfires and Hurricanes from several squadrons lined up at Digby in Lincolnshire. The aircaft had assembled there prior to a massed flypast over cities in the Midlands to mark Empire Air Day on 20 May 1939. (No. 72 Squadron Archive)

Spitfires first saw action on 6 September 1939, during the so-called 'Battle of Barking Creek'

was east of the radar. It looked as if the Luftwaffe was about to launch an onslaught on the capital. The operators at Canewdon reported 20 unidentified aircraft heading towards London from the east.

> **For the next hour chaos, utter and complete, reigned over the Thames estuary**

Within minutes the formations being tracked on the radar, all of them now designated as 'hostile', increased to twelve.

A GERMAN PILOT'S OPINION OF THE SPITFIRE

Below: Spitfires in captivity: by the beginning of the Battle of Britain the Germans had captured four Spitfires in flying or repairable condition.
Bottom: A captured Spitfire painted in bogus British markings and used in propaganda photographs.

'I was able to fly a captured Spitfire at Jever. My first impression was that it had a beautiful engine. It purred. The engine of the Messerschmitt 109 was very loud. Also the Spitfire was easier to fly, and to land, than the Me 109. The 109 was unforgiving of any inattention. I felt familiar with the Spitfire from the very start. That was my first and lasting impression. But with my experience with the 109, I personally would not have

traded it for a Spitfire. I had the impression, though I did not fly the Spitfire long enough to prove it, that the 109 was the faster, especially in the dive. Also, I think the pilot's view was better from the 109. In the Spitfire one flew further back, a bit more over the wing.'

OBERLEUTNANT HANS SCHMOLLER-HALDY, MESSERSCHMITT 109 PILOT, FIGHTER GESCHWADER 54

Soon afterwards an anti-aircraft gun battery opened fire at 'twin-engined bombers' passing overhead. Shortly after that, the leader of a Spitfire squadron broadcast a 'Tally Ho!' call, to indicate that he had enemy planes in sight and was about to engage. For the next hour chaos, utter and complete, reigned over the Thames Estuary. Squadrons of fighters cruised between the banks of cloud, seeking enemy planes

but finding only friendly ones. There were several brief fire fights, each one broken off when it became evident that the 'opponents' were 'friendly ones'. The shortage of fuel forced the Spitfires and Hurricanes to return to their airfields. There had never been any German aircraft in the area. The fiasco cost the RAF three aircraft destroyed; two Hurricanes shot down by Spitfires of No. 74 Squadron and a Blenheim shot down by anti-aircraft fire. One RAF pilot was killed.

Following the action Fighter Command launched an official inquiry to determine what had gone wrong and prevent a recurrence. One lesson, which has to be re-learned for each war, was the folly of opening

Top: *Spitfires of No. 41 Squadron photographed during the Battle of Britain.*
Above: *Spitfires of Nos 222 and 603 Squadrons at Hornchurch at the time of the Battle of Britain.*

Note the steam roller in the background, to roll flat the filled-in bomb craters on the airfield.
Below: *The Messerschmitt 109E was the most formidable opponent facing RAF Fighter Command.*

"YOU WON'T SURVIVE TEN MINUTES IN BATTLE"

'During the Battle of Britain one had to take every opportunity to train new pilots. Young pilots would arrive on the squadron with only six or seven hours' flying time on the Spitfire. One or two practice sorties could make all the difference to their ability to survive in combat. When we were at 30 minutes available, I might ring operations and ask permission to take one of the new pilots into the air for "follow my leader" practice. If one could take them up, one could point out their failings and tell them: "You won't survive ten minutes in battle if you fly like that!"'

SQUADRON LEADER DONALD MacDONELL, COMMANDER OF NO. 64 SQUADRON

Left: Spitfire X4110 had a service life of only 15 minutes! On the morning of 18 August 1940 this brand new aircraft arrived at No.602 Squadron at Westhampnett as a replacement. Before there was time to paint on the squadron markings Flight Lieutenant Dunlop Urie took it into action and in an encounter with Me 109s the fighter suffered severe damage.

Spitfires and Hurricanes flew large numbers of sorties to cover the evacuation of Dunkirk

fire on aircraft that had not been positively identified as 'hostile'. Another was the looking at the reports from one radar in isolation (stations had reported seeing no aircraft, but the absence of plots had been ignored). A further lesson was the need to fit IFF (identification friend or foe) radar equipment in all RAF fighters, and the programme to build and install this equipment received top priority.

The Spitfires first encountered German aircraft en masse on on 21 May 1940, when rapid advance of the German army into Belgium and France brought the war to within reach of RAF fighters operating from airfields in Kent. During the following weeks, Spitfires and Hurricanes flew large numbers of sorties to cover the evacuation of Allied troops from Dunkirk.

BATTLE OF BRITAIN

By July 1940 RAF Fighter Command possessed fifty squadrons of single-seat fighters, thirty-one with Hurricanes and nineteen with Spitfires. The Battle of Britain opened with

Above: Pilot Officer Robert Doe of No. 234 Squadron was credited with eleven enemy aircraft destroyed and two shared destroyed. He then moved to a Hurricane squadron and shot down three more. Doe suffered serious injuries during a crash landing in January 1941, and these prevented him flying for several months.
Above right: Dunlop Urie, his feet bandaged, waiting to be taken to hospital.
Right: Squadron Leader Donald MacDonell commanded No. 64 Squadron during the Battle and was credited with nine enemy aircraft destroyed and one shared destroyed.

WAITING AT READINESS

During the Battle of Britain RAF fighter squadrons waiting to go into action were held on the ground at what was known as Readiness 5 Minutes. The fighters sat in their earth-and-brick revetments around the perimeter of the airfield, and from time to time the ground crews would run the engines to warm the oil and ensure the planes could take off immediately. Squadron Leader Don MacDonell, commander of No. 64 Squadron during the Battle, explained what it was like.

'When we were at Readiness the pilots would be relaxing at the dispersal area – reading, chatting, playing cards. Each Flight had a separate crew room, so no pilot was too far from his Spitfire. I would be out of my office, wearing flying kit and Mae West, with the Flight I was to lead on that day. Each pilot's parachute was laid out on the seat of his aircraft, with the straps laid over the armour plating at the back of the cockpit.

Every time the telephone rang there would be a ghastly silence. The orderly would answer it and often hear something like: "Yes, Sir... yes Sir...Sergeant Smith wanted on the phone." And everyone would breath again.'

Luftwaffe attacks on convoys of shipping passing through the English Channel, in an effort to disrupt the coastal traffic and also to force the RAF into action.

Above left: *Flying Officer Leonard Haines of No. 19 Squadron was credited with eight enemy 'kills' and four shared destroyed. He died in a flying accident in April 1941.*

Above right: *Squadron Leader Derek Boitel-Gill commanding No. 152 Squadron was credited with eight aircraft destroyed. He died in a flying accident in September 1941.*

There were repeated attacks on Fighter Command airfields in the south of England

These actions were a prelude to the main Luftwaffe campaign, which began on 13 August, aimed at destroying Fighter Command. That day German aircraft launched multi-pronged attacks on the Royal Navy bases at Portland and Southampton and on the airfields at Detling and Eastchurch.

Every major airfield in the No. 11 Group area took hard knocks. However, there was an efficient damage-repair organisation and in the event only

'SCRAMBLE'

In Fighter Command the code-word 'Scramble' meant 'get airborne as soon as possible'. When pilots received the order they ran as if their lives depended on it. Each 30-second delay in getting airborne meant 1,000 feet (305m) less altitude they had when they met the enemy. Everyone knew that a Spitfire caught in the climb was easy meat for a Messerschmitt attacking in a dive. Squadron Leader Donald MacDonell explained the procedure for getting airborne:

'The orderly answering the telephone would shout "SCRAMBLE!" and each pilot would dash for his aircraft. One mechanic would already have started the engine; the other would be holding the parachute up and help me strap it on. Then I would climb into the cockpit and he would pass my seat straps over my shoulders and help me fasten them. When I gave the thumbs-up he would slam shut the side door and I would pull tight the various straps. I would pull on my helmet, plug in the R/T lead and check that the engine was running properly. If all was well I would wave to the groundcrew to pull away the chocks, open the throttle, and move forward across the grass to the take-off position. There I would line up, open the throttle wide and begin my take-off run with the rest of my pilots following as fast as they could. The whole thing, from the scramble order to the last aircraft leaving the ground, took about a minute and a half.'

SPITFIRE DEPLOYMENT, SEPTEMBER 1940

Spitfire units, at 14th September, before the Battle of Britain on the next day. First figure aircraft serviceable, in brackets aircraft unserviceable.

No. 10 GROUP, HQ BOX, WILTSHIRE
Middle Wallop Sector
No. 152 Squadron 17 (2) Warmwell
No. 609 Squadron 15 (3) Middle Wallop
St Eval Sector
No. 234 Squadron 16 (1) St Eval
Group Total **48 (6)**

No. 11 GROUP, HQ UXBRIDGE, MIDDLESEX
Biggin Hill Sector
No. 72 Squadron 10 (7) Biggin Hill
No. 92 Squadron 16 (1) Biggin Hill
No. 66 Squadron 14 (2) Gravesend
Hornchurch Sector
No. 603 Squadron 14 (5) Hornchurch
No. 41 Squadron 12 (6) Rochford
No. 222 Squadron 11 (3) Rochford
Tangmere Sector
No. 602 Squadron 15 (4) Westhampnett
Group Total **92 (28)**

No. 12 GROUP, HQ WATNALL, NOTTINGHAMSHIRE
Duxford Sector
No. 19 Squadron 14 (0) Fowlmere
Coltishall Sector
No. 74 Squadron 14 (8) Coltishall
Wittering Sector
No. 266 Squadron 14 (5) Wittering
Digby Sector
No. 611 Squadron 17 (1) Digby
Kirton-in-Lindsey Sector
No. 616 Squadron 14 (4) Kirton-in-Lindsey
No. 64 Squadron 7 (3) Leconfield
6 (3) Ringway
Group Total **86 (24)**

No. 13 GROUP, HQ NEWCASTLE, NORTHUMBERLAND
Catterick Sector
No. 54 Squadron 15 (2) Catterick
Usworth Sector
No. 610 Squadron 14 (5) Acklington
Turnhouse Sector
No. 65 Squadron 15 (5) Turnhouse
Group Total **44 (12)**

Spitfires at Operational Training Units
26 (24)

Spitfire Production During Week Prior to 14 September 38

Replacement Spitfires held at Maintenance Units, 14 September 1940
Ready for immediate issue to units 47
Ready for issue within four days 10

Below left: *Sergeant Basil Whall flew with No.602 Squadron and was credited with seven enemy aircraft destroyed and two shared destroyed. In October 1940 he* suffered fatal injuries when he tried to land his damaged aircraft after a combat sortie.
Below right: *Lieutenant Arthur 'Admiral' Blake, a Fleet Air Arm* pilot loaned to RAF Fighter Command, flew with No.19 Squadron. Credited with four enemy aircraft destroyed, he was shot down and killed in October 1940.

one airfield, that at Manston in Kent, was put out of action for more than a few hours. Only in rare instances were the raiders able to catch RAF fighters on the ground. By the time the German bombers arrived to deliver their attack on an airfield, the Spitfires and Hurricanes based there were usually airborne and well clear. Fighters able to fly but not fight took off on 'survival scrambles' with orders to keep clear of the area until the threat had passed. Aircraft unable to fly were wheeled into the protective revetments, or dispersed around the airfield where they were difficult to hit. As a result, the frontline fighter units lost less than twenty fighters destroyed on the ground, despite the almost daily attacks on airfields.

On 7 September the Luftwaffe shifted its attack to London, concentrating its main effort against the sprawling dock area to the east of the city. During the following week there were three further attacks on the capital. Then on 15 September, Battle of Britain Day, the Luftwaffe mounted two separate raids on London.

'IT DEMONSTRATED THE DETERMINATION AND BRAVERY WITH WHICH THE TOMMIES WERE FIGHTING OVER THEIR OWN COUNTRY'

Early on the afternoon of 15 September 1940, as the Heinkel 111s of Bomber Geschwader 26 were passing Maidstone on their way home, the formation suddenly came under attack from Spitfires. Leutnant Roderich Cescotti, one of the German pilots, recalled:

'A few Tommies succeeded in penetrating our fighter escort. I saw a Spitfire dive steeply through our escort, level out and close rapidly on our formation. It opened fire, from ahead and to the right, and its tracers streaked towards us. At that moment a Bf 109, which we had not seen before, appeared behind the Spitfire and we saw its rounds striking the Spitfire's tail. But the Tommy continued his attack, coming straight for us, and his rounds slashed into our aircraft. We could not return the fire for fear of hitting the Messerschmitt. I put my left arm across my face to protect it from the plexiglass splinters flying around the cockpit, holding the controls with my right hand. With only the thin plexiglass between us, we were eye-to-eye with the enemy's eight machine guns. At the last moment the Spitfire pulled up and passed very close over though out of control, and went down steeply trailing black smoke. Waggling its wings, the Messerschmitt swept past us and curved in for another attack. The action lasted only a few seconds, but it demonstrated the determination and bravery with which the Tommies were fighting over their own country.'

Cescotti's Heinkel had taken several hits, but he was able to hold position in formation. He made a normal landing at his base at Wevelghem in Belgium.

Almost certainly the courageous Spitfire pilot was Flying Officer Peter Pease of No.603 Squadron, who was shot down at the time, the place, and in the manner described by Cescotti. When the blazing fighter smashed into the ground a few miles southeast of Maidstone, Pease was still in the cockpit.

The son of Sir Richard Pease, Arthur Peter Pease studied at Eton and Cambridge University before joining the Royal Air Force at the beginning of the war. In July 1940 he was posted to No 603 Squadron based at Dyce airfield near Aberdeen and later that month he shared in the destruction of a Heinkel 111. Early in August the Squadron moved to Hornchurch, north-east of London, to take part in the defence of southern England. On 3 September Pease was credited with shooting down a Messerschmitt 109, and four days later his Spitfire suffered battle damage and he made a crash landing at Hornchurch. Just over a week later, on 15 September Peter Pease died in action.

Above: *Flying Officer Peter Pease of No.603 Squadron.*

'I FELT JOLLY GLAD TO BE DOWN ON THE GROUND WITHOUT HAVING CAUGHT FIRE'

'We were just going in to attack when somebody yelled 'Messerschmitts' over the R.T and the whole squadron spilt up. Actually It was a false alarm. The bombers were my object, so I snooped in under the 110s and attacked the bombers (about 40–50 Heinkel 111s) from the starboard beam.

'I got in a burst of about three seconds when – Crash! and the whole World seemed to be tumbling in on me. I pushed the stick forward hard, went into a vertical dive and held it until I was below cloud. The chief trouble was petrol gushing into the cockpit at the rate of gallons all over my feet, and a sort of lake of petrol in the bottom of the cockpit. My knee and leg were tingling all over as if I had pushed them into a bed of nettles. There was a bullet hole in my windscreen where a bullet had come in and entered the dashboard, knocking away the starter button. Another bullet, I think an explosive one, had knocked away one of my petrol taps in front of the joystick, spattering my leg with little splinters and sending a chunk of something through the back-side of my petrol tank near the bottom. I made for home at top speed to get there before all my petrol ran out. I was about 15 miles from the aerodrome and it was a heart-rending business with all that petrol gushing over my legs and the constant danger of fire. About five miles from the 'drome smoke began to come from under my dashboard. I thought the whole thing might blow up at any minute, so I switched off my engine. The smoke stopped. I glided towards the 'drome and tried putting my wheels down. One came down and the other remained stuck up. There was nothing for it but to make a one-wheel landing. I switched on my engine again to make the aerodrome. It took me some way and then began to smoke again, so I hastily switched off. I was now near enough and made a normal approach and held off. I made a good landing, touching down lightly. The unsupported wing slowly began to drop. I was able to hold it up for some time and then down came the wing tip on the ground. I began to slew round and counteracted as much as possible with the brake on the wheel which was down. I ended up going sideways on one wheel, a tail wheel and a wing tip. Luckily, the good tyre held out and the only damage to the aeroplane, apart from that done by the bullets, was a wing tip that is easily replaceable.

'I hopped out and went off to the M.O. to get a lot of metal splinters picked out of my leg and wrist. I felt jolly glad to be down on the ground without having caught fire.'

PILOT OFFICER ERIC MARRS of No.152 Squadron describing his action on 30 September 1940

Left: A pilot of No. 313 (Czech) Squadron running to his Spitfire during a scramble take off.

Two hours later there was a heavier attack on a series of targets in the London dock area.

No. 11 Group of Fighter Command, possessed 310 serviceable single-seat fighters. Of that total 218 were Hurricanes, and 92 were Spitfires. About one third of the available squadrons, Hurricanes and Spitfires, engaged the raiding forces as they made their way across Kent to the capital. The main body of defending fighters assembled over the outskirts of London. It was there that the two great clashes occurred and most of the aircraft were shot down.

BATTLE OF BRITAIN DAY

The first attack took place shortly before noon in a force comprised of twenty-one Messerschmitt 109 fighter-bombers and twenty-seven Dornier 17 bombers, with an escort of about a hundred and eighty Me 109s. The fighter-bombers were to attack rail targets throughout the London area, while the Dorniers were to hit the concentration of rail lines and junctions at Battersea.

Above: WAAF mechanics helping the pilot strap into a Spitfire Mark II of No.411 (Canadian) Squadron, at Digby in Lincolnshire in 1941.
Right: A few Mark II Spitfires were modified for the Air Sea Rescue role, carrying two cylindrical drums in parachutes in the rear fuselage holding an inflatable rubber dinghy and ration packs for survivors.

During the afternoon of the 15th, the Luftwaffe also launched smaller attacks on targets on the south coast. Twenty-six Heinkels bombed the Royal Navy base at Portland, and a small force of Messerschmitt 109 and 110 fighter-bombers tried unsuccessfully to hit the Supermarine plant at Southampton.

That day fifty-five German aircraft were destroyed, most of them falling to fighter attack. The RAF lost eight Spitfires and twenty-one Hurricanes. The Spitfire force suffered a loss rate of 4.2 per hundred sorties, while the Hurricane force suffered a loss rate of 6.4 per hundred sorties. In

action the Spitfire's superior performance meant it had a 50 per cent better chance of survival compared with the Hurricane. The German losses on 15 September fell far short of the 185 aircraft the defenders claimed as destroyed. Yet the action is rightly deemed to mark the climax of the Battle. Two days later Adolf Hitler ordered an indefinite postponement of Operation Sealion, the planned invasion of Britain. The ships and barges concentrated at ports along the Channel coast returned to their normal tasks and it was clear that the threat of invasion had passed.

THE MARK II

Near the end of the Battle of Britain the Spitfire Mark II entered service. Similar to the Mark I, it was powered by the Merlin 12 engine giving an additional 110 hp. With its armour protection and additional equipment, the Mark II weighed 350lb (159kg) more than the early Mark I. The Spitfire emerged from the Battle of Britain with a proven record of success in the limited role of home-defence fighter. If the Spitfire was to play a major part in the war, it would have to modify its role.

MAINTAINING SPITFIRE PRODUCTION

On 26 September 1940 a raiding force of fifty-nine Heinkel 111s mounted a devastating attack on the two main Supermarine factories at Woolston and Itchen. The bombers wrecked most of the factory buildings at both sites, striking a body blow at Spitfire production.

On the day following the attack Lord Beaverbrook, Winston Churchill's tireless Minister of Aircraft Production, visited Southampton to inspect the damage. On his decision the two wrecked factories were abandoned. Production of Spitfires was to be dispersed into several smaller units in towns and cities. Fortuitously most of the machine tools and production jigs at Woolston and Itchen had survived the attack. Also, the final assembly hangers at Eastleigh airfield had not been touched. Supermarine executives toured Southampton, Winchester, Salisbury, Trowbridge, Reading and Newbury and the surrounding areas, looking at every large open building. Motor repair garages, laundries and bus stations were the obvious choices. Accompanying each Supermarine executive was a policeman who carried a letter of introduction from the Chief Constable of the area, requesting cooperation but giving no reason for the visit. Where a building was considered suitable for use in the dispersed production scheme, the not-always-delighted owner received official papers requisitioning the building. As each new site was acquired, the Spitfire production jigs and tools were brought in and set up.

Never again would Spitfire production be as vulnerable to air attack as it had been in September 1940.

Above right and below: Following the attack on the Supermarine factories, Spitfire production was dispersed into several small units in the surrounding towns and cities. These photographs show Spitfire wing leading edges being manufactured at the requisitioned garage of Anna Valley Motors Ltd at Salisbury.

Far right, below: A remarkable photograph taken from a Messerschmitt 110 reconnaissance aircraft over Snodland, Kent, showing Spitfires of No. 64 Squadron climbing into position to intercept the aircraft. The Messerschmitt suffered severe damage in the ensuing engagement and the radio operator was killed.

SPITFIRE SKYPLANES

In time of war it is difficult to exaggerate the importance of aerial reconnaissance. To plan effective air attacks, staff officers require the best possible information on each target. They need to know where bombs should be aimed to cause maximum damage. They also need to know the layout of the defences around each target, so they can route the bombers to avoid the worst of them. Without such information, attacking forces will inflict less damage, and suffer heavier losses. The best source of such information is aerial photography.

Today the idea of using an unarmed reconnaissance aircraft, is well accepted. It was not always so. Before the Second World War most air forces employed modified bombers to fly long-range reconnaissance missions. These machines had to carry guns and gunners to fight their way through to targets.

Shortly before the outbreak of war, Flying Officer Maurice 'Shorty' Longbottom, suggested a better means of securing reconnaissance photographs. In a memo he set down his views on the future of strategic aerial reconnaissance. Longbottom

suggested that reconnaissance should be done 'by the use of a single small machine, relying solely on its speed, climb and ceiling to avoid detection.' Longbottom believed the ideal aircraft would be a Spitfire with the guns, ammunition, radio and other unnecessary equipment removed.

The Air Ministry greeted Longbottom's memorandum with polite interest, but initially the paper was pigeon-holed.

Main left: *Compare the 1939 inset photograph with the main one, of Bullihgen, taken in April 1944 from a Spitfire at the same altitude, with a camera fitted with a 36in lens. Far more ground detail is visible.*

Top: *Spitfire PR IC used for high-altitude photographic missions. This aircraft carried its vertically mounted cameras in a blister under the starboard wing, seen in the open position for the removal of the film magazines.*

Middle: *Spitfire PR IF. This aircraft carried its vertically mounted cameras in the rear fuselage. Blister fuel tanks under the wings gave it increased range.*
Above: *Spitfire PR IG used for low-altitude photograph targets beneath cloud. These aircraft wore a very pale shade of pink the same as clouds on an overcast day.*

RECONNAISSANCE VARIANTS

PR IA Original PR variant, one 5in (12.7cm) lens camera mounted in each wing. No additional fuel.

PR IB One 8in (20.3cm) lens camera in each wing. Additional fuel: 29-gallon (132l) tank in the rear fuselage.

PR IC As PR IB, but with the two 8in lens cameras mounted in tandem in a blister fairing under the starboard wing. Additional fuel: 29-gallon (132l) tank in the rear fuselage, 30-gallon (136.5l) blister tank under the port wing.

PR ID First major re-design of the Spitfire for the reconnaissance role. Carried two 8in or two 20in (50.8cm) lens cameras in the rear fuselage. Additional fuel: large fuel tank built integrally with the leading edge of the wing, capacity 114 gal (518l); 29-gallon tank in the rear fuselage. This variant replaced the Marks IA, IB, IC and IF in front-line service during 1941. When fitted with the Merlin 45 engine it became the PR 5D, then it was redesignated as the PR Mark 4.

PR IE Designed for the low-altitude

reconnaissance role; only one example produced. Oblique camera under each wing, pointing at right angles to the line of flight. Additional fuel: 29-gallon (132l) tank in rear fuselage.

PR IF Carried two 8in or two 20in (50.8cm) lens cameras in the rear fuselage. Additional fuel: 30-gallon (136.5l) blister tank under each wing, 29-gallon (132l) tank in the rear fuselage.

PR IG Designed for low-altitude reconnaissance role. One oblique camera mounted in the rear fuselage,

Above: A reconnaisance Spitfire at high altitude. The pilots avoided leaving condensation trails, as these betrayed their positions, making them vulnerable to fighter interception.

could point either to port or to starboard. In addition there was one 14in (36.5cm) and one 5in (12.7cm) mounted vertically in the rear fuselage. Additional fuel: 29-gallon (132l) tank in the rear fuselage.

The RAF was desperately short of modern reconnaisance aircraft fighters, needing every available Spitfire for the defence of Great Britain. Air Chief Marshal Dowding was unwilling to release these aircraft for other roles, no matter how persuasive the arguments might appear.

It took only six weeks of war to change people's minds. The main RAF reconnaissance aircraft then in use, the low performance Blenheim, was quite inadequate for the task. Rarely could they photograph targets any distance inside enemy territory, and they suffered heavy losses whenever they tried.

SECRET NEW UNIT

Air Chief Marshal Dowding reluctantly agreed to release a couple of Spitfires for the reconnaissance role. The aircraft went to a highly secret new unit based at Heston north of London, headed by Wing Commander Sidney Cotton. One of the officers who helped him set up the unit was 'Shorty' Longbottom himself.

Cotton's first step was to modify the Spitfires for the new role and commence operations over enemy territory. Each aircraft was fitted with a pair of cameras, mounted in each wing in the space previously occupied by the guns and ammunition boxes. Metal plates sealed off

Far right: Interior of the huge Spitfire production facility at Castle Bromwich, *Birmingham. Morris Motors Ltd built the factory, under contract to the British Government. The plant produced some twelve thousand Spitfires, over half of the total. At its peak it turned out 320 Spitfires a month.*

Below: Dramatic low-altitude shot of the German cruiser Hopper in dry dock, at heavily defended Brest.

SKYPLANE PILOT

'During the early [photographic reconnaissance] missions there was no heating in our Spitfires. For the high altitude missions we wore thick suits with electrical heating. Trussed up in our Mae West and parachute, one could scarcely move in the narrow cockpit of the Spitfire. When flying over enemy territory one had to be searching the sky the whole time for enemy fighters. On more than one occasion I started violent evasive action to shake off a suspected enemy fighter, only to discover that it was a small speck of dirt on the inside of my perspex canopy!

'A big worry over enemy territory was that one might start leaving a condensation trail without knowing it, thus pointing out one's position to the enemy. To avoid that we had small mirrors fitted in the blisters on each side of the canopy, so that one could see the trail as soon as it started to form. When that happened one could either climb or descend until the trail ceased. If possible, we liked to climb above the trail's layer because then fighters trying to intercept us had first to climb through the trail's layer themselves and could be seen in good time.'

PILOT OFFICER GORDON GREEN, SPITFIRE PILOT, PHOTOGRAPHIC RECONNAISSANCE UNIT

the empty gun ports, and groundcrewmen applied plaster of Paris to fill the joints in the skinning. Then each aircraft received a coat of polish to give it a smooth, high gloss, finish. With these changes the maximum speed of the reconnaissance Spitfires was about 12mph (20km/hr) faster than the fighter version.

In November 1939 the Spitfire reconnaissance unit under the cover-designation 'No. 2 Camouflage Unit', moved to Seclin in France to begin operational trials. On the 18th, Longbottom, now a Flight Lieutenant, took off to photograph the German city of Aachen. Flying at 33,000ft (10,000m), he found navigation difficult. When his films were developed, they showed a strip of Belgian territory to the south of Aachen. Longbottom learned the lesson well, and when he returned to the area four days later, he made a successful photographic run over the German border defences.

During the next few weeks, Spitfires photographed several targets in western Germany, including the Ruhr industrial area. Significantly, and in distinct contrast to the Blenheims, the Spitfires flew their missions without loss or serious interference from the German defences. Photographs taken from 33,000 ft (10,000m) with 5in (12.7cm) focal-length cameras produced very small-scale pictures, however. The interpreters could pick out roads, railways, villages and major fortifications. But even with prints enlarged as

much as the grain of the film allowed, it was not possible to see troop positions or individual vehicles. If the Spitfire's capabilities were to be fully exploited, longer lens cameras would be needed. Apart from that proviso, the flights proved the essential soundness of Longbottom's proposals. As a result Air Chief Marshal Dowding agreed to release a dozen more Spitfires for the reconnaissance role.

In January 1940 an improved photographic reconnaissance Spitfire was ready for operations, the PR IB (for details of this and other reconnaissance variants, see opposite; the earlier variant became known as the PR IA). In February, Longbottom demonstrated the usefulness of the PR IB's additional range capability when he photographed the important German naval bases at Wilhelmshaven and Emden.

Cotton's unit was renamed the Photographic Development Unit, the new title revealing its true role for the first time. In 1940 the operations in France were reorganized and a further unit, No. 212 Squadron, formed at Seclin to conduct the

Left: Seamstresses applying the fabric covering to Spitfire rudders, at Castle Bromwich. The Spitfire's rudder weighed only 18lb (8kg), but was strong enough to withstand manoeuvring at high speed.

Commander Geoffrey Tuttle replaced Sidney Cotton as its commander. The changes of name and commander made no difference to the way the unit operated, however.

> ### Longbottom took the PR IC to Kiel, the first RAF aircraft to photograph the important naval base

At the end of July a further Spitfire reconnaissance variant appeared, the 'super-long-range' PR IF. This variant had a radius of action about 100 miles (160 km) greater than the Type IC. Operating from airfields in East Anglia, it could photograph targets as far afield as Berlin.

Throughout the summer of 1940, reconnaissance Spitfires kept a daily watch on the German preparations for the invasion of Britain. Each day they sallied forth to photograph each of the ports along the Channel coast, observing the growing assemblies of barges and shipping at each. Then on 20 September, three days after Adolf Hitler's order to postpone the invasion, a reconnaissance Spitfire returned bearing the first hard evidence of the change in German plans. Its photographs of Cherbourg harbour showed that five destroyers and a torpedo boat had left the port since the previous reconnaissance. In the weeks that followed, almost every

Spitfire reconnaisance missions from there.

LONG-RANGE VISION

In March 1940 a so-called 'long-range' reconnaisance version of the Spitfire appeared, the PR IC, with a further fuel tank to increase its reach. On 7 April Longbottom took this aircraft to Kiel, the first RAF aircraft to photograph the important naval base since the outbreak of war.

Little over a month later, on 10 May 1940, German forces launched their powerful Blitzkrieg attack on France, Holland and Belgium. During the hectic weeks that followed No. 212 Squadron photographed

Below: A showpiece of the British aircraft industry, the Castle Bromwich plant had a constant stream of important visitors. Here Winston Churchill is seen chatting with Alex Henshaw, Chief Test Pilot at the factory.

each stage of the advance of the German Panzer columns. The squadron then withdrew to England, where its aircraft and personnel were incorporated in the PDU at Heston.

Thus far the reconnaissance Spitfires had flown their missions at medium or high altitude, and photographed their targets from directly above. Most of the RAF's aerial photography would continue to be done that way. A few Spitfires were fitted with the so-called oblique camera installation, with a camera pointing at right angles to the line of flight and a few degrees below the horizontal. On 7 July 1940 Flying Officer Alistair Taylor proved the value of the new installation. Despite a 700ft (213m) cloud base and heavy rain, he took good photographs of shipping inside Boulogne harbour as he flew past the outer mole. From then on low-altitude photography, nicknamed 'dicing' because of the risks involved, became an important additional role for the reconnaissance Spitfires.

Also in July 1940, the Photographic Development Unit underwent yet another name change. It became the Photographic Reconnaissance Unit (PRU) and Wing

'IT WAS ALL RATHER LIKE A FOX HUNT...'

'During the early [photographic reconnaissance] missions to cover Brest [in 1941] we lost about five pilots fairly quickly. After the first couple had failed to return the Flight Commander, Flight Lieutenant Keith Arnold, asked Benson [the headquarters of the reconnaissance units] to send some reserve pilots. They duly arrived. Both took off for Brest that evening and neither came back. That was a very sobering incident.

'The important thing with any photographic mission was to take the photos if one could, and get them back to base. As the "boss" of PRU, Wing Commander Geoffrey Tuttle, often used to say, "I want you to get home safely not just because I like your faces, but because if you don't the whole sortie will be a waste of time!" So it was no use trying to play hide and seek with the Luftwaffe. If one had lost surprise during the approach to a heavily defended target, the best thing was to abandon the mission. One could go back another time when things might be better. Looking back at my time with the PRU, I get a lot of satisfaction from the knowledge that although I played my part in the war, I never had to fire a shot in anger. In one sense we in the reconnaissance business had things easy. All the time it was impressed on us: bring back the photographs or, if you can't, bring back the aeroplane. An infantryman taking part in the Battle of Alamein could not suddenly decide "This is ridiculous, I'm going home!" He just had to go on. But if we thought we had lost the element of surprise we were not only permitted to turn back, we were expected to do so. On the other hand there were times when I knew real fear. When one was 15 minutes out from Brest on a low altitude sortie, one's heart was beating away and as the target got nearer one's mouth got completely dry. Anyone who was not frightened at the thought of going in to photograph one of the most heavily defended targets in Europe, was not human.'

PILOT OFFICER GORDON GREEN, SPITFIRE PILOT, PHOTOGRAPHIC RECONNAISSANCE UNIT

successive reconnaissance flight revealed fewer ships and barges in each port as the vessels resumed their normal tasks. The threat to Great Britain had passed.

TO STETTIN

The 'long range' and 'extra long range' versions of the Spitfire opened new vistas for photographic reconnaissance and the targets it could cover. Yet in terms of range, the modified fighter could do even better. Supermarine redesigned the wing to take a huge additional fuel tank that took up almost the entire leading edge back to the main spar. In October 1940 the first Spitfires modified in this way, the PR ID, became available for operations.

When carrying its full load of fuel the PR ID was difficult to handle, as Flight Lieutenant Neil Wheeler explained. 'You could not fly it straight and level for the first half hour or hour after take off. Until you had emptied the rear tank, the aircraft hunted the whole time. The centre of gravity was so far back that you couldn't control it.' Once part of the fuel load had been consumed, however, the Type D handled well and its extra range gave it a dramatic extension of reconnaissance cover. On 29 October 1940 one of these aircraft photographed the port of Stettin on the Baltic (now Sczecin in Poland) and returned after 5 hours and 20 minutes airborne.

The final reconnaissance variant of the Spitfire I was the Type G, optimized for the low-altitude photographic role with an oblique camera mounted in the rear fuselage. This version retained the fighter's standard armament of eight .303in (7.7mm) machine guns to enable it to defend itself against enemy fighters.

By 1941 the reconnaissance Spitfires possessed the range to photograph targets almost anywhere in western Europe.

Above: Test pilots striding out to fly brand new Spitfires off the production line at Castle Bromwich.

THE SPITFIRE
SPREADS ITS WINGS

In the spring of 1941 a new production version of the Spitfire appeared, the Mark V. This was fitted with the Merlin 45 engine which gave increases of, respectively, 440 and 330 horse power over the versions fitted to the Marks I and II. The main production version of the Spitfire V carried an armament of two 20mm cannon and four .303in (7.7mm) machine guns.

SPITFIRE V

Type Single-seat general purpose fighter.
Armament Four Hispano 20 mm cannon with 120 rounds per gun, or two Hispano 20 mm cannon with 120 rounds per gun and four Browning .303in (7.7mm) machine guns with 350 rounds per gun, or eight .303in (7.7mm) Browning machine guns with 350 rounds per gun. Maximum bomb load two 250lb (113kg) bombs.
Power Plant One Rolls-Royce Merlin 45 liquid cooled V-12 engine developing 1,470hp.
Dimensions Span 36ft 10in (10.98m), 32ft 6in (9.9m, clipped wings); length 29ft 11in (9.11m).
Weight Maximum loaded weight 6,070lb (2,752kg).
Performance Maximum speed 371mph at 20,000ft (597km/hr at 6,100m). Service ceiling 38,000ft (11,585m).

Left and inset: Spitfire VC fitted with four 20mm cannon, being loaded on the aircraft carrier USS Wasp docked at Glasgow In April 1942. The wingtips had been removed and placed in the cockpit.
Right, top: The Daimler-Benz company at Stuttgart fitted a DB605 engine Into a captured Mark V.
Right, below: Spitfire In trouble: a still from a combat film taken by the Luftwaffe fighter ace Major Gerhard Schoepfel of Fighter Geschwader 26, showing cannon shells bursting on the fuselage.

In 1941 Fighter Command moved from the defensive to the offensive. Simultaneously Spitfire production rose to a point where it exceeded losses. During the Battle of Britain nineteen squadrons had operated Spitfires. By September 1941 there were twenty-seven and by the end of 1941 Fighter Command had forty-six squadrons equipped with Spitfires.

The Mark V had a performance significantly better than the earlier variants of the Spitfire, yet it was not good enough. In the summer of 1941 the Luftwaffe introduced a new, more effective fighter into service: the Focke Wulf 190.

The Focke Wulf was 25-30mph (40-48km/hr) faster than the Spitfire V at most altitudes and it could out-climb, out-dive and out-roll the British fighter. The Spitfire V's only advantage over its new opponent was that it could turn tighter.

Fortunately for the RAF, the Luftwaffe was heavily committed to supporting the campaign in Russia. As a result the size of the fighter force retained in the west, would remain relatively small.

SPITFIRES TO MALTA

The next major challenge to face the Spitfire came early in 1942. Malta was the cornerstone of Britain's strategy in the

Left: In September 1942 the US manned 'Eagle' Squadrons of the RAF were officially transferred to the US Army Air Force with their aircraft. This aircraft went with No.121 Squadron to become part of the 335th Fighter Squadron of the 4th Fighter Group.

Mediterranean. Torpedo-bombers operating from the island took a steady toll of ships carrying supplies and reinforcements to sustain the Axis ground forces in North Africa. The island lay within 100 miles (160km) of Axis airfields in Sicily and suffered frequent and destructive air attacks. Malta's survival depended on her air defences, but the Hurricanes based on the island were outclassed by the Messerschmitt 109Fs opposing them.

Only the Spitfire V could engage the Me 109F on equal terms, but the distance from Gibraltar to Malta was far beyond the Spitfire's normal

Right: US Army Air Force mechanics carry out an engine change on a spare.
Below: Armourers of No. 72 Squadron cleaning the barrel and removing the ammunition drum from the Hispano 20mm cannon.

When the new German fighter first appeared, it came as a severe shock to Fighter Command

ferry range. The strength of the Axis naval and air forces besieging the island precluded any large delivery of fighters by sea. The Hurricanes already on Malta had been transported half way by aircraft carrier, which launched them to fly the rest of the way to the island. The Spitfires needed to use the same method; from fly-off point to Malta was approximately 660 miles (1,062km). Engineers at Supermarine designed a 90-gallon (409l) drop tank. The first delivery of Spitfires took place on 7 March 1942, fifteen taking off from HMS *Eagle*.

Above: *The flight deck of Wasp pictured late on the afternoon of 19 April, as the carrier prepared to fly off her brood of Spitfires soon after first light the following morning. Ranged in front and to the left of them are the carrier's own Wildcat fighters.*
Left: *The Focke Wulf 190 fighter was a formidable opponent for the Spitfire Mark V.*

SPITFIRE V VERSUS FOCKE WULF 190A

In July 1942, a comparative trial between a Spitfire V and a captured Focke Wulf 190 fighter took place. These trials revealed just how formidable a foe they were. Excerpts from the official RAF report on the trials are given below:

The FW 190 was compared with a Spitfire VB from an operational squadron for speed and all-round manoeuvrability at heights up to 25,000ft (7,620m). The FW 190 is superior in speed at all heights, and the approximate differences are as follows:

At 2,000ft (610m) the FW 190 is 25–30mph (40–48km/hr) faster than the Spitfire 5B
At 3,000ft (915m) the FW 190 is 30–35mph (48–56km/hr) faster than the Spitfire 5B
At 5,000ft (1,525m) the FW 190 is 25mph (40km/hr) faster than the Spitfire VB
At 9,000ft (2,744m) the FW 190 is 25–30 mph faster than the Spitfire 5B
At 15,000ft (4573m) the FW 190 is 20mph (32km/hr) faster than the Spitfire 5B
At 18,000ft (5,488m) the FW 190 is 20mph (32km/hr) faster than the Spitfire VB
At 21,000ft (6,400m) the FW 190 is 20–25mph (32–40km/hr) faster than the Spitfire VB

Climb: The climb of the FW 190 is superior to that of the Spitfire VB at all heights. The best speeds for climbing are approximately the same, but the angle of the FW 190 is considerably steeper. Under maximum continuous climbing conditions the climb of the FW 190 is about 450ft/min (137m/min) better up to 25,000ft (7,620m).

Dive: Comparative dives between the two aircraft have shown that the FW 190 can leave the Spitfire with ease, particularly during the initial stages.

Manoeuvrability: The manoeuvrability of the FW 190 is better than that of the Spitfire VB except in turning circles. The FW 190 has better acceleration under all conditions of flight and this must obviously be most useful during combat.

When the FW 190 was in a turn and was attacked by the Spitfire, the superior rate of roll enabled it to flick into a diving turn in the opposite direction. The pilot of the Spitfire found great difficulty in following this manoeuvre and even when prepared for it, was seldom able to allow the correct deflection. A dive from this manoeuvre enabled the FW 190 to draw away from the Spitfire which was then forced to break off the attack.

The above trials have shown that the Spitfire VB must cruise at high speed when in an area where enemy fighters can be expected.

Left: After each launch of Spitfires on deck, those in the hangar were brought up by lift. This required slick timing. A Spitfire is about to begin its takeoff; the aircraft ahead of it can be seen climbing away, just above the starboard wing. Meanwhile, the lift is already on the way to the hangar to pick up the next aircraft.

AMERICAN HELP

The Spitfires arrived just in time. The defending fighter units were heavily outnumbered. On 1 April Winston Churchill sent a personal telegram to President Roosevelt asking for help:

'Air attack on Malta is very heavy. There are now in Sicily about 400 German and 200 Italian fighters. Malta can only now muster 20 to 30 serviceable fighters. We keep feeding Malta with Spitfires in packets of 16 loosed from EAGLE carrier.

'This has worked quite well but EAGLE is now laid up for a month by defects in her steering gear. Would you be willing to allow your carrier WASP to do one of these trips provided details are satisfactorily agreed between the Navy Staffs? We estimate that WASP could take 50 or more Spitfires . . .'

Within three days of receiving the telegram the US President agreed to the request. Six days after that *Wasp* docked at Port Glasgow to load 47 Spitfires for the island. On the 20th April, the carrier began launching the Spitfires. Forty-six of the 47 fighters that took off reached Malta safely. These Spitfires, however, were to be destroyed in the air or on the ground, in the following days.

Middle: Scene on the flight deck of USS Wasp on the morning of 9 May 1942, as the carrier prepares to launch her aircraft for the largest resupply of aircraft to Malta. In the background, preparing to launch her Spitfires also, is HMS Eagle.

Above: A soldier, a sailor and an airman carry out refuelling and rearming of a Spitfire of No. 603 Squadron at Takali, Malta, In the spring of 1942. The blast pen was constructed from empty petrol tins filled with sand.

Right and below: Spitfire Vs of the No. 54 Squadron based at Darwin, Australia, early in 1943 providing air defence for the Northern Territory. (Australian War Memorial)

Again Malta was in crisis, and again Mr Churchill asked the US President to help. The American carrier returned to Glasgow on 29 April and took on a further forty-seven Spitfires. By then HMS *Eagle* at Gibraltar had completed her repairs, and she took on a further seventeen fighters.

MALTA SAVED

As *Wasp* entered the Mediterranean a second time, *Eagle* set sail from Gibraltar to join her. The two carriers and their escorts headed east together and shortly after dawn on 9 May they launched their Spitfires. Sixty of the 64 fighters that set out reached Malta. It was sufficient to change the course of the battle. The island's air defences were now strong enough to resist Axis air attacks, and could be topped up with 'penny packets' of Spitfires from the smaller carriers.

By late 1942 the RAF possessed a more cost-effective method of delivering Spitfires to Malta from Gibraltar. Supermarine engineers had modified the Mark V to fly the distance non-stop, by fitting a 170 gallon (772l) drop tank under the fuselage and a 29 gallon (132l) auxiliary tank in the rear fuselage. The modified Spitfire could now fly the 1,100 mile (1,770km) distance in a single hop.

During October and November 1942 seventeen Spitfires took off from Gibraltar to fly to Malta. All except one of them made it.

The Allied victory at El Alamein, and the subsequent expulsion of Axis forces from Libya, lifted the siege of Malta.

BY SPITFIRE TO MALTA

Pilot Officer Michael Le Bas of No. 601 Squadron described his take off in a Spitfire from the deck of USS *Wasp*. His heavily loaded aircraft carried a 90-gallon (409l) drop tank under the fuselage. Ahead lay a flight of 660 miles (1,062km), about as far as from London to Prague.

'The deck officer began rotating his checkered flag and I pushed forward the throttle to emergency override to get the last ounce of power out of my Merlin. The Spitfire picked up speed rapidly in its headlong charge down the deck, but not rapidly enough. The ship's bows got closer and closer and still I had insufficient airspeed and suddenly – I was off the end. With only 60 feet to play with before I hit the water, I retracted the undercarriage and eased forward on the stick to build up speed. Down and down went the Spitfire until, about fifteen feet above the waves, it reached flying speed and I was able to level out. After what seemed an age, my speed built up and I was able to climb away. It had been a hairy introduction to flying off an aircraft carrier. Things had happened so quickly that there was no time to think.'

REGAINING CONTROL
OF THE SKIES

After the initial encounters with Focke Wulf 190s, Fighter Command made strong demands for an improved fighter with the performance to meet the new challenge. There could be no question of designing, building and bringing into service a completely new aircraft; on the most optimistic time scale that would have taken at least four years. Fighter Command could not wait that long.

Rolls-Royce already had the answer to the problem in a new version of the Merlin. Previous versions of the engine used a single-stage supercharger. The new engine employed a two-stage supercharger, in which the output from the first blower fed into the second to compress the charge of air further before it entered the carburettor. The two-stage supercharger gave a spectacular improvement in high-altitude performance. At 30,000ft (9,145m) the Merlin 45 engine with a single-stage supercharger developed about 720 horse power. At the same altitude the same basic engine fitted with a two-stage supercharger developed about 1,020 horse power, an increase of more than 40 per cent. The extra plumbing added about 200 pounds (90kg) to the weight of the engine and increased its length by 9 inches (23cm).

In September 1941, an experimental Spitfire incorporating the two-stage supercharger began flight testing.

> ## There could be no question of designing, building and bringing into service a brand new aircraft

Far Left: A Spitfire VII, the high-altitude Interceptor version of the famous fighter. Note the distinctive long-span wing with pointed tips.

SPITFIRE MARK IX

Type Single-seat general purpose fighter and fighter-bomber.
Armament Two Hispano 20mm cannon with 120 rounds per gun, four Browning .303in (7.7mm) machine guns with 350 rounds per gun; or two Hispano 20mm cannon with 120 rounds per gun and two Browning .5in (12.7mm) machine guns with 250 rounds per gun. Maximum bomb load one 50-pound (226kg) bomb and two 250 pounders (113kg).

Power Plant One Rolls-Royce Merlin 61, 63 or 70 liquid cooled V-12 engine with two-stage supercharger. Merlin 65 developed 1,565 hp.
Dimensions Span 40ft 2in (12.85, pointed wing tips), 36ft 10in (10.98m, normal wing tips) or 32ft 6in (9.9m, clipped wings); length 30ft 0in (9.14m).
Weight Maximum loaded weight 7,500lb (3,400kg).
Performance Maximum speed 400mph at 25,000ft (657km/hr at 7,622m); service ceiling 43,000ft (13,110m).

Below: Spitfire IX of No. 402 (Canadian) Squadron.

TURNING POINT IN AN AIR WAR

On the afternoon of 30 July 1942 Flight Lieutenant Donald Kingaby of No. 64 Squadron scored his 16th aerial victory. Afterwards he reported:

'I sighted approximately 12 FW 190s 2,000ft [610m] below us at 12,000ft [3,658m] just off Boulogne proceeding towards French coast. We dived down on them and I attacked a FW 190 from astern and below giving a very short burst, about half a second, from 300yd. I was forced to break away as I was crowded out by other Spits. I broke down and right and caught another FW as he commenced to dive away. At 14,000ft [4,268m] approx. I gave a burst of cannon and M/G, 400 yd range hitting E/A along fuselage. Pieces fell off and E/A continued in straight dive nearly vertical It followed E/A down to 5,000ft [1,525m] over Boulogne and saw him hit the deck just outside the town of Boulogne and explode and burn up. Returned to base at 0ft.'

The combat report was little different from many others in the summer of 1942, yet this air combat marked a significant turning point in the air war over Europe. It was the first time the Spitfire Mark IX had encountered the Focke Wulf 190 in action. The latest variant of the British fighter showed that it could take on its once-feared opponent on equal terms. The Luftwaffe would never regain their superiority in the skies.

The Merlin 61 Spitfire was considerably faster than any previous version, with a maximum speed of 414mph at 27,200ft (667km/hr at 8,300m). Its service ceiling was over 41,000 ft (12,500m).

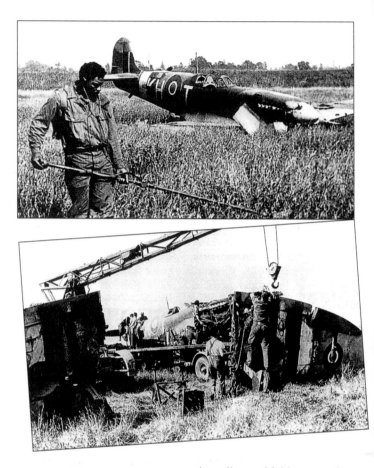

THREE NEW VARIANTS

The Spitfire VII was a high-altitude interceptor version, with a pressurized cabin and a longer wingspan giving increased area. Its airframe was redesigned and strengthened to compensate for the increases in engine power and weight the fighter had incurred previously. The second of the new variants, the Spitfire VIII, was similar to the Mark VII but lacked the pressurized cabin of that type.

These two versions required a large amount of re-design as well as retooling of the production lines. Neither version would be available in quantity until the spring of 1943.

In the meantime Fighter Command quickly needed a fighter to counter the FW 190. The solution was the Spitfire IX, which was essentially a Mark V with the minimum of modification necessary to take the Merlin 61 engine.

The Mark V was not really strong enough to accept the additional engine power. In wartime, however, the RAF was prepared to accept this deficiency in the name of operational expediency.

Left and above: *A damaged aircraft repaired and returned to service was as valuable as a new aircraft, and the RAF salvage teams and repair organization played a valuable role. This Spitfire of No. 403 (Canadian) Squadron crash-landed in a mine-field in Normandy. After a sweep of the area to ensure that it was safe, the fighter was dismantled and loaded on to a transporter.*

The first production Spitfire IXs arrived at No. 64 Squadron at Hornchurch during June 1942, and the unit resumed operations with the new variant at the end of July. The new Spitfire quickly demonstrated that it was the equal of the Focke Wulf 190 in combat. Proof of this came, when a German pilot inadvertently landed his FW 190 at Pembrey in South Wales. The RAF carried out detailed flight tests with

SPITFIRE IX VERSUS FOCKE WULF 190A

In July 1942 a Spitfire IX was flown in a comparative trial against a captured Focke Wulf 190. The similarities in performances were remarkable. Excerpts from the official trials report are given below:

Comparative Speeds: The FW 190 was compared with a fully operational Spitfire IX for speed and manoeuvrability at heights up to 25,000ft (7,620m). The Spitfire IX at most heights is slightly superior in speed to the FW 190 and the approximate differences in speeds at various heights are as follows:

At 2,000ft (610m) the FW 190 is 7–8mph (11–13km/hr) faster than the Spitfire IX
At 5,000ft (1,524m) the FW 190 and the Spitfire IX are approximately the same
At 8,000ft (2,44m) the Spitfire IX is 8mph (13km/hr) faster than the FW 190
At 15,000ft (4,573m) the Spitfire IX is 5mph (8km/hr) faster than the FW 190
At 18,000ft (5,488m) the FW 190 is 3mph (5km/hr) faster than the Spitfire IX
At 21,000ft (6,400m) the FW 190 and the Spitfire IX are approximately the same
At 25,000ft (7,622m) the Spitfire IX is 5–7mph (8–11km/hr) faster than the FW 190

Climb: During comparative climbs at various heights up to 23,000ft (7,012m), with both aircraft flying under maximum continuous climbing conditions, little difference was found between the two aircraft although on the whole the Spitfire IX was slightly better. Above 22,000ft (6,707m) the climb of the FW 190 is falling off rapidly, whereas the climb of the Spitfire IX is increasing.

Dive: The FW 190 is faster than the Spitfire IX in a dive, particularly during the initial stage. This superiority is not as marked as with the Spitfire VB.

Manoeuvrability: The FW 190 is more manoeuvrable than the Spitfire IX except in turning circles. The superior rate of roll of the FW 190 enabled it to avoid the Spitfire IX, by flicking over into a diving turn in the opposition direction.

The Spitfire IX's worst heights for fighting the FW 190 were between 18,000 and 22,000ft (5,486m and 6,707m) and below 3,000ft (914m).

The initial acceleration of the FW 190 is better than the Spitfire IX under all conditions of flight, except in level flight at such altitudes where the Spitfire has a speed advantage.

The general impression of the pilots in the trials is that the Spitfire IX compares well with the FW 190. Provided the Spitfire has the initiative, it undoubtedly has a good chance of shooting down the FW 190.

Left: The Spitfire VIII entered service after the Mark IX. This example belonged to No.457 (Australian) Squadron and was one of the 410 purchased by that air force for operations in the South Pacific area.

MARK VII

Type Single-seat high-altitude interceptor fighter with pressurized cabin.

Armament Two Hispano 20mm cannon with 120 rounds per gun, four Browning .303in (7.7mm) machine guns with 350 rounds per gun. Aircraft assigned to ultra high-altitude interception duties sometimes carried only the four .303 in machine guns.

Power Plant One Rolls-Royce Merlin 61, 64 or 71 liquid cooled V-12 engine with two-stage super-charger. Merlin 61 developed 1,565hp.

Dimensions: Span 40ft 2in (12.85m, pointed wing tips) or 36ft 10in (10.98m normal wing tips); length 30ft (9.15m).

Weight Maximum loaded weight 8,000lb (3,628kg).

Performance (Rolls-Royce Merlin 71 engine) maximum speed 424mph at 29,500ft (682km/hr at 8,994m); service ceiling 45,100ft (13.750m).

the captured aircraft to determine its exact performance and then had it fly mock combats with each of the main Allied fighters.

MARK IX IN SERVICE

The new variant had an immediate impact on the air situation. In combat it was impossible to distinguish it from the Mark V, and FW 190 pilots could never be certain which Spitfire variant they faced. The German fighters became markedly less aggressive and RAF fighter losses fell appreciably.

The first major action involving Spitfire IXs was on 19 August 1942, on the French coast. Four squadrons flew the new variant that day and they mounted 14 squadron-sized missions comprising about 150 sorties.

By the spring of 1943 the Spitfire IX equipped most of the RAF's single-seat fighter squadrons based in Great Britain. The re-engineered variants of the Spitfire intended to replace the Mark IX saw rather less use.

By the time the Mark VIII became available in quantity, in the spring of 1943, the FW 190 menace over north west Europe had been contained. The entire

Left: Spitfire Mark VIIIs of No.417 (Canadian) Squadron based at Canne, Italy, in 1944. These aircraft were fitted with pointed wing tips for high-altitude operations, as employed on the Mark VII.

Left: The Spitfire Mark XVI was similar to the Mark IX but was powered by the version of the Merlin engine built under licence by the American Packard Company. Late production Spitfire IXs and XVIs featured cut-down fuselages and bubble canopies.

Bottom left: Floatplane conversion of the Spitfire. A small number of aircraft were modified In this way but none saw action.

BUBBLE CANOPY

In most cases where Spitfires were shot down by enemy fighters, the victim never saw his assailant in time to take effective evasive action. Most such attacks were mounted from the fighter's blind zone, below and behind. Any modification that reduced the likelihood of a surprise attack would increase the fighter's chances of survival in combat.

The answer was to cutback the rear fuselage behind the cockpit, and fit the fighter with a bubble canopy. The first modified Spitfire flew in the summer of 1943. Manufacturer's trials showed little significant deterioration in the aircraft's handling. Experienced service pilots were impressed with the improvement in view from the bubble canopy. Their report stated:

'This is an enormous improvement. The pilot can see quite easily round to his fin and past it, almost to the further edge of the tailplane.

By banking the aircraft slightly during weaving action, the downward view to the rear is opened up well.'

Modified Spitfires began to reach the operational squadrons early in 1945.

entire 1,658-aircraft production run of this variant went overseas to units operating in the Middle East, the Far East and Australia.

The Mark IX, continued in production a lot longer than anyone had expected. The Supermarine and Castle Bromwich plants together turned out nearly six thousand of them.

The Spitfire XVI airframe was almost identical to that of the Mark IX, but it was powered by a version of the Merlin built by the American Packard Company. Late production Spitfire IXs and XVIs featured cut-down fuselages and bubble canopies, features which gave the pilot greatly improved vision behind and below the fighter.

The introduction of the Merlin 60 series improved the performance of the Spitfire to the point where it could fight the FW 190 on equal terms. Yet engineers at Rolls-Royce were not content to rest on their laurels. As we shall observe in the next chapter, they had something even better on offer.

ENTER THE GRIFFON

Mark XIV Spitfire of No. 402 (Canadian) Squadron. This version was the most effective variant to operate in the air superiority role during the Second World War.

In 1939 Rolls-Royce had begun development of a larger engine, later named the Griffon. With a cubic capacity of 65 gallons (36.75l), the new engine was one-third larger than its predecessor. The initial production version, with a single-stage supercharger, developed 1,735 hp. By clever positioning of components, the designers kept the length of the Griffon to within 3 inches (7.5cm), and the weight to within 600 pounds (272kg), of the equivalent figures for the Merlin. The new engine's frontal area was little greater than that of its predecessor.

In November 1941 an experimental Griffon prototype, the Mark IV, began flight testing. The aircraft had a maximum speed of 372mph at 5,700ft (600km/hr at 1,740m) which increased to 397mph at 18,000ft (640km/hr at 5,500m).

> **To counter the threat the RAF issued a requirement for a low-altitude interceptor**

At about this time the Luftwaffe commenced tip-and-run attacks on towns on the south and east coasts of England. Small forces of fighter-bombers ran in at low altitude to avoid radar detection. To counter the threat the RAF issued a requirement for a low-altitude interceptor. The Griffon Spitfire offered the best in performance at low altitude, and this became the prototype for the Mark XII fighter.

SPITFIRE XII

Type Single-seat fighter optimized for operations at low and medium altitudes.
Armament Two Hispano 20mm cannon with 120 rounds per gun, four Browning .303in (7.7mm) machine guns with 350 rounds per gun.
Power Plant One Rolls-Royce Griffon 4 liquid cooled V-12 engine with single-stage supercharger developing 1,735 horse power.
Dimensions Span 32ft 7in (9.93m); length 30ft 9in (9.37m).
Weight Maximum loaded weight 7,400lb (3,356kg).
Performance Maximum speed 389mph at 12,500ft (626km/hr at 3,810m); service ceiling 37,350ft (11,387m).

Below: The first Griffon-powered Spitfire, pictured after the aircraft had been modified to become the prototype Mark XII low-altitude fighter.

SPITFIRE XIV

Type Single-seat fighter and fighter reconnaissance aircraft.
Armament Two Hispano 20mm cannon with 120 rounds per gun, four Browning .303in (7.7mm) machine guns with 350 rounds per gun; or two Hispano 20mm cannon with 120 rounds per gun and two Browning .5in (12.7mm) machine guns with 250 rounds per gun. Fighter reconnaissance version carried an oblique-mounted camera in the rear fuselage.
Power Plant One Rolls-Royce Griffon 65 liquid cooled V-12 engine with two-stage supercharger developing 2,035hp.
Dimensions Span 36ft 1in (10.98m normal wing tips) or 32ft 7in (9.93m, clipped wings); length 32ft 8in (9.96m).
Weight Maximum loaded weight 10,065 pounds (4,565kg).
Performance Maximum speed 439mph at 24,500ft (707km/hr); service ceiling 43,000ft (13,110m).

Supermarine got a production order to build one hundred examples.

Like the Mark IX, the early production Mark XIIs used Mark V airframes with the minimum of modification necessary to take the new engine. Production Mark XIIs all had clipped wings. Compared with the Mark IX, the Mark XII was 14mph (22km/hr) faster at sea level and 8mph faster at 10,000 ft. But above 20,000ft (6,100m) performance fell away rapidly and the Mark XII became progressively slower than the Mark IX.

In the spring of 1943 Nos 41 and 91 Squadrons commenced operations with Mark XIIs from Hawkinge airfield near Folkestone. The units flew standing patrols against enemy fighter-bombers attacking coastal targets. On 25 May, No. 91 Squadron scrambled six fighters to engage FW 190 fighter-bombers attacking Folkestone. The Spitfires claimed the destruction of six raiders, without loss to themselves.

Although the Mark XII, was faster than the opposing fighter types at low and medium altitudes, this was of little value during offensive sweeps over France. German fighter pilots preferred to remain at altitude, coming down only to deliver high-speed diving attacks before making zoom climbs back to altitude. Rarely would they let themselves be drawn into turning fights with Spitfires below 20,000 ft.

An obvious next step for the Spitfire was to fit it with a Griffon with a two-stage supercharger. The new engine, the Griffon 65, appeared in the spring of 1943 and developed an impressive 1,540hp for take-off and 2,035hp at 7,000 ft (2,134m). Six Spitfire VIIIs were modified to take the new engine and became prototypes for the Mark XIV.

Flight tests with pre-production Mark XIVs revealed it to be an extremely effective fighter, giving a huge improvement in performance over the Mark IX. During comparative trials against a captured FW 190 and a Messerschmitt 109G, the Spitfire XIV showed itself to be superior to the German fighters in almost every respect.

The new variant went into production in the autumn of 1943. In the spring of 1944, Nos 91, 322 and 610 Squadrons received Mark XIVs. All three units were fully operational in June when the V.1 flying bomb attacks on London commenced.

SPITFIRE v FLYING BOMB

Although the V.1s flew a straight and predictable path, usually they were not easy targets. The majority flew at speeds around 350mph (563km/hr) and heights of between 3,000 and 4,000ft (915 and 1,220m). The highest came in at around 8,000 ft (2,440m) and the lowest flew at treetop height – which often led to their early demise!

> *Although the V.1s flew a straight and predictable path, usually they were not easy targets*

Protecting the capital were four separate layers of defences. The first layer, extending from mid-Channel to about 10 miles (16km) short of the south coast, was the Outer Fighter Patrol Area where Spitfires and other fighters could engage the flying bombs. Next came the Gun Belt, with more than 2,500 AA guns of all calibres positioned along the strip of coast between Beachy Head and Dover; this was off-limits to fighters, allowing gunners freedom to shoot at anything that came within range. From 10 miles (16km) inland to 10 miles (16km) short of London was the Inner Fighter Area where

---

SPITFIRE XIV COMPARED WITH FOCKE WULF 190A

Early in 1944 the Air Fighting Development Unit at Duxford flew a Spitfire XIV in a comparative trial against a captured Focke Wulf 190A. Excerpts from the official trials report are given below:

Maximum Speeds: From 0–5,000ft (0–1,525m) and 15,000–20,000ft (4,573–6,100m) the Spitfire XIV is only 20mph (32km/hr) faster; at all other heights it is up to 60mph (97km/hr) faster.

Maximum Climb: The Spitfire XIV has a considerably greater rate of climb than the FW 190 A at all altitudes.

Dive: After the initial part of the dive, during which the FW 190 gains slightly, the Spitfire XIV has a slight advantage.

Turning Circle: The Spitfire XIV can easily turn inside the FW 190. In the case of a right-hand turn, this difference is not quite so pronounced.

Rate of Roll: The FW 190 is very much better.

Conclusions: In defence, the Spitfire XIV should use its remarkable maximum climb and turning circle against any enemy aircraft. In the attack it can afford to 'mix it' but should beware of the quick roll and dive. If this manoeuvre is used by an FW 190 and the Spitfire XIV follows, it will probably not be able to close the range until the FW 190 has pulled out of its dive.

SPITFIRE XIV COMPARED WITH ME109G

Early in 1944 the Air Fighting Development Unit at Duxford flew a Spitfire XIV in a comparative trial against a captured Messerschmitt 109G, the latest sub-type of the famous German fighter. Excerpts from the official trials report are given below:

Maximum Speed: The Spitfire XIV is 40mph (64km/hr) faster at all heights except near 16,000ft (4,878m), where it is only 10mph (16km/hr) faster.

Maximum Climb: The same result: at 16,000ft (4,877m) the two aircraft are identical, otherwise the Spitfire XIV out-climbs the Me 109G. The zoom climb is practically identical when the climb is made without opening the throttle. Climbing at full throttle, the Spitfire XIV draws away easily from the Me 109G quite easily.

Dive: During the initial part of the dive, the Me 109G pulls away slightly, but when a speed of 380mph (611 km/hr) is reached, the Spitfire XIV begins to gain on the Me 109G.

Turning Circle: The Spitfire XIV easily out-turns the Me 109G in either direction.

Rate of Roll: The Spitfire XIV rolls much more quickly.

Conclusion: The Spitfire XIV is superior to the Me 109G in every respect.

Below: During mock combats the Me 109G was no match for the Spitfire XIV.

more fighters engaged the V.1s. The final layer, was the barrage balloon zone consisting of over a thousand balloons, which began 10 miles short of the London built-up area and ended at its outskirts.

All available squadrons with Mark XIVs redeployed to the Kent area to defend the capital.

AIR SUPERIORITY FIGHTER

At the end of August 1944, Allied ground forces advancing along the north coast of France overran the last of the V.1 launching sites in the Pas de Calais. The 8,617th and last flying bomb launched from that area crossed the south coast of England on the morning of 1 September.

Following the capture of the V.1 sites, the Spitfire XIV squadrons redeployed to airfields in Belgium, to resume operations against conventional enemy aircraft. Four further squadrons joined them soon afterwards, Nos 41, 130, 350 and 403 Squadrons.

The Mark XXI was intended as the 'definitive' fighter variant of the Spitfire. Powered by the Griffon 65 engine, it featured a completely redesigned wing with a much-strengthened internal structure. It carried the four 20mm cannon armament as standard. Early production machines had unpleasant handling characteristics. It took a few months to iron out these bugs and as a result the variant entered service only during the final few weeks of the war.

The delay in bringing the Mark XXI into action had no effect on the air war in Europe, for the Allied Air Forces defeated the Luftwaffe with the fighter types in service.

In the next chapter we shall observe the work done to improve the effectiveness of reconnaissance variants.

MORE SPITFIRE
SKYPLANES

As the war progressed, the Royal Air Force faced increasing demands to provide reconnaissance photographs of targets deep inside occupied territory in Europe. Yet, by the summer of 1942, the improving German air defences inflicted mounting losses on the reconnaissance Spitfires. The obvious answer was to produce a higher performance reconnaissance aircraft powered by the Merlin 61 engine. The new variant, the Spitfire PR XI, combined the strengthened airframe of the Mark VIII fighter with the integral wing fuel tank and rear fuselage camera installation of the PR Marks ID and VD.

Left: Spitfire PR XI in invasion markings. Note the ports in the rear fuselage for the two vertical cameras.

Until the PR XI became available, fifteen Mark IX fighters underwent modification for the reconnaissance role. Designated PR IXs, these aircraft had the armament removed and a pair of vertical cameras installed in the rear fuselage. The version had no extra internal fuel tankage, and during operations it usually flew with a 90 gallon (409l) drop tank under the fuselage. No. 541 Squadron at Benson received the first PR Mark IXs in November 1942. Although the limited tankage confined the PR IX to operations over western Europe, it restored the ability to photograph defended targets without incurring serious losses.

In December 1942 the first Spitfire PR XIs began coming off the production line. The new variant could operate at altitudes above 42,000ft (12,800m), some 10,000ft

SPITFIRE MK XI

Type Single-seat long range reconnaissance aircraft.
War Load Two vertically mounted reconnaissance cameras, could also carry one oblique mounted camera. No armament.
Power Plant One Rolls-Royce Merlin 63 liquid cooled V-12 engine with two-stage super-charger developing 1,650hp.
Dimensions Span 36ft 10in (10.98m); length 31ft 1in (9.47m).
Weight Maximum loaded weight 8,519lb (3,863kg).
Performance Maximum speed 417mph at 24,000ft (671km/hr at 7317m); service ceiling 44,000ft (13,415m).

(3,000m) higher than previous reconnaissance versions. The

Below and overleaf: Spitfire XIs of the 10th Photo Group, US Army Air Force. The unit operated this variant on photographic reconnaissance missions over occupied Europe.

SPITFIRE XIX

Type Single-seat long-range reconnaissance aircraft.

War Load Two vertically mounted reconnaissance cameras, could also carry one oblique mounted camera. No armament.

Power Plant One Rolls-Royce Griffon 66 liquid cooled V-12 engine with two-stage supercharger developing 2,035hp.

Dimensions Span 36ft 10in (10.98m normal wing tips); length 32ft 8in (0.96m).

Weight Maximum loaded weight 10,450lb (4,739kg) .

Performance Maximum speed 445mph at 26,000ft (716km/hr at 7,927m); operational ceiling in excess of 49,000ft (14,940m).

Above: PR XI of US 10th Photo Group.

Below: German pilots clamber over a captured PR XI.

Mark XI replaced all other unarmed versions of the Spitfire in front-line reconnaissance units, and 471 examples were built. For more than a year after the variant entered service, it was almost immune to fighter interception while flying at high altitude.

In the autumn of 1943 the US 8th Air Force in Great Britain received a dozen Mark XIs. These formed the 14th Photo Squadron, 10th Photographic Group, based at Mount Farm near Oxford. The unit's role was to take pre-strike and post-strike photographs of tar-

gets attacked by the US heavy bombers. Major Walt Weitner, commander of the 14th, described his impressions of flying this version on operations:

'With all the extra clothing, the parachute, dinghy, life jacket and oxygen mask, the narrow cockpit of a Spitfire was no place for the claustrophobic! With a full load of fuel, the Spit would "lean" disconcertingly during turns when one taxied. Once the gear was up and you pulled up the nose, boy would she climb!'

The Mark XI cruised at altitudes around 39,000ft, ascending above that altitude if enemy fighters tried to intercept it. Weitner found the Spitfire easy to handle at very high altitude:

'For high altitude work the Spit was unequalled. One had always to have hold of the stick, but it needed little pressure. In the reconnaissance business you were continually banking to search the sky all around for enemy fighters and to check the navigation.'

NEW VARIANTS

The system of allocating Spitfire numbers was anything but methodical, and the PR Mark X entered service more than a year later than the PR XI. The Mark X was similar to the Mark XI, but it was fitted with a pressurized cabin. Only sixteen examples were built, however, and the variant

entered service with Nos 541 and 542 Squadrons in May 1944. The commander of the latter unit, Squadron Leader Alfred Ball, remembered the PR X with no great affection:

'I flew the PR X a few times on operations. They were not popular because of the poor visibility out of the very thick perspex canopy. Outside everything looked a slightly discoloured yellow, the perspex was not as clear as on an ordinary Spitfire. The extra weight of the pressure cabin led the Mark X to feel much heavier than the Mark XI. We preferred the unpressurized Mark XI to the Mark X.'

'Once the gear was up and you pulled up the nose, boy would she climb!'

The Mark XI's near-immunity from fighter interception lasted until the spring of 1944. Then the Luftwaffe deployed its first jet fighter types, the rocket-propelled Me 163 and the turbojet powered Me 262. High flying Allied reconnaissance aircraft, unarmed and alone, offered perfect targets on which the German jet pilots could make practice interceptions.

A fighter-reconnaissance

version of the Spitfire XIV entered service in small numbers, fitted with an oblique camera in the rear fuselage.

THE MARK XIX

With the increasing threat of interception from German jet fighters, there was a requirement for a Griffon-powered long-range unarmed reconnaissance variant. This became the PR Mark XIX, with integral wing fuel tanks as fitted to the PR XI and its predecessors.

The new variant entered service in May 1944 and gave a huge advance in performance over the PR XI. Later production Mark XIXs had pressurized cabins, built to an improved design. Comfortably ensconced in their pressurized cabins, pilots often took this variant above 49,000ft (above 15,000m).

Altogether 225 examples of the PR XIX were built, before production of this version ended in the spring of 1946.

Photographic reconnaissance was one role that the Spitfire's designer had not envisaged. Another was that of fighter-bomber.

Below: The Mark XIX was the final reconnaissance version of the Spitfire, and remained in front-line service in this role until 1954. This example carries a 170-gallon (773l) ferry tank under the fuselage.

SPITFIRE
FIGHTER-BOMBER

Winston Churchill once commented that 'Air power is the most difficult of all forms of military force to measure, or even to express in precise terms.' One can apply those same words to air superiority. Certainly, once the enemy air force is driven from the skies, the side with air superiority possesses a great advantage. However, to exploit this advantage types of aircraft other than the pure fighter must be brought into play. Bombers, transports and reconnaissance aircraft can then capitalize on the situation and mount effective operations to support the land battle. To assist with this, part of the fighter force will relinquish air-to-air operations and join in the attack on ground targets.

By June 1944, the Luftwaffe had been so weakened that it was rarely able to operate over northern France. Having secured air superiority, many Spitfire units switched to the fighter-bomber role. They were the bane of the German ground troops, as they bombed and strafed anything that moved in the rear areas.

TARGET ROMMEL

An action by Spitfire fighter-bombers that had far-reaching consequences for the land battle occurred on 17 July 1944. That day Field Marshal Erwin Rommel, commander of German ground forces in Normandy, needed to travel urgently to a sector of the front where an Allied breakthrough seemed imminent. A flight of Mustangs on low-level reconnaissance observed the staff car speeding along a road near Lisieux, and reported their find. Spitfires of No. 602 Squadron, flying an armed reconnaissance over the area, were immediately ordered to investigate the sighting.

Squadron Leader Chris Le Roux, the formation leader, spotted the car and carried out a low altitude strafing attack with cannon and machine guns. He scored several hits and, its driver dead at the wheel, the car ran off the road and crashed into a tree. Rommel suffered a fractured skull and severe concussion, and was replaced at a critical stage in the land battle.

Far left: Spitfire IX fighter-bombers of No. 601 Squadron about to take off from Fano, Italy. **Below and overleaf:** *Mark IXs fitted with two 250lb (113kg) bombs under the wings.*

'THE EFFECT OF AIR SUPERIORITY'

'... we always knew when we were flying over the front line either when starting out on a reconnaissance mission or when returning: the contrast was astonishing, for in German occupied territory not a thing moved; perhaps a solitary vehicle would be observed, but as soon as the driver or look-out saw an aeroplane the vehicle stopped. Over our own territory masses of tents and convoys were to be seen, and that was the effect that air superiority, or the complete lack of it, had on land forces and their everyday existence.'

GROUP CAPTAIN G. MILLINGTON, COMMANDER NO. 285 (RECONNAISSANCE) WING IN ITALY, 1944, IN HIS BOOK THE UNSEEN EYE

BOMB LOADS CARRIED

The bomb loads carried by Spitfires depended on the nature of the target and its distance from base. The greater the distance the aircraft had to fly, the smaller the bomb load it could carry. Normally the Spitfires carried two 250 pound (113kg) bombs under the wings or a 500 pounder (226kg) under the fuselage. However, if the target was relatively close to base, the aircraft might carry the 500 pounder as well as two 250 pounders. Once the bombs had been dropped, the fighter could switch to the ground-attack role. When operating in the fighter-bomber role, Spitfires usually flew in sections of four or six, depending on the type of target and the weight of attack required.

Once the bombs had dropped, the fighter's powerful gun armament made it an effective ground-strafing aircraft

Flying Officer David Green flew Spitfires with No. 73 Squadron over Italy and Yugoslavia. He describes the normal tactics for a dive-bombing attack in a Spitfire:

'Carrying two 250lb bombs, the Spitfire made a very fine dive bomber. It could attack accurately and didn't need a fighter escort because as soon as the bombs had been released it was a fighter. The briefing beforehand had to be good enough for us to be able to fly right up to the target identify it and bomb it.

AIR SUPPORT FOR THE ARMY, 10 NOV 1944

SQUADRON	AIRCRAFT	TIME UP	REMARKS
No. 7 SAAF	6 Spitfire	0945	Bombed medium gun position.
No. 1 SAAF	6 Spitfire	1000	Bombed field guns near Forli.
No. 601	6 Spitfire	1015	Bombed field guns near Forli. Light AA fire. One aircraft failed to pull out of dive possible due to flak hit, pilot killed.
No. 2 SAAF	6 Spitfire	1020	Two aircraft returned early. Rest bombed gun position and carried out strafing attacks. Heavy AA from target, no losses.
No. 92	6 Spitfire	1025	Bombed gun positions S. Faenza.
No. 92	6 Spitfire	1030	Bombed and strafed gun and mortar positions near S. Faenza.
No. 4 SAAF	6 Spitfire	1040	Dive-bombed gun positions.
No. 2 SAAF	6 Spitfire	1105	Bombed 3 gun positions, target well strafed. Light AA from target.
No. 4 SAAF	6 Spitfire	1135	Bombed gun positions.

We normally operated in sections of four, and would fly to the target at 10,000 feet in finger-four battle formation.

'As the target came into view I would position it so that it appeared to be running down the line of my port cannon. When the target emerged from under the trailing edge I would pull the aircraft up, roll it over on its back and let the nose drop until the target was lined up in the gunsight graticule. That way, one got the Spitfire to go down in the correct angle of dive of 60 degrees. The other aircraft in the section, Nos 2, 3, and 4, would be following me down still in echelon.'

When the leader's dive took him to an altitude of 4,000 feet (1,219m) above the ground, he released his bombs.

'It was a pretty steep dive, it felt as if one was going down vertically.'

'I would let go my bombs and call "Bombs gone!"; the other chaps in the section would then release theirs. If there had been little flak, I would pull hard on the stick to bring the aircraft out of the dive and into a slight climb, so that I could look over my shoulder to see where the bombs had gone. But if we were being fired at, we would use our high forward speed to get us down to ground level where there was cover.'

During the final months of the war almost every attack launched by the British army

received strong fighter bomber support. The example above shows the scale of air support for the British advance on the Montone River in Italy, on 10 November 1944, over a two hour period.

VERSATILITY

Given the ability of the Spitfire in the fighter-bomber role, the reader should remember that attacks on ground targets were far from everyone's thoughts when the Spitfire was conceived.

The Spitfire remained in front-line service in the RAF for nearly a decade after the end of the war. In the next chapter we shall observe the final stages of its lengthy career in that service and also in foreign air forces.

THE AVRO LANCASTER

1 Two .303in (7.7mm) Browning machine guns
2 Frazer-Nash power-operated nose turret
3 Nose blister
4 Bomb-aimer's panel (optically flat)
5 Bomb-aimer's control panel
6 Side windows
7 External air temperature thermometer
8 Pitot head
9 Bomb-aimer's chest support
10 Fire extinguisher
11 Parachute emergency exit
12 F-24 camera
13 Glycol tank/step
14 Ventilator fairing
15 Bomb-bay doors forward actuating jacks
16 Bomb-bay doors forward actuating jacks
17 Control linkage
18 Rudder panels
19 Instrument panel
20 Windscreen sprays
21 Windscreen
22 Dimmer switches
23 Flight-engineer's folding seat
24 Flight-engineer's control panel
25 Pilot's seat
26 Flight-deck floor level
27 Elevator and rudder control rods (underfloor)
28 Trim tab control cables
29 Main floor/bomb-bay support longeron
30 Fire extinguisher
31 Wireless installation
32 Navigator's seat
33 Canopy rear/down-view blister
34 Pilot's head armour
35 Cockpit canopy emergency escape hatch
36 D/F loop
37 Aerial mast support
38 Electrical services panel
39 Navigator's compartment window
40 Navigator's desk
41 Aircraft and radio compass receiver
42 Wireless-operator's desk
43 Wireless-operator's seat
44 Wireless-operator's compartment window
45 Front spar carry-through/fuselage frame
46 Astrodome
47 Inboard section wing ribs
48 Spar join
49 Aerial mast
50 Starboard inboard engine nacelle
51 Spinner
52 Three-blade de Havilland constant-speed propellers
53 Oil cooler intake
54 Oil cooler radiator
55 Carburettor air intake
56 Radiator shutter
57 Engine bearer frame
58 Exhaust flame-damper shroud
59 Packard-built Rolls-Royce Merlin 28 liquid-cooled engine
60 Nacelle/wing fairing
61 Fuel tank bearer ribs
62 Intermediate ribs
63 Leading-edge structure
64 Wing stringers
65 Wingtip skinning
66 Starboard navigation light
67 Starboard formation light
68 Aileron hinge fairings
69 Wing rear spar
70 Starboard aileron
71 Aileron balance tab

72 Balance tab control rod
73 Aileron trim tab
74 HF aerial
75 Split trailing-edge flap (outboard section)
76 Emergency (ditching) exit
77 Crash axe stowage
78 Fire extinguisher
79 Hydraulic reservoir
80 Signal/flare pistol stowage
81 Parachute stowage box/spar step
82 Rear spar carry-through
83 Bunk backrest
84 Rear spar fuselage frame
85 Emergency packs
86 Roof light
87 Dinghy manual release cable (dinghy stowage in starboard wingroot)
88 Mid-gunner's parachute stowage
89 Tail turret ammunition box
90 Ammunition feed track
91 Emergency (ditching) exit
92 Flame floats stowage
93 Sea markers stowage
94 Roof light
95 Dorsal turret fairing
96 Frazer-Nash power-operated dorsal turret

Avro Lancaster Mk III

97 Two .303in (7.7mm) Browning machine guns
98 Turret mounting ring
99 Turret mechanism
100 Ammunition track cover plate
101 Turret step bracket
102 Header tank
103 Oxygen cylinder
104 Fire extinguisher
105 DR compass housing
106 Handrail
107 Crew entry door (starboard)
108 Parachute stowage
109 First-aid pack
110 Starboard tailplane
111 Rudder control lever
112 Starboard tailfin
113 Rudder balance weights
114 Starboard rudder
115 Rudder datum hinge
116 Rudder tab actuating rod
117 Rudder tab
118 Starboard elevator
119 Elevator balance tab
120 Roof light
121 Tail main frame
122 Parachute stowage
123 Fire extinguisher
124 Tail turret entry door
125 Frazer-Nash power-operated tail turret
126 Four .303in (7.7mm) Browning machine guns
127 Cartridge case ejection chutes
128 Rear navigation light
129 Elevator trim tab
130 Fin construction
131 Rudder balance weights
132 Port rudder frame
133 Rudder trim tab
134 Rudder tab balance weight
135 Rudder tab actuating rod
136 Rudder horn balance
137 Trim tab actuating jack
138 Tailplane construction
139 Elevator torque tube
140 Tailplane carry-through
141 Non-retractable tailwheel
142 Elsan closet
143 Ammunition track cover plate

144 Elevator and rudder control rods
145 H2S (radar-bombing) ventral antenna fairing
146 Dorsal turret step
147 Ammunition feed track
148 Tail turret ammunition box
149 Bomb-bay aft bulkhead
150 Bomb-bay doors
151 Bomb-bay doors aft actuating jacks
152 Reserve ammunition boxes
153 Main floor support structure
154 Flap operating hydraulic jack
155 Flap operating tube
156 Flap toggle links
157 Flap tube connecting link
158 Rear spar
159 Split trailing-edge flap (inboard section)
160 Split trailing-edge flap (outboard section)
161 Aileron control lever
162 Aileron trim tab control cable linkage
163 Aileron trim tab
164 Aileron balance tab control rod
165 Aileron balance tab
166 Aileron hinge fairings
167 Port aileron
168 Port wingtip
169 Port formation light
170 Port navigation light
171 Retractable landing lights (port wing only)
172 Cable cutters
173 Fuel vent pipe
174 Aileron control rod
175 Port outer (No. 3) fuel tank (114 gal/518 litres)
176 Outboard engine support frame/rear spar pick-up
177 Fuel booster pump
178 Fire extinguisher
179 Engine sub-frame
180 Filler cap
181 Outboard engine oil tank
182 Firewall/bulkhead
183 Carburettor air intake
184 Outboard engine support frame
185 Port mainwheel
186 Undercarriage oleo struts
187 Flame-damper shroud
188 Outboard engine support frame/main spar pick-up
189 Undercarriage retraction jacks
190 Oleo strut attachment pin
191 Undercarriage support beam (light-alloy casting)
192 Centre-section outer rib/undercarriage support
193 Location of port intermediate (No. 2) fuel tank (383 gal/1741 litres)
194 Mainwheel well
195 Emergency retraction air valve
196 Retraction cylinder attachment
197 Port inner (No. 1) fuel tank (580 gal/2637 litres)
198 Oxygen bottle stowage
199 Rest bunk
200 Main spar
201 Hinged inboard leading-edge
202 Cabin heater installation
203 Air intake
204 Inboard engine support frame
205 Inboard engine oil tank
206 Carburettor intake anti-ice guard
207 Port inner nacelle
208 Flame-damper shroud
209 Detachable cowling panels
210 Bomb shackles
211 Bomb-bay doors (open)
212 8000lb (2532kg) bomb

THE MANCHESTER

The origins of the Lancaster lay in Air Ministry Specification P13/36, issued in September 1936, but it was some time before the definitive aircraft emerged. The requirements included a maximum bomb load of 8,000lb (3.63 tonnes), a six-man crew, which included a ventral gunner, and the ability to operate from existing 4,500ft (1,375m) long grass strips. Power was to be provided by two Rolls-Royce Vultures, a 24 cylinder liquid-cooled engine which was expected to develop about 2,000hp.

The Handley Page Company had early doubts about the Vulture, and switched to the proven Merlin, for what was to become the Halifax. At A. V. Roe, chief designer Roy Chadwick persevered with the bomber, with Napier's Sabre as a fall-back engine.

Two prototypes of the Avro Type 679, later to be named the Manchester, were ordered with-

Left: The Lancaster Mk I, originally known as the Manchester III, was developed around the Manchester fuselage and wing centre section.

AVRO 679

Dimensions
Wing span 80ft 2in (24.43m)
Tailplane span 22ft 0in (6.70m)
Length 70ft 0in (21.33m)
Height 19ft 6in (5.94m)

Weights
Maximum take-off 45,000lb (20,400kg)
Maximum bomb load 10,000lb (4,500kg)

Power
Two Rolls-Royce 24 cylinder Vulture I liquid-cooled engines rated at 1,720hp each.

Performance
Maximum speed 256mph (412km/hr) at 12,500ft (3,800m)
Range with maximum bomb load c1,200 miles (1,930km) Service ceiling c18,000ft (5,500m)

Armament
Two .303 Browning machine guns in each of three Nash and Thompson power-operated turrets, nose, tail, and a retractable ventral 'dustbin'. None fitted on first flight.

in a week of Specification P13/36 being issued, and the first flight took place at Ringway Airport on 25 July 1939. It was a large aircraft, with the wing in the mid position, and with twin fins and rudders. Handling problems were immediately apparent; the

controls were heavy, and lateral stability left much to be desired. The take-off run was far longer than anticipated, with no bomb load, with the gun turrets omitted and their positions faired over. Meanwhile the second prototype, already well advanced, was modified to try to cure these faults. The outer wing sections were redesigned, extending the span to 90ft 1in (27.46m); the control surfaces (ailerons and elevators) were improved, and larger fins and rudders fitted.

In the expectation that the faults of the first prototype would soon be overcome, contracts were placed for the production of 1,200 Manchesters. The first flight of the second prototype took place on 26 May 1940, handling had improved but directional stability, especially at low airspeeds, was still far from adequate. It was then decided to fit a central fin, which went some way towards improving matters.

Below: The twin-engined Manchester was the forerunner of the Lancaster. This No.61 Squadron aircraft failed to return from a raid on Hamburg in April 1942.

Above: The Manchester IA left off the central fin, but the span of the tailplane was greatly increased.

There were problems with the Vulture whose design had been started in 1935. It had two V-12 engines on a common crankcase, one upright, with the other inverted beneath it. With a capacity of 42.48 litres, it was expected to deliver over 2,000hp at 3,000rpm for take-off, and 1,710hp at an altitude of 15,000ft (4,570m).

The Vulture was just that bit too clever for the time

Lubrication, excessive wear, metal fatigue and overheating all gave cause for concern. But with the build-up of RAF Bomber Command, it was decided to continue with the Manchester, in the hope that the problems would be solved.

DEFENSIVE

The gun turrets were installed in the second prototype; two .303 Brownings in the nose, tail, and in a retractable ventral 'dustbin' arrangement. These also gave rise to handling problems. When rotated, they interfered with the slipstream. The nose turret caused the aircraft to veer to one side, while the rear turret caused vibration in the elevators.

Battle experience in 1939 led to a rethinking of the defensive armament for bombers. The ventral turret was deleted and a twin-gun mid-upper turret installed. The armament of the tail turret was to be doubled to four machine guns, but various weight restrictions prevented this being put into practice for some considerable time.

Despite the problems, the Manchester had many good points. The layout of the spacious cabin was highly praised, while the bomb bay could hold either four 2,000 pounders (900kg) or four sea mines; or one of the new 4,000lb (1,800kg) bombs together with six 1,000 pounders (450kg). The structure was sturdy, and adjustments to the flight control system resulted in an aircraft that was quite pleasant to fly.

Continuing problems with the Vulture engines limited it to 52,000lb (23.59 tonnes) and to 12,000ft (3,660m) with maximum bomb load and 50 per cent fuel.

STOP GAP

Further testing revealed an average of only 76 flying hours between engine failures, and generally the Manchester was only able to maintain height on one engine at fairly light all-up weights. The Manchester was rushed into service even though it would be only an interim type with Bomber Command.

The first operational Manchester squadron was No. 207, formed at Waddington late in 1940. Composed mainly of experienced crews, conversion onto type proceeded, and the Manchester was released for short-range operations with a reduced bomb load.

The target was the German cruiser Admiral Hipper

The first operation was flown by six aircraft on the night of 24/25 February 1941 with six aircraft. The target was the German cruiser *Admiral Hipper*, which was in the French port of Brest. None of these early aircraft were fitted with the mid-upper gun turret, and the ventral dustbin

remained unmanned for the raid. The bomb load consisted of twelve 500lb (225kg) semi-armour piercing bombs. Only moderate flak was encountered, and all aircraft returned safely. *Admiral Hipper* was not hit, which was only to be expected in those early days of the night-bombing war.

The first Manchester lost to enemy action came over England on 13 March, when a

No. 207 Squadron aircraft was caught shortly after take-off.

The Vultures claimed their first victim exactly a week later, when a Manchester crashed shortly after take-off following an engine fire. On 13 April, all Manchesters were grounded for engine changes. Several aircraft were now entering service with the mid-upper turret, while the grounding period allowed others to have this fitted.

The Manchester still continued to be plagued by engine problems. The summer of 1941 saw the introduction of the Manchester 1A, which had a tailplane of increased span, taller twin fins and rudders, and no central fin.

LANCASTERS

The Manchester was being overtaken by events. The first Lancasters reached the squadrons late in 1941, and the fate of the twin-engined aircraft was sealed. It was finally withdrawn from Bomber Command operations after a raid on Bremen on 25/26 June 1942.

MANCHESTER SQUADRONS

Sqn No.	Bases	1st Operation	Last Operation
207	Waddington	24 Feb 1941	
	Bottesford		11/12 March 1942
97	Waddington	8/9 April 1941	
	Coningsby		9/10 Jan 1942
61	N. Luffenham	14/15 Aug 1941	
	Syerston		1/2 June 1942
83	Scampton	28 Jan 1942	1/2 June 1942
106	Coningsby	20 March 1942	25/26 June 1942
50	Skellingthorpe	8/9 April 1942	
	Swinderby		25/26 June 1942
49	Scampton	2/3 May 1942	25/26 June 1942

The operational careers of the last four squadrons listed were very short, partly due to the fact that the similarities between the Lancaster and the Manchester allowed for an easy switch over.

MANCHESTER 1A

Dimensions
Wingspan 90ft 1in (27.46m); Tailplane span 33ft 0in (10.06m); Length 70ft 0in (21.33m); Height 19ft 6in (9.54m).

Weights
Maximum take-off 56,000lb (25,400kg); Maximum bomb load 10,350lb (4,700kg).

Power
Two Rolls-Royce 24 cylinder Vulture II liquid-cooled engines rated at 1,845hp each.

Performance
Maximum speed 265mph (426km/hr) at 17,000ft (5,200km/hr); Range with maximum bomb load 1,200 miles (1,930km); Service ceiling 19,200ft (5,850m).

Armament
Two Browning .303 machine guns in nose and dorsal turrets; four .303 Browning machine guns in tail turret.

THE LANCASTER
DESCRIBED

It has been said that the Lancaster arose from the failure of the Manchester but in the autumn of 1938, long before the first flight of the Manchester prototype, A.V. Roe's design office considered the possibility of a four-engined variant of the Type 679. But only the most basic work was done at this stage on what was to become the Avro Type 683.

Early in the following year, a new specification was issued; B.1/39. Its ultimate purpose was to produce a heavy bomber which would start to replace the four-engined Stirlings and Halifaxes (neither of which had yet flown), and the Manchester itself in four to five years' time.

The requirements were stringent; a cruising speed of 280mph (450km/hr) at 15,000ft (4,570m) while carrying a bomb load of 9,000lb (4.08 tonnes); only slightly

Left: As a safeguard against a shortage of Merlins, the Mk II Lancaster was powered by Bristol Hercules radial engines.

less than the maximum of 10,000lb (4.54 tonnes) specified. Range under these conditions was to be a minimum of 2,500 miles (4,000km). This was pushing the state of the art very hard, with the requirement for defensive armament, which was to consist of tail and ventral turrets each carrying four 20mm cannon. These turrets did not even exist at that time, and the complexity, weight and drag of such planes ensured that they never would. Prototype aircraft were ordered from both Handley Page and Bristol, but neither got past the mock-up stage. The Air Ministry

Above: The first four-engined bomber to enter service with Bomber Command was the Short Stirling. It was inferior to the Lancaster in both performance and load-carrying.

was however interested in A.V. Roe's proposal for a four-engined bomber developed from the Manchester. Initial progress with the four-engined machine was slow. Not until the production Manchester was finalized could serious work start on its derivative.

The advantages of four-engined bombers seem glaringly obvious. Because they were

BRITISH BOMBER COMPARISONS 1941

A/C type	Cruise Speed at Altitude	Bomb Load for Max Radius	Radius with Max Bomb
Wellington	170mph (273km/hr) at 11,300ft (3,450m)	2,500lb (1,130kg) for 1,100 miles (1,770km)	560 miles (900km) with a 4,500lb (2,040kg)
Stirling	208mph (335km/hr) at 13,800ft (4,200m)	3,500lb (1,590kg) for 855 miles (1,37km)	285 miles (460km) with (6,350kg)
Halifax	203mph (327km/hr) 15,100ft (4,600m)	5,800lb (2,630kg) for 910 miles (1,465km)	580 miles (930km) with 8,000lb (3,630kg)
Manchester	205mph (330km/hr) 13,650ft (4,160m)	8,100lb (3,675kg) for 885 miles (1,425km)	500 miles (805km) with 10,350lb (4,700kg)

From the above table it can be seen that the payload/range of the twin-engined Manchester was significantly better than either of its four-engined contemporaries. It totally outclassed the Wellington.

Above: The Rolls-Royce Merlin XX engine installation package for the Beaufighter IIF was adapted for the Lancaster.

bigger than their twin-engined counterparts, they could carry heavier loads of fuel and weaponry. In 1939, the twin-engined Manchester could carry a 40 per cent greater bomb load than the four-engined Halifax over a comparable distance. Two engines required fewer systems, less weight, less maintenance, and lower costs for spares and replacements. Aerodynamically, with only two engines instead of four, there was less drag to overcome in flight. The difficulty was producing an engine of sufficient power to do the job. The Napier Sabre was scheduled to power the Manchester II, but delays ensured this leading variant was never built.

The Merlin was the obvious choice for the Type 683, but

The overall wingspan was increased to accommodate engines

demand for this engine for Spitfires and Hurricanes was high. As a backup, the more powerful but heavier and draggier Bristol Hercules radial was selected. Increased demand for the Hercules caused by Stirling production eventually led to the IIF variant. Rolls-Royce had developed an engine installation package, which, with minor changes, proved eminently suitable for the new bomber.

Type 683, known in the design office as the Lancaster from a very early stage, was developed around the Manchester fuselage and wing centre section. The cavernous bomb bay met all current requirements. The overall wingspan was substantially increased to accommodate the outboard engines, which also had the effect of improving take-off performance.

FOUR ENGINES

At the end of August 1940, the decision was taken that Bomber Command's strategic force would be entirely equipped as soon as possible with four-engined bombers. In retrospect this decision seems extraordinary. The four-engined heavy bomber had yet to prove itself, but there remained one sound operational reason for the decision. Even reliable engines

Left: The Avro Type 683 prototype was initially known as the Manchester III, and only later renamed the Lancaster I.

Above: The second Lancaster prototype introduced a ventral turret that was fitted to early production aircraft.

failed occasionally, and all were vulnerable to flak and fighters. The failure of one engine in a four-engined type was much less serious than the same case in a twin, in which a full 50 per cent of the available power was lost, and asymmetric handling problems, with all the remaining power on one side, were far more extreme.

Trials at Boscombe Down showed good handling qualities but directional stability was lacking

The decision to proceed with the four-engined Avro bomber was taken, although as a security measure the name Lancaster was dropped and the Type 683 became known as the Manchester Mark III, the Mark II designation having been reserved for the Napier Sabre-powered aircraft, which in fact was never built. The prototype used a Manchester I airframe powered by Merlin Xs, and retained the short-span tailplane and triple fin layout of that aircraft. The first flight took place on 9 January 1941.

Trials at Boscombe Down showed good handling qualities although, directional stability was lacking. With the new Merlin XXs fitted, the prototype reached a maximum speed of 310mph (500km/hr) at 21,000ft (6,400m) – an outstanding performance for a heavy bomber of that era. The use of Manchester sub-assemblies speeded up the output.

SECOND PROTOTYPE M

The second Lancaster prototype, which made its maiden flight on 13 May 1941, was rather nearer to the production

LANCASTER

Dimensions
Wingspan 102ft 0in (31.09m); Length (tail up) 69ft 6in (21.18m); Height (tail up) 20ft 6in (6.25m); Wing area 1,297 sq ft (120.45m²)

Weights
Empty 36,900lb (16,740kg); Normal loaded 53,000lb (24,040kg); Maximum overload 65,000lb (29,480kg); B.I Special with 22,000lb (9,980kg); Grand Slam 70,000lb (31,750kg); Maximum internal bomb load 14,000lb (6,350kg).

Power
Four Rolls-Royce Merlin 12 cylinder liquid-cooled engines each rated at 1,460hp (variable depending on type) driving a three-bladed variable-pitch, constant-speed propeller. Lancaster B.III powered by four Bristol Hercules 14 cylinder air-cooled radial engines each rated at 1,650hp.

Fuel and Oil
Total fuel 2,154gal (9,790 litres) in six wing tanks. 580gal (2,637 litres) in each inboard wing tank; 383gal (740 litres) in each intermediate wing tank, and 114gal (518 litres) in each outboard wing tank. One or two overload 400gal (1,818 litre) tanks could be mounted in the bomb bay. Oil tank capacity 150gal (682 litres) carried in four wing tanks.

Performance
Maximum speed 270mph (434km/hr) at 19,000ft (5,800m); Cruise speed 210mph (338km/hr); 19.3 min to 11,000ft (3,350m); 43.5min to 20,000ft (6,100m); Service ceiling 21,500ft (6,550m); Range with 14,000lb (6,350kg) bomb load 1,160 miles (1,870km); with 7,000lb (1,795kg) bomb load and one overload fuel tank 2,230 miles (3,590km).

Armament
Two .303 Browning machine guns with 1,000rpg in a Frazer-Nash power-operated turret in the nose; ditto in the mid-upper position, and four Browning machine guns with 2,500 rpg in a Frazer-Nash power-operated turret in the tail. A few aircraft retained the ventral gun position, while many others had the mid-upper turret removed. Others were fitted with two .50 Browning heavy machine guns.

machine standard, stressed for an all-up weight of 60,000lb (27.22 tonnes), and with a dorsal gun turret fitted. It retained the ventral turret for the time being. The third prototype followed on 26 November of that year, which was powered by Hercules VI radials, and became the prototype Lancaster Mark II. But long before the radial-engined machine took to the air, production Mark Is were rolling off the lines.

All-up weight had been increased to 65,000lb (29.48 tonnes) maximum; maximum bomb load had been increased to 14,000lb (6.35 tonnes); two extra fuel tanks had been fitted in the wings, and the ventral turret had been removed. A collar fairing had been added around the mid-upper turret to stop the guns being depressed enough to damage the aircraft, and a four-gun turret was standard in the tail position. The crew consisted of seven men; the pilot, who was also the aircraft captain, regardless of rank; a second pilot, who was quickly replaced by the new category of flight engineer; a bomb-aimer, who also manned the front

Above: The standard camouflage scheme was dark green and dark earth disruptive pattern above and matt black below.

turret; a navigator, a wireless operator, and mid-upper and tail gunners.

THE LANCASTER CLOSE UP

The Lancaster is a lady, and for that reason is never described as 'it', but always as 'she'. Very much the grand dame, the indomitable dowager, yet with a twinkle in her eye to hint at a racy past in her younger days. Her attire is sombre, a staid dull black on undersides of wings and tail and fuselage sides complemented by a tasteful camouflage scheme on top. Guns protrude from turrets in

her nose and tail and mid-way down her upper fuselage. The first impression is that she is big. Her huge main wheels, suspended on sturdy legs beneath the inboard engine nacelles, are almost shoulder-height, while the front fuselage towers high above us. Her mid-mounted wings spread 50ft (15m) to either side, carrying the four sleek cowlings which house the Rolls-Royce Merlin engines with their shrouded exhausts, fronted by large three-bladed propellors.

In the front of her nose is a hemispherical transparent dome, with a round optically flat panel

Below: Figures on the ground give scale to the first production Lancaster, seen prior to delivery to Boscombe Down for type testing.

LANCASTER GUN TURRET

Type	FN 5	FN 50	FN 20	FN 64
Position	Nose	Mid-upper	Tail	Ventral
Guns	2 x .303 Browning Mk II	2 x .303 Browning Mk II	4 x .303 Browning Mk II	2 x .303 Browning Mk II
Rounds	1,000	1,000	2,500	500
Gunsight	Mk III Reflector	Mk IIIA Reflector	Mk III Reflector or Gyro Mk IIc	Periscopic
Traverse	+/-95°	360°	+/-94°	+/-90°
Elevation	60°	20°	60°	0°
Depression	45°	2°	45°	60°

looking downwards. Above is a turret from which project two .303 Browning machine guns. Immediately behind the turret is a glazed cabin for the pilot and his flight engineer, but we see little of this as we walk beneath the giant bird.

What we do see is the huge bomb bay, which starts almost immediately beneath the front of the cabin and reaches back to a point almost level with the dorsal turret. As is usual before engine start-up, the bomb bay doors are open, revealing the sinister outlines of the contents. In the centre is a large, dark green cylinder, a 4,000lb (1,800kg) high explosive 'cookie'. It is surrounded by twelve SBCs (Small Bomb Containers) filled with incendiaries. This is the most usual Lancaster bomb load.

We climb up and in, then it's down onto the central catwalk

Astern of the bomb bay is a teardrop-shaped fairing. This houses the scanner for H2S, the latest radar bombing and navi-gational aid. We enter the Lancaster through a small hatch in the starboard side. A short metal ladder hooks onto the sill, and we climb up and in, onto an inner step, then it's down onto the central catwalk.

REAR GUNNER

Once inside, the interior of a Lancaster is bleak indeed. The structure, fuselage formers and longerons are bare, showing the metal skin. Running the length of the fuselage walls are pipes, rods, all manner of plumbing and wiring. These are for carry-ing hydraulic fluid and power to where it is needed.

At this point, the first member of the crew leaves us. He passes the primitive Elsan toilet to his right, scrambles over the tailplane spar structure, pauses to stow his parachute, then squeezes into his cold and cramped position, shutting the armoured doors behind him. He is the rear gunner, and his job is arguably the most danger-ous, and certainly the coldest, the most lonely and isolated, of any Lancaster crewman.

From now until the end of the mission, his only human contact will be the disembodied voices of other crew members over the intercom. The German night fighters almost always attack from astern. If he is given the opportunity to use his skills, his four rifle-calibre machine guns are far outranged by the cannon of the German night fighters which, if visibility is good enough, can stand off and shoot at him. They can also slip below, where they are difficult to see, and pick off the bomber with their upward-firing guns.

Even in defeat, the rear gun-ner's fate is a lonely one.

Below: The open doors give some idea of the vast size of the bomb bay. The bombs were released In a preset sequence.

stowing his parachute in its place high on the right, he climbs into his turret via a step on the left of the fuselage.

The mid-upper gunner has only two machine guns. His field of fire is obstructed, however, to the rear by the tailplane and fins on each side, and straight ahead by the navigator's astrodome. The turret is surrounded by a fairing which contains a cam track. By restricting the movement of the guns, this ensures that he cannot damage his own aircraft when firing. When the guns are elevated at 20 degrees or more, turret traverse is fast and smooth, but below this it is much slower. This is to avoid damage to the

The call to bale out is 'Abracadabra Jump, Jump! Abracadabra Jump, Jump!'. It sounds silly, but it has one advantage. It cannot possibly be misunderstood but was seldom used, and the order given in plain language. On hearing the command to bale out, the rear gunner opens his armoured doors at the rear of his turret, reaches back for his parachute and clips it onto his chest harness. He swivels his turret right round until the open doors are facing outwards, then does a backward roll out into the night sky above a hostile country. This is of course presupposing that his parachute has not been burnt or shot to pieces, that he is still able to turn his turret to the escape position, and that his out-of-control bomber will allow him to make these necessary moves.

The rest of the crew turn to the right along the catwalk. On the far wall is a handrail, very necessary for moving about in flight. Next to reach his station is the mid-upper gunner. After

Above: *Up the ladder and in. A crew from No. 9 Squadron board their Lancaster ready for a mission.*

LANCASTER BOMB LOADS

Bombing, and especially night bombing, was a very imprecise art in the Second World War. Even finding the target was difficult enough; hitting it often seemed next to impossible. The solution adopted was to saturate the target area with bombs; high explosive to demolish buildings and incendiaries to set the ruins on fire. It was crude, but it was the only practicable means available to Bomber Command. There were of course specialized weapons which called for greater accuracy, but these were less common.

Blast and demolition
1) 1 x 8,000lb (3,630kg) HE plus 6 (max) 500lb (225kg) HE.
2) 14 x 1,000lb (450kg) HE.

Blast, demolition and fire
3) 1 x 4,000lb (1,800kg) HE plus 3 x 1,000lb HE plus up to 6 SBCs (Small Bomb Containers) each holding either 236 4lb (2kg) or 24 x 30lb (14kg) incendiaries.
4) 1 x 4,000lb (1,800kg) HE plus up to 12 SBCs.

Maximum incendiary
5) 14 SBCs.

Deployed tactical targets
6) 1 x 4,000lb (1,800kg) HE plus up to 18,500lb (225kg) HE.

Low-level attacks
7) 6 x 1,000lb (450kg) HE with delayed action fuses.

Hardened targets, naval installations, ships etc.
8) 6 x 2,000lb (900kg) armour piercing with very short delay fuses.

Minelaying
9) Up to six 1,500lb (680kg) or 1,850lb (840kg) mines.

Above: *Emergency escape from the rear turret was made by turning it sideways as seen here, then rolling out backwards.*
Left: *The mid-upper turret, showing the fairing which prevented the gunner from damaging his own aircraft.*
Below: *H2S position in the Lancaster. Top left is the curtain which shuts out light; to the right is the flight engineer's position, with his seat folded. (Alfred Price)*

carry-through. We arrive at the main crew positions through a 7mm-thick armoured door. Situated on the left is the wireless operator's small table and radio. There is a small window which is level with the leading edge of the wing, but at night a curtain is drawn across it. This is mainly because he needs artificial light by which to work, and this must not be allowed to betray the presence of the bomber to any roving fighters which might be in the area. The wireless operator has the warmest place in the aircraft; often he is overheated while other crew members are freezing.

H2S, a blind bombing aid which shows a radar picture of the ground

In front of the wireless operator sits the navigator, sideways on. He also has a table on which he spreads out charts and a computer. Above him is an astrodome, through which the navigator can estimate a very approximate position. There is also another piece of equipment.

This is H2S, a blind bombing aid which shows a radar picture of the ground below on a television-type screen. It needs good interpretation to get good results, and like all electronic aids of this era, it can be temperamental. But it helps.

THE PILOT

Up front, his seat on a raised floor section to the left of the main cabin, is the pilot, who is also the aircraft captain.

turret fairing at full depression, but in action, it is a serious disadvantage as it makes tracking a fast-moving enemy fighter very difficult.

In an emergency the mid-upper gunner must get out of the turret, retrieve his parachute, and depart through the door by which he entered. Just ahead of the mid-upper turret is an escape hatch in the fuselage roof, which is used in the event of a crash landing or a ditching at sea. In the latter event, a dinghy is housed in the upper surface of the starboard wing-root, which hopefully can be released manually from inside the aircraft, and which should then inflate automatically if the Lancaster comes down in the 'drink', as it is generally known.

The walls in this area of the fuselage are cluttered with fire extinguishers and flame float and sea marker canisters.

Further up the fuselage is the rear wing spar carry-through, with a step on the far side which contains more parachute stowage. To the left of this is the rest bunk, which is normally used only for casualties.

A few feet along is yet another obstacle, the main wing spar

Above left: The H2S scanner housing supplanted the ventral turret position on many aircraft. This is a late war model.
Above right: Lancaster pilot's position, showing the sliding hatch through which escape was barely possible. However, the extensively glazed cabin gave a good all-round view.

He has a good all-round view through the canopy. There is a direct-vision panel on either side of the windshield, and in the canopy roof is an escape hatch. Behind him is a 4mm-thick sheet of armour.

In front of the pilot is the control column which directs the elevators in the tail, causing the aircraft to climb or dive. A wheel-type yoke moves like a car steering wheel, controlling the ailerons in the wings to make the aircraft bank to left or right. At his feet are the rudder pedals, which are used for flat turns to either side.

Low to the pilot's left is the compass, but for convenience a compass repeater is mounted on the divided windshield. The dash contains many dials and switches, while the throttle levers and propellor speed con-trols are mounted on a central console where they can be reached by both the pilot and the flight engineer.

The flight engineer sits to the right of the pilot on a folding seat, allowing access to the bomb aimer's and front gunner's positions. His task is to look after the engines, throttle settings and propellor pitch settings, fuel flow, and also act as the pilot's assistant.

He has two panels to monitor. One, on the starboard side, contains oil and fuel gauges, booster pump switches, fuel pressure warning lights, and fuel tank selector cocks. The other is part of the main dash, and contains revolution counters, boost gauges, ignition switches, engine fire extinguisher buttons and propellor feathering buttons.

BOMB AIMER

Squeezing past the flight engineer's station, we clamber down into the nose. This is the territory of the bomb aimer, who usually mans the nose turret when not actually on the bombing run, although he can also be called upon to assist the naviga-tor by map-reading.

The bomb aimer lies prone, his chest propped on an adjustable support. Beneath him is the forward escape hatch. which may also be used by the flight engineer and the pilot.

To the right of the bomb aimer is the bomb fusing and selection panel. It is essential that the bombs are released in a predetermined order from the long bay. For this, a selector box is used. Also featured are camera controls and photo-flares which enable a picture to be taken of the aim point.

BOMBS GONE

The bomb sight is of the vector type, into which the aircraft speed and altitude are set, together with the ballistic data, and the estimated wind speed and direction. The sight is gyro-stabilized, which allows banked turns to be made during the run up to the target. Two lines of light on a reflecting screen form a cross which indicates where the bomb will drop. Over the intercom the bomb aimer guides the pilot to a position where the extension of the

Left: Bomb release switch in hand, the bomb aimer lies prone facing his Mk XIV vector sight.
Above: All late-production Lancasters, regardless of mark, were fitted with an enlarged nose transparency.

vertical line passes through the aim point. When the bomber is lined up correctly, the aim point appears to slide gradually down the vertical line. Then when the cross touches the target, the bomb aimer presses the button and down go the bombs, bringing destruction to the target below. When not engaged in dropping bombs, the bomb aimer occupies the nose turret, with its two machine guns. At night he will probably have little

to do; rarely is visibility clear enough to allow the night fighters to attack from head-on. In daylight or at low level the situation could be different, and the turret might be occupied even on the bombing run. The gunner had no footrest, and in moments of excitement may well have tread on the bomb aimer's head, to say nothing of showering him with hot 'empties' when he fires.

This then is the Lancaster, a bomber in which many thousands of men went to war, and for which many thousands of crewmen had affection, and faith that she was the best.

Below: When not actually on the bombing run, the bomb aimer normally manned the front gun turret. This Lancaster was visiting the USA on a goodwill mission in 1942.

The first unit to receive the Lancaster was No. 44 (Rhodesia) Squadron at Waddington. The first Lancaster prototype arrived in mid September 1941, while several Manchester pilots were transferred to the squadron to ease the task of conversion. Not until Christmas Eve did the first three operational aircraft arrive, followed by four more on 28 December.

No. 44 Squadron had flown Hampdens, but as from January 1942, seven of the Manchester squadrons were progressively re-equipped with the Lancaster. Brand new Manchesters were still coming off the production lines, and Lancaster production was not yet in full swing. Also, the similarities of the two aircraft made it relatively easy to convert Manchester crews to the Lancaster; the latter could therefore be introduced into service faster by bringing more Manchesters on stream. The first Lancasters reached No. 97 Squadron in January, and No. 207 Squadron in March 1942.

The first Lancaster operation took place on the night of 3/4 March 1942. Four Lancasters of No. 44 Squadron laid mines (an operation codenamed 'Gardening') off the German coast. All returned safely. In the first excursion over Germany, two aircraft of the same squadron joined a raid on Essen, again without loss. The first Lancaster to be lost in action failed to return from another Gardening sortie on 24/25 March.

Above: This former No. 44 Squadron aircraft flew the Atlantic to Canada to serve as a pattern aircraft for Lancaster production. **Far left:** Fitters swarm all over the port inner engine of this Lancaster Mk 11 of No. 408 'Goose' Squadron, RCAF.

THE AUGSBURG RAID

In the Spring of 1942 U-boat production facilities became priority targets, and one of the most important was the MAN works at Augsburg, where their diesel engines were made. Augsburg was not far from Munich, a round trip of some 1,250 miles (2,000km), mostly over enemy territory.

On the afternoon of 17 April, 12 Lancasters took off for Augsburg. The first wave of six, flying in two Vics of three, was from No. 44 Squadron, led by Squadron leader John Nettleton. Two miles (3km) astern and about 3 miles (5km) to starboard was the second wave, six Lancasters from No. 97

AUSBERG RAID REPORT, EXTRACT

Aircraft Attacking	Bombs Dropped	Release Height	Time at Target	Results observed
8	14.3 tons	50/400ft	1955/2015	Huge red flames seen. One a/c claimed hits on main building, two others claim bombs in target area.

Owing to poor light and low altitude, photographs lacked all essential detail. No bomb bursts are shown, but a large fire is seen probably in the city of Augsburg, and it is clear that at least one and probably all the aircraft passed directly over the target. A PR photograph taken on 25/4 reveals severe damage chiefly to the S end of the works. The main Diesel Assembly Shop has suffered heavy damage.

Above: Squadron Leader John Nettleton led the daring daylight raid on the U-boat engine factory at Augsburg, for which he was awarded the Victoria Cross.

LANCASTER SQUADRONS, OPERATION MILLENNIUM

Sqn No.	Base	Date of 1st Op.
144	Waddington	3 March 1942
97	Woodhall Spa	20/21 March 1942
207	Bottesford	24/25 April 1942
83	Coningsby	29/30 April 1942
61	Syerston	5/6 May 1942
106	Coningsby	30/31 May 1942
50	Skellingthorpe	30/31 May 1942 (one a/c only)

Squadron, led by Squadron leader John Sherwood. Each aircraft carried four 1,000lb (450kg) bombs with 11-second delayed action fuses.

Diversionary attacks were planned to keep German fighters occupied, but these miscarried. Between 20 and 30 Messerschmitt 109s of JG.2 returning to base encountered the rear Vic of Nettleton's wave. They shot down all three before turning their attention to the leading trio. One more Lancaster went down and the others were damaged before the Germans, by now low on fuel and ammunition, broke off the running battle. The second wave, although only a few miles away, was not spotted.

Nettleton and Flying Officer J. Garwell, the other survivor of the first wave, bored eastwards on track for Munich until over the Ammer lake they swung north towards Augsburg, followed at a distance of about 10 miles (16km) by the No. 97 Squadron formation.

Augsburg finally came into sight, and the two remaining Lancasters of No. 44 Squadron detoured around some tall factory chimneys and commenced their bombing run. At this point Garwell's aircraft was hit by flak and, shortly after releasing his bombs, he had to slide the burning Lancaster onto the ground. Four of the seven crewmen aboard survived, to be taken prisoner. Nettleton's Lancaster alone escaped into the gathering gloom.

Minutes later, the first Vic of the second wave from 97 Squadron arrived to find a thoroughly alerted defence. Unlike Nettleton, Sherwood did not attempt to dodge around the factory chimneys, but climbed above them. All three aircraft bombed accurately, but Sherwood's Lancaster was mortally hit by ground fire, and crashed in flames shortly after. By some miracle, Sherwood

Below: Wellingtons were the most numerous bombers participating in Operation Millennium. However, they were soon to be phased out in favour of the Avro Lancaster. (via Flypast)

Above: No. 83 Squadron Lancasters took part in the 1,000 bomber raid on Cologne. This unit was also the first Lancaster Pathfinder squadron.
Right: Cologne at the end of the war, showing the devastation around the cathedral. Wrecked bridges block the Rhine.

himself survived with only minor injuries.

Meanwhile the final Vic, now came racing in from the south. They were met by a storm of anti-aircraft fire, and all three were badly damaged. One blew up just as its bombs fell clear, but the other two got through.

Seventeen bombs hit the factory buildings, causing extensive damage. Nettleton was awarded the Victoria Cross for his exploit, and many other survivors were decorated for this, the first Lancaster raid to be made public. But with a loss rate exceeding 50 per cent it was not repeatable.

OPERATION MILLENNIUM

By the end of May 1942, seven squadrons had Lancasters. This was just in time for them to take part in a raid which for Bomber Command was a turning point in the night air offensive.

The strategic bombing of the Third Reich was, in its early days, an haphazard affair, with individual crews plotting their own courses and timings. Navigation was inexact, and only one crew in three managed to place their bombs within 5 miles (8km) of the target. To make matters worse, the German night fighter defences had taken the measure of this form of attack, and losses were steadily increasing. The future of Bomber Command looked increasingly uncertain. This was the situation when Air Marshal Arthur Harris assumed command in February 1942.

Harris realized that a raid by 1,000 bombers would be the biggest raid ever; the magic number of 1,000 would attract interest and demonstrate that RAF Bomber Command was truly a force to be reckoned with.

All aircraft would follow the same route from a merge point off the coast

The target chosen was Cologne. The city was within range of a new radio navigational device called Gee, and on a moonlit night the Rhine was easily identifiable from the air. All aircraft would follow the same route from a merge point off the coast. The entire attack was to

Above: Mk I R5609 flew with No. 97 Squadron on the Cologne and Essen thousand-bomber raids. Later it took part in the Battles of the Ruhr, Berlin, Hamburg and Peenemunde. It survived the war. (Alfred Price)

last just 90 minutes, an average of more than 11 aircraft bombing every minute! The German defences would be saturated by weight of numbers, minimizing losses.

The Cologne raid took place on the night of 30/31 May, 1942. The attack was in three waves, the first consisting of Gee-equipped Wellingtons and Stirlings with selected crews. The second wave consisted of the remaining Stirlings and Wellingtons, and the other twin-engined types; Hampdens, Whitleys and Manchesters. The third wave consisted of more than 125 Halifaxes and about 75 Lancasters which were scheduled to be over the target during the final 15 minutes of the attack. As the fastest and most heavily armed aircraft in the force, they were the least vulnerable to German night fighters. Losses to the third wave

amounted to a mere 1.9 per cent, compared with 4.8 per cent to the first wave and 4.1 per cent to the second.

For Bomber Command, it opened a new era in strategic bombing. Within three years, Lancasters would make up virtually the whole of the raiding force, and the damage they wrought upon German industry and communications was incalculable.

The secret of success for Operation Millennium had been the ability to find the target and mark it for the following crews. Gee was a useful navigation aid, but it not only lacked accuracy but was too short-ranged to cover many important targets. A special target-finding force was eventually formed in July 1942.

THE PATHFINDERS

Bomber Command introduced a competition to promote increased efficiency in the form of a photographic ladder. It became standard procedure for each bomber to photograph its aim point, and each squadron's position on the ladder was

determined by the accuracy of these. The ladder indicated which squadrons (and also which crews) were consistently finding their targets.

The first loads to go down contained a high proportion of incendiaries

Path Finder Force (PFF) was formed, commanded by Group Captain Don Bennett, an Australian navigation expert and prewar trail-blazer.

Bomber Command was divided into operational areas called Groups. The squadron heading the photographic ladder in each of the four Bomber Groups was transferred to the newly formed No. 8 Pathfinder Group, based in Huntingdon. By the end of the war, there were 14 Lancaster-equipped PFF Squadrons.

Regrettably PFF did not manage to bring about an instant improvement in bombing effectiveness. This had to wait for new navigational devices, for special pyrotechnic markers, and the development of methods which made the best use of them.

The former duly arrived in the shape of Oboe, an accurate but range-limited radio bombing device carried by Mosquitos. Dependent on signals from ground transmitters in England, it took in the highly industrialized Ruhr area but not much else.

The heavy bombers had H2S a radar navigation and blind bombing aid, but it was much less accurate than Oboe.

Above: *Flak bursts punctuate the night sky over Germany as Pathfinder markers go down on a target in Germany. Two other bombers are just visible.*

Parachute flares had long been used as an aid to target finding. They had however two drawbacks. Unless visibility was good, they would not light up the ground sufficiently well for crews to visually identify a target, or even pinpoint their own location. Then, of course, unless the flares were released in the right area, they simply illuminated a strange and often unrecognisable area of Germany, which was not a lot of help. Used in conjunction with Oboe or H2S, flares became far more effective.

In Operation Millennium, the first loads to go down contained a high proportion of incendiaries, to start fires which would lead the following bombers to the target area. Something more accurate was needed, and this duly arrived in the form of markers, known as Target Indicators, or TIs.

Each TI contained 60 pyrotechnic candles. A barometric fuse preset to operate at low altitude blew the TI open, cascading the candles onto the ground, igniting as they went. Seen from above, the contents of each TI would appear as an intense pool of light, about 900ft (275m) in diameter. Burning time was about three minutes, so they needed to be replenished at frequent intervals.

By now the Germans had started to produce dummy targets to mislead the bombers. Their obvious reaction to TIs was to copy them and, when a raid was imminent, set them off on a dummy target. To circumvent this, TIs were produced in a combination of colours; red, yellow, green, etc., and used in a predetermined order which varied from raid to raid.

When cloud covered the target, sky markers were used. These were parachute flares in a variety of colours. Dropped by Oboe or H2S aircraft. they demanded a complicated offset bomber technique.

Skymarking gave accuracy far superior to the early years of the war, when 'agricultural bombing' – the accidental bombing of fields – was a common occurrence.

With the new equipment available, all that remained was to find the best methods of employing it. Oboe Mosquitos were used for the initial marking of all targets within its range. Outside Oboe 1 reach, H2S was used. Tactics were roughly as follows. The first aircraft to arrive, typically five minutes before the main attack was scheduled to start, were the Finders, backed by a few Supporters. The Finders dropped flares where they thought that the aiming points were likely to be. Having visually identified the aim point, they would drop further flares directly above it.

The Finders would be followed by the Illuminators, who would drop sticks of flares directly across the aim point. Then would come the Primary Markers, to put TIs on the aim point itself. Backers-Up would continue to drop TIs at intervals, to give the Main Force an aiming point throughout the attack.

This form of visual marking was codenamed Newhaven. When, due to poor visibility or broken cloud, the marking was carried out using H2S, it became Parramatta, while skymarking was dubbed Wanganui.

As with all new methods, teething troubles occurred, mainly due to the precise timing required. The first real success achieved by PFF came during the Barmen-Wuppertal raid on 29/30 May 1943. The target was accurately marked, and the subsequent bombing highly concentrated. How was this done?

BARMEN/WUPPERTAL

A total of 719 aircraft were despatched. Of these, 272 were Lancasters, of which 20 aircraft were Lancaster Is and IIIs of PFF. The attack was spearheaded by 11 Mosquito IVs fitted with Oboe.

Main Force, following on behind, included 31 Lancaster Is and IIIs of No. 8 Pathfinder Group; 76 Lancaster Is and IIIs of No. 1 Group; 16 Hercules-engined Lancaster IIs of No. 3 Group; and 129 Lancaster Is and IIIs of No. 5 Group. Loads consisted of a mixture of high explosives; 4,000lb (1,800kg) cookies in the case of the Lancasters, and incendiaries.

The bombing was heavy and concentrated

Visibility in the target area was poor, but the first Mosquitos marked accurately at 00.47 hours, with red target indicators. They were followed

Above: Incendiary bomb containers are loaded.

by PFF backers-up with green TIs, and PFF 'fire-raisers' with incendiaries. Four of these, equipped with H2S, also marked with yellow TIs. Main Force aircraft were instructed to aim at the reds if visible; otherwise at the centre of the greens.

The bombing was heavy and concentrated; 611 aircraft claimed to have bombed the primary target. A total of 33 aircraft were lost on this raid. Lancaster losses amounted to seven; barely half the average losses for the raid.

A factor common to all forms of warfare is confusion, and the Pathfinder-led attacks on Germany were no exception. If a Pathfinder put down his TIs in the wrong place,

inevitably a proportion of Main Force would use them as an aim point. The Germans grew very adept at detecting decoys. A third factor was creep-back where crews over a heavily defended target released their bombs early. This resulted in the Main Force bomb pattern extending further back. A raid controller was needed to direct the marking, giving a running commentary on which TIs were to be used for aiming; which was the real target and a decoy.

A possible solution appeared to be that pioneered by Wing Commander Guy Gibson for Operation Chastise, the destruction of the Mohne and Eder dams in the Ruhr. He controlled his force very effectively using VHF voice radio to communicate. Possibly a Master Bomber could control an orthodox raid in the same way. There was only one way to find out; lay on a small-scale experiment.

OPERATION BELLICOSE

The target chosen, Friedrichshafen, called for a high degree of accuracy. It lies on the

---

EXTRACT FROM BOMBER COMMAND NIGHT RAID REPORT No. 340

611 aircraft, out of a force of 719, attacked the Barmen district of Wuppertal with great success. The fire-raising technique was effectively employed, as a complement to ground marking, resulting in the best concentration yet achieved by the Pathfinder Force. Immense damage was caused in the town, covering over 1,000 acres and affecting 113 industrial concerns, as well as totally disrupting the transport system and public utilities.

north shore of the Bodensee, the south shore of which is in Switzerland. In 1943, it was the largest production centre for radar parts for the Third Reich, and its destruction would be a severe blow to the German air defences.

Main Force crews were to orbit the target, with no more than two aircraft at the same altitude. Once a TI landed on the target, the Master Bomber would issue a special signal, and all available aircraft would attack immediately. It was of course possible that the target could quickly become obscured by smoke; in this case the crews were to make their attack run from a certain point, sighting on a second point, but delaying bomb release long enough for the aircraft to cover 6,000ft (1,800m) to the actual target.

This raid required special training and picked crews. Piloted by Flight Lieutenants Rodley, a survivor of the Augsburg raid, and John Sauvage, and Pilot Officers D.I. Jones and Jimmy Munro, the latter a Canadian, they were flown north to Scampton for two days' intensive training.

For this trial mission the Master Bomber was not a Pathfinder, but the very experienced Group Captain Leonard Slee. His deputy was the Wing Commander G.L. Gomm. There were also two controllers, either of whom could take charge in the event of an emergency. The force took off late in the evening of 20 June 1943 and headed south, crossing the Channel at maximum altitude. Once over France they progressively lost height down to 10,000ft (3,050m) as they passed Orleans, then lower still

to between 2,500 and 3,000ft (750-900m). After crossing the Rhine, they climbed to attack altitude. At about this time, Wing Commander Gomm, of No. 467 (Australian) Squadron, took over as Master Bomber.

Exactly on time, Munro and Jones released a string of flares parallel to, and on either side of, the target. Gomm ordered all aircraft to gain another 5,000ft (1,500m). Realizing that this would make visual identification very difficult, the four Pathfinders stayed at their original altitude.

The Master Bomber ordered all aircraft to attack at once

Sauvage put down a green TI just north of the Zeppelin sheds. He was followed by Rodley, who dropped a green TI accurately. On seeing this, the Master Bomber ordered all aircraft fitted with the Mk XIV bombsight to attack at once. Jones had to abandon one run to

Below: Prototype Lancaster Mk III. Externally indistinguishable from the Mk I, the main difference was American-built Packard Merlins with Hamilton propellers.

W4114

Above: Aircraft of No. 50 Squadron at Swinderby. The nearest was struck off charge when it crashed at Thurlby, Lincs, on 19 September 1942.

steady his aircraft. More flares were dropped along the shoreline around the two predesignated points. After the attack, all 59 Lancasters headed for Maison Blanche and Blida airfields in Algeria.

For 'Rod' Rodley, however, it was an eventful trip. Unknown to him, a TI had hung up. When, far out over the Mediterranean he lost height, the barometric fuse operated and the candles ignited. An evil red glow suddenly appeared beneath his Lancaster. Thinking he was under attack from a night fighter, Rodley took evasive action, while Sergeant Duffy, his flight engineer, checked for damage. The bomb bay was a mass of flames, but the cause was obvious. A quick pull on the jettison toggle and the blazing remnants of the TI fell clear, leaving the Lancaster damaged but flyable.

The Master Bomber concept was rated a success. Six of the Lancasters were damaged by anti-aircraft fire, one beyond repair. The 'shuttle' concept of flying on to North Africa was also rated a success, and was later used by both Bomber Command and the USAAF.

As the strategic bombing of the Third Reich continued, PFF methods became ever more sophisticated. At the same time, the proportion of Lancasters to other heavy bomber types grew ever greater. On 23/24 July 1944, a force of 619 heavy bombers was sent against the German naval base at Kiel. Of these, no fewer than 84 per cent were Lancasters.

PATHFINDER PROGRESS

The concept of the Master Bomber was tried and proven. His function was to check on the accuracy of the marking, call by radio for adjustments or back-up where necessary, and, while loitering in the area until the bombing was completed, do everything possible to ensure

that the munitions went down exactly where they were intended to go.

It was not long before the standard aircraft became the fast and agile twin-engined Mosquito. This was the case for the Kiel raid, in which the Master Bomber and his deputy flew two of the 10 Mosquitos

AIRCRAFT IN RAID ON KIEL, 23/24 JULY 1944

Group	Type	No	Missing
8	Mosquito IX	1	–
	Mosquito XVI	6	–
	Mosquito XX	3	–
	Lancaster III	89	1
1	Lancaster I	85	1
	Lancaster III	104	1
6	Lancaster II	14	–
	Lancaster X	28	–
5	Lancaster I	46	1
	Lancaster III	53	–
3	Lancaster I	59	–
	Lancaster II	14	–
	Lancaster III	27	–
4	Halifax III	100	–

Total
10 Mosquitos, 519 Lancasters, 100 Halifaxes.

Top: *Detailed models were made by the Central Intelligence Unit. Seen here is Kiel harbour.*
Above: *Lancaster Mk I of No. 83 Squadron. Alter a distinguished career with PFF, this aircraft came down in Holland after raiding Essen on 3/4 April 1943.*

allocated for primary marking.

'The method employed for the raid on Kiel was controlled Newhaven marking. Blind Illuminators, 21 Lancasters, were to drop red TIs at H-6 (six minutes before zero hour), and white flares if the weather was suitable. If there was more than 6/10ths cloud, they were to retain their white flares, and drop green flares with red stars instead. If their H2S should prove unserviceable, they were to retain their markers and act as Main Force. These were to be followed by the Primary Visual markers, 6 Lancasters, at H-4, who were to drop red and green TIs using the red TIs dropped by the Illuminators as a guide. If they could not identify the target visually they were to retain their markers and act as Main Force. Visual Centerers, 16 Lancasters, distributed throughout the attack, were to aim green TIs with one second overshoot at: 1) the centre of mixed red and green TIs; 2) the centre of red TIs; 3) the centre of green TIs; in that order of priority. If no TIs were visible, they were to act as Main Force. The Secondary Blind Markers, 7 Lancasters at H+10 and 4 at

H+11, were to drop red TIs by H2S. If there was more than 6/10ths cloud they were to release skymarking flares green with red stars. If their H2S was unserviceable they also were to act as Main Force. 28 Lancasters of 8 Group were to act as supporters, bombing at H-6 on H2S, or if that was unserviceable, visually or on a good dead reckoning.'

KIEL

The Main Force was scheduled to attack in four very concentrated waves, putting 516 heavy bombers over the target in the space of just 15 minutes. Scattered among them would be 15 ABC (Airborne Cigar) Lancasters of No. 101 Squadron, each carrying an extra crewman whose function was to jam the German night fighter radio frequencies. Bombing instructions were, in order of priority: 1) centre of mixed red and green TIs or red TIs; 2) centre of green TIs; 3) centre of skymarking flares.

During the raid on Kiel, the target was covered with 10/10ths cloud. No contact could be made with the Master Bomber, and his deputy assumed control of proceedings. Marking was considered accurate with Main Force bombing on the glow of TIs and many explosions and fires were reported.

Only four Lancasters were lost on this mission; a mere 0.7. per cent of the total.

PFF led the way to the targets, but Main Force, was the mighty sledgehammer that came crashing down on them.

For all practical purposes Main Force was Bomber Command. Main Force delivered the greatest weight of bombs against the war machine that was the Third Reich, and Main Force took the greatest number of casualties. Nor should it be forgotten that Main Force was the training ground for those who became Pathfinders or who smashed the Ruhr Dams and sank the *Tirpitz*.

As the war continued, the Lancaster progressively became the backbone of Main Force. In numbers of sorties flown and tonnages of bombs delivered, it outstripped all other bombers in service by a large margin.

The strategic bombing of Germany, and to a lesser extent its Axis partner Italy, consisted of a number of what amounted to protracted set-piece battles, interspersed with many highly individual actions. The thousand bomber raids of May and June 1942 had only been achieved by milking training units of aircraft and crews. This tremendous effort could not be sustained. During the months following June 1942, Bomber Command restricted itself to raids of up to 300 aircraft against single targets roughly twice a week, weather permitting.

The number of Lancaster squadrons steadily grew. Prior to October 1942, conversion onto the new type was carried

out by a specially formed third flight within each squadron. Later, conversion flights were centralized and merged into Heavy Conversion Units.

Special weapons often featured in the Lancaster story. One of these was the huge Capital Ship Bomb, which had a shaped charge designed to cut through armour.

Top: Crew returning from a raid.
Above: Wing Commander Guy Gibson (right) led No. 106 Squadron to Gdynia, before forming the Dam Busters.
Far Left: The devastated oil refinery at Harburg, just to the south of Hamburg.

FRIEDRICHSHAFEN, BOMB LOADS

Leader/Deputy Leader	2 x Lancaster III	1 x 4,000lb (1,800kg) 7 x 500lb (227kg)
97 Sqn PFF	2 x Lancaster III	3 x red TI; 3 x green TI 16 x white flares 2 x 500lb (227kg) 2 x red TI 2 x green TI 32 x white flares 2 x 500lb (227kg)
9,49,50,57,61,106 Sqns No. 5 Grp	32 x Lancaster III	1 x 4,000lb (1,800kg) 7 x 500lb (227kg)
44,207,467,619 Sqns No. 5 Grp	Lancaster III fitted with Mk XIV bombsight	14 x 500lb (227kg)
44,207 Sqns, No. 5 Grp	Lancaster III not fitted with Mk XIV bombsight	Full incendiary load

SEARCHLIGHTS

'One of my worst moments of the whole raid was when, during one of my five successful runs over the target, T-Tommy was caught in a cone of searchlights. I fought desperately to lose those probing beams of light which had caught my aircraft in their web. Shrapnel hit the fuselage like hailstones until, by diving at near maximum speed, I escaped into the darkness. Poor Jack Hannah, my wireless operator, stationed at the astrodome on the lookout for enemy fighters, protested as he was tossed about like a pea in a pod.'

PILOT OFFICER D. I. JONES,
No. 97 SQUADRON

In August 1942, the German's only aircraft carrier *Graf Zeppelin* and the battle cruiser *Gneisenau* were reported at Gdynia in Poland. A raid was mounted on 27 August by adapted Lancasters of No. 106 Squadron and led by Wing Commander Guy Gibson and Squadron Leader Arthur Richardson.

ANTICLIMAX

The result was, perhaps inevitably, an anticlimax. Visibility was poor, and the

Top: To carry bombs of 8,000lb (3,600kg) or more, Lancaster bomb bay doors were bulged, as seen on this Mk II.
Above: A gaggle of Lancasters at low level. Not the Le Creusot raid, but these in Far Eastern finish show up much better.

defences stronger than expected. Arriving over Gdynia, 106 Squadron was unable to locate *Graf Zeppelin*, but managed to find what was believed to be *Gneisenau*.

Gibson made several runs but the bomb missed the battle cruiser by about 1,200ft (360m).

Early in September, 8,000lb (3,600kg) bombs started to arrive on the squadrons. These needed modifications both to the bomb bay and doors, and Gibson's squadron with its aircraft already adapted for the Capital Ship Bomb, pioneered their use. The following month saw another Bomber Command set-piece attack.

PARTICIPANTS IN OPERATION ROBINSON

Squadron	No. of A/C	Base
No. 9	10*	Waddington
No. 44	9	Waddington
No. 49	10	Scampton
No. 50	12	Skellingthorpe
No. 57	10	Scampton
No. 61	7*	Syerston
No. 97	9	Woodhall Spa
No. 106	12*	Syerston
No. 207	15	Langar

NB. * denotes two aircraft to Montchanin.

Left: *The ice cream cornets among the bombs denote raids on Italian targets.*
Below: *A decorated 8,000lb (3,600kg) bomb on its loading trolley in front of a Mk II of No. 426 Squadron RCAF.*
Bottom: *Lancaster Mk II of No. 426 Thunderbirds Squadron RCAF. It was lost over Stuttgart on 7/8 October 1943.*

OPERATION ROBINSON

Vital targets were not always in Germany. One such was the Schneider armaments factory at south-eastern France. Although covering nearly 300 acres, the need to avoid civil casualties demanded a standard of accuracy that could only be attained in daylight. The nine Lancaster squadrons operational in No. 5 Group began to practise low-level flying early in October.

The lessons of the Augsburg raid had been well learnt. The bombers were scheduled to reach the target just before dusk, making their escape into the darkening sky. This time, however, the inbound route of the raiding force was carefully planned to minimize the possibility of fighter interception.

After take-off, on 17 October, 96 Lancasters from 5 Group assembled over Upper Heyford in Oxfordshire, and from there proceeded to Land's End. Descending to 1,000ft (300m) over the sea to avoid radar detection, they turned south-easterly over the Bay of Biscay. When about 60 miles (95km) from the French coast, they dropped down to 300ft (90m) and turned almost due east.

4,000ft, the minimum release height for the 4,000lb cookies

Unhindered by the German defences, the low-level armada thundered on. The sole incident occurred as a Lancaster of No. 57 Squadron took a partridge through the windscreen. The formation climbed to its attack altitude of 4,000ft (1,200m), the minimum release height for the 4,000lb (1,800kg) cookies that were carried by 15 aircraft. As they climbed, they edged a few degrees southwards in the direction of Le Creusot and took up their attack formation.

Navigation and timing were spot on, and surprise was almost

OVERSEAS LANCASTER SQUADRONS

Sqn	Nationality	First Op	Base
460	Australian	22/23 Nov 42 Stuttgart	Breighton
467	Australian	2/3 Jan 43 Gardening	Bottesford
426	Canadian	17/18 Aug 43 Peenemunde	Linton-on-Ouse
405	Canadian	17/18 Aug 43 Peenemunde	Gransden Lodge
408	Canadian	7/8 Oct 43 Stuttgart	Linton-on-Ouse
432	Canadian	18/19 Nov 43 Sea Search	East Moor
463	Australian	26/27 Nov 43 Berlin	Waddington
75	New Zealand	9/10 April 44 Villeneuve St George	Mepal
300	Polish	18/10 April 44 Rouen	Faldingworth
419	Canadian	27/28 April Friedrichschafen	Middleton St George
428	Canadian	July 44	Middleton St George
431	Canadian	December 44	Croft
434	Canadian	2/3/Jan 45 Nuremburg	Croft
424	Canadian	February 44	Skipton-on-Swale
433	Canadian	1/2 Feb 45 Ludwigshaven	Skipton-on-Swale
427	Canadian	11 March 45 Essen	Leeming
429	Canadian	April 45	Leeming

complete. In an attack lasting just nine minutes, over 200 tonnes of high explosive and incendiaries rained down.

At the same time, six Lancasters attacked a transformer station at Montchanin. They carried ten 500lb (225kg) bombs each, and were briefed to attack from 500ft (150m). The transformer station was wrecked, but two of the pilots were over-enthusiastic and attacked from well below the minimum safe height. One aircraft was damaged and the other crashed, both victims of their own bomb explosions.

One Lancaster forced to turn back with engine failure was intercepted by three Arado Ar 196 floatplanes of the Kriegsmarine. The flight engineer was killed in the attack.

In all, damage to the Lancasters was remarkably light, with just a few holes in some aircraft. Although limited production was resumed at Le Creusot after a period of about three weeks, major repair work was still in progress eight months later.

The battle of El Alamein commenced just five days after the raid on Le Creusot, while Operation Torch, in north-west Africa, was scheduled for 11 November. Lancaster squadrons played an indirect part in these operations by bombarding targets in northern Italy.

Above left: *The projection at the bottom of the turret is the Monica aerial; damage was caused by flak.*
Left: *Star of Wings for Victory Week in Trafalgar Square, this No. 207 Squadron Lancaster was one of the first production aircraft.*

Between October and December, 936 sorties were flown. Italian air defences were ineffective and losses were light. But the long distances involved, plus a double crossing of the Alps, made raiding Italy a tremendous test of endurance for the Lancaster crews.

If the weather was too bad for the Alpine crossing to be attempted, German targets were substituted instead at the last moment.

Lancaster output soon reached the stage where squadrons could start equipping with the type. The first three to do so were No. 460 (Australian) Squadron at Breighton; No. 101 Squadron at Holme-on-Spalding Moor; and No. 103 Squadron at Elsham Wolds.

The conversion of the Australian squadron onto the Lancaster highlighted a trend. Although No. 44 Squadron had been dubbed 'Rhodesia', there were not enough Rhodesians to man it fully. Of the 48 aircrew on the Augsburg raid, only eight were Rhodesians. Two, including Nettleton himself, were South Africans. Two Canadians, two New Zealanders, and a single Australian completed the overseas contingent. The remaining 33 were British.

From the outbreak of war, volunteers from the British Empire, or Commonwealth, as it is now called, had hastened to the aid of the mother country. A high proportion of Australians, Canadians or New Zealanders in one squadron gave it a uniquely national flavour. No. 460 was the first of many such Lancaster squadrons, but numerically the Canadians took pride of place; No. 6 Group was for all practical purposes an all Canadian Bomber Group.

ELECTRONIC WARFARE

The year of 1943 commenced with raids on Berlin, with the Pathfinders honing their marking techniques on the city. Electronic warfare took on greater significance with the introduction of new jamming and threat detection systems. Of these, Tinsel could be tuned to transmit engine noise on the German fighter control frequencies; Monica was a tail warning radar; while Boozer could detect German radar emissions. Many other systems followed in the years to come.

Tinsel was initially successful, though the Germans gradually introduced measures to limit its effectiveness. Monica, in contrast, was a minor disaster from the outset. Quite unable to discriminate between friend and foe, it constantly gave false alarms as friendly aircraft came into its search area. The Germans developed a detector codenamed Flensburg which could home on Monica's emissions from long ranges. Naxos-Z was another German detector, designed to home on H2S.

Above right: Lancaster Mk I of No. 106 Squadron damaged by a night fighter during the Battle of the Ruhr in April 1943.
Right: This Lancaster collided on the ground with an American B-17 Fortress.

Above: Hamburg showed up well on the H2S screen, when compared to the map on the left. (Alfred Price)

Boozer, was rather better; if the bomber was illuminated by ground radar, a red warning light came on. If fighter radar emissions were detected, an orange light glowed. Once a night fighter gained visual contact its radar was often switched to standby, upon which the warning light went out precisely at the moment of greatest danger.

WINDOW OVER HAMBURG

Many references to the difficulties caused by Window to the ground and fighter defences were overheard in intercepted wireless traffic. Some enemy aircraft reported interference. One very interesting remark was "it is impossible, too many hostiles". This indicates that the Window echoes, besides producing general interference of the (German) display tube, were also confused with true aircraft echoes.

115 sorties by night fighters were overheard 33 of which mentioned British aircraft. Our crews reported 49 interceptions, but only seven of these developed into attacks. Enemy aircraft frequently seemed unaware of the presence of bombers in their vicinity. Only two instances of fighter damage were reported, and all of the five bombers seen to be shot down in combat were at least 20 miles (32km) away from Hamburg.

BOMBER COMMAND NIGHT RAID REPORT No 383

THE BATTLE OF THE RUHR

The Ruhr was the industrial heart of Germany, invariably heavily cloaked by industrial haze, making targets notoriously difficult to locate. However, with the introduction of Oboe it could be attacked accurately for the first time.

Below: This 550 Squadron Lancaster survived the war with a tally of over 100 sorties against targets.

The Battle of the Ruhr opened on 5/6 March with a heavy raid on Essen the home of the Krupps steelworks, one of the most important targets in Germany. It was marked by PFF, then bombed by Main Force in three waves. The final wave consisted of 145 Lancasters from 14 squadrons, about half the Main Force total. One-third of the Krupps works was heavily damaged, more than all previous raids on this target combined had achieved.

Raids on Munich, Nuremberg and Stuttgart followed. Just over a week later, Bomber Command returned to Essen. A third raid on Essen took place on 3/4 April, and a fourth on 30 April/1 May. Duisburg had been raided twice. Dortmund and Dusseldorf were hit during May with over 300 Lancasters on each raid. Raids on targets in the Ruhr continued until 14/15 June, culminating in a heavy attack on the steel and coal centre of Oberhausen.

The Battle of the Ruhr conclusively demonstrated Bomber Command's ability to hit targets in this area, while taking only moderate casualties. But the Ruhr was within range of Oboe. The pressing need was to carry the battle deeper into Germany with similar results.

OPERATION GOMORRAH

Hamburg's strategic importance lay in its shipbuilding activities, and the manufacturing of U-boats. Situated close to the coast, and with a large and very easily recognizable river running through it, Hamburg was suitable for locating by H2S.

A new counter-measure codenamed Window was available for the first time. It consisted of bundles of aluminium foil strips, which would each give the appearance of a heavy bomber on German radars, making tracking impossible.

On the night of 24/25 July 1943, 791 bombers set course for Hamburg. Of these, 347, were Lancasters, but they carried nearly three-quarters of the total tonnage of bombs. They

Above: Time exposure of German flak over a defended area.
Right: Flight Lieutenant William Reid VC of No. 61 Squadron. Twice wounded, his aircraft badly damaged and two crewmen dead, he continued the mission and bombed the target.

were monitored by German ground radar until the bomb aimers started to drop bundles of Window down their flare chutes at one minute intervals.

The result was complete chaos for the defenders. The radar screens filled up, giving the appearance of a raid by 11,000 bombers! All semblance of control was lost, and fighters already airborne were ordered to the vicinity. They spent most of their time chasing clouds of Window, while the flak was reduced to firing at random, in the hope of scoring a lucky hit.

Bombing accuracy was marred only by an element of 'creepback' in the later stages, caused by over-eager crews releasing their bombs a fraction too early on the attack run. Only four Lancasters failed to return, but three of these were from the high-flying No. 103 Squadron,

which had gained least protection of all from Window.

FOLLOW-UPS

Daylight raids by the USAAF 8th Air Force were made on 25 and 26 July. Bomber Command returned in force on the night of 27/28, with 787 aircraft, 353 of them Lancasters. A third raid followed on 29/30 July, and the fourth and final one on 2/3 August. The damage assessment report stated: 'The city of Hamburg is now in ruins. The general destruction is on a scale never before seen in a town or city of this size.'

losses started to rise again.

The next heavy raid was on the weapons research centre at Peenemunde, a high-risk mission; Peenemunde was a small target on the Baltic coast, and good visibility was needed for bombing accuracy. A full-moon night was chosen, 17/18 August. Deep penetrations were seldom made at this time of year, as the northern sky was never completely dark. Conditions were therefore ideal for the night fighters.

The course to the target suggested that the bombers were heading for Berlin. Over 200 German fighters converged on the capital. Once bombs started going down on Peenemunde there was no disguising the real

Top: This Heavy Conversion Unit aircraft died in flames following a training accident.
Left: Lancaster Mk I ME703 of No. 576 Squadron survived the Nuremburg raid in March 1944, only to receive a direct flak hit five weeks later.
Below: Chaos in the Juvissy marshalling yards after a raid by 200 Lancasters on 18/19 April 1944.

In this short campaign, some 3,095 sorties were flown, 1,373 of them by Lancasters. In total, more than 8,600 tons of bombs fell on Hamburg. Losses were 86 bombers, 39 of them Lancasters. The German defence system, fire and rescue services were left in complete disarray.

Measures taken by the Germans included a looser form of fighter control, new airborne radar of a different wavelength, emission detectors as described earlier, and saturating the target area with 'cat's eye' single seaters. Before long, bomber

A further 11 heavy raids on the German capital were carried out by the middle of February, interspersed with other targets. In all, 6,209 Lancaster sorties were flown in this period, losing 321 aircraft in action. This represented an unsustainable loss rate of 5.2 per cent, which rose to 8 per cent for a final raid in March.

Peenemunde was heavily damaged, but the price was high

These figures do not include operational attrition. Fog and low cloud over England on 17 December caused the loss of 28 Lancasters, in addition to 25 missing, while two more had collided after take-off. The loss rate for this one mission was an appalling 11.4 per cent.

Berlin was too large an area, too heavily defended, too far inland, and much harder to identify with any precision. And by this time, the advantages of Window were much less as the German defences adapted themselves to it. While extensive damage was caused, the concentrated destruction of Hamburg was not repeated.

NUREMBERG

If the Battle of Berlin was a defeat for Bomber Command, the raid on Nuremberg on 30/31 March 1944 was a disaster. For Bomber Command, the Nuremberg raid was the night when it all went wrong.

Deception attacks on Kassel and Cologne were recognized early, which enabled the defences to concentrate on the

Top: This Canadian Lancaster visited Berlin on at least seven occasions, with three different squadrons; Nos 432, 426 and 408.
Above: *Shot down over Berlin, this Lancaster broke up in mid-air and its tail landed in a garden. (Alfred Price)*

target. Those fighters with enough fuel headed north to intercept the final two waves.

Peenemunde was heavily damaged, but the price paid for the raid upon it was high. Losses amounted to 40 aircraft, of which 24 were Lancasters. It is believed that the majority fell to fighters. Diversions and feints became a standard tactic in

Bomber Command's armoury, followed later by simultaneous attacks on multiple targets.

THE BATTLE OF BERLIN

The operations so far described were successful, but Bomber Command also had setbacks. The Battle of Berlin was one such. It commenced on 18/19 November 1943 with an attack by an all-Lancaster force, but on this occasion PFF marking was not up to scratch, and the bombing was scattered. The absence of a Master Bomber did not help matters. Four days later they tried again, this time with better results.

that night, while 13 crashed on their arrival at base. One was written off with battle damage, whilst seventy more aircraft returned with varying degrees of damage.

Most of the losses occurred on the outward leg. Night fighters accounted for 78 aircraft, including 55 Lancasters; two bombers collided and another one was lost to an unknown cause. Of the 440 Lancaster crewmen who failed to return home, only 107 survived. Worst of all was that the raid was an almost complete failure.

Top: *The V-weapons site at Wizernes after a raid by Lancasters of No. 5 Group, 20 July 1944.*
Left: *Repair was a vital part of aircraft replacement.*
Below: *Before and after. A raid on the oil storage depot at Bec d'Ambes on 4 August 1944.*

main raid of 781 heavy bombers, of which 569 were Lancasters from 34 different squadrons. The twin-engined night fighters were scrambled, and ordered to assemble over a radio beacon. Unfortunately the course of the bombers took them towards this beacon, running them straight into the trap. Forecast winds were incorrect, and the bomber stream became spread out. Atmospheric conditions were such that long condensation trails formed behind the bombers visible under a half moon. The track of the bombers was visible from miles away.

94 bombers failed to return that night, while 13 crashed on their return

An incredible total of 94 bombers failed to make the return journey from Germany

RETURN TO EUROPE

The outcome of the entire war in Europe hinged on the successful invasion of Normandy. From April 1944 the majority of Lancaster sorties were against targets in France and Belgium, mainly railway centres and airfields, radar stations and coastal gun batteries.

The weeks following D-Day saw road and rail communications, enemy troop concentrations and fuel depots all accorded priority, but as the V-1 and V-2 assault on London had begun, a great deal of effort was diverted to their launching sites.

There was a large-scale return to daylight operations for Bomber Command. Allied air superiority in the area kept up the pressure around the clock. Then, as the Allied armies pushed further inland, heavy attacks were made on German-held airfields in Holland.

During the concluding six months of the war, the Lancaster force grew to an enormous 57 squadrons; over 1,200 aircraft.

Above: Lancaster assembly line at Baginton. The wartime censor has rather clumsily airbrushed out the aircraft number.

Concentrated attacks on synthetic oil plants were made during the winter of 1944/45, vastly reducing supplies. Dresden, at that time a key road and rail target, was attacked in strength on 13/14 February 1945; Essen by more than 1,000 bombers in daylight on 11 March, and Kiel on 9/10 April. Berlin, once the most heavily defended area in Germany, was raided five nights later by more than 500 Lancasters, of which only two failed to return. But by this time major targets were in short supply and the majority of raids were on a comparatively small scale, and as the Allied armies pushed into Germany the strategic bombing war gradually drew to a close.

FINAL OPERATIONS

The Lancaster ended the war on more peaceful tasks. Operation Manna saw 17 Lancaster squadrons dropping containers of food to the population of Holland; Operation Exodus involved the repatriation of released British prisoners of war. This was followed by Operation Dodge, the return of 8th Army veterans from the Mediterranean area. It was an honourable finish to a hard-fought campaign.

Left: Edith, veteran of 84 sorties during which she destroyed a German fighter, completed a further 14 trips dropping food and repatriating prisoners of war.

BOMBERS VS
FIGHTERS

A heavily defended target could put up a storm of light flak, but most bombing was carried out at altitudes beyond its reach. Heavy flak could not be avoided by high flying, but it had a far slower rate of fire than the light automatic guns. Far fewer shells came up at any one time, and they took up to 30 seconds to arrive at typical operational altitudes. Radar-predicted heavy flak was pretty accurate, but one method of avoiding it was to change course and altitude at frequent intervals. Hopefully the shells would then burst in the spot where the bomber would have been had it not evaded.

Pilots felt that the best course was to take no evasive action and to drop the nose and accelerate out of the flak zone. The Lancaster's deadliest enemy was the fighter. As the vast majority of Lancaster sorties were made in darkness, we will concentrate on the night fighter threat.

Countermeasures were used to hinder the defenders but they could not prevent a fighter

from searching visually. If a night fighter succeeded in entering the bomber stream, it was in a target-rich environment. Even with its radar and radio communications jammed solid, it was often possible for the fighter to make a visual sighting. And once the fighter was in visual contact, an attack usually followed.

Normal Lancaster defensive armament consisted of two machine guns in each of nose and dorsal positions, and four more in the tail, all in power-

Above: Radar-predicted heavy flak guns were mainly deployed along the coast or around cities.
Below left: Searchlights illuminated the bomber for flak or fighters;
Opposite: Two .50 calibre machine guns in the tail gave a mightier punch than the usual four .303 Brownings.

operated turrets. The guns were Browning .303 calibre, with a high cyclic rate of fire. They could pour out a lot of rounds, but the bullets themselves were small and lacked hitting power. Four types of ammunition were in general use; ball, tracer, armour-piercing and incendiary.

The four guns in the rear turret were usually harmonized on a point at 750ft (225m) for night missions, and on a 7ft 6in (2.29m) square pattern at 1,200ft (365m) by day. The nose and mid-upper turrets were often harmonized 5ft (1.52m) apart at 1,200ft (365m), although it was generally accepted that the maximum effective range of the .303 Browning was 900ft (275m). The main defence at night was the tail and mid-upper turret, in that order.

Left: This Lancaster example, from No. 15 Squadron, also carries G-H radar bombing equipment.
Below: Mk I Lancaster used for trials of a periscopically sighted ventral turret in 1942. It was not a success.

their high rate of fire.

From June 1944, a number of Lancasters were fitted with the Rose Rice tail turret, which mounted two .50 calibre Brownings. While the combination of a much heavier projectile and a slightly higher muzzle velocity gave a rather better effective range, the cyclic rate of fire of this weapon was at most 850 rounds per minute. The standard four-gun Lancaster turret could spew out 306 bullets in a four second burst, compared with just 113 for the Rose Rice turret. However, the weight of fire of the latter was about 50 per cent heavier provided that all bullets struck home.

The primary task of the Lancaster was to deliver bombs and return safely

The primary task of the Lancaster was to deliver bombs on target and return safely. Shooting it down was the cherry on the cake. On dark nights, when the fighters were forced to get in close, the four-gun turret of the Rose Rice, had much to commend it. Few German night fighter pilots would press home an attack while they were taking hits themselves. The final advantage of the standard four-gun turret

Few nights were clear enough to allow fighters to make frontal attacks, and it was unlikely that a Lancaster would overhaul a fighter from astern, so the nose turret was of most use in discouraging the ground defences during low-level missions.

Wartime British bomber armament has often been criticized as inadequate, because it was both out-ranged and out-gunned by the German fighter weapons. British bombers were far more heavily defended than those of any other nation except the Americans, and that included their German counterparts. The Heinkel He 111 typically carried a single rifle-calibre machine gun in each of just five positions, with limited fields of fire and no power-operated turrets. At night, German fighters often had to get very close before they could identify the bomber and take aim. This brought them well into the range of the British machine guns, which compensated for their small projectiles by

LANCASTER, DEFENSIVE GUNS

Browning MG	.303 calibre	.50 calibre
Cyclic rate of fire	1,150rpm	750/850rpm
Weight	22lb (10kg)	64lb (29kg)
Muzzle Velocity	2,660ft/sec (811m/sec)	2,750ft/sec 838m/sec)
Projectile Weight	174 grains	710 grains

Above: The nose turret was rarely of use at night, but daylight raids became more frequent. No. 100 Squadron – 128 ops.

was that it had no less than 130 seconds' firing time, compared with a mere 24 seconds for the Rose Rice. This was rarely called for; against enemy fighters 24 seconds' firing time was usually adequate.

From late 1944 Lancasters carried out a surprising number of daylight operations; the heavier gun with its longer range was by far the most preferable. Among the squadrons equipped with the Rose Rice rear turret were Nos 83, 101, 153 and 170.

The other major variation in Lancaster defensive armament was the Glenn Martin 250 mid-upper turret, which also mounted two .50 calibre Brownings. This was carried by the Lancaster B.VII. 150 planes were built but as deliveries of this model did

not commence until April 1945, it was just too late to see action.

GUNSIGHTS

The main gunsight used in Lancaster turrets was the Barr & Stroud G Mk III reflector sight. In use, this showed an illuminated orange circle with a central dot, both focused at infinity. A brightness control adjusted it according to conditions; bright in sunlight, dim at night. The radius of the circle was approximately equal to the wingspan of a single-engined fighter at a range of 1,200ft (365m), while the radius of the circle gave the deflection (the amount of aiming ahead) needed to hit a target with a relative crossing speed of 50mph (80km/hr).

In 1944, the Mk IIc gyroscopic sight entered service as a turret sight. This could actually predict the point of aim, if the

approaching fighter could be tracked for a short while, and its wingspan set on a dial. A gun-laying radar code-named Village Inn was introduced in the final months of the war, which allowed opponents to be engaged from beyond visual range. While potentially devastating, the problem was obtaining positive identification of the radar contact as hostile.

The essence of effective defence against fighters was always to see them first. At night this was far from easy. As a general rule, they came from

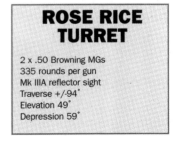

ROSE RICE TURRET

2 x .50 Browning MGs
335 rounds per gun
Mk IIIA reflector sight
Traverse +/-94°
Elevation 49°
Depression 59°

Above: Mk I with an experimental arrangement of remote barbettes and the sighting position in the tail.

below, where they were masked by the dark ground and most difficult to see. The bomber would be lined against the sky, even on a starless night. Attacks generally came from astern, with the fighter swimming up from the depths and attacking in a slight climb with its fixed frontal armament. Its target was rarely the fuselage, as if the bombs detonated the resulting explosion could quite easily destroy the night fighter too. Normally the wings, with the vulnerable engines and fuel tanks, were selected.

Later on, the German night fighters used Schrage Musik, cannon pointing upwards at an angle of about 60 degrees, aimed by a reflector sight mounted in the cabin roof. This allowed them to attack from almost directly underneath, and out of sight of the gunners. The fighter had to formate beneath the bomber and take careful aim at the fuel tanks between the engines. A short burst of fire was then usually sufficient.

SCHRAGE MUSIK

The German fighters did not use tracer in a Schrage Musik attack, so Bomber Command was rather slow in identifying it.

If a bomber set out then failed to return there was no one to tell the tale. Only those few aircraft that survived such attacks limped back bearing the tell-tale scars, and gradually the tactic became known.

Methods of dealing with night fighters varied. Often, if one was sighted that was not making any overtly aggressive moves, the policy was to leave it well alone, hoping that the bomber had not been seen. Other crews maintained that an aggressive attitude was best, opening fire even at long range in order to show the fighter the kind of welcome it could expect if it made an attacking move. Sometimes these ploys worked; at other times they didn't.

Flight Lieutenant Tony Weber's Pathfinder crew developed their own unique brand of defence against attack from below. The Lancasters of No. 405 Squadron had had their dorsal turrets removed to improve performance, which left the mid-upper gunner as a spare bod. A small viewing hole was cut in the fuselage floor aft of the bomb bay, fitted with safety straps, oxygen connection for a heated flying suit. This

Below: Canadian-built Mk X, fitted with the small and neat Glenn Martin mid-upper turret.

Above: 'Village Inn' gunlaying radar was fitted to a few tail turrets towards the end of the war.
Left: The most widely used German night fighter was the radar-equipped Messerschmitt Me 110G.

position was then manned by the mid-upper gunner. When a fighter was spotted coming in below, the pilot was warned. He immediately throttled back and lowered 10 degrees of flap, which killed a lot of speed and gave the aircraft greater manoeuvrability. As the Lancaster slowed, the fighter started to overshoot beneath it.

Then, at the critical moment, Weber shoved the yoke fully forward, putting his huge bomber into a dive.

The result was a steep descent right on top of the offending fighter, accompanied by the fervent hope that the German pilot's reflexes were fast enough for him to get out of the way in time. Negative 'g'

made the Merlins cut through fuel starvation, temporarily extinguishing the exhaust flames and probably adding to the German pilot's visual problems. One dose of this nerve-racking treatment usually convinced him to go look for someone who didn't play so rough. No. 405 Squadron later adopted the ventral viewing hole on all its aircraft.

The other, official counter to fighter attack was the corkscrew. Few people (and fighter pilot's are no exception) are any good

Above: The upward slanting cannon installation known as Schrage Musik allowed the night fighters to attack from the blind spot below the Lancaster. (Alfred Price)

at deflection shooting, and the object of the corkscrew was to give the fighter a difficult target rather than a sitting duck.

It consisted of a steep turn of about 30 degrees combined with a dive of about 500ft (150m), followed immediately by a steep turn of about 30 degrees in the opposite direction combined with a climb of about 500ft (150m). These manoeuvres would be repeated as long as the fighter was in an attacking position. In this way, course and altitude could both be maintained, while few German fighter pilots were good enough to follow a

corkscrewing Lancaster and still get into a good firing position.

Instructions for the corkscrew were given by the rear gunner, although the mid-upper gunner or the bomb aimer, from a position in the astrodome, could also act as controller for the engagement. On spotting a fighter moving into position, the man making the sighting would call over the intercom, 'Prepare to corkscrew left [or right]', the rule being to break into the direction of the attack where possible. Then as the fighter moved into firing range, the executive order of 'Go' would be given, launching the bomber into a series of wild gyrations. The controls had to be handled roughly, making the corkscrew violent, if it was to be really effective. The Lancaster

could corkscrew very well even with a 12,000lb (5,400kg) bomb on board, while unladen it was extremely manoeuvrable for such a large machine.

McLean was credited with five German fighters shot down plus one probable

Survival depended on teamwork; total co-operation and trust between pilot and gunners. A classic engagement occurred on 15/16 March 1944, following an abortive raid on an aero engine factory at Metz, near the Franco-German border.

The Lancaster was from No. 617 Squadron, the Dam Busters, and had a mainly Canadian crew. The rear gunner

THE CORKSCREW MANOEUVRE

The corkscrew was a manoeuvre designed to make it very difficult for an enemy fighter to gain a firing position.

Above: Some Lancaster squadrons removed their dorsal turrets to improve performance.

was a Scot with original ideas about defensive tactics.

Men are born with differing abilities. Some have a natural flair for ball games; others play the piano outstandingly well. Flight Sergeant T.J. McLean's individual talent was for air-to-air gunnery. Credited with five German fighters shot down plus a probable on a previous tour of operations, he had volunteered to join No. 617 Squadron, widely regarded at that time as a suicide outfit, and had been assigned to Flying Officer Bill Duffy's crew as the tail gunner.

Past experience had convinced Tom McLean that the most effective loading for his guns was 45 per cent tracer and 55 per cent armour piercing, rather than the ball, tracer,

incendiary and armour piercing mix laid down in regulations. On this trip he had unofficially arranged for his preferred mix to be loaded for the first time, to his rear turret only. Not even the crew knew about this; the nose turret and the mid-upper, which was manned by Canadian Red Evans, both had standard loadings.

All aircraft were recalled without bombing as the target was under heavy cloud, but on the return trip across France the sky was cloudless, the stars shone brightly, and visibility was exceptionally good.

The first warning came from Monica, the tail warning radar, which picked up a contact to port at a range of about 3,600ft (1,100m). McLean strained his eyes, finally making out a dark

shape which appeared to be four-engined. At first it was assumed to be another returning bomber. Gradually the shape closed, which was unusual, and when it was about 2,700ft (820m) away, McLean realized that it was actually two night fighters in close proximity to one another. Following standard procedure, he told his pilot: 'Prepare to corkscrew port!'

THREE FIGHTERS

A Messerschmitt 109 single-seater fighter was sighted, flying abreast of the Lancaster about 1,500ft (450m) distant with navigation lights burning! The only explanation for this behaviour seemed to be that it was trying to distract the gunners from the fighters astern. At this moment, one of the two broke towards the Lancaster with obviously aggressive intentions. As it closed, McLean gave the order 'Go!' and Duffy commenced a violent corkscrew just as the fighter opened fire at extreme range. The Lancaster was hit, but not seriously, and

Above: German night fighters relied on ground control to position them in the bomber stream.

the German pilot broke away before lining up for another firing pass.

The Me 110 closed right in. Once again the big bomber corkscrewed, spoiling its aim, while McLean poured an angry burst of fire at it, hitting its port engine, then called 'Drop' over the intercom. Immediately, the flight engineer throttled back all four engines and the Lancaster rapidly lost speed, reducing the range faster than the German pilot had expected. On hearing his guns, the flight engineer once more opened the throttles in what was a very well-rehearsed manoeuvre.

On fire, the first Me 110 fell away into the void, and after making sure that the second fighter still remained in its original position, the rear gunner passed the word 'Easy' over the intercom. Upon hearing this, Bill Duffy relaxed the corkscrew manoeuvre.

The second night fighter, moved out to a position almost abeam of the Lancaster before commencing a curving attack from slightly below it. Again a violent evasive corkscrew, again a torrent of fire from both rear and mid-upper turrets, and the second fighter plunged earthwards, trailing a comet-like fiery tail.

The Me 109 shadowed them, just out of range. A visual search (Monica had been switched off) showed another Me 110 coming up behind, moving from port to starboard, then finally to dead astern.

Duffy spotted some cloud ahead and below, and pushed over into a shallow dive towards it. As he did so, the 110 came in, and the Lancaster went into a hard corkscrew, this time to starboard. McLean called: 'Drop!' The combination of corkscrew and speed loss spoiled the German pilot's aim completely, and he was met by a barrage of tracer and armour piercing bullets at close range. With pieces flying off, his aircraft entered a flat spin down into the abyss. A red glow lit the cloud layer below.

The second fighter plunged earthwards, trailing a comet-like fiery tail

At this, the Me 109 switched off its lights and turned in for an attack. The tail turret could not be brought to bear, but Red Evans in the mid-upper position returned fire, then, as the Me 109 passed beneath the bomber, quickly traversed his turret to speed it on its way on the far side. It never returned.

At this stage of the war, night fighters were encountered quite frequently. Sometimes, by dint of hard manoeuvring or escaping into cloud, the bomber managed

Below: In March 1944, a Lancaster of No. 617 Squadron accounted for three Me 110 night fighters like these in a single action. (Alfred Price)

to shake them off. At other times, the air gunners managed to beat off the attack.

There are several footnotes to this outstanding action. As noted in the preceding chapter, Monica could be homed on from very long ranges. It was almost certainly this which drew as many as four fighters to a single Lancaster.

The corkscrew saved the lives of hundreds of bomber crewmen

The role of the Me 109 was more mysterious. It seems hardly likely that it was acting as a controller, and it is doubtful that it was acting as a station-keeping aid for the twin-engined fighters; The most probable explanation is that it was a day fighter on a night cross-country that had forgotten to switch off its navigation lights, that just happened to be in the right place at the right time.

Flight Sergeant McLean's ammunition mix had much to commend it, inasmuch as the 'fright factor' of so much tracer, combined with the penetrative power of armour-piercing bullets, was potentially very effective. Some bomber crews preferred to fire no tracer at all on the grounds that this merely demonstrated the inadequate range of the .303 Brownings, thereby encouraging the night fighters to stand off and shoot back. In fact, McLean's idea would only be effective if the fighter could be lured in close, which of course was done.

There can be no doubt that the corkscrew saved the lives of hundreds of bomber crewmen.

RAF LANCASTER SQUADRONS, FORMED NOV 42–DEC 45

Sqn No.	First Op	Base Formed
101	20/21 Nov 42 Turin	Holme-on-Spalding Moor
103	21/22 Nov 42 Gardening	Elsham Wolds
12	3/4 Jan 43 Gardening	Wickenby
156	26/27 Jan 43 Lorient	Warboys
100	4/5 March 43 Gardening	Grimsby
115	20/21 March 43 Gardening	East Wretham
617	16/17 May 43 Dams Raid	Scampton
619	11/12 June 43 Dusseldorf	Woodhall Spa
7	8/9 July 43 Cologne	Oakington
514	3/4 Sept 43 Dusseldorf	Foulsham
166	22/23 Sept 43 Hanover	Kirmington
625	18/19 Oct 43 Hanover	Kelstern
626	10/11 Nov 43 Mondane	Wickenby
550	26/27 Nov 43 Berlin	Grimsby
576	2/3 Dec 43 Berlin	Elsham Wolds
630	18/19 Dec 43 Berlin	East Kirby

RAF LANCASTER SQUADRONS, FORMED JAN 44–MAY 45

Sqn No.	First Op	Base Formed
622	14/15 Jan 44 Brunswick	Mildenhall
15	January 44 not known	Mildenhall
635	22/23 March 44 Frankfurt	Downham Market
35	April 44 not known	Gravely
582	9/10 April 44 Lille	Little Staughton
90	June 44 not known	Tuddenham
149	17 Sept 44 Boulogne	Methwold
218	Sept 44 not known	Methwold
153	7 Oct 44 Emmerich	Kirmington
227	11 Oct 44 Walcheren	Bardney
186	18 Oct 44 Bonn	Tuddenham
170	19/20 Oct 44 Stuttgart	Kelstern
195	26 Oct 44 Leverkusen	Witchford
189	1 Nov 44 Homburg	Bardney
150	2 Nov 44 not known	Kiskerton
138	29 March 44 Hallendorf	Tuddenham

However, to be really effective it had to be violent, as if it was too gently executed, an experienced fighter pilot could simply follow the bomber through the manoeuvre. Properly carried out, it made the bomber a very difficult target, even by day.

In the closing months of the war, Lancasters carried out many daylight raids over Germany. Whereas American heavy bombers flew in tightly packed formations to take advantage of the massed firepower of their heavy machine guns, the reach of the Lancaster guns was less. The combination of fire and movement generally proved an effective defence.

SPECIAL SQUADRONS

As a weapon of war the Lancaster was a bludgeon rather than a rapier. But circumstances alter cases, and when precision weapons were devised for special targets, the Lancaster became a scalpel.

Ruhr industry was dependent on hydroelectric power and water, supplied by several huge dams. The destruction of the largest of these would have a devastating effect on German armaments output. But no ordinary bomb was capable of the task. In the Weybridge offices of Vickers, a quiet genius called Barnes Wallis applied himself to the problem.

The solution he came up with was a large mine, which had to be placed with absolute precision against the inner face of the dams by flying at exactly

Right: Provisioning Lancaster, with modified bomb bay for Upkeep, and dorsal turret removed.
Below: An inert Upkeep falls clear of the dropping aircraft during trials at Reculver.
Left: To mark the 34th anniversary of the raid, a Lancaster reflew the mission in 1977.

220mph (354km/hr) and 60ft (18m), releasing the weapon to an accuracy of less than one fifth of a second. A special squadron was trained specifically for the task. To lead it, Wing Commander Guy Gibson was chosen, and his aircrews were hand-picked from the best that Bomber Command could offer. They were predominantly British, but included 26 Canadians, 12 Australians, two New Zealanders and a single American. It is less widely known that the ground crews and support tradesmen were also hand-picked. Thus was the birth of No. 617 Squadron at Scampton in March 1943.

The mine, codenamed Upkeep, was a large cylindrical weapon weighing 9,250lb (4,200kg), over two-thirds of which was high explosive. Aircraft were taken from squadrons in No. 5 Group. The bomb bay doors were removed and special brackets fitted, together with an electric motor to get Upkeep rotating at 500 revolutions per minute before release. The bomb bay was faired to front and rear of the mine in order to reduce drag and the mid-upper turret was removed. Transformed in this manner, the Mk Is became Type 464 Provisioning Lancasters.

Above: Dr Barnes Wallis, creator of Upkeep, Tallboy and Grand Slam, pictured with the standard of No. 617 Squadron.

Other changes were made as they were found necessary. The entire raid was to be flown at low level, so bomb aimers assisted navigation using a specially prepared roller map. The nose turret had to be manned continually, which gave a role to the otherwise redundant mid-upper gunner, and stirrups were fitted to prevent him treading on the bomb aimer's head in moments of excitement.

Achieving the exact height

over water at night proved difficult, but was solved by fitting Aldis lamps in the nose camera port and behind the bomb bay, angled so that the two spots of light touched at exactly 60ft (18m) and offset to starboard where they were easily seen by the navigator, who monitored height on the attack run.

This was the first use of the 'Master Bomber' technique, later to become standard

Standard bombsights could not be used, but the Dann sight, made up from a plywood triangle, an eyepiece and a couple of nails, worked well in practice, while pilots had marks on the windshield to aid them in lining up on a target.

Close control of the operation was vital, and for this Gibson had all Lancasters fitted with fighter-type VHF radios. This was the first use of the 'Master Bomber' technique, later to become standard throughout Bomber Command

At low level, the Lancasters

might have to fight their way into and out of the target area, while the Mohne Dam at least was known to be defended. Three thousand rounds per gun was carried, giving 157 seconds of firing time. All of it was tracer, to keep the heads of the German gunners down.

OPERATION CHASTISE

The attack on the dams was set for 16/17 May, when good weather was forecast the moon was full, and the water level behind the dams was at its highest. Nineteen Lancasters took off in three waves. The first wave consisted of nine aircraft in three Vics of three, led by Gibson. Its primary targets were the Mohne and Eder Dams. The second wave, of five Lancasters flying individually, took a more northerly route. Their target was the Sorpe Dam, of different construction to the first two and needing a

Below: Provisioning Lancaster at dispersal, showing the drive belt that rotated Upkeep at 500rpm before release.

Above: *Gibson leads his crew aboard Lancaster ED932, AJ-G, prior to taking off on the Dams Raid. His aircraft survived the war, only to be scrapped.*
Left: *ED825, AJ-T, was the reserve aircraft for the Dams Raid, and was flown by Flight Lieutenant McCarthy when his own machine went unserviceable.*

different mode of attack, albeit with the same weapon. The third and final wave of five air-craft also flew individually. Taking off two hours after the others, it was a reserve to be used against the main targets if needed, otherwise to attack sec-ondary dams in the area.

Opposition to the passage of the first wave was moderate, but Bill Astell's Lancaster fell to

light flak. The remainder arrived over the Mohne Dam on time. Gibson later wrote, 'In that light it looked squat and heavy and unconquerable; it looked grey and solid in the moonlight, as though it were part of the countryside itself and just as immovable. A struc-ture like a battleship was show-ering out flak all along its length.'

After circling to make an assessment of the situation, Gibson began his attack run, curving in down-moon, past the hills and low over the water. He had his spotlights on for height and the light flak saw him coming and opened up with everything they had. Bomb Aimer Spam Spafford released the mine and they swept low over the dam. From the air it

Above: Dams Raid debrief. Standing L to R; Air Chief Marshal Arthur Harris, Air Marshal Cochrane. Seated; intelligence officer, Spafford and Taerum of Gibson's crew.

looked like a perfect drop, but in fact the mine had fallen short.

Next came Hopgood, whose aircraft caught fire and crashed, while his mine bounced clear; Gibson then ordered Australian Mick Martin to attack. Martin's Lancaster was hit, and its mine was released off course to detonate harmlessly. Dinghy Young made a perfect run and deposited his Upkeep right against the dam wall. Even as Maltby made his run, the parapet crumbled and the dam burst. His mine added to the breach made by Young.

ON TO THE EDER

Martin and Maltby headed for home, while Gibson and Young led the three remaining armed Lancasters to the Eder Dam. Australian David Shannon made three attempts without being able to line up correctly. Henry Maudslay then tried twice, with no luck. On Shannon's fourth attempt his mine exploded against the dam, causing a small breach.

Maudslay tried once more, but his mine hit the parapet with him just above it. It was assumed that he and his crew died in the explosion, but badly damaged, he had limped some 130 miles (210km) towards home before falling to flak.

Only one armed Lancaster remained, and on the second attempt its pilot, Les Knight, made a perfect run. His mine punched a hole clean through the giant dam wall,

The first aircraft to be lost during Operation Chastise was that of Byers. Les Munro's Lancaster was damaged by flak had to abandon the mission, while Geoff Rice, flying as low as possible, hit the sea and lost his mine. He also was forced to

OPERATION CHASTISE, PARTICIPANTS

Pilot	Letters	A/C No.
First Wave		
Wg Cdr G.P. Gibson	AJ-G	ED 932/G
Flt Lt J. V. Hopgood	AJ-M	ED 925/G
Flt Lt H.B. Martin	AJ-P	ED 909/G
Sqn Ldr H. M. Young	AJ-A	ED 887/G
Flt Lt D.J. H. Maltby	AJ-J	ED 906/G
Flt Lt D.J. Shannon	AJ-L	ED 929/G
Sqn Ldr H.M. Maudslay	AJ-Z	ED 937/G
Flt Lt W. Astell	AJ-B	ED 864/G
Plt Off L. G. Knight	AJ-N	ED 912/G
Second Wave		
Flt Lt J.C. McCarthy	AJ-T	ED 825/G
Flt Lt R.N.G. Barlow	AJ-E	ED 927/G
Flt Lt J. L. Munro	AJ-W	ED 921/G
Plt Off V.W. Byers	AJ-K	ED 934/G
Plt Off G. Rice	AJ-H	ED 936/G
Third and Reserve Wave		
Plt Off W.H.T. Ottley	AJ-C	ED 910/G
Plt Off L.J. Burpee	AJ-S	ED 865/G
Flt Sgt K.S. Brown	AJ-F	ED 918/G
Flt Sgt W.C. Townsend	AJ-O	ED 886/G
Flt Sgt C.T. Anderson	AJ-Y	ED 914/G

NB: McCarthy was originally scheduled to fly ED 923/G, but this aircraft developed a hydraulic leak.

return. Barlow, an Australian, was claimed by flak just inside the German border, and of the ill-fated second wave, only the American, Joe McCarthy, survived. After making nine runs against the Sorpe he dropped his mine on the tenth, but without any visible results.

The final wave fared only slightly better. Burpee, a young Canadian from Gibson's previous squadron, went down over Holland, while Ottley lasted only a little longer. Both fell to light flak. Of the other three, Anderson was the least lucky. Last off, the fates conspired to force him to abandon the mission without attacking.

One Victoria Cross and no fewer than 33 other awards were made

Brown attacked the Sorpe after several attempts, like McCarthy with no visible result, while Townsend, on course for the Mohne Dam, was diverted to the Ennerpe Dam instead. After several brushes with flak, he emerged into an area made unrecognisable by floods from the already breached Mohne and Eder. Finally Townsend arrived at what appeared to be the Ennerpe and dropped his mine, but post-war evidence seems to indicate that he attacked the Bever Dam 5 miles (8km) away.

The entire German air defence system was by now alert to the events. Apart from Maudslay, the only other loss was Dinghy Young. Hit by flak as he recrossed the coast, he went down into the sea. Others,

Above: The Dortmund-Ems Canal, scene of the Dam Busters' worst disaster, was finally breached in 1944. (Alfred Price)
Below: Under the leadership of Group Captain Leonard Cheshire VC, No.617 Squadron became the most accurate heavy bomber squadron of the war.

including McCarthy, Brown and Townsend, had eventful return flights, but recovered safely to Scampton.

Success had been expensive. Eight Lancasters failed to return home; of the 56 men on board, only three survived. Guy Gibson

was awarded the Victoria Cross, Britain's highest decoration, and 33 other awards were made to participants in the raid.

The Dams Raid has long passed into legend. No. 617 Squadron had established itself as an elite unit.

A new role was sought for No. 617 Squadron. The modified Lancasters were replaced by standard Mk IIIs, and the crews started intensive high- and low-level training. Wing Commander Guy Gibson was replaced by Squadron Leader George Holden. On 30 August 1943, the squadron was ordered to Coningsby for low-level attacks.

DORTMUND-EMS

The next target was the well defended Dortmund-Ems canal, a strategic artery in the German transport system. 617 squadron was to try, using the new 12,000lb (5,440kg) high-capacity bomb.

Low cloud in the target area caused the first attempt to be recalled, minus Maltby, who went into the sea after hitting someone's slipstream at low level. The next night they tried again. It was a disaster. Heavy mist in the target area foiled all

Above: No. 9 Squadron, pictured with its famous W4964 Johnny Walker, *was something of an elite outfit. Its total of 106 operations took in the Ruhr, Hamburg, Berlin and Peenemunde and Tirpitz.*

attempts to bomb accurately, while the defences claimed five Lancasters, among them those of Holden and Les Knight. The squadron rapidly gained the reputation of being a suicide outfit. Six aircraft, with six more from No. 619 Squadron, went out again the next night to attack the Antheor Viaduct in southern France at low level. This was another failure and the squadron was withdrawn from operations while changes took place.

One was the introduction of the Stabilizing Automatic Bomb Sight, or SABS, introduced by Arthur 'Talking Bomb' Richardson, whom we last saw over Gdynia with Guy Gibson. No. 617 was now to become a medium and high-level 'sniper' squadron. The other was the arrival of Wing Commander Leonard Cheshire to command on 11 November.

A more exacting test came on the night of 8/9 February

Cheshire was introspective and unconventional, and arguably the most inspirational bomber leader of the war. Always leading from the front, he was described by David Shannon as a pied piper; people followed him gladly. He set out to make the squadron live, breathe and eat bombing accuracy.

Several missions followed against pin point targets, but they were not a great success. Oboe marking was too inaccurate against small targets. Cheshire and Martin worked out between them that only low-level marking in a dive would be good enough, and on 3/4 January 1944, they tried it against a flying bomb site at Freval. By the illumination of flares, they marked from 400ft (120m), and 12,000lb (5,440kg) bombs from the remainder of the formation as they obliterated the target.

A more exacting test came on 8/9 February, by which time No. 617 has moved to Woodhall Spa. The aero engine works at

Limoges were almost totally destroyed, while damage to French houses close by was minimal. Other raids followed with equal success, the only failure during this time being another attempt against the Antheor Viaduct.

To mark heavily defended targets, a smaller and faster aircraft was needed. The obvious choice was a Mosquito, which Cheshire duly acquired, bringing the low-level marking career of the Lancaster to an end. At the same time, 617 became pathfinders and Main Force leaders to No. 5 Group.

D-DAY DECEPTION

The first of these was Operation Taxable, a deception ploy that was designed to make the Germans think that a vast invasion fleet was moving towards Cap d'Antifer, some 20 miles (30km) north of Le Havre. This was done by 16 Lancasters, flying precise speeds and courses, dropping Window at five-second intervals. Packed with Window bundles,

Above: Lurking in the Norwegian fjords, the German battleship Tirpitz *kept strong British naval forces tied down.*

they maintained the deception for some eight hours until dawn broke to reveal only an empty sea to the expectant Germans.

The second was the introduction of the Tallboy, a new 12,000lb (5,440kg) bomb with exceptionally good ballistic qualities and penetrative power. Like Upkeep, Tallboy was the idea of Dr Barnes Wallis, and only the SABS equipped Dam Busters could bomb accurately enough to make the best use of this new and devastating weapon.

One of the few south-to-north rail routes still open in France at this time passed through a tunnel near Saumur, on the Loire. Shortly after midnight on 8/9 June the squadron arrived, and Cheshire placed two red spot fires in the mouth of the tunnel. Nineteen Tallboy armed Lancasters moved in, plus another six with conventional loads. The result was a series of enormous craters that tore the line to pieces. One Tallboy had

impacted the hillside and bored its way down to explode inside the tunnel almost 60ft (18m) below, completely blocking it.

More precision raids followed; concrete E-boat pens at Le Havre, and V-Weapon sites scattered around the Pas-de-Calais and elsewhere. In July, command of the squadron passed from Cheshire to Wing Commander Willie Tait DSO DFC.

617 VERSUS *TIRPITZ*

The German battleship *Tirpitz* lying in Alten Fjord in Norway, tied down British naval units which would have been better employed elsewhere.

Even from the most northerly of British airfields Alten Fjord was outside Lancaster range. A deal was struck with the Russians, who made Yagodnik,

---

MOHNE DAM

'The gunners had seen us coming. They could see us coming with our spotlights on for over two miles away. Now they opened up and tracers began swirling towards us; some were even bouncing on the smooth surface of the lake. This was a horrible moment: we were being dragged along at four miles a minute, almost against our will, towards the things we were going to destroy. I think at that moment the boys did not want to go. I know I did not want to go.'

WING COMMANDER G. PENROSE GIBSON VC, DSO, DFC.

EVADING RADAR

LEGEND
- ⚓ Tirpitz at Tromso
- —— Bombers' Route
- ⌒ 1500 Foot Radar cover
- ◉ Radar Stations

NORTH SEA

TROMSO

NORWAY SWEDEN

LOSSIEMOUTH

0 ——— 100
MILES

Evading the German radar cover by flying in over Sweden, Nos 617 and 9 Squadrons achieved complete surprise in their third attack on the *Tirpitz*.

near Arkhangelsk, available as a refuelling stop. For this and subsequent anti-*Tirpitz* operations, No. 617 was joined by No. 9 Squadron, which, although fitted with the Mk XIV vector bombsight, was also something of an elite outfit. Of the 36 Lancasters detailed, 24 carried Tallboys; the others were loaded with 12 Johnny Walker Diving Mines each, an original but ineffective weapon.

The arid nearly ended in disaster when bad weather over Russia forced many Lancasters to land where they could. Six were abandoned in the marshes. On 15 September the attack was finally mounted, and the German early warning system proved equal to the task and a smokescreen quickly obscured the battleship. A single Tallboy hit was scored, but *Tirpitz* was still afloat. The Kriegsmarine

her south to Tromso for use as a floating German gun battery; she would never sail again, but this was not known either.

Calculations showed that fitting internal fuel tanks in the fuselage of the Lancasters would allow *Tirpitz* to be attacked from Lossiemouth. On 20 October, 40 aircraft of 617 and 9 Squadrons set out on the long haul to Tromso. A combination of poor weather and enemy fighters made this attack a failure, and few crews even so much as saw the battleship.

They achieved complete surprise and scored multiple hits

The final attack on *Tirpitz* was mounted on 12 November, with 31 Lancasters from both squadrons. Approaching from the Swedish side, they achieved complete surprise and scored multiple hits. The *Tirpitz* slowly sank, but the water was too shallow for her to sink completely.

Tait was now replaced by 617's final wartime commander, Group Captain John Fauquier,

Below: 'Twas a famous victory!' Tirpitz *lies in Tromso Fjord, having capsized after multiple bomb hits.*

a Canadian. Tallboys now rained down on the U-boat pens at Bergen, and the Bielefeld Viaduct. The latter proved hard to hit and 54 Tallboys were aimed at it during February 1945 without result. But now Barnes Wallis' 22,000lb (10 tonne) Grand Slam was ready for use.

Only the Lancaster B.I Special could carry Grand Slam. This aircraft had strengthened main gear, nose and dorsal turrets deleted, and the bomb doors removed, plus other minor modifications. The crew was reduced to four.

The first Grand Slam raid took place on 14 March 1945. Five days later, six Grand Slams and 13 Tallboys were hauled to the rail viaduct at Arnsberg, where, every bomb fell within a 600ft (180m) radius. To underline the astounding level of the bombing accuracy, when the

bridge at Nienberg was attacked on 22 March the first four aircraft sent in to bomb scored direct hits from a Grand Slam at one end and a Tallboy at the other and lifted the entire centre span into the air, where it was hit straight in the middle by another Tallboy!

The final mission was against Berchtesgaden, Hitler's redoubt

One more bridge was smashed, then the U-boat pens at Farge were attacked. Two Grand Slams went clean through the 23ft (7m) thick reinforced concrete roof and exploded inside, while shock waves from 10 near misses shattered the foundations. 617 Squadron's final mission was against Berchtesgaden, Hitler's southern redoubt, in the final days of the war.

Above: *Lancasters of No. 101 Squadron were identifiable by their Air-borne Cigar masts. This one is unloading incendiaries.*

There was one other special Lancaster squadron, No. 101, whose aircraft, distinguished externally by three large aerials, carried the top secret ABC (Air-borne Cigar) from October 1943. ABC was a jammer working on the German night fighter frequency, and required an additional member of crew to operate it. Lancasters of No. 101 Squadron carried a full load of bombs and, scattered throughout the bomber stream, accompanied Main Force on nearly every raid. In the later stages of the war, with multi-pronged raids the norm, 101 became the biggest Lancaster squadron of all, with a final complement of 42 aircraft.

THE MESSERSCHMITT
109

Messerschmitt Me 109G-14

1 Starboard navigation light
2 Starboard wingtip
3 Fixed trim tab
4 Starboard Frise-type aileron
5 Flush-riveted stressed wing-skinning
6 Handley Page leading-edge automatic slot
7 Slot control linkage
8 Slot equalizer rod
9 Aileron control linkage
10 Fabric-covered flap section
11 Wheel fairing
12 Port fuselage machine-gun ammunition-feed fairing
13 Port Rheinmetall-Borsig 13mm MG 131 machine-gun
14 Engine accessories
15 Starboard machine-gun trough
16 Daimler Benz DB 605AM 12-cylinder inverted-vee liquid-cooled engine
17 Detachable cowling panel
18 Oil filter access
19 Oil tank
20 Propeller pitch-change mechanism
21 VDM electrically-operated constant-speed propeller
22 Spinner
23 Engine-mounted cannon muzzle

24 Blast tube
25 Propeller hub
26 Spinner back plate
27 Auxiliary cooling intakes
28 Cooling header tank
29 Anti-vibration rubber engine-mounting pads
30 Elektron forged engine bearer
31 Engine bearer support strut attachment
32 Plug leads
33 Exhaust manifold fairing strip
34 Ejector exhausts
35 Cowling fasteners
36 Oil cooler
37 Oil cooler intake
38 Starboard mainwheel
39 Oil cooler outlet flap
40 Wing root fillet
41 Wing/fuselage fairing
42 Firewall/bulkhead
43 Supercharger air intake
44 Supercharger assembly
45 20mm cannon magazine drum
46 13mm machine-gun ammunition feed
47 Engine bearer upper attachment
48 Ammunition feed fairing

49 13mm Rheinmetall-Borsig MG 131 machine-gun breeches
50 Instrument panel
51 20mm Mauser MG 151/20 cannon breech
52 Heelrests
53 Rudder pedals
54 Undercarriage emergency retraction cables
55 Fuselage frame
56 Wing/fuselage fairing
57 Undercarriage emergency retraction headwheel (outboard)

58 Tail trim handwheel (inboard)
59 Seat harness
60 Throttle lever
61 Control column
62 Cockpit ventilation inlet
63 Revi 16B reflector gunsight (folding)
64 Armoured windshield frame
65 Anti-glare gunsight screen
66 90 mm armourglass windscreen
67 Galland-type clear-vision hinged canopy
68 Framed armourglass head/back panel
69 Canopy contoured frame
70 Canopy hinges (starboard)
71 Canopy release catch
72 Pilot's bucket-type seat (8 mm back armour)
73 Underfloor contoured fuel tank (88 Imp gal/400 litres of 87 octane B4)
74 Fuselage frame

348

75 Circular access panel
76 Tail trimming cable conduit
77 Wireless leads
78 MW50 (methanel/water) tank
   (25 Imp gal/114 litres capacity)

79 Handhold
80 Fuselage decking
81 Aerial mast
82 D/F loop
83 Oxygen cylinders (three)
84 Filler pipe
85 Wireless equipment packs
   (FuG 16ZY communications and
   FuG 25a IFF)

86 Main fuel filler cap
87 Aerial
88 Fuselage top keel
   (connector stringer)
89 Aerial lead-in
90 Fuselage skin plating sections
91 U-stringers
92 Fuselage frames (monocoque
   construction)
93 Tail trimming cables
94 Tailfin root fairing
95 Starboard fixed tailplane
96 Elevator balance
97 Starboard elevator
98 Geared elevator tab
99 All-wooden tailfin construction
100 Aerial attachment
101 Rudder upper hinge bracket
102 Rudder post
103 Fabric-covered wooden rudder
    structure
104 Geared rudder tab
105 Rear navigation light
106 Port elevator
107 Geared elevator tab

108 Tailplane structure
109 Rudder actuating linkage
110 Elevator control horn
111 Elevator connecting rod
112 Elevator control quadrant
113 Tailwheel leg cuff
114 Castoring non-retractable
    tailwheel
115 Lengthened tailwheel/leg
116 Access panel
117 Tailwheel shock-strut
118 Lifting point
119 Rudder cable
120 Elevator cables
121 First-aid pack
122 Air bottles
123 Fuselage access panel
124 Bottom keel
    (connector stringer)
125 Ventral IFF aerial
126 Master compass
127 Elevator control linkage
128 Wing root fillet
129 Camber-changing flap
130 Ducted coolant radiator
131 Wing stringers
132 Wing rear pick-up point
133 Spar/fuselage upper pin joint
    (horizontal)
134 Spar/fuselage lower pin joint
    (vertical)
135 Flaps equalizer rod
136 Rüstsatz R3 auxiliary fuel tank
    ventral rack
137 Undercarriage electrical
    interlock
138 Wing horizontal pin forward
    pick-up
139 Undercarriage retraction jack
    mechanism

140 Undercarriage pivot-bevel
141 Auxiliary fuel tank (Rüstsatz
    R3) of 66 Imp gal (3000
    litre) capacity
142 Mainwheel leg fairing
143 Mainwheel oleo leg
144 Brake lines
145 Mainwheel fairing
146 Port mainwheel
147 Leading-edge skin
148 Port mainwheel well
149 Wing spar
150 Flap actuating linkage
151 Fabric-covered control surfaces
152 Slotted flap structure
153 Leading-edge slot actuating
    mechanism
154 Slot equalizer rod
155 Handley Page automatic
    leading-edge slot
156 Wing stringers
157 Spar flange decrease
158 Wing ribs
159 Flush-riveted stressed wing-
    skinning
160 Metal-framed Frise-type aileron
161 Fixed trim tab
162 Wingtip construction
163 Port navigation light
164 Angled pitot head
165 Rüstsatz R6 optional
    underwing cannon gondola
166 14-point plug connection
167 Electrical junction box
168 Cannon rear mounting bracket
169 20mm Mauser MG 151 20mm
    cannon
170 Cannon front mounting
    bracket
171 Ammunition feed chute
172 Ammunition magazine drum
173 Underwing panel
174 Gondola fairing
175 Cannon barrel

The story of the Messerschmitt 109 began in 1934. Early that year the Air Ministry issued a requirement for an advanced monoplane fighter to replace the Heinkel 51 and Arado 68 biplanes then about to enter service, and invited aircraft companies to submit designs.

The early 1930s saw rapid advances in aviation technology, especially in the design of fighter planes. The new generation of fighters was quite different in shape and in performance from those that had gone before. Out went the fabric-covered strut-braced biplane with its open cockpit and fixed undercarriage. In its place came the sleek low-wing monoplane with an all-metal structure, enclosed cockpit and a retractable undercarriage. These new fighters were much faster than their predecessors in the climb, in the dive and in level flight. Also, in their developed versions, they were more heavily armed.

Chief designer Willi Messerschmitt had no previous experience of designing fighter aircraft

---

At that time the Bavarian Aircraft Company (Bayerische Flugzeugwerke) was a little-known aircraft firm. It was turning out small batches of planes built under licence for the Luftwaffe. Willi Messerschmitt, the company's brilliant young chief designer, had no previous experience of designing a fighter. He did have great flair and originality and ambition.

Messerschmitt's new fighter used almost every innovation of the period. It was a clean-lined all-metal low-wing monoplane with a retractable undercarriage and an enclosed cockpit. The small wing was fitted with retractable flaps and leading-edge slots. Messerschmitt designed the fighter around the new 610hp Junkers Jumo 210 engine. Work on the airframe advanced more rapidly than that on the power plant, and it was clear that the latter would not be ready in time. Messerschmitt had to look elsewhere for an engine to get his prototype into the air. Ironically, in view of later events, his choice of engine was a 695hp Rolls-Royce Kestrel imported from Great Britain.

Opposite: Ground crewmen reloading the wing and engine-mounted 7.9 mm machine guns of a 'Caesar' of IIIrd Gruppe of Fighter Geschwader 51. Scrupulous cleanliness was essential, any grit or dirt on the rounds was liable to cause a stoppage during firing.
Below: The first prototype Me 109 ground-running its Rolls-Royce Kestrel engine, at about the time of its maiden flight in September 1935. (via Ethell)

MESSERSCHMITT 109 B-1

Type Single-seat interceptor fighter.
Armament Two Rheinmetall-Borsig 7.9mm machine guns mounted on top of the engine and synchronized to fire through the airscrew (500 rounds per gun).
Power Plant One Junkers Jumo 210 Da inverted V-12 liquid cooled engine developing 635 horse power for take off.
Dimensions Span 32ft 4$^1/_2$in (9.87m); length 28ft (8.55m).
Weight Normal operational take off, 4,741lb (2150kg).
Performance Maximum speed 289mph at 13,100ft (465km/hr at 4,000m). Service ceiling 26,900ft (98,200m).

MESSERSCHMITT 109 C-1

Type Single-seat interceptor fighter.
Armament Four Rheinmetall-Borsig MG 17 7.9 mm machine guns. Two synchronized to fire through the airscrew (500 rounds per gun), two mounted in wings (420rpg).
Power Plant Junkers Jumo 210 Ga inverted V-12 liquid cooled engine developing 700 hp for take off. This and subsequent versions were fitted with direct fuel injection engines.
Dimensions Span 32ft 4in (9.87m); length 28ft (8.55m).
Weight Normal operational take off 5,060lb (2,290kg).
Performance Maximum speed 292mph (470km/hr) at 14,770ft (4,500m). Service ceiling 27,570ft (8,400m).

Initially called the Bayerische Flugzeugwerke (Bf) 109, the new fighter made its maiden flight in September 1935. That was one month before the prototype Hurricane and six months before the prototype Spitfire, its two main rivals.

The Arado, Heinkel and Focke Wulf companies also designed for the Luftwaffe. Messerschmitt's design had a maximum speed of 290mph (467km/hr) which was 17mph (27km/hr) faster than any of the rivals and its handling characteristics were also superior.

Below: Line up of early production Me 109 'Bertas', awaiting delivery at the Bayerische Flugzeugwerke factory early in 1937. At this time the aircraft was the most potent fighter in service anywhere in the world. (via Schliephake)

Above: An Me 109 'Caesar' of Fighter Gruppe 152.

INTO PRODUCTION

Following the service trials, the Luftwaffe placed an order for ten more Me 109 prototypes. A second prototype, powered by the Jumo 210A engine, joined the test programme in January 1936. In the autumn of 1936 the Luftwaffe announced that the Me 109 was to be its standard single-engined fighter type. The Me 109B, the 'Berta', was the initial production variant. It was powered by the Jumo 210 engine and carried an armament of three (later four) 7.9 mm machine guns.

In February 1937 production Me 109Bs began emerging from the Augsburg factory. The first Luftwaffe unit to receive the new fighter was IInd Gruppe of Fighter Geschwader 132 based at Jueterbog near Berlin.

Early in 1938 the next major version of the Me 109 appeared, the Me 109C 'Caesar'. This featured several detailed improvements and its Jumo 210 engine was fitted with fuel injection. The initial version carried four machine guns, two on top of the engine and one each wing close to the root. The 'Caesar' was built in moderately large numbers and the variant equipped several fighter units.

MESSERSCHMITT 109 D-1

Type Single-seat interceptor fighter.
Armament Two Rheinmetall-Borsig MG 17 7.9 mm machine guns mounted on top of the engine synchronized to fire through the airscrew (500 rounds per gun). One Oerlikon MG FF 20mm cannon mounted under the engine and firing through the spinner (60 rounds).
Power Plant One Daimler Benz DB 600Aa inverted V-12 liquid cooled engine developing 986hp for take off.
Dimensions Span 32ft 4in (9.87m); length 28ft 2in (8.60m).
Weight Normal operational take off, 5,336lb (2,420kg).
Performance Maximum speed 356mph (574km/hr) at 11,490ft (3,500m). Service ceiling 32,800ft (10,000m).

Following hard on the heels of the 'Caesar' came the Me 109D 'Dora'. This was fitted with the new Daimler Benz 600 engine which developed 960 horse power. The more powerful engine gave a much better

MESSERSCHMITT 109 E-1

Type Single-seat general purpose fighter.
Armament Four Rheinmetall-Borsig MG 17 7.9mm machine guns in fuselage and wings. Or two MG17 machine guns and two MG FF cannon. Some aircraft were modified to carry a rack for single 110lb (45kg) bomb.
Power Plant One Daimler Benz DB 601A inverted V-12 liquid cooled engine developing 1,175hp for take off.
Dimensions Span 32ft 4in (9.87m); length 28ft 4in (8.64m).
Weight Normal operational take off, 5,535lb (2,510kg).
Performance Maximum speed 356mph at 13,130ft (573km/hr at 4,000m). Service ceiling 34,450ft (10,500m).

The fine performance of the 'Dora' was undermined by difficulties with the DB 600 engine

performance and the 'Dora' could reach a maximum speed of 356mph at 11,400ft (574km/hr at 3,500m). It also had greater fire power, with a 20 mm cannon firing through the propeller spinner and two machine guns mounted on top

Above: The Heinkel 51 biplane was the main fighter type serving with the Condor Legion during the early stages of the Civil War in Spain. It was outclassed by the Soviet-built fighter types that it came up against.

of the engine cowling. The DB 600 engine suffered serious teething troubles, and the 'Dora' was not popular with pilots. Fewer than two hundred were built before this variant passed out of production.

In September 1938 the so-called Munich Crisis broke, as a result of Adolf Hitler's claim that the Sudetenland area of Czechoslovakia should be incorporated into Germany. It seemed that Great Britain might go to war to help the Czechs retain this territory, but in the end the British prime minister, Neville Chamberlain, acceded to Hitler's demand. Several commentators have said that the move was necessary to

allow Britain time to re-arm. They neglect the fact that the Luftwaffe, too, was in no state to engage in a major conflict. Its fighter force possessed 583 Me 109s of all versions, of which 510 were serviceable. Most of these aircraft were the 'Bertas', with smaller numbers of the later 'Caesar' and 'Dora' variants. Eight fighter Gruppen had equipped, or were in the process of re-equipping, with the Me 109. The rest operated outdated biplane fighter types.

The next version of the Me 109, the first built in really large numbers, was the 'Emil' powered by the new Daimler Benz 601 engine. Based on the DB 600 engine that powered the 'Dora', the new engine was fitted with fuel injection and a more effective supercharger. It was more reliable than the earlier engine. The initial batches of Me 109Es reached the Luftwaffe early in 1939. The main production

version was armed with two 7.9 mm machine guns in the fuselage and two 20 mm cannon in the wings.

MESSERSCHMITT AG

The management of the Bayerische Flugzeugwerke decided to capitalize on the international reputation won by its now-famous chief designer, and so they appointed Willi Messerschmitt to the posts of Chairman and Managing Director, changing the company's name to Messerschmitt AG. The firm's two factories were turning out the fighter in large numbers, yet there were insufficient to meet the needs of the expanding Luftwaffe. Four other aircraft companies, Arado, Erla, Fieseler and Focke Wulf, were producing the Me 109E under licence. Production of the fighter reached 130 per month and it quickly replaced most of the earlier versions.

IN ACTION IN SPAIN

In the summer of 1936 civil war broke out in Spain. General Franco, the Nationalist leader, appealed to Adolf Hitler for help. The Luftwaffe dispatched a force, the Condor Legion, to fight alongside the Nationalists. The Soviet Union had been supplying aircraft to Spain's Republican government. The Luftwaffe pilots found that the Soviet-built Polikarpov I-16 monoplane had a clear edge in performance over their Heinkel 51 biplanes.

To test the new fighter under combat conditions, late in 1936 the Luftwaffe shipped three Me 109 prototypes to Spain. These operated from a primitive airfield near Seville and there were severe problems. Each of the handmade prototypes had components unique to itself, which made it difficult to keep them serviceable. After a few weeks, and without seeing action, the fighters returned to Germany.

Below: The Soviet Polikarpov I-16 was the best fighter in the Nationalist Air Force in Spain. It was clearly superior to the He 51.

THE 109 TRIUMPHS

The trial highlighted the need for better ground support for the Me 109. Several Luftwaffe pilots flew the prototypes in Spain, and they had no doubt that the Me 109 was superior to any of the Soviet-built fighters.

Production Me 109 'Bertas' emerged from the Augsburg factory in February 1937. Sixteen of these machines were loaded, in crates, on a freighter which delivered them to the Condor Legion.

The first unit in Spain to re-equip with the Me 109B was the 2nd Staffel of Fighter Gruppe 88. When it became operational in April 1937 there was a lull in the ground fighting. Then, in July, the Republican forces launched a powerful offensive near Madrid. The Me 109 Staffel joined the battle, escorting Junkers 52 bombers in delivering attacks on Republican troop positions.

The Me 109 proved superior to the Soviet-built I-16. It was faster in level flight and in the dive and had a higher operational ceiling. The I-16 was more manoeuvrable, especially below

10,000ft (3,048m). Republican fighter pilots tried to lure the Messerschmitts into turning fights below 10,000ft, but with little success. German fighter pilots soon learned that their machine's better performance at altitude gave them the advantage of being able to accept or refuse combat, as they chose.

The new German fighter carried radios but the sets gave such poor reception, that many pilots flew with them turned off.

The Me 109 would deliver a series of high-speed diving attacks to break up the enemy

---

Normally the Me 109s would patrol at altitudes between 16,000ft (4,877m) and 20,000ft (6,096m), which gave them a big height advantage over their opponents. On sighting enemy aircraft, the German formation leader would usually move his force into an attacking

Above: The arrival of the Me 109B in Spain in the spring of 1937 gave German pilots a machine in which they could engage the I-16 with confidence. This example belonged to 2nd Staffel of Fighter Gruppe 88 and wears the markings carried by aircraft of the Condor Legion.

position above the prey. The Messerschmitts then delivered a series of high-speed diving attacks. They repeated the process until the enemy formation broke up, or the German fighters ran low on fuel or ammunition. Provided the Me 109s maintained their high speed and did not get drawn into turning fights, they were almost unbeatable.

Some of the fiercest aerial fighting over Spain took place early in 1938, during the Republican offensive near Teruel. By then both Staffeln of Fighter Gruppe 88 had re-equipped with the Me 109. On 7 February Hauptmann Gotthardt Handrick, the Gruppe commander, was leading his unit during a bomber escort mission. Over the battle area he sighted a formation of twenty-two Soviet-built Tupolev SB-2 bombers moving in to attack a Nationalist troop position. Seeing no Republican fighters in the area, he led a concerted attack on the enemy bombers. Several of the latter were shot down, and when I-16s finally arrived on the scene they too suffered losses. The Me 109s destroyed ten enemy bombers and two fighters, without loss to themselves.

Leutnant Wilhelm Balthasar delivered a succession of diving attacks on an escorted bomber formation and shot down three bombers and a fighter, all within a space of six minutes.

The Me 109 achieved striking success over Spain, although the number of these fighters sent to fight in the conflict was never large. Up to December 1938 only fifty-five 'Bertas', 'Caesars' and 'Doras' had reached Spain and only thirty-seven were currently on the strength of Fighter Gruppe 88.

However, such was the 109's superiority that these few aircraft had been sufficient to establish air supremacy over the entire country.

In March 1939, after suffering heavy losses, the Republicans were forced to surrender. Following the cessation of hostilities the Condor Legion returned home to Germany, leaving behind some fifty Me 109s for incorporation in General Franco's Air Force.

POISED FOR POLAND

By the summer of 1939 Adolf Hitler judged that he had gained as much as he could in Europe by bluff alone. To advance further, he would have to demonstrate Germany's military might and commit its armed forces. Now his forces were poised to launch an all-out onslaught against Poland. In the next chapter we shall observe how the Me 109 units fared during the early months of the Second World War.

On 1 September 1939 German ground forces invaded Poland, with full support from the Luftwaffe. At that time the Me 109 force was comprised of twenty-four Gruppen and five independent Staffeln, with a total of nearly 1,100 fighters. More than two-thirds of the units flew the 'Emil', the rest operated the older 'Berta', 'Caesar' and 'Dora' versions. Only about one-fifth of the Me 109 force, five of the twenty-four Gruppen operating the type, was earmarked to take part in the campaign in Poland. The other units remained in western Germany, ready to meet any onslaught from the Royal Air Force and the French Air Force. There was no large-scale Allied reaction and German fighters saw little action. The number of Me 109s assigned to support the attack on Poland proved sufficient to counter the meagre forces at the disposal of the Polish Air Force. The latter possessed only about three hundred combat planes, almost all of them outdated types. The PZL 11, the most modern Polish fighter type then in service, had a maximum speed of only 242 mph (389 km/hr). It was no match even for the early versions of the Me 109. Two weeks into the campaign the Luftwaffe felt sufficiently confident to move two Me 109 Gruppen from Poland to bolster the air defences in the west. On 28 September the Polish forces laid down their arms and the campaign came to an end.

Left: *Instrument panel of an Me 109 'Emil'. The cockpit was small and the outside view restricted, but pilots came to love the machine.*

Me 109 FRONT-LINE UNITS

2 SEPTEMBER 1939 - Units marked with asterisk took part in the campaign in Poland.

Aircraft Unit	Aircraft Serviceable/Total	Aircraft Unit	Aircraft Serviceable/Total
Tactical Development Division		Destroyer Geschwader 26	
Tactical Development (Lehr) Geschwader 2		I. Gruppe	46/52B&D
Staff Flight	3/3E*	II. Gruppe	47/48B&D
I.Gruppe	34/36E*	III. Gruppe	44/48B&C
10.Staffel	9/12E		
		Air Fleet 3 (SW Germany)	
Air Fleet 1 (NE Germany)		Fighter Geschwader 51	
Fighter Geschwader 1		I. Gruppe	39/47E
I. Gruppe	54/54E*	Fighter Geschwader 52	
Fighter Geschwader 2		I. Gruppe	34/39E
II. Gruppe	39/42E	Fighter Geschwader 53	
10 Staffel	9/9C	I. Gruppe	39/51E
Fighter Geschwader 3		II. Gruppe	41/43E
Staff Flight		Fighter Geschwader 70	
I. Gruppe	3/3E	I. Gruppe	24/24E
Fighter Geschwader 20		Fighter Geschwader 71	
I. Gruppe	42/48E	I. Gruppe	18/39C&E
Fighter Geschwader 21		Destroyer Geschwader 52	
I. Gruppe	20/21E	I. Gruppe	43/44B
Destroyer Geschwader 1			
I.Gruppe	28/29E*	**Air Fleet 4** (SE Germany)	
Destroyer Geschwader 2		Fighter Geschwader 76	
I. Gruppe	36/36B*	I. Gruppe	45/49E
	40/44D*	Fighter Geschwader 77	
		I. Gruppe	43/50E
Air Fleet 2 (NW Germany)		II. Gruppe	36/50E
Fighter Geschwader 26		Destroyer Geschwader 76	
I. Gruppe	48/48	II. Gruppe	39/40B&C
II. Gruppe	44/48E	Assigned to German Navy	
Staffel	8/10C	Traegergruppe 186	24/24C
		5., 6. Staffel	24/24

This table shows the serviceable and total number of 'Berta'(B), 'Caesar'(C), 'Dora'(D) and 'Emil'(E) versions of the Me 109 in action.

IN ACTION OVER FRANCE

'Relatively few Me 109s were lost in combat and only at the end of the campaign during the Dunkirk evacuation, was there much in the way of fighter-versus-fighter combat. During the campaign in France it was difficult to compare our [Me] 109 with the French Morane or Curtiss fighters, because I never had a dogfight with either of them. I saw only one Morane during the entire campaign and it was disappearing in the distance. Our Geschwader had very little dogfighting experience until the Dunkirk action, where we met the Royal Air Force for the first time in numbers. Our pilots came back with the highest respect for the [new] enemy.'

OBERLEUTNANT JULIUS NEUMANN,
ME 109 PILOT, FIGHTER GESCHWADER 27

Above: Me 109 'Emil' of Fighter Geschwader 27. The oversized markings on the wings were to help recognition, after some incidents when aircraft had been engaged in error by 'friendly' forces.

In the west the aerial activity was limited, as each side probed the other's strengths and weaknesses. On 30 September the Royal Air Force learned a hard lesson when five Fairey Battle light bombers flew a daylight armed reconnaissance mission over the Saarbrucken area. Me 109s of Fighter Geschwader 53 intercepted the force and shot down four bombers without loss to themselves. On 18 December 1939 a force of Vickers Wellingtons flew an armed reconnaissance mission

Right: A pilot boards his Me 109 'Emil' for a scramble take off. The aircraft, bears the 'Scalded Cat' insignia of Fighter Geschwader 20, in the summer of 1939.

off the coast close to Wilhelmshaven, intending to attack any German warships. The twenty-four bombers flew in close formation and depended on their combined crossfire to deter fighter attacks. Thirty-four Me 109s, drawn from Fighter Geschwader 26 and 77 and Destroyer Geschwader 1, engaged the bombers, together with sixteen Me 110s. The German fighters shot down twelve of the Wellingtons. Two more bombers crashed on land-ing. The Wellingtons' gunners shot down only two Me 109s. The RAF made the decision that future attacks on targets in Germany would take place almost exclusively at night.

On 10 May 1940 German forces launched their offensive in the west. There were 1,346 Me 109s serving with the front line units, of which just over a thousand were serviceable. Three-quarters of these aircraft were to support the offensive, while the rest stayed in position to defend targets in Germany. The Luftwaffe established air superiority over the Dutch, Belgian and French Air Forces, and over the Royal Air Force units based in France. Everywhere the Me 109 reigned supreme, with no effective fighter opposition. Without any hindrance from the air or ground the Luftwaffe bombers carried out destructive attacks on air-fields ahead of the fast-moving Panzer thrusts.

At the end of May the German advances pushed the battle front to within range of RAF fighter units flying from bases in southern England. Only during the Dunkirk evacuation was there any serious fighter-versus-fighter combat.

THE FIRST PHASE OF THE BATTLE OF BRITAIN

On 13 July a convoy of freighters passed through the Straits of Dover. Half a dozen Junkers 87 'Stuka' dive bombers were attacking the ships when they were engaged by eleven Hurricanes of No. 56 Squadron.

'Unfortunately for them [the Hurricanes], they slid into position directly between the Stukas and our close-escort Messerschmitts. We opened fire, and at once three Hurricanes separated from the formation, two dropping and one gliding down to the water smoking heavily. I saw a Stuka diving in an attempt to reach the French coast, being chased by a single Hurricane. Behind the Hurricane was a 109, and behind that, a second Hurricane, all of the fighters firing at the aircraft in front. I saw the deadly dangerous situation and rushed down. There were five aircraft diving in a line towards the water. The Stuka was badly hit and both crewmen wounded, it crashed on the beach near Wissant. The leading Messerschmitt, flown by Feldwebel John, shot down the first Hurricane into the water. My Hurricane dropped like a stone close to the one that John had shot down.'

MAJOR JOSEF FOEZOE, LEADING ME 109s OF FIGHTER GESCHWADER 51 ESCORTING THE STUKAS

[No. 56 Squadron lost two Hurricanes destroyed and two damaged. On the German side two Ju 87s were seriously damaged but Fighter Geschwader 51 suffered no losses.]

In the course of the evacuation the Luftwaffe learned the same hard lesson as that impressed on the RAF earlier: bombers operating by day without fighter escort could expect heavy losses if they came under attack from well-handled enemy fighters. From then on the Me 109 force would fly an increasingly large proportion of its missions in the fighter escort role.

BATTLE OF BRITAIN

The Battle of Britain was the first major action in which Me 109s confronted similar numbers of enemy fighters of comparable performance and flown by pilots of equal skill.

During the Battle of Britain Me 109 fighter units flew three types of operation. First was the free hunting sweep across enemy territory used to break up defending fighter formations, to clear the sky for a bomber formation coming behind. Second, were the 'intermediate escort' operations where fighters stayed in formation until enemy fighters approached their charges, and only then were they free to break away and go into action. Third, were the close escort operations which occupied the greater part of the fighter force during any large scale attack. German fighter units assigned to this role had to remain with their allotted bomber formation at all times. Frequently the Me 109s would drive the Spitfires or Hurricanes away from the bombers, but had then to break off the pursuit and return to positions close to their allocated bomber unit. The British fighters

Below: Two 'Emils' in factory markings.

Me 109 VERSUS SPITFIRE AND HURRICANE

'I cannot compare the Me 109 with the Spitfire or the Hurricane – I never flew either of those. We were told that there was no better fighter in the world than the 109 and we believed it. Why shouldn't we – it was certainly a very effective fighter. We knew that the Spitfire and the Hurricane were good fighters too and thought they might be closely comparable with our aircraft. So everything depended on the tactics used and how experienced and aggressive the pilots were. Of course, the RAF had some young and inexperienced pilots. But we had the feeling that there was a strong backbone of very well-trained and experienced pilots. The longer-serving RAF pilots had considerable flying experience. We in the Luftwaffe did not have this advantage. Very few of those who fought on our side in the Battle of Britain had more than four years' flying experience. Overall, we felt that we were dealing with an aircraft-pilot combination as good as our own.'

**OBERLEUTNANT JULIUS NEUMANN,
ME 109 PILOT**

Left: *Julius Neumann pictured in the cockpit of the Me 109 at the RAF Museum at Hendon in 1979. He recalled 'Immediately I sat in the cockpit I felt at home. Everything came easily to hand. Had the tank been full and there been enough room in front of me, I should have loved to have been allowed to take it up.'*

Opposite (top left): 'Emils' of Fighter Geschwader 27 at their airfield at Boenninghard near Wesel, shortly before the campaign in the west in May 1940. (Neumann)
(top right): Me 109s of Fighter Geschwader 27 at St Trond in Belgium.
(bottom left): Me 109 'Emils' of IInd Gruppe of Fighter Geschwader 53 preparing to take off from Dinan in western France during the Battle of Britain.
(bottom right): Battle formation of Me 109Es of IInd Gruppe of Fighter Geschwader 27, photographed early in the Battle of Britain when the unit was based at Crepon in western France as part of Air Fleet 3. (Neumann)

would then return to the fray and the frustrating process had to be repeated. From these duels between the two air forces the strengths and weaknesses of 'Emil', compared with the Mark I versions of the Spitfire and the Hurricane, quickly became evident.

At altitudes above 20,000 ft (6,000m) the 'Emil' was slightly faster in level flight and in the climb than the Spitfire. At all altitudes the German fighter was much faster than the Hurricane. Below 15,000 ft (4,600m) the Spitfire was the faster in level flight. Both British

The British Spitfire and the Hurricane could out-turn the Messerschmitt 109

fighter types could out-turn the Me 109 at any altitude. Me 109 pilots found the fuel injection system fitted to the Daimler Benz 601 gave a useful advantage when they had a Spitfire or a Hurricane on their tail. The Messerschmitt pilot would push down the nose of his fighter and 'bunt' away from his pursuer. If an RAF fighter tried to follow

Me 109 FRONT-LINE UNITS
7 SEPTEMBER 1940

Aircraft Unit	Aircraft Serviceable/Total	Aircraft Unit	Aircraft Serviceable/Total
Air Fleet 2 (Holland, Belgium, NE France)		Fighter Geschwader 53	
Fighter Geschwader 1		Staff Flight	2/2
Staff Flight	3/4	II. Gruppe	24/33
Fighter Geschwader 3		III. Gruppe	22/30
Staff Flight	3/3	Fighter Geschwader 54	
I. Gruppe	14/23	Staff Flight	2/4
II. Gruppe	21/24	I. Gruppe	23/28
III. Gruppe	23/25	II. Gruppe	27/35
Geschwader 26		III. Gruppe	23/28
Staff Flight	3/4	Fighter Geschwader 77	
I. Gruppe	20/27	I. Gruppe	40/42
II. Gruppe	28/32	Trials Gruppe 210	17/26
III. Gruppe	26/29		
Fighter Geschwader 27		**Air Fleet 3 (NW France)**	
Staff Flight	4/5	Fighter Geschwader 2	
I. Gruppe	27/33	Staff Flight	2/5
II. Gruppe	33/37	I. Gruppe	24/29
III. Gruppe	27/31	II. Gruppe	18/22
Fighter Geschwader 51		III. Gruppe	19/30
Staff Flight	4/5	Geschwader 53	
I. Gruppe	33/36	I. Gruppe	27/34
Inglevert		Development (Lehr) Geschwader 2	
II. Gruppe	13/22	II. Gruppe	27/32
Inglevert			
III. Gruppe	31/44	**Air Fleet 5 (Norway)**	
Fighter Geschwader 52		Fighter Geschwader 77	
Staff Flight	1/2	II. Gruppe	35/44
I. Gruppe	7/21		
II. Gruppe	23/28	This table shows the serviceable and total number of Me 109s in action on the western front in 1940, leading up to the Battle of Britain.	
III. Gruppe	16/31		

WAR DIARY OF 1ST GRUPPE, FIGHTER GESCHWADER 3

The entry for 15 September 1940, now commemorated as Battle of Britain Day. At the time this unit was part of Air Fleet 2, based at Samer near Boulogne under the command of Hauptmann Hans von Hahn.

On 7 September the unit reported a strength of twenty-three Messerschmitt 109Es of which 14 were serviceable after four weeks of heavy fighting. 1200 [hours, take-off time] Escort (by 12 aircraft) of Do 17s against London. Oblt Keller shot down a Spitfire, Leutnant Rohwer a Hurricane. Fw Wollmer dived into the Channel, the impact was seen by Lt Springer. This crash appears not to have been caused by enemy action. After a long dive Vollmer's machine rolled a quarter turn into a vertical dive and he did not succeed in bailing out. A motor boat detached from a German convoy near Cap Gris Nez and went to the scene of the crash. 1510 [hours] Operation by 9 aircraft to escort He 111s against London.

At 1500h there was almost total cloud cover. Over the Thames estuary and to the north of London there were gaps in the cloud. During the flight in there was contact with Spitfires. The bombers flew in loose formation to the north of London. The Spitfires came from above, fired, and dived away. H von Hahn shot down a Spitfire, Lt Rohwer probably destroyed a Hurricane. During an attack by Spitfires Oblt Reumschuessel became separated from his wing man, Obfw Olejnik, and has not returned [this aircraft crashed near Charing, Kent; the pilot bailed out and was taken prisoner]. Obfw Hessel was heard on the radio, but he failed to return [this aircraft crashed near Tenterden; the pilot bailed out and was taken prisoner]. Obfw Buchholz's aircraft was hit and forced down in the Channel. Oblt Keller made contact with a rescue aircraft nearby, which picked up Buchholz. He had [minor] injuries and was taken to the military hospital at Boulogne. The body of Lt Kloiber has been washed ashore and buried. Lt Meckel and 2 Feldwebels attended the funeral. News has been received from the Red Cross that Oblt Tiedmann, Oblt Rau, Oblt Loidolt, Lt Landry and Obfe Lamskemper have been captured by the British.

Scenes at the airfield at Caffiers near Calais, home of the Me 109 'Emils' of IIIrd Gruppe of Fighter Geschwader 26 during the Battle of Britain. The photos come from the personal album of Gerhard Schoepfel. **Top left:** *Ground crewmen making a sandbag blast pen to protect a fighter on the ground.* **Above left and middle right:** *Aircraft in their camouflaged blast pens.* **Top right:** *Engine change of a fighter in the open.* **Bottom right:** *Officers of IIIrd Gruppe of Fighter Geschwader 26 discussing the next mission. Seated second from left is the unit commander, Major Adolf Garland. To his immediate left is Gerhard Schoenfel.*

Above and right: 'Emils' loaded with 550-pound bombs during attacks on England in the closing stages of the Battle of Britain.

this manoeuvre, the negative 'G' shut off the fuel supply from the float carburettor fitted to the Merlin engine. There would be a warning splutter, and unless the RAF pilot restored positive 'G' immediately his engine would stop dead.

RADIUS OF ACTION

Throughout the Battle of Britain, and during its final phases when the capital was the target, the Me 109's limited radius of action was of crucial importance. During that contest the Me 109, the Spitfire and the Hurricane each had an effective radius of action of about 100 miles (160km). For RAF fighters engaged in home defence

operations, fighting over airfields where they could land to refuel, that distance was adequate. However, for Me 109s flying in the bomber escort or support roles deep into enemy territory, it was inadequate. The German fighter pilots could not afford to spend long engaged in combat, their engines running at full throttle and guzzling fuel. If they were close to the limit of their radius of action the Messerschmitts had to break off the action, and head for home. This factor greatly reduced the

effectiveness of the German single-engined fighter force.

There is another point to consider. The cliché image of the Battle of Britain is that of a sky full of Spitfires and Hurricanes engaged in one-to-one turning fights with Me 109s. That might make for a spectacular film shot, but it was far from the reality of air combat. Any pilot who fastened his attention too long on one enemy fighter ran the serious risk of setting himself up for a surprise attack by another.

PROVIDING CLOSE ESCORT FOR THE BOMBERS

'Sometimes we had to provide close escort for a bomber formation, which I loathed. It gave the bomber crews the feeling they were being protected, and it might have deterred some of the enemy pilots. We needed the advantages of altitude and speed so we could engage the enemy on favourable terms. The British fighters had the initiative of when and how to attack. The Heinkels cruised at about 4,000 m [13,000 ft] at about 300km/hr [190mph]. On close escort we flew at about 370km/hr [230mph], weaving from side to side. We needed to maintain speed, or the Me 109e would have taken too long to accelerate to fighting speed if we were bounced by Spitfires. We had to stay with the bombers until our formation came under attack. When we saw the British fighters approaching we would want to accelerate to engage them. But our commander would call "Everybody stay with the bombers." We handed to the enemy the initiative of when and how they would attack us. Until they did we had to stay close to the bombers, otherwise their people would complain and there would be recriminations when we got back.'

OBERLEUTNANT HANS SCHMOLLER-HALDY, ME 109 PILOT, FIGHTER GESCHWADER 54

Above: *At the end of the Battle of Britain the top-scoring Luftwaffe pilot was Major Werner Moelders, commander of Fighter Geschwader 51. On 22 October 1940 he scored his fiftieth aerial victory.*

On both sides, the successful fighter pilots stalked their prey like hunters, using the sun and cloud to remain unseen for as long as possible, as they edged into a favourable position before launching an attack. They then dived on their often unsuspecting prey, announcing their presence with a sudden and accurate burst of fire.

Usually the first thing the victim knew of the danger was when his aircraft shuddered under the impact. A textbook example of this type of action appears in the Prologue (see page 139).

From the start of the Battle of Britain one Gruppe operated the Me 109 in the fighter-bomber role, attacking targets in southern England. The fighter carried a bomb load of up to 550 pounds (249kg). In the final part of the Battle, from the end of September, several Me 109 units flew aircraft modified for the fighter-bomber role. The defending fighters found the fast, high-flying German fighter-bombers difficult targets to engage. As a result the latter suffered minimal losses. The Me 109 carried only a small weight of bombs, and their scattered bombing meant that the attacks had only nuisance value.

REPUTATION INTACT

The Me 109 force emerged from the Battle of Britain with its reputation still intact, although it had suffered losses at the hands of the RAF pilots.

The new variant of the German fighter about to enter service, the Me 109 'Friedrich', would be even better.

Left: *Hauptmann Horst Tietzen, the commander of 5th Staffer of Fighter Geschwader 51, with his personal 'Emil' with eighteen victory bars on the tail. On the afternoon of 18 August 1940, when his victory score stood at twenty, he was shot down and killed during an action with Hurricanes of No. 501 Squadron.*

THE MOST SERIOUS AND UNPARDONABLE ERROR

'On 23 September our mission was a free hunting sweep in the triangle Ramsgate-Canterbury-Folkestone. With three of my pilots I took off at 10.27 and headed towards Ramsgate in a slow climb to 4,500 m [about 15,000 ft]. The weather was strange, with layers of cloud in which aircraft could easily hide. There were several aircraft about but we never knew if they were British or German. It was uncanny. We flew in wide curves, always changing altitude, never flying straight for long. We had been flying for 60 minutes, I thought that was enough and we were turning for home when I suddenly observed Hurricane squadron between Ramsgate and Dover, twelve aircraft in four "pulks" flying one behind the other. They were about 1,000 m (2,873ft) below us and climbing in wide curves, like a creeping worm. My impression was that it was a Hurricane squadron on a training mission. The Hurricane pilots had no idea that four 109s were above them following each of their movements. The display was so fascinating that we forgot what was going on around us. That is the most serious and unpardonable error a fighter pilot can commit, and catastrophe immediately followed. Four Spitfires, of which we had been unaware due to our carelessness, attacked us from out of the sun. They fired at us from behind, roared close over our heads at high speed and disappeared back into the sky. As we broke formation fearing another attack from the Spitfires, I saw a 109 going down in flames on my right. It was Obfw Knipscher, we never heard what happened to him.'

OBERLEUTNANT HANS SCHMOLLER-HALDY ME 109 PILOT, FIGHTER GESCHWADER 54

Top: An 'Emil' crash-landed on a French beach. During the Battle of Britain this fighter was not fitted with drop tanks. Several were lost when they ran out of fuel on their way home following air combats or after encountering strong headwinds.
Above: Me 109E-7s of Fighter Geschwader 1, a unit that spent most of the war operating in the defence of the German homeland. (via Obert)
Right: Major Adolf Galland climbing out of the cockpit of his 'Emil' after a sortie over England during the Battle of Britain.

ENTER THE 'FRIEDRICH'

During 1940 the Messerschmitt company improved the Me 109's fighting capability. The new variant was known as the Me 109 'Friedrich'. The most obvious external changes were the more rounded spinner and nose contours, the rounded wing tips and the partially retractable tail wheel. The main production version was fitted with the new Mauser 15mm cannon, one of which fired through the propeller hub. This weapon had nearly twice the firing rate of the older 20mm Oerlikon cannon, and its far higher muzzle velocity made it a much more effective weapon than its predecessor.

The 'Friedrich' was faster than the 'Emil' and it handled better in the air. It was a 'fighter pilot's fighter'. The 'Friedrich' entered service in the spring of 1941. Also at this time the RAF introduced the Mark V Spitfire into its home defence squadrons, a move that restored the balance between the fighter forces of the two sides.

NORTH AFRICA

That balanced existed only over northwest Europe. Until the

MESSSERSCHMITT 109 F-2

Type Single-seat general purpose fighter.
Armament One Mauser 15mm cannon firing through the propeller spinner (200 rounds). Two Rheinmetall-Borsig 7.9mm MGs synchronized to fire through airscrew (500 rounds per gun).
Power Plant One Daimler Benz DB 601N inverted V-12 liquid cooled engine developing 1,200hp for take off.
Dimensions Span 32ft 6in (9.92m); length 29ft 4in (8.94m).
Weight Normal operational take off, 6,174lb (2,800kg).
Performance Max. speed 373mph at 19,700ft (600km/hr at 6,000m). Service ceiling 36,100ft (11,000m).

Top: A brand new Me 109 'Friedrich' in factory markings shows off its distinctive rounded wing form above the Alps.
Above: A 'Friedrich' of Fighter Geschwader 26 returning to its base at Liegescourt in northern France in the summer of 1941. (Schoepfel)
Opposite: Two 'Emils' of Fighter Geschwader 27 on patrol over the North African desert.

Top: 'Friedrich' wearing the personal markings of the commander of IIIrd Gruppe of Fighter Geschwader 2 based in northern France, photographed in 1941.
Above: An Me 109F of Fighter Geschwader 26 outside its camouflaged dispersal hangar in northern France.

spring of 1942 the Spitfire fighter units operated only from bases in Great Britain. Units equipped with the 'Friedrich' were involved in the campaigns in North Africa and the Soviet Union where the new fighter easily out flew the less modern types. For the German fighter pilots this was a 'happy time' when many of them amassed large victory scores.

The leading 'Friedrich' fighter pilot was Leutnant Hans-Joachim Marseille. He gained seven victories during the Battle of Britain, flying the 'Emil'. From

THE ATTACK ON RUSSIA

During the weeks following the invasion of Russia, German fighters ranged far and wide over enemy territory. Close to the ground the Polikarpov I-16, the main Soviet fighter type, was almost as fast as the Me 109F. But the Type 24's radial engine was optimized for low-altitude operations and as height increased its performance fell away steadily; at 20,000ft (6,096m) the I-16 was about 100mph (160km/hr) slower than the German fighter. Although the Soviet fighters were more manoeuvrable than their adversaries, in a fighter-versus-fighter combat that advantage did no more than allow a pilot to avoid being shot down, provided he saw his attacker in good time. For the most part, the Soviet fighter pilots had to dance to their enemies' tune. Typical of the scrappy actions taking place that morning was one near Brest-Litovsk, described by Unteroffizier Reibel of Ist Gruppe of Fighter Geschwader 53: 'I was flying as wing man to Lt Zellot. We flew in the direction of Brest from Labinka. As my leader ordered a turn about, I saw two biplanes in front of us. I immediately reported them and we brought them under attack. When we were about 200m [61ft] from them they both pulled into a tight turn to the right. We pulled up high and then began a new attack, but though we both opened fire it was without success. Soon there were about ten other [enemy] machines in the area. My leader ran in to attack one of the planes while I remained high in order to cover him. Then an I-15 became separated from the others. I prepared to attack it, but had to break away when another enemy machine suddenly appeared 50m [15ft] in front of me. I opened fire with machine guns and the cannon and it burst into flames and spun out of control. Apparently the pilot had baled out. I had to turn away, as I had two [enemy] machines behind me.' Using their superior speed, the two German fighters easily pulled away.

Me 109 'Emils' of Fighter Geschwader 52 pictured at Kabaracie, Rumania, in the spring of 1941 shortly before the attack on the Soviet Union. The 'snake' marking on the rear fuselage indicated that these aircraft belonged to the IIIrd Gruppe.

Top left: *Me 109 'Emil' fighter-bomber of Fighter Geschwader 54 over the Eastern Front in 1942.*
Middle: *Me 109 'Friedrich' of Fighter Geschwader 54 pictured beside a captured Soviet I-16 fighter. The German fighter had a considerable speed advantage over its enemy counterpart, especially at high altitude.*
Bottom: *Me 109 'Friedrich' of Fighter Geschwader 53, with the unit's 'Ace of Spades' insignia on the cowling, at an airfield in the Leningrad sector on the Eastern Front during the winter of 1941-2.*

the start of 1942, in North Africa, his victory total rose rapidly. With no Spitfires yet operating in that area, the 'Friedrich' was superior to the Hurricane and Tomahawk fighters flown by the RAF and its allies. During a remarkable action on 3 June 1942, Marseille shot down six Tomahawks in rapid succession. The action is well documented and the combat is confirmed in the records of the victim unit, No. 5 Squadron South African Air Force. By the time of his death in September 1942, Marseille's tally stood at 158.

Me 109s IN NORTH AFRICA

1. Hauptmann Karl-Wolfgang Redlich of Ist Gruppe Fighter Geschwader 27 (left, with papers), briefing pilots before taking off from Sicily to fly to North Africa. The 'Emil' in the background is fitted with a dust filter over the engine air intake. (Schroer)
2. Ground running an 'Emil' engine in Sicily, to warm the engine before setting out for North Africa. (Schroer)
3. Me 109 'Emils' of Fighter Geschwader 27 dispersed around the forward landing ground in Libya. The photograph gives a good impression of the primitive conditions under which the unit had to operate. (Schroer)
4. Ground crewmen turning the handle for the inertia starter of the Daimler Benz 601 engine. The handle rotated a heavy flywheel which, when it was turning fast enough, was clutched to the engine to turn it over and start it.
5. 'Emils' of Fighter Geschwader 27 on patrol over the desert.
6. Me 109F of Fighter Geschwader 27 preparing to get airborne. This aircraft is missing its spinner.
7. Hauptmann Hans-Joachim Marseille of Fighter Geschwader 27, the most successful German fighter pilot in North Africa. At the time of his death in September 1942, his victory score was 158.
8. Fighter ace Leutnant Werner Schroer, adjutant of IInd Gruppe of Fighter Geschwader 27, with his personal aircraft. At the end of the war his victory score stood at 114. (Schroer)

The 15mm cannon on the 'Friedrich' was replaced with a fast firing 20mm Mauser cannon. Mounted above the engine cowling, the weapons gave a dense pattern of fire. This was very effective against light bombers. Against the four-engined bombers, it was another matter however.

FIRE POWER

From mid-1942 the Me 109F units operating over western Europe and North Africa encountered the American B-17 Flying Fortress and B-24 Liberator heavy bombers with increasing frequency. On average it needed about twenty hits with 20mm rounds to knock down one of these rugged aircraft. When in formation the heavy bombers put up a powerful defensive cross-fire which forced the fighters to make high-speed firing passes. Only an exceptionally good shot could achieve the required number of

Above: 'Friedrich' of Fighter Geschwader 77 operating on the Leningrad front in 1942. (Pichler via Obert)

hits using a single cannon.

The Friedrich was modified to carry a blister under each wing containing an extra 20mm cannon and ammunition. This trebled the fighter's fire power, but reduced its performance. It was the first sign of a problem that would afflict the Me 109 for the remainder of the war.

That critical shortcoming would become all too evident when the next variant entered production, the 'Gustav'.

THE EASY TIMES IN RUSSIA

Initially the German fighter pilots had an easy time over Russia. In the summer of 1942 Unteroffizier Walther Hagenah was posted to Ist Gruppe of Fighter Geschwader 3 operating the Me 109F. He flew as wing man to Obfw Otto Wessling. Hagenah told this author: 'Wessling was a superb leader who seemed to be able to score hits from ranges as great as 400m [1,312ft]. He would manoeuvre into a position of advantage above his enemy, open fire from long range, hit his enemy and pull away without getting close to his foe. My first weeks as an operational fighter pilot were a disappointment. I was beginning to get discouraged. One day Wessling took me to one side on the ground and said "Now it is time that you made your first victory!" On 12 August 1942 we were on patrol on the central Russian front and he spotted a pair of LAGG-3 fighters. He took us into an attacking position on their tails and down we went. We moved from out of the sun and achieved surprise. He hit one of them from about 400m [1,312ft] and down it went. Then he called me and said "Now you go ahead and hit the other one!" But the second Russian tried to shake us off his tail. Wessling joined the dogfight, but at the same time telling me what I had to do to get "my" kill. Eventually he succeeded in manoeuvring both me and the Russian fighter into a position where I could open fire at it. I followed Wessling's instructions and fired when he said, hitting the enemy fighter. I was very proud. Wessling was big enough to keep quiet about how I got it.'

'GUSTAV' AND 'KURFURST'

During the Second World War the principal fighter types in the major warring nations underwent courses of development to improve their fighting capability. They were fitted with more powerful (and heavier) engines, more effective (and heavier) armament, larger (and heavier) fuel tankage and additional (and heavier) protective armour and equipment.

As the fighter steadily gained weight, the airframe had to be stiffened to restore its original strength factors. That added a further twist to the spiral of increasing weight. Since the fighter's wing area usually remained constant, each increase in weight led to increase in wing loading. And that, inevitably, led to a deterioration in the fighter's handling characteristics. Stalling speeds became higher, control forces heavier, turning performance worsened and, in many cases, the aircraft developed vicious traits.

The Me 109G-2 was 660 pounds heavier than its predecessor, the Me 109F

No fighter design suffered more from this remorseless process than the Me 109. Even at the start of the war, it will be remembered, the Me 109 had already passed through several variants. By the spring of 1942 it had reached the end of its effective development and should then have passed out of production. Messerschmitt's replacement, the Me 209, was still on the drawing board.

At that time the war was still going well for Germany and her leaders confidently expected that the campaign on the Eastern Front would come to a victorious end in the autumn of 1942. Until a replacement fighter type was ready, the Luftwaffe opted to squeeze greater speed from the Me 109 and keep the fighter in full production.

The new variant, the Me 109 'Gustav', was designed around the Daimler Benz 605 engine. In essence this was a DB 601 with the cylinder block rebored to increase the engine's capacity from 33.9 litres to 35.7 litres. The additional capacity gave an extra 175 hp at full throttle, for no significant increase in the

Top: Me 109 'Gustav' of Fighter Geschwader 54 seen at an airfield in Russia.
Above: Me 109 'Gustav' of Fighter Geschwader 53 at an airfield in Sicily in 1943. (via Rigglesford)
Opposite: Pilots of Fighter Geschwader 53 snatching a quick meal beside one of their aircraft. (via Schliephake)

engine's external dimensions. The first major production version, the 'Gustav-2', was 660lb (300kg) or about 10per cent heavier than the earlier 'Friedrich' and its handling characteristics were much worse. During May 1942 a total of 234 Me 109s came off the production lines in Germany and Austria, most of them 'Gustavs'.

MESSERSCHMITT 109 G-2

Type Single-seat general purpose fighter.
Armament One Mauser 20mm cannon firing through the spinner (150 rounds) Two Rheinmetall-Borsig 7.9mm MGs synchronized to fire through the airscrew (500 rounds per gun).
Power Plant One Daimler Benz DB 605A inverted V-12 liquid cooled engine developing 1,475hp for take off.
Dimensions Span 32ft 6in (9.92m); length 29ft 0in (8.85m)
Weight Normal operational take off 6,832lb (3,100kg)
Performance Maximum speed 406mph at 28,535ft (654km/hr at 8,700m) Service ceiling 39,360ft (12,000m).

Soon after the 'Gustav' entered service with Fighter Geschwader 27, Hans-Joachim Marseille lost his life while flying the type. In September 1942 his victory score passed the 150 mark, making him the first fighter ace in history to achieve this total. On the final day of the month he flew a newly-delivered 'Gustav-2' on a bomber escort mission over Egypt. There was no contact with the enemy and the flight was uneventful, until on the return flight the aircraft's engine started to smoke. Then it caught fire. The cockpit filled with fumes and, escorted by his comrades, Marseille stayed with the aircraft until he reached German-held territory. Then he

Marseille jumped from his aircraft but for once luck had deserted him

jumped from the stricken fighter, but his luck had deserted him. As he left the Messerschmitt it appears that his head struck some part of its structure and he was knocked unconscious. His parachute did not open and he was killed on hitting the ground. Subsequent examination of his parachute revealed that it was still in the pack, held

closed by the ripcord which had not been pulled.

Small numbers of 'Gustav-2s' were modified for the tactical reconnaissance role, with the cannon removed and a vertical camera mounted in the rear fuselage. The use of the Me 109 (and also the FW 190) for this purpose became necessary because the increasing enemy fighter opposition

meant that slower reconnaissance types incurred heavy losses. Modified versions of each of the new main variants of the Me 109 would be used for tactical reconnaissance for the remainder of the war.

The next major production version of the fighter, the 'Gustav-6', started to leave the assembly lines in the autumn of 1942. This differed from the G-2 in that it carried two 13mm heavy machine guns on top of the engine cowling, in place of the earlier rifle-calibre weapons. To cover the larger breech mechanism of the 13mm guns, the fighter had two large bulges on the cowling in front of the windscreen.

'WILD BOAR' MESSERSCHMITT 109s

Me 109G-2s operating in the 'Wild Boar' single-engine nightfighter role to counter RAF bomber attacks, summer 1943.

From mid-1943 the Luftwaffe began to employ small numbers of single-engined fighters, including Me 109s, to engage RAF night bombers attacking cities in Germany. Over the target the concentrations of searchlights, the fires on the ground and the Pathfinders' marker flares often combined to illuminate the bombers. The single-seaters patrolling high above the target could then make visual attacks on the raiders. To prevent conflict with the flak defences it was agreed that the latter would engage bombers flying below a certain altitude typically 18,000ft (5,500m). Above that altitude the fighters would engage bombers. The single-engined night fighter tactics bore the apt title 'Wild Boar'. For the remainder of the war these methods were an integral part of the German night air defence system.

The Weapons Installation Fitted to the Me 109G-5 and G-6

Key:
a. MG 31 13mm heavy machine guns
b. Electrical synchronization unit for firing MG 131s through the airscrew disc
c. Magazine for MG 131 ammunition
d. Empty case chute for port MG 131
e. Mountings for MG 131s
f. Ignition coil, to provide high voltage for electrically fired MG 131 ammunition
g. Mounting brackets for nose fairing
h. MG 151 20mm cannon firing through propeller spinner
i. Front mounting of MG 151
k. Magazine for MG 151 ammunition
l. Feed chute for MG 151 ammunition
m. Control column, with firing button for weapons
n. Revi 16B reflector sight
o. Arming switch for weapons

B 5950

210mm ROCKETS

The Luftwaffe issued a range of field modification kits to allow units to 'customize' the new fighter for specific operational roles. The R-1 kit, for example, provided an under-fuselage rack to carry a single bomb weighing up to 550lb (249kg). The R-2 kit provided for a tubular launcher under each wing to carry a 210mm rocket, for use against enemy bomber formations or ground targets. The R-4 kit provided a blister mounting for a 30mm heavy cannon and ammunition, one to fit under either wing.

The 'Gustav-6' could carry one or two separate power-boosting systems, to inject a fluid into the supercharger of the DB 605 engine. To boost power at altitudes above

Above: Diagram from an official Luftwaffe handbook, showing the fuselage armament fitted as standard to Me 109 Gustav-5 and Gustav-6. These fighters had a 20mm Mauser cannon firing through the airscrew hub, and two 13mm Rheinmetall-Borsig heavy machine guns above the engine cowling synchronized to fire through the airscrew. On some later aircraft the engine-mounted cannon was replaced by a Rheinmetall-Borsig 30mm weapon.

20,000ft (6,096m), the GM-1 system injected nitrous oxide (laughing gas) into the engine. The nitrous oxide was held in liquid form in a heavily lagged pressurized container in the

Below: The 'Gustav' did not suffer fools gladly. If the pilot opened the throttle too quickly during take-off, the powerful engine torque was liable to lift the fighter off the ground before it attained flying speed. Often the fighter rolled upside down and smashed on the ground under full power, giving the pilot little chance of escape. (Schliephake) on the defensive. More fighters were required and the 'Gustav' was built in ever-greater numbers. In 1943 production of the Me 109 was twice that in the previous year, more than 6,400 'Gustavs' were delivered to the Luftwaffe.

Daylight attacks by US heavy bombers on targets in Germany had grown into deep penetration attacks by several hundred bombers. Several fighter Gruppen were withdrawn from the battle fronts to bolster the defences of the homeland.

In the summer of 1943 Unteroffizier Hans Seyringer was posted to IInd Gruppe of Fighter Geschwader 27, a day fighter unit equipped with the 'Gustav-6'. The young pilot had only about 200 flying hours in his logbook. His recollections give a good impression of what it was like to serve with such a unit.

During bomber-interception missions, fighters usually carried a 66-gal (300l) drop tank under the fuselage. Standard armament fitted to 'Gustavs' on Seyringer's unit was three 20mm cannon and two 13mm machine-guns. Some aircraft also carried two 210mm rocket launchers under the wings.

Aircraft were usually drawn up by Staffeln in line abreast on the ground. The four Staffeln, each with about a dozen 'Gustav-6s', were dispersed separately at 90-degree intervals around the perimeter of the grass airfield. Once the pilots had been brought to cockpit readiness, the order to scramble was given by firing a flare from the control tower. From then on

Top: Me 109 'Gustav-2s' of a tactical reconnaissance Gruppe. This version had the nose-mounted cannon removed, and a vertical camera fitted in the fuselage immediately behind the cockpit.
***Above:** Me 109 'Gustav-2' of Fighter Geschwader 11 at Jever during 1943, fitted with underwing launchers for two 210 mm air-to-air rockets for use against US heavy bomber formations.*

rear fuselage and the system weighed 670lb(304kg). To boost power at altitudes below 20,000ft, the MW system injected a water/methanol mixture into the engine. The complete MW system weighed 300lb (136kg).

As the 'Gustav-6' entered service Germany's war fortunes deteriorated. On each battle front the Luftwaffe was thrown

Above: A close-up of the rocket installation on a 'Gustav'.
Left: Me 109 'Gustav' of the Finnish Air Force. The type entered that service in March 1943 and remained in use until 1954

it was important to get the Gruppe into the air and assembled into battle formation as rapidly as possible. To achieve this two of the Staffeln on opposite sides of the airfield began simultaneous take-off runs, moving on parallel headings separated by a few hundred yards. As the first two Staffeln passed each other at the centre of the airfield, the other two Staffeln began their take-off runs also heading in opposite directions. After take-off the leader orbited once over the airfield so the individual Staffeln could start to move into position behind him. Then he turned on to his intercept heading and began a slow climb away. Once the formation was fully assembled he increased his rate of climb.

These tactics provided the most rapid means of getting a Gruppe into the air and assembled into formation. There was little small margin for safety if anything went wrong, however. Seyringer recalled a nerve-racking incident when, due to incor-rect fitting, a fighter taking off in the opposite direction accidentally loosed off a couple of rockets. The missiles came scorching past Seyringer's Staffel just as the fighters were getting airborne. Their proximity caused considerable consternation but, fortunately for the pilots involved, no damage!

TACTICS

Once the ground controller had brought a fighter Gruppe within visual range of an enemy formation, the Gruppe leader decided on the type of attack to employ. Usually Seyringer's Gruppe attacked bombers from the rear, the fighters flying in four-aircraft units in line abreast

Above: 'Gustav-6' carrying the white fuselage band and wing tips of a unit operating on the Mediterranean front.
Right: Unteroffizier Hans Seyringer of Fighter Geschwader 27, whose experiences are described in the text, pictured with his 'Gustav-6'. With a victory score of four enemy aircraft destroyed, he was shot down and wounded during an engagement with American escort fighters in February 1944. (Seyringer)

or line astern. The fighters split into pairs to make further firing runs. Sometimes Seyringer's Gruppe made head-on attacks, though he did not like this method. He felt that the time spent manoeuvring into position for such an attack was out of proportion to the very short firing pass that resulted.

Until late in 1943 the American escort fighters lacked the range to penetrate deep into Germany. Seyringer's unit had few encounters with them and he thought that was as well, for a heavily laden 'Gustav-6' was no match for a Thunderbolt.

To Hans Seyringer the effect of the fighter's extensive development process on handling was all too evident. To put it simply, the 'Gustav' was too heavy and its engine too powerful for the fighter's small wing and tail surfaces. When carrying a full armament and drop tank the aircraft required careful handling during the take-off. If there was heavy-handedness of the controls the fighter was liable to react viciously. If, for example, the pilot opened the throttle too quickly the powerful engine torque was liable to

lift the fighter off the ground before it attained flying speed. The 'Gustav' would drop its left wing, roll on its back and smash into the ground, giving the pilot little chance of escape.

During 1943 the Luftwaffe tactics to counter the American heavy bomber raids were in a continual state of development. Home defence units used any type of weapon that came to hand. Fighter Geschwader 11 carried out experiments in air-to-air bombing, using time-fused 550lb (249kg) released from above the bomber forma-

DISASTER FOR THE GERMAN DAY FIGHTER FORCE

In the spring of 1944 the American escort fighters were able to reach almost every part of Germany. The new Mustang was superior in performance to the Me 109 and it was usually present in greater numbers. As a result the German day fighter units took increasingly heavy losses. At the end of April 1944 Generalmajor Adolf Galland reported: 'Between January and April 1944 our day fighter arm lost more than 1,000 pilots. They included our best Staffel, Gruppe and Geschwader commanders.The time has come when our force is within sight of collapse.' Now the German pilots had to fight for their very survival, and one by one even the best of them were being picked off. Gone were the days when the aces could 'play' enemy planes to allow their less experienced colleagues to get easy kills, as over Russia a couple of years earlier. One of those who died in action with the American fighters in April 1944 was Leutnant Otto Wessling, then credited with 83 victories, who had set up Walther Hagenah's first 'kill' described earlier.

tion. If the bombs did not destroy the enemy planes, they might damage some of them sufficiently to force them to leave their formation. There were serious problems with this method. Carrying a bomb in place of a drop tank, the 'Gustav' had a short radius of action. Also it proved difficult to vector the heavily laden fighter into position above a high-flying bomber formation. Since there was no effective proximity fuse then available, the problem of getting the bomb to detonate as it passed the target aircraft defied

MESSERSCHMITT 109 G–2 VERSUS HAWKER TEMPEST

At the beginning of 1944 a captured Me 109 'Gustav-2' was flown in a comparative trial against the latest RAF fighter type, the Hawker Tempest Mark V. These extracts from the official report show that the German fighter was outclassed in almost every respect. **Maximum Speed:** The Tempest possesses an advantage of 40-50mph [64-80km/hr] at heights below 20,000 feet [5,850m] but at heights in excess of 20,000 feet [6,096m] the advantage possessed by the Tempest rapidly diminishes. **Climb:** The climb of the Me 109 is superior to that of the Tempest at all heights but this advantage is not pronounced at heights below 5,000 feet [1,520m]. When both the aircraft commence a dive at the same speed and are put into climbing attitude, the Tempest is slightly superior, but providing the Tempest possesses the initial advantage in speed, it has no difficulty in holding it providing the speed is kept in excess of 250mph [400km/hr]. **Dive:** Comparative dives between these aircraft show that the Tempest will pull away from the Me 109. This is not so marked in the early stages of the dive, but in a prolonged descent the Tempest is greatly superior. **Turning Circle:** It was found that in this aspect of manoeuvrability the Tempest was slightly superior to the Me 109. **Rate of Roll:** At speeds below 350 IAS [mph indicated, 564km/hr] there is practically nothing to choose between the two aircraft, but when this speed is exceeded the Tempest can out-manoeuvre the Me 109 by making a quick change of bank and direction. **Conclusions:** In the attack the Tempest can always follow the Me 109, except in a slow steep climb. In the combat area the Tempest should maintain a high speed, and in defence may do anything except attempt a climb at low speed.

Comparative trials revealed that the Hawker Tempest Mark V, which entered service in the RAF early in 1944, was superior to the Me 109 'Gustav-2' in almost every respect.

solution. Most of the bombs detonated well clear of their intended victims, and after a month or so the unit abandoned this form of attack.

During the spring of 1944, following the introduction of new and larger drop tanks, the American escort fighters were able to reach almost every part of Germany. The new Mustang fighters were superior in performance to the defending Me 109s, Me 110s, Me 410s and FW 190s. Moreover the escort fighters operated in large numbers and as a result the German fighter units took heavy losses.

HOME DEFENCE

By now the greater part of the Luftwaffe fighter force was committed in the defence of the homeland. And it was losing pilots faster than the German flying training schools could provide replacements. The Luftwaffe was being bled white. The only possibility of reversing this trend was with the large-scale deployment of the Messerschmitt 262 jet fighter.

Below: Me 109G-6s of IIIrd Gruppe Fighter Geschwader 27 waiting at readiness at Wiesbaden-Erbenheim in 1944. The broad red band around the rear fuselage indicated that the aircraft belonged to a Reich air defence unit. (Schroer)

Above: Damaged Me 109 'Gustav' trailing glycol smoke, after being hit in the cooling system during an engagement with a US escort fighter.

Yet this type was still not ready to enter mass production.

Although the 'Gustav' was now well beyond its effective development life, new subtypes continued to appear. By optimizing it for a narrow range of combat roles, the fighter might survive in action. Thus the 'Gustav-10', was built specifically to engage in high altitude fighter-versus-fighter combat. These aircraft carried the new Daimler Benz 605D engine with an enlarged supercharger and the GM-1 power boosting. Their armament was reduced to one 20mm cannon and two 13mm machine guns. They were assigned to units to provide top cover for heavily armed fighters delivering attacks on bomber for-

mations. Small numbers of 'Gustav-10s' were modified for the tactical reconnaissance role with the two heavy machine guns removed and a fixed vertical camera mounted in the rear fuselage.

A DESPERATE TIME

In the spring of 1944 the German aircraft industry underwent a major reorganization. The Luftwaffe needed every modern fighter it could lay its hands on. Under the new

IN ACTION DURING THE FINAL MONTHS OF THE WAR

'Leutnant Hans-Ulrich Flade flew the Me 109 'Gustav' and the 'Kurfurst' with IInd Gruppe of Fighter Geschwader 27 early in 1945. In previous months the production of these fighters had reached an all-time high, and if an aircraft was damaged it was usually simpler to get a new fighter than repair the old one: 'We simply went to the depot nearby, where they had hundreds of brand-new 109s – G-10s, G–14s and even the very latest K models. There was no proper organization any more; the depot staff just said: "There are the aircraft, take what you want and go away." But getting fuel, that was more difficult. Flade's Gruppe had a strength of about twenty pilots, but it was losing these at a rate of two or three each day. Morale on the unit was low. 'Each morning we pilots had breakfast together, and the replacements would come in. The older pilots regarded the newcomers as though they had only days to live – and with reason, for the standard of fighter conversion training was now so low that most of the new pilots flew only two or three missions before they were shot down. I remember many conversations along these lines – not exactly a cheerful subject for a young man who had just joined his first operational unit!' The Gruppe operated in the top-cover role, to keep the American escort fighters off the backs of other German fighters making for the bombers. 'We followed the old rules: dive as a pair or a four out of the sun, make a quick attack to break up their formation and make them drop their tanks, then climb out of danger and assess the situation. If conditions were favourable, we would go down for a second attack. Always the escorts were so numerous that it would have been foolish to get into a dog-fight.'

Top: The Me 109G-14 featured a larger rudder and a redesigned cockpit canopy to give better vision to the sides and the rear. This example belonged to IIIrd Gruppe of Fighter Geschwader 3, a unit that flew escort missions for more heavily armoured fighters delivering attacks on US heavy bomber formations. (Romm)

Above: Me 109 'Kurfurst', the final version of the fighter to go into production in Germany before the end of the war. As well as the revised tail surfaces and redesigned canopy fitted to the late production 'Gustavs', this variant featured a more powerful Daimler Benz 605 engine and carried two 15 mm cannons mounted on top of the engine.

Luftwaffe procurement plan, almost the entire capacity of the industry was turned over to the manufacture of fighter-type aircraft. At the same time, to render the industry less vulnerable to air attack, a large part of the aircraft construction and assembly work was dispersed into small factories and workshops dotted throughout the country.

Once the new system was in place, production of the Me 109 rose in leaps and bounds, despite the heavy and continual raids on German cities and industrial centres. For the Me 109 September 1944 was the peak month, with the Luftwaffe taking delivery of 1,605 new aircraft. That year 14,212 examples of this type of aircraft were delivered, more than twice as many as in the previous year which had itself been a record. At this stage of the war the units equipped with Me 109s always had plenty of aircraft, although there were shortages of trained pilots and fuel as the tide turned against the German forces.

Above and left: The unusual 'Mistel' weapon, a Me 109 mounted rigidly on top of a Junkers 88 bomber that had the cabin removed and a large warhead fitted In its place. The Me 109 pilot aligned the bomber on the target, then fired explosive bolts to separate his aircraft so he could make his escape.

Despite the poor handling qualities of the Me 109 'Gustav', work continued in attempts to squeeze yet more speed and combat capability out of the basic design. The final variant of the Me 109 to enter large-scale production was the 'Kurfurst', deliveries of which began at the end of September 1944. The initial production sub-type, the 'Kurfurst 2', had a pair of 15 mm cannon in place of the 13 mm weapons mounted above the engine. The 'Kurfurst-4' was a high altitude fighter with a pressurized cabin. The 'Kurfurst-6' was a specialized bomber-destroyer version, with a 30 mm high-velocity cannon firing through the airscrew spinner.

The final sub-type to enter production before the end of the war was the 'Kurfurst-14', which was powered by a DB 605L engine with a two-stage supercharger. This aircraft was the fastest Me 109 of them all, with a maximum speed of 452mph at 19,700 ft (728km/hr at 6,000m).

During the early months of 1945 the Allied ground forces were thrusting into Germany from both the east and the west. As the factories building components and assemblies for the Me 109 came under threat from these forces, they were blown up to prevent capture. Also at this time attacks on the German road, rail and canal systems made it difficult to deliver air-craft components to the assembly plants. However, despite these obstacles, the Me 109 continued to be turned out in large numbers until the very end of the war.

In the final four months of the conflict the Luftwaffe took delivery of nearly three thousand Me 109s. It is estimated that several hundred more of these aircraft were probably completed, but they never reached the units for which they were intended, remaining in the factories where they had been assembled.

The precise number of Me 109s built will never be known with certainty, but without doubt it can be stated that the figure exceeded 33,000. So, to the type's other 'firsts' can be added the distinction that no other fighter design, anywhere else in the world, was produced in greater numbers.